T0180399

Communications in Computer and Information Science   1704

More information about this series at https://link.springer.com/bookseries/7899

KC Santosh · Ayush Goyal · Djamila Aouada ·
Aaisha Makkar · Yao-Yi Chiang ·
Satish K Singh (Eds.)

Recent Trends in Image Processing and Pattern Recognition

5th International Conference, RTIP2R 2022
Kingsville, TX, USA, December 1–2, 2022
Revised Selected Papers

 Springer

Editors
KC Santosh ⓘ
University of South Dakota
South Dakota, USA

Ayush Goyal
Texas A&M University - Kingsville
Texas, USA

Djamila Aouada
University of Luxembourg
Luxembourg, Luxembourg

Aaisha Makkar
University of Derby
Derby, UK

Yao-Yi Chiang ⓘ
University of Minnesota
Minnesota, USA

Satish K Singh
IIIT Allahabad
Allahabad, India

ISSN 1865-0929   ISSN 1865-0937 (electronic)
Communications in Computer and Information Science
ISBN 978-3-031-23598-6   ISBN 978-3-031-23599-3 (eBook)
https://doi.org/10.1007/978-3-031-23599-3

This Springer imprint is published by the registered company Springer Nature Switzerland AG
The registered company address is: Gewerbestrasse 11, 6330 Cham, Switzerland

Preface

It is our pleasure to introduce this collection of research papers in Springer's Communication in Computer and Information Science (CCIS) series from the fifth International Conference on Recent Trends in Image Processing and Pattern Recognition (RTIP2R 2022). RTIP2R 2022 took place in-person at the University of Texas - Kingsville during December 1–2, 2022, in collaboration with the 2AI: Applied Artificial Intelligence Research Lab at the University of South Dakota.

As announced in the call for papers, RTIP2R 2022 attracted current and/or recent research on image processing, pattern recognition, and computer vision with several different applications, such as document understanding, biometrics, medical imaging, and image analysis in agriculture. Altogether, we received 69 submissions and selected 31 papers for conference presentations. On average, each paper selected for a conference presentation received at least three reviews in a single blind process. For publication, the conference chairs decided not to include no-show papers as well as those papers that were not revised in accordance with the chairs' reports. Taking this into account, the conference chairs decided to move forward with 31 papers for publication. As a result, the acceptance rate for this volume is 44.9%.

In brief, the event was a great platform bringing together research scientists, academics, and industry practitioners. We genuinely believe that the conference was full of innovative ideas, and we are grateful to the following keynote speakers for their insightful talks: Sameer Antani (Principal Investigator – tenure-track, US National Library of Medicine, National Institutes of Health), Tracy Anne Hammond (Professor, Texas A&M University), and Patrick S.P. Wang (Professor Emeritus, Northeastern University and Founding Editor of IJPRAI).

We would like to thank everyone who contributed to the success of RTIP2R 2022.

November 2022

KC Santosh
Ayush Goyal
Djamila Auoada
Aaisha Makkar
Yao-Yi Chiang
Satish K Singh

Organization

Patron

Heidi Taboada   Texas A&M University - Kingsville, USA

Honorary Chairs

Scott Smith   Texas A&M University - Kingsville, USA
Habib Ammari   Texas A&M University - Kingsville, USA
Jean-Marc Ogier   La Rochelle Université, France

General Chairs

KC Santosh   University of South Dakota, USA
Ayush Goyal   Texas A&M University - Kingsville, USA
Djamila Auoada   University of Luxembourg, Luxembourg

Program Chairs

Aaisha Makkar   University of Derby, UK
Yao-Yi Chiang   University of Minnesota, USA
Satish K Singh   IIIT Allahabad, India

Local Chairs

Robert Diersing   Mais Nijim Texas A&M University - Kingsville, USA
Afzel Noore   Mais Nijim Texas A&M University - Kingsville, USA
Mahesh Hosur   Mais Nijim Texas A&M University - Kingsville, USA
Lifford McLauchlan   Mais Nijim Texas A&M University - Kingsville, USA
Mehrube Mehrubeoglu   Texas A&M University - Corpus Christi, USA

Special Track Chairs

Szilard Vajda   Central Washington University, USA
Anuradha Kar   Paris Brain Institute, France

Surya Prakash	IIT Indore, India
Marzieh Khakifirooz	Tecnológico de Monterrey, Mexico
Kaushik Roy	West Bengal State University, India

Workshop Chairs

David Hicks	Texas A&M University - Kingsville, USA
Hubert Cecotti	California State University, USA
Alice Othmani	Université Paris-Est Créteil, France
Ravindra Hegadi	Central University of Karnataka, India
Alaa Ali Hameed	Istinye University, Turkey
Loveleen Gaur	Amity University, India

Area Chairs

Sunil Aryal	Deakin University, Australia
Sema Candemir	Ohio State Medical Center, USA
Antoine Vacavant	Université Clermont Auvergne, France
Hoda Al Khzaimi	New York University, Abu Dhabi, UAE
Akhtar Jamil	National University of Computer and Emerging Sciences, Pakistan
Manju Khari	Jawaharlal Nehru University, India

Local Advisory Committee

Robert Diersing	Texas A&M University - Kingsville, USA
Afzel Noore	Texas A&M University - Kingsville, USA
Mahesh Hosur	Texas A&M University - Kingsville, USA
Mehrube Mehrubeoglu	Texas A&M University - Corpus Christi, USA

Publicity Chairs

Sam O'Neill, UK
Sameer Antani, USA
Justin Smith, USA
Sema Candemir, USA
Sivaramakrishnan Rajaraman, USA
Mufti Mahmud, UK
Mamoun Alazab, Australia
Giancarlo Fortino, Italy
Laurent Wendling, France
Xianqing Mao, Luxembourg
Virach Sornlertlamvanich, Japan
Thanaruk Theeramunkung, Thailand

Patrice Boursier, Malaysia
Shishir Shandilya, India
M. Shamim Kaiser, Bangladesh
Usha Batra, India
Randy Hoover, USA

Technical Program Committee

David Zeng	Dakota State University, USA
Alice Othmani	Université Paris-Est Créteil, France
Akhtar Jamil	Natational University of Computer and Emerging Sciences, Pakistan
Yashbir Singh	Mayo Clinc - Rochester, USA
Hoda Al Khzaimi	New York University, Abu Dhabi, UAE
Alaa Ali Hameed	Istinye University, Turkey
Deepak Jain	Chongqing University, China
Abdelkrim Haqiq	Université Hassan 1er, Morocco
Louisa Kessi	ORPALIS, PSPDFKit, France
Vishnu Pendyala	San Jose State University, USA
Rajkumar Saini	Lulea University of Technology, Sweden
Vikas Chouhan	University of New Brunswick, Canada
Sivaramakrishnan Rajaraman	National Library of Medicine, USA
Hamam Mokayed	Lulea University of Technology, Sweden
Mickael Coustaty	La Rochelle Université, France
Zhiyun Xue	National Library of Medicine, NIH, USA
Ghada Zamzmi	National Library of Medicine, NIH, USA
Feng Yang	National Library of Medicine, NIH, USA
Kruttika Sutrave	University of South Dakota, USA
Fayadh Alenezi	Jouf University, Saudi Arabia
Randy Hoover	South Dakota School of Mines and Technology, USA
Janmenjoy Nayak	Maharaja Sriram Chandra Bhanja Deo University, India
Ripal Ranpara	Amitya University, India
Sunil Aryal	Deakin University, Australia
Somenath Chakrabortty	West Virginia University, USA
Ameni Boumaiza	Hamad Bin Khalifa University, Qatar
Kaushik Roy	West Bengal State University, India
Mallikarjun Hangarge	KASCC, India
Debnath Bhattacharya	KL University, India
Thippa Reddy Gadekallu	VIT, India
Vedika Gupta	Jindal Global Business School, India
Ghanapriya Singh	NIT Uttarakhand, India

Hari Prabhat Gupta	IIT BHU, India
Millie Pant	IIT Roorkee, India
Darshan Ruikar	MIT World Peace University, India
Onur Dogan	Izmir Bakircay University, Turkey
Ravinder M.	IGDTUW, India
Shishir Shandilya	VIT Bhopal, India
Kiran Sood	Chitkara University, India
Sachi Pandey	SRM Institute of Science and Technology, Delhi NCR Campus, India
Vandana Sharma	Galgotias University, India
M. Rasel Mahmud	University of Texas at San Antonio, USA
Seshu Kumar Damarla	University of Alberta, Canada
Pethuru Raj Chelliah	Reliance Jio Platforms Ltd., India
Ankit Bansal	Chitkara University, India
Rajesh Kumar Korupalli V.	Woxsen University, India
Preeti Nagrath	Bharati Vidyapeeth College of Engineering, India
Gayathri Nagasubramanian	Galgotias University, India
Kritika Bansal	IIT Delhi, India
C. H. Patil	MIT World Peace University, India
Vishwanath Karad	MIT World Peace University, India
Virendra Malemath	KLE Dr. MSS CET Belagavi, India
Azmain Yakin Srizon	Rajshahi University of Engineering and Technology, Bangladesh
Abhishek Bhatt	College of Engineering Pune, India
Edgar Steven Correa Pinzon	Pontificia Universidad Javeriana, Colombia
Johnson Adekunle Owolabi	Bowen University, Nigeria
Rohini A. Bhusnurmath	Karnataka State Akkamahadevi Women's University, India
Sarbagya Shakya	Eastern New Mexico University, USA
Suleyman Eken	Kocaeli University, Turkey
Amrit Pal	Vellore Institute of Technology, Chennai, India
Priti Rai	Institute of Management Studies, India
Shivani Saluja	Indian School of Hospitality, India
Sofia Pillai	Noida Institute of Engineering and Technology, India
Sumegh Tharewal	MIT World Peace University Pune, India

Conference Secretaries

Casey Wall (Communication)	University of South Dakota, USA
Suprim Nakarmi (Production)	University of South Dakota, USA
Padam Jung Thapa (Production)	University of South Dakota, USA

Contents

Computer Vision and Pattern Recognition

Internet of Things and Security

Signal Processing and Machine Learning

Healthcare: Medical Imaging and Informatics

Data Characterization for Reliable AI in Medicine

Sivaramakrishnan Rajaraman, Ghada Zamzmi, Feng Yang, Zhiyun Xue, and Sameer K. Antani

Computational Health Research Branch, National Library of Medicine, National Institutes of Health, Bethesda, MD 20894, USA
{sivaramakrishnan.rajaraman,ghadazamzmi.alzamzmi,feng.yang2, zhiyun.xue,sameer.antani}@nih.gov

Abstract. Research in Artificial Intelligence (AI)-based medical computer vision algorithms bear promises to improve disease screening, diagnosis, and subsequently patient care. However, these algorithms are highly impacted by the characteristics of the underlying data. In this work, we discuss various data characteristics, namely *Volume, Veracity, Validity, Variety,* and *Velocity,* that impact the design, reliability, and evolution of machine learning in medical computer vision. Further, we discuss each characteristic and the recent works conducted in our research lab that informed our understanding of the impact of these characteristics on the design of medical decision-making algorithms and outcome reliability.

Keywords: Data characteristics · Artificial intelligence · Machine learning · Deep learning · Medical imaging · Data-driven design · Reliability · Generalizability · Robustness

1 Introduction

Machine learning (ML) algorithms are performing on par with or surpassing human performance in medical computer vision applications [1]. ML methods are inherently data-driven, which greatly influences the network design. Further, data characteristics impact outcomes and their interpretation of the desired problem. Modern approaches to artificial intelligence (AI) systems encapsulate ML design appropriate for specific applications and, therefore, are implicitly affected by data characteristics used in its training or learning. These observations are particularly critical for healthcare and other applications where AI decisions are of high consequence. A vast majority of AI and ML applications in medicine have been in the domain of medical imaging [2]. Unlike natural images, medical images are often available in limited quantity with sparse annotations. Further, medical images are acquired in a variety of modalities (e.g., radiological imagery, optical imagery, ultrasound, as well as microscopic, to name a few) using several imaging sensors with varying characteristics and acquisition parameters. The acquired images can be multidimensional with varying channel depth as well as spatial and temporal resolution. This variety has a direct impact on not only network design but also learning.

KC Santosh et al. (Eds.): RTIP2R 2022, CCIS 1704, pp. 3–11, 2023.
https://doi.org/10.1007/978-3-031-23599-3_1

Additional impacts include the variety and distribution of the patient population and disease representation in the images. Post-acquisition steps to handle these issues include quality control and curation of images as well as relevant non-imaging patient metadata. As such, data characteristics must be considered as a critical component of the ML and prediction pipeline design toward developing robust, repeatable, and reproducible models for use in clinical applications.

In this manuscript, we discuss key data characteristics that impact ML design, particularly for medical imaging analyses. We itemize these characteristics as "5-V"s, viz., *Volume, Veracity, Validity, Variety*, and *Velocity*. These characteristics are not necessarily independent of each other and may be correlated. Also, discussions on big data have mentioned three terms that are analogous to our discussion, but not necessarily, the same [3]. The discussed characteristics must be considered as a lens through which the ML model is designed, evaluated, and its results analyzed or interpreted. To illustrate these characteristics, this paper reflects relevant published literature from our laboratory during 2019–2022 that were significantly influential to our proposal. Our laboratory focuses on methodical research in medical imaging, medical informatics, ML, and AI for computational health as a part of intramural research at the National Library of Medicine (NLM), part of the United States National Institutes of Health (NIH). We believe understanding and analyzing these data characteristics will help derive more value from data while enabling the improved design of appropriate learning models/methods and allowing the AI systems to better generalize to real-world conditions.

The rest of this paper is organized as follows. We discuss the 5-Vs of data in Sect. 2. Relevant recent works addressing these data characteristics are elaborated in Sect. 3 followed by conclusions in Sect. 4.

2   Data Characteristics: Definitions

Volume: Volume is the amount of data used for training, validation, and testing of the ML model. The term overlaps with and does not intend to replace the definitions of imaging data dimensionality (e.g., 2D, 3D, 4D). A data-driven architecture relies heavily on the volume of training data to develop reliable, i.e., repeatable, and reproducible models. Insufficient data can result in model overfitting and poor generalization.

Veracity: Truthful and factual representation of the nature of the problem is necessary for training reliable AI. This term implies that the data used for training must represent the problem exhaustively including all variations that are used for human expert-based decision-making. It is an open question whether future variations in the reality of the problem, such as evolution or understanding of the etiology, need to be accounted for in support of active/open-world learning-based scenarios.

Validity: Validity singularly reflects the quality of data being logically or factually sound. It could be considered in the sense of the image being of "good technical quality", i.e., in focus, complete coverage of the anatomy, appropriate resolution, brightness, etc.; or the image could be considered acceptable from a clinical evaluation perspective, where the clinician or clinician's aide can adequately discriminate and accurately assess the extent/severity disease on the image. Note, however, that human acceptance of a valid image does not necessarily mean that the image is of perfect technical quality. Not only does valid data help in reducing inter- and intra-person variability but can also increase real-world variety. In this context, valid data extends beyond just the raw sensor-acquired data to also include expert annotations or labeling and considerations for their granularity and accuracy. Another perspective of validity is the completeness of the data acquired over time.

Variety: Variety in data may be considered in the following broad categories, viz., acquisition variety, population variety, and disease variety. Acquisition variety considers the differences in data when it is acquired using devices from different manufacturers or different device models/generations. This variety may be accidental, i.e., the AI designer has no control over the selection of a particular device, or programmatically ensured to increase data variation toward strengthening the AI. Population (ethnicity, geographic, disease prevalence) diversity is highly desirable to increase the resilience and fairness of the AI to unseen cases. Similarly, disease variety in terms of severity, extent, and comorbidities may help AI become more useful to aid in wider clinical adoption. However, diversity without supporting volume may not always be useful.

Velocity: Velocity relates to the temporal sensitivity of the acquisition device and the corresponding generation of data. At the patient level, the velocity could refer to the completeness in recording/sampling data across patient encounters which could be hours, days, or months apart. At a technical level, it could refer to the sampling rate at which a sensor operates. There is an overlap with data veracity characteristics since the sampling rate must be meaningful to the disease or condition for which data acquisition is being performed.

3   Recent Works Addressing Data Characteristics

In this section, we illustrate how these 5-Vs drive the design of the methods through references to our prior works. These works were influential in informing us of the significance of these data characteristics. We use them to indicate their importance toward achieving desired robustness in ML design and outcomes.

Volume: Our works have explored different techniques to tackle issues with the limited availability of training data. Our methods use a combination of direct and indirect techniques for either increasing data or responding to limited data through ML design methods. Direct techniques include achieving gains through traditional data augmentation, generative adversarial networks (GANs)-based data augmentation methods, and synthetic minority over-sampling (SMOTE) techniques. Indirect methods for responding to limited data volume include transfer learning, medical modality-specific pretraining and fine-tuning, semi-supervised learning, self-supervised learning, and federated learning. For example, in [4], we studied the utility of GAN-synthesized images and those generated by conventional data augmentation toward training the convolutional neural network (CNN)-based deep learning (DL) models for classifying chest X-rays (CXRs) as showing normal or abnormal lungs. We trained a progressive-growing GAN (PG-GAN) to synthesize high-resolution CXRs and used traditional augmentation methods like flipping, rotation, and pixel shifting to increase training data volume. We trained an abnormality classifier using different augmented training sets – traditionally augmented (TA), GAN-augmented (GA), and baseline non-augmented (NA) data. We observed that compared to using NA data, both TA and GA improved performance, however, TA resulted in superior performance compared to GA. We attribute the reduction in performance to the limited variance exhibited by GA images. Another technique for increasing volume was explored in [5, 6] in which SMOTE techniques were applied to imbalanced drug-resistant tuberculosis (DR-TB) and drug-sensitive tuberculosis DS-TB clinical datasets to avoid biased predictions in favor of the majority class. In this work, we extracted three clinical features and 26 radiological features and trained ML classifiers using different combinations of extracted features to evaluate their ability to differentiate between DR-TB and DS-TB. We observed that automatic discrimination based on SMOTE oversampling technique with a combination of 25 statistically signifi-cant features achieved the best performance. Further, in [7], we proposed a novel design of a shared trunk and multiple task-specific heads (Hydra) to simultaneously reduce computational complexity and improve performance even with limited data. The trunk learned a CXR modality-specific super-resolution task where the trained CNN-based model learned the mapping from low-resolution to high-resolution CXR images. The learned super-resolution trunk was appended with multiple task-specific heads for simul-taneous learning of multiple visual tasks such as image enhancement, lung segmentation, and abnormality classification. We observed that the use of modality-specific represen-tation, which was constructed using unlabeled data, enhanced the quality of images and improved the performance of target visual tasks with limited datasets. In another study [8], we discussed the multi-task learning (MTL) approach that used a medical image modality-specific backbone as a unified representation (UMS-Rep) to transfer modality-specific knowledge and fine-tune them to improve performance in several target tasks. We explored different fine-tuning strategies to demonstrate the impact of the proposal on the performance of several medical computer vision tasks including image denoising, segmentation, and classification, among others, using two medical imaging modalities, viz., CXR and Doppler echocardiography. We observed that the UMS-Rep approach reduced the overall demand for a large amount of labeled data as well as computational resources and improved generalization and performance. For a non-radiology modality, in [9], we examined semi-supervised learning with the ResNeSt50 architecture together with transfer learning and image augmentation for cervix precancer identification which brings significant performance improvements to the baseline approaches. We also pro-posed self-supervised learning (SSL) approaches (both centralized SSL and federated SSL) to utilize unlabeled data for cervix image classification to address the challenges of label scarcity and variability issues [10]. Medical data famously suffers from a higher class imbalance where the number of cases is much fewer than controls. In [11], we proposed a distance metric learning (DML) based method to respond to the data scarcity and bias training issues due to class imbalance data in cervical cancer screening.

Veracity: We explored different techniques that considered data veracity as a central aspect of ML design. For example, in [12], we explored the benefits of training CNN and vision transformer (ViT)-based DL models using the lateral CXRs compared to the widely used frontal CXRs and constructing their ensembles to detect pulmonary abnormalities consistent with TB. Lateral views are routinely used in clinical protocols to confirm retrocardiac expression of the disease. However, almost all publications in the literature use only frontal CXR projection images for analysis. To bring the ML predictions closer to clinical routine, we demonstrated that our model ensemble had superior classification and TB disease-specific localization performance. This study demonstrated that like the frontal CXR projections, the lateral CXRs could help improve the detection of disease-specific biomarkers and meaningfully supplement clinical decision-making.

Given that obtaining a truthful and factual representation of the data can be hard, in [13], we proposed a method that can learn initially from a limited representation of the data, and then actively update its knowledge based on new variations in the data. Specifically, an open-world active learning method was proposed to handle the dynamic and changing nature of medical data in the real world as follows. First, the network learned to classify an initial set of data into a limited set of classes while labeling upcoming unknown or new data as unknown. Then, a clustering approach was used to cluster new data into various groups to be labeled by human experts. These newly labeled data samples were then used to update the classifier knowledge. This process of actively labeling unknown clusters of data samples and integrating them into the classification model increased the robustness of the classifier as it allowed to update the classifier based on new and unknown data samples. Our results of applying this method for echocardiography view classification showed the superiority of the proposed approach as compared to the closed-world classification approaches (i.e., trained once on a limited dataset).

Validity: The granularity and specificity of expert annotations can have a significant impact on the training of ML models. These annotations are impacted by both the experience of the annotator as well as the setting in which the ML application is intended to be used. During the high days of the COVID-19 pandemic, a medical researcher might desire pixel-accurate disease prediction from the algorithm, while a clinician at a busy hospital might be satisfied with a highlighted region to help focus treatment decisions. To study this effect, we compared ML learning from annotations by two radiologists from different settings. Our findings were published in [14] where we observed that the variability in their annotations significantly affected the learning and ML predictions. To overcome inter-personal annotation variability, a Simultaneous Truth and Performance Level Estimation (STAPLE)-based annotation consensus was derived as a faithful measure of the ground truth to ensure validity. In a separate effort, to advance the state of the art for image segmentation methods toward improving the performance of the fine-grained segmentation of TB-consistent findings in digital chest X-ray images, in [15], we published a collection of the first pixel-level annotations/segmentations of pulmonary radiological manifestations that are consistent with TB. The annotation collection comprises lung pattern abnormalities for TB patients, mask files for each abnormality, and metadata that summarizes lung abnormality types. Another aspect of validity is image quality. We note that controlling image quality plays a key role in ML as it can affect the downstream pipeline performance significantly. Many factors can adversely affect or degrade image quality. Some are related to the clinical aspect while others are related to the technical aspect of the imaging device and the illumination condition, such as blur, noise, glare, low contrast, etc. While care providers can be trained to take high-quality images and use advanced hardware, it is critical to developing automated techniques to remedy the image quality problem in existing data sets as well as during acquisition. On this aspect, we proposed DL-based methods to filter out the images of irrelevant types [16, 17], evaluate the degradation of disease identification performance under different levels of image noise and the effectiveness of denoising on classification [18], and develop a general image quality classifier using the data labeled by expert clinician annotators based on their judgment [19] where we also applied Confident Learning to identify mislabeled samples automatically.

Variety: In [4], we studied the gains achieved through introducing variety into the training process by augmenting the training data using conventional affine transformation-based and GAN-based augmentations. The augmented data was used to train DL models for classifying CXRs as showing normal lungs or other pulmonary abnormalities. We observed that the classification performance achieved through training the models using traditionally augmented data was superior compared to using GAN-augmented data. However, both traditional and GAN-based augmentation improved performance. In another study [20], we augmented the training data using a *weak* augmentation method toward classifying CXRs as showing normal lungs or other COVID-19-consistent abnormalities. We expanded the training data distribution by adding CXRs pooled from publicly available resources that manifest pneumonia-consistent findings to introduce variability into the training process. The augmented data was used to train DL models and the performance was evaluated with a hold-out test data consisting of only CXRs manifesting COVID-19 consistent findings. The classification performance was compared to those achieved with non-augmented training. We observed that weak data augmentation demonstrated superior classification performance compared to non-augmented training. Variety in the visual characteristics of medically important regions in images may be different across imaging devices. This cross-device disparity could be a significant confounding factor for automatic disease identification using ML. Hence, there is a need to examine and assess to what extent the images taken by one device are visually different from those taken by another device based strictly on their appearance with no knowledge of any abnormality exhibited on them for the same patient population at the same geographical location. In [21], we proposed a simple but effective DL-based clustering approach to investigate whether the images taken by three different devices can be well distinguished from each other concerning the visual appearance/content within their cervix regions. The results of this work indicate a large number of training images from different sources is needed for enabling generalizability in a classifier for worldwide use that is independent of the device and robust to both technique and device characteristics.

Velocity: This characteristic is often difficult to control in downstream ML analysis. This is because the sampling rate of the acquired data is controlled by the imaging device and is important for human clinical assessment of the imagery. Further, limitations are introduced when the human experts reduce the acquisition rate to support manual analysis which might not be needed for automated predictions. As such, this factor can vary significantly across data sets as well as ML design decisions. Another thing to consider is the data acquisition over time when the advance of technology can make obsolete or adversely affect the reproducibility of data used for the analyses. For example, in a large study conducted decades ago on cervix cancer screening, images were captured using the CerviScope [22], a film-based imaging device specially designed for taking images of the cervix that has now been out of the market and is no longer accessible. The data collected by new devices, such as cell phones have a different appearance and sampling rate from the old data. Therefore, DL models designed with digitized versions of film images may not translate to new images and need to be retrained to retain performance gains [23].

The impact of velocity or sampling rate on the method's design has been demonstrated in [24]. Specifically, we propose in [24] a lightweight and fast echocardiography segmentation network called TaNet to accommodate the sampling rate (>30 frames per second [fps]) of the acquired data. Our results showed that current echocardiography segmentation methods (e.g., UNet and FCN) cannot perform frame-by-frame segmentation and analysis in real-time as these methods are deeper and tend to segment 5 fps on average. The ability of the proposed TaNet network to perform real-time cardiac region segmentation allows to temporally quantify cardiac biomarkers over longer periods (i.e., a higher number of heartbeats). Note that human experts in clinical practice might decide to acquire echocardiography clips with a lower acquisition rate (e.g., 2–3 heartbeats) to facilitate manual analysis, which is not needed for automated real-time analysis.

4 Conclusion

Medical data is a significant contributor to the design, generalizability, and reliability of ML models. Therefore, it is mandatory to recognize and understand the various characteristics of data and assess what can be achieved using this data. Further, new strategies and technologies should be developed to understand the nature, complexity, and volume of data to derive meaningful information. Such strategies could provide further insights into procedural, technical, and other improvements in medical decision-making. Data collected across heterogeneous platforms need to be properly integrated and implemented for faithful clinical decision-making. In this paper, we highlight our works that helped identify these data characteristics and define them to help advance the reliability of AI/ML in medicine.

Acknowledgments. This research was supported by the Intramural Research Program (IRP) of the National Library of Medicine (NLM), National Institutes of Health (NIH).

Conflicts of Interest. The authors declare no conflict of interest.

References

1. Alzubaidi, L., et al.: Review of deep learning: concepts, CNN architectures, challenges, applications, future directions. J. Big Data **8**(1), 1–74 (2021). https://doi.org/10.1186/s40 537-021-00444-8
2. Suzuki, K.: Overview of deep learning in medical imaging. Radiol. Phys. Technol. **10**(3), 257–273 (2017). https://doi.org/10.1007/s12194-017-0406-5
3. Younas, M.: Research challenges of big data. SOCA **13**(2), 105–107 (2019). https://doi.org/10.1007/s11761-019-00265-x
4. Ganesan, P., Rajaraman, S., Long, R., Ghoraani, B., Antani, S.: Assessment of data augmentation strategies toward performance improvement of abnormality classification in chest radiographs. In: Proceedings of the Annual International Conference of the IEEE Engineering in Medicine and Biology Society, EMBS (2019). https://doi.org/10.1109/EMBC.2019.8857516
5. Yang, F., et al.: Differentiating between drug-sensitive and drug-resistant tuberculosis with machine learning for clinical and radiological features. Quant. Imaging Med. Surg. **12**, 675–687 (2022). https://doi.org/10.21037/qims-21-290
6. Yang, F., et al.: Automated drug-resistant TB screening: importance of demographic features and radiological findings in chest X-ray. In: Proceedings of Applied Imagery Pattern Recognition Workshop, 9–12 October 2021. https://doi.org/10.1109/AIPR52630.2021.976 2198
7. Zamzmi, G., Rajaraman, S., Antani, S.: Accelerating super-resolution and visual task analysis in medical images. Appl. Sci. **10** (2020). https://doi.org/10.3390/app10124282
8. Zamzmi, G., Rajaraman, S., Antani, S.: UMS-Rep: unified modality-specific representation for efficient medical image analysis. Inform. Med. Unlocked. **24**, 100571 (2021). https://doi.org/10.1016/j.imu.2021.100571
9. Angara, S., Guo, P., Xue, Z., Antani, S.: Semi-supervised learning for cervical precancer detection. In: Proceedings of International Symposium on Computer-Based Medical Systems, pp. 202–206, June 2021. https://doi.org/10.1109/CBMS52027.2021.00072
10. Pal, A., Xue, Z., Antani, S.: Deep cervix model development from heterogeneous and partially labeled image datasets. In: Proceedings of the 7th International Conference on Emerging Applications of Information Technology (EAIT 2022), Kolkata, India, 30–31 March 2022
11. Pal, A., et al.: Deep multiple-instance learning for abnormal cell detection in cervical histopathology images. Comput. Biol. Med. **138**, 104890 (2021). https://doi.org/10.1016/j.compbiomed.2021.104890
12. Rajaraman, S., Zamzmi, G., Folio, L.R., Antani, S.: Detecting tuberculosis-consistent findings in lateral chest X-rays using an ensemble of CNNs and vision transformers. Front. Genet. **13**, 1–13 (2022). https://doi.org/10.3389/fgene.2022.864724
13. Zamzmi, G., Oguguo, T., Rajaraman, S., Antani, S.: Open world active learning for echocardiography view classification. In: Proceedings of SPIE Medical Imaging (2022): Computer-Aided Diagnosis, vol. 120330J, 4 April 2022. https://doi.org/10.1117/12.2612578
14. Rajaraman, S., Sornapudi, S., Alderson, P.O., Folio, L.R., Antani, S.K.: Analyzing inter-reader variability affecting deep ensemble learning for COVID-19 detection in chest radiographs. PLoS ONE (2020). https://doi.org/10.1371/journal.pone.0242301
15. Yang, F., et al.: Annotations of lung abnormalities in the Shenzhen chest pulmonary diseases. MDPI Data **7**(7), 95 (2022). https://doi.org/10.3390/data7070095
16. Guo, P., et al.: Ensemble deep learning for cervix image selection toward improving reliability in automated cervical precancer screening. Diagnostics **10** (2020). https://doi.org/10.3390/diagnostics10070451

17. Xue, Z., et al.: Cleaning highly unbalanced multisource image dataset for quality control in cervical precancer screening. In: Santosh, K.C., Hegadi, R., Pal, U. (eds.) RTIP2R 2021. CCIS, vol 1576, pp. 3–13. Springer, Cham (2022). https://doi.org/10.1007/978-3-031-070 05-1_1

18. Xue, Z., Angara, S., Levitz, D., Antani, S.K.: Analysis of digital noise reduction methods on classifiers used in automated visual evaluation. In: SPIE International Society of Optical Engineering, p. 28 (2022). https://doi.org/10.1117/12.2610235

19. Xue, Z., et al.: Image quality classification for automated visual evaluation of cervical precancer. In: Zamzmi, G., Antani, S., Bagci, U., Linguraru, M.G., Rajaraman, S., Xue, Z. (eds.) MILLanD 2022. LNCS, vol. 13559, pp. 206–217. Springer, Cham (2022). https://doi.org/10. 1007/978-3-031-16760-7_20

20. Rajaraman, S., Antani, S.: Weakly labeled data augmentation for deep learning: a study on COVID-19 detection in chest X-rays. Diagnostics **10**, 1–17 (2020). https://doi.org/10.3390/ diagnostics10060358

21. Xue, Z., et al.: A deep clustering method for analyzing uterine cervix images across imaging devices. In: Proceedings of the IEEE Symposium on Computer-Based Medical Systems, pp. 527–532, June 2021. https://doi.org/10.1109/CBMS52027.2021.00085

22. Rodríguez, A.C., et al.: Cervical cancer incidence after screening with HPV, cytology, and visual methods: 18-year follow-up of the Guanacaste cohort. Int. J. Cancer. **140**, 1926–1934 (2017). https://doi.org/10.1002/ijc.30614

23. Xue, Z., et al.: A demonstration of automated visual evaluation of cervical images taken with a smartphone camera. Int. J. Cancer **147**, 2416–2423 (2020). https://doi.org/10.1002/ijc.33029

24. Zamzmi, G., Rajaraman, S., Hsu, L.-Y., Sachdev, V., Antani, S.: Real-time echocardiography image analysis and quantification of cardiac indices. Med. Image Anal. **80**, 102438 (2022). https://doi.org/10.1016/j.media.2022.102438

Alzheimer's Disease Detection Using Ensemble Learning and Artificial Neural Networks

Ahana Bandyopadhyay[1], Sourodip Ghosh[1], Moinak Bose[1(✉)], Arun Singh[3], Alice Othmani[2], and KC Santosh[4]

[1] Applied AI Research Lab, Vermillion, SD 57069, USA
moinakbose12@gmail.com
[2] Universitè Paris-Est, LISSI, UPEC, 94400 Vitry sur Seine, France
alice.othmani@u-pec.fr
[3] Basic Biomedical Sciences, University of South Dakota, Vermillion, SD 57069, USA
arun.singh@usd.edu
[4] Applied AI Research Lab, Computer Science Department, University of South Dakota, Vermillion, SD 57069, USA
santosh.kc@usd.edu

Abstract. This paper presents an ensemble method using machine learning classification algorithms and an artificial neural network-based scheme using the popular and widely used open access series of imaging studies (OASIS) dataset for Alzheimer's disease (AD) detection. The proposed work performs an in-depth feature examination and a training-test split in a 70 : 30 ratio on the dataset and applies 8 different ML algorithms. The AD detection outcome is obtained using two procedures, first by an ensemble approach applied to different machine learning algorithms, and secondly by using an artificial neural network (ANN). The use of ANN achieves an overall test accuracy of 0.9196 whereas two ensemble techniques, namely gradient boosting and voting classifier achieve an overall test accuracy of 0.857 and 0.8304. The precision and sensitivity scores demonstrate the superior detection performance of the ANN over the ensemble method on ML algorithms.

Keywords: Alzheimer's disease detection · Machine learning · ANN · Ensemble learning

1 Introduction

1.1 Context

Alzheimer's disease (AD) is a type of dementia that affects a person's memory, thought, and behaviour. It is a disease that begins with mildly affecting parts of the brain, which makes an individual have difficulty in remembering any newly learned information, constant changes in mood, and confusion with events, times,

KC Santosh et al. (Eds.): RTIP2R 2022, CCIS 1704, pp. 12–21, 2023.
https://doi.org/10.1007/978-3-031-23599-3_2

and places. AD usually starts in an individual after the age of 60 years and its risk increases as the person ages. So the early detection of the disease can help the doctors start the treatment which can significantly help alleviate some symptoms, reduce their intensity, and thus contribute to a better quality of life for patients and their families. In recent years, various MRI biomarkers have been proposed for grouping AD patients in various illness stages. Despite numerous endeavours, distinguishing effective AD-explicit biomarkers for the early determination and expectation of ailment movement is still awaited and requires more research.

1.2   Related Works

Ensemble learning and neural networks have increased various individual results that are obtained from non-linear network designs [1, 2]. Various conventional AI strategies, for instance, SVM and feedforward neural networks are used effectively to analyze AD through MRI pictures as given in [3, 4]. One such ongoing technique is [4], where a dual-tree complex wavelet transform is utilized to extricate features, and a feed-forward neural network is utilized to characterize the pictures. Expound conversation and 1167 similar outcomes with other famous conventional strategies can likewise be found. A mix of patches extricated from an autoencoder followed by convolutional layers for feature extraction was utilized in [5]. While these profound learning strategies give great precision results, our proposed method for determining the training information and utilization of transfer learning, we get equivalent and in fact slightly better accuracy while utilizing just a small amount of the training information and computation. The information mining strategies in an MRI signal give an approach to separate the useful information from the MRI data comprising a huge number of voxels. The insignificant arrangement of voxel values is important to accomplish an adequately high precision for the expectation and conclusion of Alzheimer's Disease. Multivariate methodologies, for example, PCA [6], ICA [7], SEM [8], and SVM [9] are potential applicants yet have not been applied to several useful neuroimaging information up until this point. As of late, such multivariate strategies have been received for the examination of basic MRI to distinguish spatial examples of decay in Alzheimer's Disease [10–12]. The use of such classifiers of a spatial example of decay in MCI has indicated promising outcomes for the expectation of Alzheimer's Disease [10, 11]. Ding et al. [13] validated an algorithm to cater diagnosis of Alzheimer's disease with PET scans of brain images with a ROC curve of 0.98.

1.3   Problem Identification

Recently, different imaging tools for Alzheimer's disease detection have been proposed by impactful research findings [14–17]. Some works [18] propose segmentation and identification frameworks to differentiate Alzheimer's disease from mild cognitive impairment. Some have worked towards stratification of Alzheimer's by creating a risk-score neural network model [19].

Currently, different imaging and screening procedures using deep learning tools for feature extraction like convolutional neural networks (CNNs), deep

CNNs, or recurrent neural networks (RNNs) are being widely used. Each learning algorithms extract patterns using convolutional, pooling, activation functions/layers, batch normalization layers, and multiple other layers, depending upon the type of network. The aforementioned procedure processes around millions of trainable points (trainable parameters). Note that the size of the training data is a primary factor for the total number of trainable parameters.

Therefore, the above-mentioned process differs from machine learning approaches in terms of computational efficiency. Traditional machine learning models (SVM, kNN, Gradient boosting, etc) efficiently classify patterns using statistical approaches with lowered computation time.

1.4   Contribution Outline

This paper proposes a comparative analysis between machine learning algorithms and a multi-layered perceptron or artificial neural network (ANN) when trained on a classification dataset. The problem statement is currently a topic of utmost significance due to the challenges faced by subjects exposed to Alzheimer's disease or other dementia-related disorders.

Towards this, the proposed AD detection scheme consists of two different approaches. Firstly, the model is trained with conventional machine learning architectures, and then two ensemble learning architectures termed Gradient Boosting and Voting Classifier are used to get the decision of the class to which it belongs. The gradient Boosting algorithm consists of results acquired from the decision tree classifier and random forest classifier whereas the voting classifier considers the results from the SVM, XGBoost, Adaboost, random forest, and decision tree classifiers. Furthermore, an artificial neural network (ANN) architecture is also trained and used for AD detection, and the results are evaluated using evaluation parameters. The workflow is demonstrated in Fig. 1. The following section gives a highlight of the experimentation conducted with the OASIS dataset (373 subjects).

2   Experiments

2.1   Data and Pre-processing

For our experiments, the training and testing examples comprising MRI reports and other information about AD patients have been collected from the popular open access series of imaging studies (OASIS) dataset [20]. It contains two sets of data containing cross-sectional MRI information in young, moderately aged, Non-demented, and demented established grown-ups, and the longitudinal MRI information of the Non-demented and grown-ups. The first set has a cross-sectional assortment of 416 subjects aged 18 to 96 years. The second set comprises a longitudinal assortment of 150 subjects aged 60 to 96 years. Classes in the independent categories were ID (patient ID), M/F (male or female), Hand (which hand is more dominant, L/R), Age, Educ (level of education), SES (socio-economic status), MMSE (mini-mental state examination), CDR (clinical dementia rate), eTIV

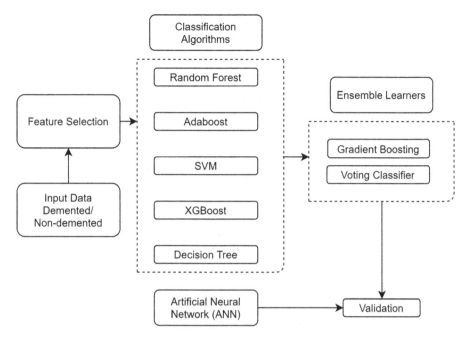

Fig. 1. Proposed workflow

(estimated total intracranial volume) and nWBV (Normalize whole brain volume) (see Sect. 2.2 for more about MMSE, CDR, eTIV, nWBV, and ASF) along with target column (Non-demented/Demented) were assessed from the OASIS dataset. The data contains 373 examples and 15 features. Violin plots of CDR by Gender and Age are shown in Fig. 2a and 2b, respectively. Label Encoder was used to encode the columns into numeric data values, test size was set to 30% (112), keeping 70% (261) for training the classifiers.

2.2   Abbreviations

The classes taken for experimentation are discussed in brief:

(a) The Mini-Mental State Examination (MMSE) or Folstein test is a 30-point survey that is utilized broadly in clinical and exploratory settings to quantify subjective disability.

(b) The Clinical Dementia Rating (CDR) is a 5-point scale used to portray six spaces of intellectual and practical execution appropriate to Alzheimer's infection and related dementias: Memory, Orientation, Judgment and Problem Solving, Community Affairs, Home and Hobbies, and Personal Care. The vital data to make each evaluation is acquired through a semi-organized meeting of the patient and a solid witness or guarantee source (e.g. relative). The CDR table gives observations that control the clinician in making proper validations, dependent on information and clinical evaluations.

(c) Estimated Total Intracranial Volume (eTIV) is efficiently used as a proxy to maximize brain volume (pre-morbid), sometimes accounting for cognitive reserve [21].
(d) Normalize whole brain volume (nWBV) shares an estimate of the relative percentage of the intracranial cavity that is occupied by the brain.
(e) Atlas Scaling Factor (ASF) is a methodology for morphometric and useful information investigation in young, old, and demented adults utilizing mechanized atlas-based head size standardization.

2.3   Model Architectures

The proposed work compares two learning frameworks. One is the ensemble learning applied over several ML algorithms and the other is an ANN-based classification scheme.

Machine Learning Algorithms. The popular Random Forest Classifier, SVM, Decision Tree Classifier, XGBoost, Voting Classifier, Gradient Boosting Classifier, and Adaboost Classifier were used for the disease classification. In Random Forest Classifier, the max depth was set to 8, keeping the number of estimators as 200. For SVM, C (regularization parameter) was set to 0.1 by applying hyperparameter tuning. In the Decision Tree Classifier, the max depth was set to 5. For the XGBoost classifier, regularization parameters were appropriately set for min child weight, gamma, subsample, colsample by tree, and max depth. Voting Classifier was applied on all these algorithms with the individual weights and parameters, as were functional on the individual classifiers. Feature importance for all the classifiers was evaluated along with ROC curves, accuracy, precision, and sensitivity. Another ML framework, Adaboost combines multiple stumps who are technically weak learners thus increasing their learning strength. The number of stumps was set to 60 signifying decision trees have one node and two leaves. Adaboost assigns equal sample weights to all records which are then fed into a model and based on the performance of each stump, weights of incorrectly classified records are increased and correctly classified are decreased. Gradient boosting is an ensemble boosting technique that basically optimizes the classification loss function. Decision trees used in gradient boosting are comparatively larger in size than Adaboost. Voting Classifier uses the technique of ensemble learning using which the results of various ML models operating simultaneously are merged together. This helps in reducing over-fitting and improving accuracy. Therefore, it combined the outputs of machine learning algorithms like Random Forest, Adaboost, XGBoost, Decision Tree and SVM. The final class prediction was done using hard voting.

Artificial Neural Networks. ANNs are computational networks comprised of highly interconnected neurons that work together simultaneously to analyse and process information similar to the way the human brain does. It consists of dropout layers, dense layers and activation functions stacked together. We

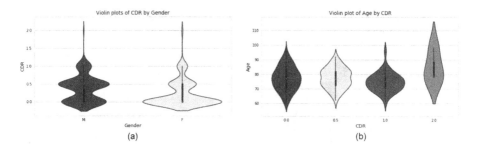

Fig. 2. Violin plots of CDR with (a) Age and (b) Gender

used a dense layer consisting of 8 neurons. A dropout rate of 0.5 was used which randomly disables half of the neurons of a layer which helps in reducing over-fitting and the training time required for each epoch. Activation functions are differentiable functions that help to decide which of the neurons will get activated and will push forward their values onto the next layer. They provide neurons with the ability to learn complex and complicated data. Adam optimizer [22] was used to update weights and bias. The Sequential ANN architecture is considered as follows: Dense(8) ⇒ Dropout(0.5) ⇒ Activation['ReLU'] ⇒ Flatten ⇒ Dense(1) ⇒ Activation['Sigmoid'].

The individual machine learning models were trained with the described specifications and the ANN model was trained with 500 epochs. The validation accuracy converged at 0.92, suggesting the highest performance.

2.4 Evaluation Protocol and Performance Metrics

The equations for accuracy, precision and sensitivity are given as follows:

$$\text{Accuracy} = \frac{TP + TN}{TP + TN + FP + FN} \tag{1}$$

$$\text{Precision} = \frac{TP}{TP + FP} \tag{2}$$

$$\text{Sensitivity} = \frac{TP}{TP + FN} \tag{3}$$

2.5 Results Analysis

The models were first evaluated with respect to the individual architectures, and ensembled architectures are then compared to the ANN architecture. The models used are compared in Table 1 with respect to their Accuracy, Precision, and Sensitivity. ANN outperforms other models, with an accuracy of 0.9196, with a misclassification value of 0.0804. This signifies that the model evaluates 103

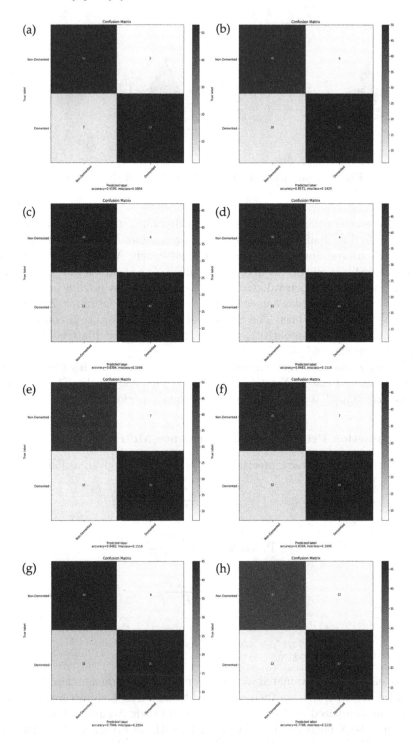

Fig. 3. Confusion matrices for (a) ANN, (b) Gradient boosting, (c) Voting classifier, (d) Random forest, (e) Adaboost, (f) Decision tree, (g) XGBoost, and (h) SVM.

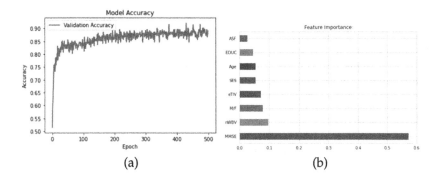

Fig. 4. (a) ANN training: 500 epochs (b) Feature importance analysis.

Table 1. Performance evaluation of all architectures used.

Classifier	Accuracy	Precision	Sensitivity	F-1 Score
ANN	0.92	0.962	0.877	0.917
Gradient Boosting	0.857	0.85	0.857	0.851
Voting Classifier	0.830	0.885	0.78	0.828
Random Forest	0.848	0.85	0.85	0.844
Adaboost	0.848	0.80	0.80	0.841
Decision Tree	0.830	0.86	0.86	0.825
XGBoost	0.795	0.846	0.746	0.792
SVM	0.777	0.769	0.755	0.761

test cases correctly, out of 112. The ensembled architectures, namely Gradient Boosting and Voting Classifier show accuracy close to 0.857 and 0.8304, respectively. The confusion matrix in Fig. 3 shows the true positives and false negative rates, which further determine the Accuracy, Precision, and Sensitivity of all the algorithms used in our experiment. The accuracy, precision, and sensitivity scores for the classifiers are mentioned in Table 1 and are calculated from the equations as mentioned.

Figure 4(a) demonstrated validation accuracy of the model after 500 epochs. The validation set was kept the same as the test set. Feature importance maps shown in Fig. 4(b), demonstrate that the MMSE parameter (around 0.6) highly accounts for the target column, i.e., Demented/Non-demented. This ensures that slight changes in MMSE can re-evaluate the class of the subject, where other columns are given lesser importance (around 0.1).

The ANN classifier outperforms the ensemble and individual machine-learning classifiers due to the following reasons:

1. The performance of the multi-layer perceptron architecture (ANN) can be optimized by a variable number of epochs, governing validation of model convergence, when training and validation losses are monitored.

2. The regularization of the cost function of machine learning algorithms is concluded after a certain number of attempts of tuning the concerned hyper-parameters.
3. The performance of the ANN architecture is expected to optimize when the multi-labelled features are data engineered with more correlation.

3   Conclusion

The proposed scheme was experimented with and analysed using the ensembled learners on ML algorithms and the ANN model. The ANN model outperforms the rest of the defined classifiers. Furthermore, investigation and analysis of different methods for predicting Demented and Non-demented labels are aimed as a future scope, along with the increase of data, to precisely address the Alzheimer's Disease problem.

References

1. Ghosh, S., Bandyopadhyay, A., Sahay, S., Ghosh, R., Kundu, I., Santosh, K.: Colorectal histology tumor detection using ensemble deep neural network. Eng. Appl. Artif. Intell. **100**, 104202 (2021)
2. Paul, D., Tewari, A., Ghosh, S., Santosh, K.: OCTx: ensembled deep learning model to detect retinal disorders. In: 2020 IEEE 33rd International Symposium on Computer-Based Medical Systems (CBMS), pp. 526–531. IEEE (2020)
3. Plant, C., et al.: Automated detection of brain atrophy patterns based on MRI for the prediction of Alzheimer's disease. Neuroimage **50**(1), 162–174 (2010)
4. Jha, D., Kim, J.-I., Kwon, G.-R.: Diagnosis of Alzheimer's disease using dual-tree complex wavelet transform, PCA, and feed-forward neural network. J. Healthc. Eng. **2017**, 13 p., 9060124 (2017). https://doi.org/10.1155/2017/9060124
5. Gupta, A., Ayhan, M., Maida, A.: Natural image bases to represent neuroimaging data. In: International Conference on Machine Learning, pp. 987–994 (2013)
6. Friston, K.J., Poline, J.-B., Holmes, A.P., Frith, C.D., Frackowiak, R.S.: A multivariate analysis of pet activation studies. Hum. Brain Mapp. **4**(2), 140–151 (1996)
7. McKeown, M.J., et al.: Analysis of fMRI data by blind separation into independent spatial components. Hum. Brain Mapp. **6**(3), 160–188 (1998)
8. McIntosh, A., Grady, C., Ungerleider, L.G., Haxby, J., Rapoport, S., Horwitz, B.: Network analysis of cortical visual pathways mapped with PET. J. Neurosci. **14**(2), 655–666 (1994)
9. Mourao-Miranda, J., Bokde, A.L., Born, C., Hampel, H., Stetter, M.: Classifying brain states and determining the discriminating activation patterns: support vector machine on functional mri data. NeuroImage **28**(4), 980–995 (2005)
10. Davatzikos, C., Genc, A., Xu, D., Resnick, S.M.: Voxel-based morphometry using the RAVENS maps: methods and validation using simulated longitudinal atrophy. NeuroImage **14**(6), 1361–1369 (2001)
11. Teipel, S.J., et al.: Multivariate deformation-based analysis of brain atrophy to predict Alzheimer's disease in mild cognitive impairment. Neuroimage **38**(1), 13–24 (2007)
12. Vemuri, P., et al.: Alzheimer's disease diagnosis in individual subjects using structural MR images: validation studies. Neuroimage **39**(3), 1186–1197 (2008)

13. Ding, Y., et al.: A deep learning model to predict a diagnosis of Alzheimer disease by using 18F-FDG PET of the brain. Radiology **290**(2), 456–464 (2019)
14. Al-Khuzaie, F.E., Bayat, O., Duru, A.D.: Diagnosis of Alzheimer disease using 2D MRI slices by convolutional neural network. Appl. Bion. Biomech. **2021** (2021). https://pubmed.ncbi.nlm.nih.gov/33623535/
15. Venugopalan, J., Tong, L., Hassanzadeh, H.R., Wang, M.D.: Multimodal deep learning models for early detection of Alzheimer's disease stage. Sci. Rep. **11**(1), 1–13 (2021)
16. Mehmood, A., Maqsood, M., Bashir, M., Shuyuan, Y.: A deep Siamese convolution neural network for multi-class classification of Alzheimer disease. Brain Sci. **10**(2), 84 (2020)
17. Islam, J., Zhang, Y.: Early diagnosis of Alzheimer's disease: a neuroimaging study with deep learning architectures. In: Proceedings of the IEEE Conference on Computer Vision and Pattern Recognition Workshops, pp. 1881–1883 (2018)
18. Suh, C., et al.: Development and validation of a deep learning-based automatic brain segmentation and classification algorithm for Alzheimer disease using 3D T1-weighted volumetric images. Am. J. Neuroradiol. **41**(12), 2227–2234 (2020)
19. Nagaraj, S., Duong, T.: Risk score stratification of Alzheimer's disease and mild cognitive impairment using deep learning. medRxiv, 2020–11 (2021)
20. Marcus, D.S., Fotenos, A.F., Csernansky, J.G., Morris, J.C., Buckner, R.L.: Open access series of imaging studies: longitudinal MRI data in nondemented and demented older adults. J. Cogn. Neurosci. **22**(12), 2677–2684 (2010)
21. Perneczky, R., et al.: Head circumference, atrophy, and cognition: implications for brain reserve in Alzheimer disease. Neurology **75**(2), 137–142 (2010)
22. Kingma, D.P., Ba, J.: Adam: a method for stochastic optimization. arXiv preprint arXiv:1412.6980 (2014)

Semi-supervised Multi-domain Learning
for Medical Image Classification

Ruchika Chavhan[1], Biplab Banerjee[2], and Nibaran Das[3](✉)

[1] School of Informatics, University of Edinburgh, Scotland, UK
[2] Center of Machine Intelligence and Data Science, IIT Bombay, Mumbai, India
bbanerjee@iitb.ac.in
[3] Department of CSE, Jadavpur University, Kolkata, India
nibaran@ieee.org

Abstract. The limitations of domain dependence in neural networks and data scarcity are addressed in this paper by analyzing the problem of semi-supervised medical image classification across multiple visual domains using a single integrated framework. Under this premise, we learn a universal parametric family of neural networks, which share a majority of their weights across domains by learning a few adaptive domain-specific parameters. We train these universal networks on a suitable *pretext task* that captures a meaningful representation for image classification and further fine-tune the networks using a small fraction of training data. We perform our experiments on five medical datasets spanning breast, cervical, and colorectal cancer. Extensive experiments on architectures of domain-adaptive parameters demonstrate that our data-deficient universal model performs equivalently to a fully supervised setup, rendering a semi-supervised multi-domain setting with lower numbers of training samples for medical data extremely feasible in the real world.

Keywords: Multi-domain learning · Semi-supervised learning · Medical image classification

1 Introduction

The adoption of machine learning techniques for medical data and image analysis has significantly expanded and gathered immense attraction from researchers in recent decades [24,26,38]. Consequently, several deep learning techniques are being rapidly utilized to automate and improve predictions in the fields of genomics research [12], cancer prognosis [4,32], and medical imaging [25,34]. The effect of this permeation can also be seen widely in the the field of medical disorder classification, tumor/lesion segmentation, abnormality detection in areas like neurology [2], ophthalmic [11] and thoracic imaging [39], and digital and microscopic pathology [17]. Observing research from the past few decades, it can be deduced that the

Supplementary Information The online version contains supplementary material available at https://doi.org/10.1007/978-3-031-23599-3_3.

proliferation of computer automation in medical research has led to an unprecedented expansion of algorithms and datasets catering to medical researchers.

However, owing to the data-centric nature of machine learning, a surge in research implies an escalated need for labeled data collection, which is both time consuming and laborious. The lack of labeled data has motivated myriad research in the field of unsupervised [33], self-supervised [7], and semi supervised [10] learning. Semi-supervised learning considers a few labeled samples available with a large amount of unlabeled data. The goal of a semi-supervised learning model is to make effective use of all of the available data, labeled and unlabeled. Self-supervised learning is an elegant subset of machine learning where a model can generate output labels intrinsically from unlabeled data. The *self-supervised* , also known as the *pretext task* guides a supervised loss function by learning inherent properties or semantic representations of the objects which are further used for related downstream tasks. A convolutional neural network (CNN) is trained to solve the pretext task and generate pseudo labels for the dataset based on the attributes learnt from the objective function of the pretext task. In some works, intrinsic latent representations learnt by solving a pretext task are utilized for semi-supervised learning with scarce annotations [22,30,37]. Parameters of the model trained on the self-supervised task are finetuned on a few annotated samples to perform a downstream visual task. The semi-supervised setup holds immense utility in real world applications, especially for medical data on account of limited annotations, patients, and means of data collection. As a result, a rich body of literature exists for semi-supervised learning and self-supervised learning for medical data as well [1,3,5,15,16,20].

Another hindrance in enhancing the scalability of machine learning techniques is that models understand multiple image datasets independently by learning separate models for every visual domain. Furthermore, these restrictions are amplified for medical datasets due to factors like scarcity, the rarity of the disease, the risk of data misuse, and lack of data-sharing incentives. Recently, research in the field of multi-domain learning [29,31] is proliferating guided by the aim of learning universal representations and feature extractors that can operate over several different visual domains. The primary goal is to develop models that can compactly represent multiple domains by leveraging associative knowledge between low and mid-level features of visually distinct domains. The underlying working principle behind these models is that multiple domains should share majority of their parameters except for certain weights, named adapters, that depend on the distribution of individual domains. Details of the multi-domain setup is described in detail in subsequent sections.

Although, there has been remarkable research in learning models for multiple domains in medical data [8,21,23,35], we argue that the methodology and goals of the proposed frameworks are significantly different from ours. We would like to indicate that learning models for multiple domains and a multi-domain setting are substantially different. For example, [6] introduced a framework for early Alzheimer's disease detection that utilize transfer learning to simultaneously learn the task and leverage information from multi-auxiliary domains to excel on the target domain. In the same spirit, [27] considers a self-supervised domain adaptation setting using multiple datasets for glaucoma detection. The above methods mainly focus on a transfer learning and domain adaptation pipeline that assume a certain degree of similarity between visual domains related to one body part. In contrast, our model is capable of operating without any assumptions about similarities between datasets as we consider domains from different body parts and sources to perform different image classification tasks. We would like to point out that the above works perform detection of only a single disease, implying that detection of different disease would require us to train a completely new model. Contrarily, our multi-domain universal models can perform detection of different diseases using a single universal model with only a few domain-specific adapters. Hence, this setup evinces itself to be extremely practical in a real life scenario where it is unfeasible to perpetually keep shifting between neural networks for different types of diagnosis.

In this paper, we jointly tackle the problem of scarce annotations and multi-domain training on medical datasets from distinct visual domains. We perform semi-supervised training on multiple domains by learning generalized representations using a vast majority of shared parameters and a few domain-specific adapters. Essentially, this is equivalent to learning a single framework for multiple domains with the addition of a very few dependent parameters. By virtue of training only a singular universal model on multiple domains, a major merit of the proposed method is that we can use a single model for scarce datasets corresponding to distinct organs and tissues or obtained from different laboratories using disparate preparation methods. To demonstrate this, we perform our experiments on the task of image classification for five medical datasets spanning over breast, cervical, and colorectal cancer which are collected for either tissue (Histology) or cell (cytology) study. Our contributions in this paper are three-fold:

- A framework to perform medical image classification on a distinct variety of datasets under the multi-domain setting.
- Moreover, we challenge ourselves by introducing restrictions on annotated data collected from multiple domains, operating in a semi-supervised setting.
- We perform several experiments on different architectures of adapters to analyse and compare their behaviour in the presence of limited supervision.

2   Methods

2.1   Preliminaries

Under the multi-domain setting, we aim to train neural networks that share a majority of their parameters across domains with exception of a few adaptive ones denoted by θ_d for $d = 1, 2, ...D$, where D is the total number of domains. We denote input images of each domain by $\mathcal{X}_d \in \mathbf{R}^{H \times W \times 3}$, projected onto a feature space $\mathcal{F}_d \in \mathbf{R}^{H_f \times W_f \times C_f}$ by a convolutional feature extractor $\mathcal{E}_\Theta : \mathbf{R}^{H \times W \times 3} \rightarrow$

$\mathbf{R}^{H_f \times W_f \times C_f}$. Here, $\Theta = \{\theta_d \cup \psi\}$ denotes the complete set of domain-dependent θ_d and independent parameters ψ for the feature extractor, such that $\theta_d \cap \psi = \emptyset$. Subsequently, we obtain the labels for an image from domain d using a domain-specific linear classifier $\mathcal{L}_{\phi_d} : \mathbf{R}^{H_f \times W_f \times C_f} \rightarrow \mathbf{R}^{|C|_d}$, where $|C|_d$ is the number of categories in the domain. It is assumed that $\mathcal{L}_d$ consists of a softmax layer which returns a normalized probability distribution $\mathcal{P}_d = \mathcal{L}_d(\mathcal{E}(\mathcal{X}_d))$ over all classes in domain d. For notational convenience, we drop the parameters Θ_d and ϕ_d from the feature extractor and the linear classifier. To sum up, the domain-agnostic parameters are denoted by ψ while θ_d and ϕ_d are the domain-specific parameters.

2.2 Residual Adapters

A ResNet block [13] is a function $r_w : \mathbf{R}^{H \times W \times C} \rightarrow \mathbf{R}^{H \times W \times C}$ parametrised by weights w that performs the operation $r_w(x) = x + w \star x$. Here, the operation $\star$ consists of convolutional with batch normalization and ReLU function.

The primary idea behind residual adapters [29] is to modify the conventional residual network to contain domain-specific parameters. Naturally, to adapt a residual block $r_{i,w,d}$ for domain d, its parameters w need to be replaced by domain-specific weights $\theta_{i,d}$, $i = 1, 2, ... |R|$, where $|R|$ is the number of residual adapters in the universal neural network. In order to restrict the number of domain-dependent parameters, the convolution layers in θ_d are implemented in the form of a filter bank of size 1×1. Apart from convolution filters, the scaling parameters of batch-normalization are also incorporated in the residual adapter modules by virtue of normalized outputs and stable training. It is worth noting that batch-normalization inherently consists of domain-specific scaling parameters that adds a certain degree of adaptation in the network. These residual adapters can be positioned in two ways [31] with respect to the domain-agnostic parameters: parallel and in series. We direct the readers to [31] for a thorough analysis of parallel and series residual adapters.

2.3 Multi-domain Semi-supervised Training

Let us denote the pretext task/self-supervised task and the downstream task by $\mathcal{T}_p$ and $\mathcal{T}_m$ respectively. In this paper, we consider the downstream task to be multi-class image classification. Under this premise, a suitable pretext task performs auxiliary classification on d domains over $|C|_d^p$ categories obtained inherently from unlabeled data. We denote the datasets corresponding to pretext tasks and downstream tasks for domain d by $D_{p,d} = \{\mathcal{X}_i^{p,d}, \mathcal{Y}_i^{p,d}\}_{i=1}^{N_{p,d}}$ and $D_{m,d} = \{\mathcal{X}_i^{m,d}, \mathcal{Y}_i^{m,d}\}_{i=1}^{N_{m,d}}$ respectively. Since, we operate in a semi-supervised setup, we assume that a few annotated samples are available to us for each domain such that $N_{p,d} >> N_{m,d} \forall d$. These annotated samples for task $\mathcal{T}_m$ are further used to finetune the parameters of the network trained on the pretext task $\mathcal{T}_p$.

We consider a neural network for image classification consisting of convolutional and fully-connected layers given by $\mathcal{N}(\cdot) = \mathcal{L}_d(\mathcal{E}(\cdot))$ such that $\mathcal{E} = \{\theta_d \cup \psi\}$. In multi-domain learning works [29,31], the domain-agnostic parameters ψ are obtained from a model pre-trained on a large dataset such as ImageNet while the domain-specific parameters are finetuned on corresponding domains. This ensures that a predominant number of parameters of the neural network are shared across domains. In the same spirit, we finetune only the domain-specific parameters θ_d, ϕ_d while solving both $\mathcal{T}_p$ and $\mathcal{T}_m$, while the domain-independent parameters ψ remain frozen and shared amongst all domains throughout the training process.

The entire training setup is demonstrated by Fig. 1. Initially, we train the network $\mathcal{N}$ to solve the pretext task $\mathcal{T}_p$ using $D_{p,d}$. In order to perform the classification based pretext task, we introduce a different linear classifier $\hat{\mathcal{L}}_{\phi_{d'}} : \mathbf{R}^{H_f \times W_f \times C_f} \rightarrow \mathbf{R}^{|C|^p_d}$, which provides a probability distribution over auxiliary categories. The output of the network for the pretext task is obtained as $\mathcal{Y}_i^{p,d} = \hat{\mathcal{L}}(\mathcal{E}(\mathcal{X}_i^{p,d}))$. Thereafter, the domain-specific parameters for the pretext task $\Theta_{d'} = \theta_d \cup \phi_{d'}$ are updated according to Eq. 1, where $L_{p,d}(\cdot, \cdot)$ stands for cross-entropy loss for each domain and $B_{p,d}$ stands for the size of a minibatch.

$$\Theta_{d'} \leftarrow \Theta_{d'} - \eta \sum_{i=1}^{B_{p,d}} \frac{dL_{p,d}(\hat{\mathcal{Y}}_i^{p,d}, \mathcal{Y}_i^{p,d})}{d\Theta_d}, \forall d \tag{1}$$

By training our network on a befitting pretext task, we have ensured that our network comprises a meaningful semantic representation capable of supplementing knowledge for a downstream task. Consequently, the final step is to finetune only the parameters of the classification layer $\mathcal{L}_{\phi_d}$ on the downstream task using a few annotated samples and update its parameters using Eq. 2. Here, $\mathcal{Y}_i^{m,d} = \mathcal{L}(\mathcal{E}(\mathcal{X}_i^{m,d}))$ denotes the output of the downstream classification task and $L_{m,d}(\cdot, \cdot)$ stands for cross-entropy loss for corresponding domains.

$$\phi_d \leftarrow \phi_d - \eta \sum_{i=1}^{B_{m,d}} \frac{dL_{m,d}(\hat{\mathcal{Y}}_i^{m,d}, \mathcal{Y}_i^{m,d})}{d\phi_d}, \forall d \tag{2}$$

During testing, domain-specific parameters $\theta_d \cup \phi_d$ corresponding to the domain d of the input image are retrieved from stored models to perform classification over $|\mathcal{C}_d|$ categories.

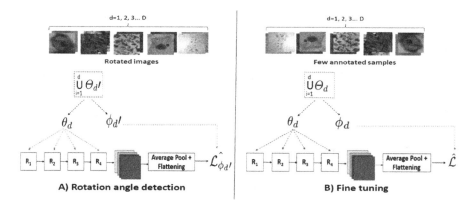

Fig. 1. Overview of the Multi-domain semi-supervised setup. The domain-specific parameters for a domain are chosen from the union of all parameters given a domain index d. The green and red dashed arrows denote trainable and frozen domain-dependent parameters respectively. (Color figure online)

Algorithm 1. Training Algorithm

Stage 1: Self supervised training
Input: Pre-trained Resnet-26 model. Initialise parameters $\Theta_{d\prime}$. while not done do
1: **for** $epoch = 1$ to epochs **do**
2:    Rotate $\mathcal{X}_i^{p,d}$ by an arbitrary angle from the set $Y_i^{p,d} = \{0, 90, 180, 270\}$.
3:    $\hat{\mathcal{Y}}_i^{p,d} = \hat{\mathcal{L}}(\mathcal{E}(\mathcal{X}_i^{p,d}))$;
4:    Update $\Theta_{d\prime}$ using Equation 1;
5: **end for**
Stage 2: Fine-tuning
Input: Frozen parameters θ_d. Initialise parameters ϕ_d.
6: **for** $epoch = 1$ to epochs **do**
7:    **for** $i = 1$ to $N_{m,d}$ **do**
8:       $\mathcal{Y}_i^{m,d} = \mathcal{L}(\mathcal{E}(\mathcal{X}_i^{m,d}))$;
9:       Update ϕ_d using Equation 2;
10:    **end for**
11: **end for**

---

3 Experimental Setup

Datasets: We perform experiments on five distinct datasets related to various types of cancers namely breast, colorectal and cervical. The data are collected by two techniques, i.e. Histology and Cytology.

– **Mendeley:** [14] This dataset consists of total 963 liquid based cytology pap smear images divided into four classes ($|C|_d = 4$) of pre-cancerous and cancerous lesions of cervical cancer namely High squamous intra-epithelial lesion, Low squamous intra-epithelial lesion, Negative for Intraepithelial malignancy, and Squamous cell carcinoma.

- **Herlev:** [18] This dataset contains 917 images of healthy and cancerous pap smears categorized into seven classes ($|C|_d = 7$) which are carcinoma, light dysplastic, moderate dysplastic, normal columnar, normal intermediate, normal superficiel, and severe dysplastic.
- **SIPaKMeD:** [28] This dataset is comprised of 4049 images pap smear slides divided into five categories ($|C|_d = 5$) containing normal, abnormal and benign cells specifically the superficial-intermediate, parabasal, koilocytotic, dysketarotic, and metaplastic cells.
- **Kather:** [19] This dataset is a collection of histological images of human colorectal cancer sub-divided into eight classes ($|C|_d = 8$) of benign and malignant cancer.
- **BreakHis:** [36] This dataset contains 9,109 microscopic images of benign and malignant breast tumor tissue further subdivided into eight categories. However, for our experiments, we consider only two classes ($|C|_d = 2$) due to high inter-class similarity.

Pretext Task: We choose rotation angle prediction (RotNet) [9] as the self-supervision task for our experiments. We rotate the image arbitarily by choosing one of the angles out of the set $\mathcal{A} = \{0, 90, 180, 270\}$. This implies that $|C|_d^p = 4$, $\forall d$. The parameters $\Theta_{d'}$ are trained to predict the angle by which the input image has been rotated. For all domains, we trained this proxy task for 200 epochs.

Architecture: We consider the baseline model to be a ResNet module in the 26-layer configuration as done in [31]. The network consists of 3 blocks of convolutional layers that output features containing 64, 128 and 256 channels respectively. Each block further consists of 4 residual blocks ($|R| = 4$) each, containing a domain-independent 3×3 convolutional layers followed by 1×1 domain-specific filter banks with a skip connection. The spatial resolution of the data is halved from a block to the next. The residual adapters are distributed throughout all the feature extractors modules which are followed by domain-specific classifiers. The model in Fig. 1 depicts only one such convolutional block for ease of visualization of the training method.

Training Details: We use the 80:20 training and validation set split for all the five datasets. We train the entire model using stochastic gradient optimization with a learning rate of 10^{-3}, momentum and weight decay. In contrast to [31], we do not use dropout in any of the residual adapters. We perform finetuning on the domain-specific classifier for 200 epochs for each domain. The training algorithm is mentioned in Algorithm 1.

4   Results and Discussion

In this section, we discuss the results obtained by our proposed methodology on the five datasets mentioned in Sect. 3. For every dataset we finetune the domain-specific parameters of the network with 10/25/50/100 labeled samples per class. In Fig. 2, we present the performance of parallel residual adapters in the universal model on each dataset while varying the number of samples. Table 1

Table 1. Results of the parallel and series adapters on five medical datasets by varying the number of samples per class. We report the accuracies in % of each model under different cases of limited supervision. "Full" denotes training with the complete training set. We also report the deviation of accuracy throughout the validation set. The greatest value in reach row is highlighted in **bold**.

Dataset	Model	Number of samples				
		10	25	50	100	Full
Mendeley	Parallel	76.52 ± 1.04	91.15 ± 0.52	97.40 ± 0.41	98.44 ± 0.52	$\mathbf{98.96 \pm 0.07}$
	Series	82.21 ± 1.12	91.67 ± 1.04	96.35 ± 0.52	$\mathbf{98.96 \pm 1.04}$	97.40 ± 1.86
Kather	Parallel	78.63 ± 0.61	90.63 ± 0.81	93.75 ± 1.41	$\mathbf{96.88 \pm 0.25}$	96.87 ± 2.02
	Series	74.60 ± 0.10	81.45 ± 0.20	88.21 ± 0.30	90.83 ± 0.20	$\mathbf{93.75 \pm 0.41}$
SipaKMed	Parallel	75.63 ± 0.38	90.63 ± 0.13	93.75 ± 0.28	94.13 ± 0.48	$\mathbf{94.63 \pm 1.63}$
	Series	78.13 ± 1.30	89.84 ± 0.25	92.19 ± 1.06	$\mathbf{96.88 \pm 0.88}$	95.25 ± 1.50
BreakHis	Parallel	43.75 ± 0.07	84.38 ± 0.52	87.50 ± 0.88	92.49 ± 0.30	$\mathbf{92.97 \pm 2.35}$
	Series	59.38 ± 0.02	84.64 ± 2.34	96.88 ± 0.21	$\mathbf{96.88 \pm 1.04}$	97.73 ± 0.85
Herlev	Parallel	50.63 ± 1.25	87.50 ± 2.13	93.75 ± 1.25	$\mathbf{98.86 \pm 0.63}$	98.66 ± 0.29
	Series	53.13 ± 1.48	75.00 ± 2.28	92.19 ± 0.63	96.36 ± 1.24	$\mathbf{97.32 \pm 0.85}$

demonstrates the results of our universal model on all five medical datasets considered in this paper. We perform experiments on two architectural possibilities of the residual adapters: series and parallel and compare their performance. To demonstrate the generalization capability of our model under the constraints on labeled data, we also compare our results with the fully-supervised multimodal training setup. We also provide an extensive qualitative visualisation of the performance of our models in the supplementary material.

Discussion: From Table 1, we observe that our model provides an accuracy that is almost equivalent to the performance of a fully-supervised model, inspite of severe data scarcity. As expected, the performance of all models increase with the introduction of more training samples. In some cases, addition of 15–25 samples provides a sharp boost in accuracies. We observe that in most cases the accuracy obtained with only 100 samples is appreciably close to model with full supervision. Interestingly, in many cases, the accuracy provided by some models with just 100 samples is better than full supervision.

- **Mendeley:** For this dataset, we observe a better performace with the series adapters in all the cases. In case of parallel adapters, the precision obtained with full supervision is greater than limited supervision of 100 samples by merely 0.52%. Interestingly, the accuracy provided by the series adapters by 1.56%.
- **Kather:** The parallel adapters outperform the series adapters by 3.12% in a fully supervised setup. However, for 100 samples, this difference increases to 6.05%. The average performance of parallel adapters on 100 samples and full supervision is almost equal.
- **SipakMed:** From Table 1, we conclude that both adapters perform almost equally for this dataset. However, the series adapters with supervision of

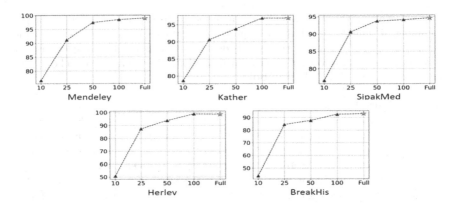

Fig. 2. Comparison of accuracy of parallel adapters by varying the number of samples per class. x-axis denotes the number of samples and y-axis denotes accuracy of the model. The green star denotes the accuracy of the model under full supervision. (Color figure online)

100 samples provides greater accuracy than full supervision by 1.63%. It is interesting to note that there is very little fluctuation in accuracy (0.38%) when number of samples are increased from 50 to 100.

- **BreakHis:** We observe that the series adapter models perform consistently better than parallel adapters. The performance of the series adapters on 100 samples is appreciably close to model with full supervision. A stark increase in accuracy is observed when number of samples increase from 10 to 25.
- **Herlev:** In this case, the parallel adapters perform better than series adapters with 100 samples by 2.5%. Furthermore, parallel adapters with 100 samples perform slightly better (0.2%) than full supervision.

5   Conclusion

In this paper, we proposed the concept of semi-supervised multi-domain learning in the domain of medical images. Our aim is to tackle two major restrictions that hinder the growth of machine learning in the medical domain, namely data scarcity and domain-dependence of models. To accomplish this, we introduce a universal family of models that share majority of their parameters except a few domain-specific parameters termed as adapters that leverage information from pretext tasks to perform image classification. We perform extensive experiments on five medical image datasets from different sub-domains namely, Medeley, Kather, SipakMed, BreakHis, and Herlev spanning breast, colorectal, and cervical cancer. Ultimately, we demonstrate that the performace of our models trained with as few as 100 samples is congruous with those trained under full supervision. This opens up riveting and exciting possibilities for a semi-supervised multi-domain setup for medical images under multiple scenarios. In the future, we wish to extend this setup to dense prediction tasks like semantic segmentation and object detection for tumor/lesion detection.

References

1. Bai, W., et al.: Self-supervised learning for cardiac MR image segmentation by anatomical position prediction. In: Shen, D., et al. (eds.) MICCAI 2019. LNCS, vol. 11765, pp. 541–549. Springer, Cham (2019). https://doi.org/10.1007/978-3-030-32245-8_60
2. Brosch, T., Tam, R.: Manifold learning of brain MRIs by deep learning. In: Mori, K., Sakuma, I., Sato, Y., Barillot, C., Navab, N. (eds.) MICCAI 2013. LNCS, vol. 8150, pp. 633–640. Springer, Heidelberg (2013). https://doi.org/10.1007/978-3-642-40763-5_78
3. Chaitanya, K., Erdil, E., Karani, N., Konukoglu, E.: Contrastive learning of global and local features for medical image segmentation with limited annotations In: Proceedings of the 34th International Conference on Neural Information Processing Systems-NIPS 2020, pp. 2546–12558 (2020)
4. Cheerla, A., Gevaert, O.: Deep learning with multimodal representation for pan-cancer prognosis prediction. Bioinformatics **35**(14), i446–i454 (2019)
5. Chen, L., Bentley, P., Mori, K., Misawa, K., Fujiwara, M., Rueckert, D.: Self-supervised learning for medical image analysis using image context restoration. Med. Image Anal. **58**, 101539 (2019)
6. Cheng, B., Liu, M., Shen, D., Li, Z., Zhang, D.: Multi-domain transfer learning for early diagnosis of Alzheimer's disease. Neuroinformatics **15**(2), 115–132 (2016)
7. Chhipa, P.C., Upadhyay, R., Grund Pihlgren, G., Saini, R., Uchida, S., Liwicki, M.: Magnification prior: a self-supervised method for learning representations on breast cancer histopathological images. arXiv e-prints arXiv:2203.07707, March 2022
8. Feng, Y., Liu, Y., Luo, J.: Universal model for multi-domain medical image retrieval (2020). https://doi.org/10.48550/arxiv.2007.08628
9. Gidaris, S., Singh, P., Komodakis, N.: Unsupervised representation learning by predicting image rotations. In: 6th International Conference on Learning Representations, ICLR 2018 (2018). https://openreview.net/forum?id=S1v4N2l0-
10. Guillaumin, M., Verbeek, J., Schmid, C.: Multimodal semi-supervised learning for image classification. In: 2010 IEEE Computer Society Conference on Computer Vision and Pattern Recognition, pp. 902–909. IEEE (2010)
11. Gulshan, V., et al.: Development and validation of a deep learning algorithm for detection of diabetic retinopathy in retinal fundus photographs. JAMA **316** (2016). https://doi.org/10.1001/jama.2016.17216
12. Hajiramezanali, E., Zamani Dadaneh, S., Karbalayghareh, A., Zhou, M., Qian, X.: Bayesian multi-domain learning for cancer subtype discovery from next-generation sequencing count data. In: Bengio, S., Wallach, H., Larochelle, H., Grauman, K., Cesa-Bianchi, N., Garnett, R. (eds.) Advances in Neural Information Processing Systems, vol. 31, p. 9133–9142. Curran Associates, Inc. (2018)
13. He, K., Zhang, X., Ren, S., Sun, J.: Identity mappings in deep residual networks. In: Leibe, B., Matas, J., Sebe, N., Welling, M. (eds.) ECCV 2016. LNCS, vol. 9908, pp. 630–645. Springer, Cham (2016). https://doi.org/10.1007/978-3-319-46493-0_38
14. Hussain, E., Mahanta, L.B., Borah, H., Das, C.R.: Liquid based-cytology pap smear dataset for automated multi-class diagnosis of pre-cancerous and cervical cancer lesions. Data Brief **30**, 105589 (2020)
15. Imran, A.A.Z., et al.: Self-supervised, semi-supervised, multi-context learning for the combined classification and segmentation of medical images (student abstract). In: Proceedings of the AAAI Conference on Artificial Intelligence, vol. 34, pp. 13815–13816 (2020). https://doi.org/10.1609/aaai.v34i10.7179

16. Jamaludin, A., Kadir, T., Zisserman, A.: Self-supervised learning for spinal MRIs. In: Cardoso, M.J., et al. (eds.) DLMIA/ML-CDS 2017. LNCS, vol. 10553, pp. 294–302. Springer, Cham (2017). https://doi.org/10.1007/978-3-319-67558-9_34

17. Janowczyk, A., Basavanhally, A., Madabhushi, A.: Stain normalization using sparse autoencoders (StaNoSA): application to digital pathology. Comput. Med. Imaging Graph. **57**, 50–61 (2017). Recent Developments in Machine Learning for Medical Imaging Applications

18. Jantzen, J., Norup, J., Dounias, G., Bjerregaard, B.: Pap-smear benchmark data for pattern classification. In: Nature inspired Smart Information Systems: EU Coordination Action, NiSIS 2005, 01 January 2005, pp. 1–9 (2005)

19. Kather, J.N., et al.: Collection of textures in colorectal cancer histology (2016)

20. Khosravan, N.: Semi-supervised multi-task learning for lung cancer diagnosis, vol. 2018, pp. 710–713 (2018). https://doi.org/10.1109/EMBC.2018.8512294

21. Kraljevic, Z., et al..: Multi-domain clinical natural language processing with MedCAT: the medical concept annotation toolkit. Artif. Intell. Med. **117**, 102083 (2021)

22. Laine, S., Aila, T.: Temporal ensembling for semi-supervised learning. In: 5th International Conference on Learning Representations, ICLR 2017, Toulon, France, 24–26 April 2017 (2017)

23. Li, H., Wang, Y., Wan, R., Wang, S., Li, T.Q., Kot, A.: Domain generalization for medical imaging classification with linear-dependency regularization, vol. 33, pp. 3118–3129 (2020)

24. Litjens, G., et al.: A survey on deep learning in medical image analysis. Med. Image Anal. **42**, 60–88 (2017)

25. Lundervold, A.S., Lundervold, A.: An overview of deep learning in medical imaging focusing on MRI. Zeitschrift für Medizinische Physik **29**(2), 102–127 (2019). Special Issue: Deep Learning in Medical Physics

26. Mitra, S., Das, N., Dey, S., Chakraborty, S., Nasipuri, M., Naskar, M.K.: Cytology image analysis techniques toward automation: systematically revisited. ACM Comput. Surv. **54**(3) (2021).https://doi.org/10.1145/3447238

27. Mojab, N., et al.: Real-world multi-domain data applications for generalizations to clinical settings. In: 2020 19th IEEE International Conference on Machine Learning and Applications (ICMLA), pp. 677–684 (2020). https://doi.org/10.1109/ICMLA51294.2020.00112

28. Plissiti, M.E., Dimitrakopoulos, P., Sfikas, G., Nikou, C., Krikoni, O., Charchanti, A.: SIPaKMeD: a new dataset for feature and image based classification of normal and pathological cervical cells in pap smear images. In: 2018 25th IEEE International Conference on Image Processing (ICIP), pp. 3144–3148 (2018). https://doi.org/10.1109/ICIP.2018.8451588

29. Rebuffi, S.A., Bilen, H., Vedaldi, A.: Learning multiple visual domains with residual adapters. In: Guyon, I., et al.. (eds.) Advances in Neural Information Processing Systems, vol. 30, pp. 1–11. Curran Associates, Inc. (2017)

30. Rebuffi, S.A., Ehrhardt, S., Han, K., Vedaldi, A., Zisserman, A.: Semi-supervised learning with scarce annotations. In: 2020 IEEE/CVF Conference on Computer Vision and Pattern Recognition Workshops (CVPRW), pp. 3294–3302 (2020)

31. Rebuffi, S.A., Vedaldi, A., Bilen, H.: Efficient parametrization of multi-domain deep neural networks. In: 2018 IEEE/CVF Conference on Computer Vision and Pattern Recognition, pp. 8119–8127 (2018). https://doi.org/10.1109/CVPR.2018.00847

32. Santosh, K., Das, N., Ghosh, S.: Cytology image analysis. In: Santosh, K., Das, N., Ghosh, S. (eds.) Deep Learning Models for Medical Imaging, Chap. 4. Primers in Biomedical Imaging Devices and Systems, pp. 99–123. Academic Press (2022)

33. Schmarje, L., Santarossa, M., Schröder, S.M., Koch, R.: A survey on semi-, self-and unsupervised learning for image classification. arXiv:2002.08721 (2020)
34. Sen, A., Mitra, S., Chakraborty, S., Mondal, D., Santosh, K., Das, N.: Ensemble framework for unsupervised cervical cell segmentation. In: 2022 IEEE 35th International Symposium on Computer-Based Medical Systems (CBMS), pp. 345–350 (2022). https://doi.org/10.1109/CBMS55023.2022.00068
35. Shen, L., et al.: Multi-domain image completion for random missing input data. IEEE Trans. Med. Imaging **40**(4), 1113–1122 (2021)
36. Spanhol, F.A., Oliveira, L.S., Petitjean, C., Heutte, L.: Breast cancer histopathological image classification using convolutional neural networks. In: 2016 International Joint Conference on Neural Networks (IJCNN), pp. 2560–2567 (2016)
37. Tarvainen, A., Valpola, H.: Mean teachers are better role models: Weight-averaged consistency targets improve semi-supervised deep learning results. In: Advances in Neural Information Processing Systems 30, pp. 1195–1204 (2017)
38. Wang, R., Lei, T., Cui, R., Zhang, B., Meng, H., Nandi, A.K.: Medical image segmentation using deep learning: a survey. IET Image Process. **16**(5), 1243–1267 (2022)
39. Zhou, X., Ito, T., Takayama, R., Wang, S., Hara, T., Fujita, H.: Three-dimensional CT image segmentation by combining 2D fully convolutional network with 3D majority voting. In: Carneiro, G., et al. (eds.) LABELS/DLMIA 2016. LNCS, vol. 10008, pp. 111–120. Springer, Cham (2016). https://doi.org/10.1007/978-3-319-46976-8_12

Significant CC400 Functional Brain Parcellations Based LeNet5 Convolutional Neural Network for Autism Spectrum Disorder Detection

Alice Othmani[1]([✉]) [iD], Thibaut Bizet[2], Tanguy Pellerin[2], Badr Hamdi[2],
Marc-Antoine Bock[2], and Soumyabrata Dev[3] [iD]

[1] Université Paris-Est, LISSI, UPEC, 94400 Vitry sur Seine, France
`alice.othmani@u-pec.fr`
[2] Engineering School - EFREI Paris, 94800 Villejuif, France
[3] School of Computer Science, University College Dublin, Dublin, Ireland

Abstract. Machine learning and computer vision have opened new pathways to investigate imaging data captured from different sensors. Numerous application areas are getting benefit from these advancements and one of these areas is medical imaging. Despite rapid advancements in machine learning based medical condition diagnosis systems (CADs), some ailments and disorders are hard to diagnose/classify due to the absence or the lack of consensus on biomarkers for specific disorders, like the Autism Spectrum Disorder (ASD). In this study, the challenging problem of classification of ASD using the magnetic resonance imaging (MRI) data is tackled. Hence, we propose an interpretable deep neural network based approach for ASD detection from MRI images. Our proposed explanation method is based on the selection of four regions of interest from the MRI images. The four significant CC400 functional brain parcellations are then concatenated and fed to a LeNet-5-based convolutional neural network to predict ASD. The performances of the proposed approach are evaluated on ABIDE dataset and promising results are achieved. Three augmented datasets are considered and an accuracy of 95% is achieved by using LeNet-5 which outperforms VGG16 and ResNet-50. The achieved accuracy outperforms also the existing deep neural networks based approaches on ABIDE dataset. The use of the four significant CC400 functional brain parcellations makes our approach more interpretable and more accurate.

Keywords: Deep learning · Convolutional Neural Network · Autism Spectrum Disorder · ABIDE I · MRI images

1 Introduction

Autism Spectrum Disorder (ASD) is a neurodevelopmental disorder that is perceived by a lack of emotional intelligence and social interaction. It is also

KC Santosh et al. (Eds.): RTIP2R 2022, CCIS 1704, pp. 34–45, 2023.
https://doi.org/10.1007/978-3-031-23599-3_4

recognized by repetitive, exaggerated, extreme and stigmatized behaviour [1]. This syndrome is not a rare condition, but a spectrum with several disabilities. According to DSM-IV APA (American Psychiatric Association) and ICD-10 WHO (World Health Organization 1993), behavioral and social characteristics is used to distinguish and to define ASD [2,3]. WHO reports, ASD affects one child in 160. An ASD subject has an abnormal social interaction with a limited enjoyment and interests in specific tasks and activities, and a limited of verbal and nonverbal communication skills. Children with ASD can improve their quality life, improve their social skills and reduce communication problems with an early diagnosis during childhood. However, ASD is difficult to diagnose because there is no medical test, like a blood test, to find the disorder. Regarding that, a lot of people are not diagnosed until they are teenagers or adults. This delay in diagnosis may affect the life of the ASD person and it delays to get help and needed health care services.

Magnetic-resonance Imaging (MR) examination provides a powerful tool for studying brain structural changes in people with ASD. In fact, MRI is a non-invasive technique universally used to study the brain and its structure thanks to regional network(s). Thus, subtle variations in neural patterns/networks are disclosed using this technique and new and relevant biomarkers can be defined for ASD. MRI scans are further divided into: (1) functional MRI (f-MRI) and (2) structural MRI (s-MRI) [4]. fMRI is a non-invasive technique for measuring brain activity and identifying changes associated with blood flow. Combining fMRI alongside with deep learning have been found to be the most essential and fruitful tool to yield significant results [5].

In this paper, a new and explainable deep learning-based approach is proposed to detect ASD from MRI images and evaluated on ABIDE dataset. The proposed approach is based learning deep patterns from significant CC400 functional brain parcellations for ASD detection. In addition to the high performance of our proposed approach, it offers an accurate ASD decision support system with interpretability ability for more trust in machine learning approaches. The paper is organized as follows: in the next Sect. 2, the literature review is presented, then the proposed approach is presented (refer to Sect. 4). After, experimental setups and achieved results are discussed in Sect. 5. The last Sect. 6 dispense our conclusion and our planned future work.

2   Related Work

Numerous approaches have been proposed in the literature for the detection of psychological and neurodevelopmental disorders [6,7]. Among these approaches, several ones are reported for ASD detection from MRI images. Brain activation patterns are recorded using fMRI of 17 adults diagnosed with high functioning autism (HFA) and 17 normal adults as control group [7]. These 17 adults who participated in the experiment were scanned while they imagined 16 social interaction scenarios. Authors presented machine learning technique based on Gaussian Naive Bayes (GNB) classifiers to classify autistic and control group.

Proposed approach achieved average recognition accuracy of 97%.

Sabuncu et al. [8] employed three different machine learning algorithms i.e. Support Vector Machine (SVM) [9], Neighborhood Approximation Forest (NAF) [10] and Relevance Vector Machine (RVM) [11] to analyze different neurological disorders, which include Alzheimer, schizophrenia, autism, attention deficit and hyperactivity disorders. Authors conducted machine learning experiments on structural MRI (s-MRI) data (s-MRI presents morphological features of brain) collected from 2800 individuals, gathered from six publicly available datasets[1]. Study conducted by Sabuncu et al. achieved average recognition accuracies of 59%, 70% and 86% for Autism, Schizophrenia and Alzheimer respectively using 5-fold cross-validation learning strategy.

Recent studies are based on deep learning algorithms that uses large brain imaging datasets for ASD detection. A transfer learning strategy is performed in [1]. Another Convolutional Neural Networks (CNN) based approach is proposed in [3] by using parallel filters to study the brains regions. In order to analyze MRI images, some researchers employed Convolutional Neural Networks (CNN) which are special deep neural networks well suited for analyzing structures present in the images. Sherkatghanad et al. [12] proposed architecture for ASD detection based on CNN. They also used resting-state functional magnetic resonance imaging (rsfMRI) data from ABIDE dataset and an average accuracy of 70.22% is achieved. Apart from achieving recognition accuracy, Zeinab et al. have also graphically shown which areas of brain are significant/salient in detecting ASD. Huang et al. [13] proposed a graph based model for detection of ASD. Authors have used a three-layer deep belief network (DBN) [14], where DBNs are probabilistic generative models. Proposed model is tested using resting-state functional magnetic resonance imaging (rsfMRI) data from ABIDE dataset and 76.4% of mean accuracy is achieved.

3D CNN based approach is proposed in [15]. Researchers have also proposed models that exploit the time-series nature of rs-fMRI Data. One such model is proposed by Dvornek et al. [16]. They utilized long short-term memory (LSTMs) for ASD classification. Authors have conducted experiment using data from ABIDE-I dataset [17] and they have achieved accuracy of 68.5%. In another article by Dvornek et al. [18], different methodologies/scenarios were proposed that incorporated phenotypic data with resting-state functional magnetic resonance imaging (rsfMRI) into recurrent neural networks (RNN) for classifying ASD. Proposed model achieved average recognition accuracy of 70.1% on the ABIDE dataset [17] when raw phenotypic data was combined directly with the baseline RNN model.

More recently, researchers applied autoencoders to detect ASD and augmented datasets to achieve a strong trained classifier. One such framework is proposed by Eslami et al. [19]. They proposed a framework (ASD-DiagNet) for automatic detection of ASD using functional magnetic resonance imaging (fMRI) data. Their proposed method is based on application of autoencoders and single layer perceptron (SLP). For robust training of proposed architecture, authors not

---

[1] https://www.nmr.mgh.harvard.edu/lab/mripredict.

only used ABIDE dataset but also its augmented version (linear interpolation). By using autoencoders, proposed architecture was able to reduce feature vector, thus reducing time complexity of model training as well. Proposed architecture achieved average recognition accuracy of 82% on data from 10 sites. Another framework that utilizes autoencoders to detect ASD is proposed by Wang et al. [20]. Wang et al. [20] proposed multi-atlas feature representation based method. Multi-atlas feature representation was deduced by applying stacked denoising autoencoder (SDA). Classification of features was achieved using Multi-Layer Perceptron (MLP) and Ensemble learning method. Proposed architecture was tested on ABIDE dataset and a mean accuracy of 74.52% is achieved.

3   Motivations and Contributions

As shown in the previous section, deep learning is the new trend in ASD diagnosis from MRI images. Despite the high performances and the accurate predictions of deep learning-based approaches, they remain black boxes and we cannot fully explain their predictions. Healthcare is one the applications that impact human lives and interpretability is crucial in healthcare decision support systems. A model's output is not very meaningful or accountable if it can't be explained. To trust a system and to deploy it in real-world healthcare applications, we must be able to explain why it has given an output. To the best of our knowledge, no explainable deep learning-based approach have been proposed for ASD diagnosis from MRI images in the literature.

In this paper, we aim to reach high performances by leveraging high advances in deep learning, while having the ability to interpret and to explain the deep neural network predictions. Thus, the main contributions of this paper are:

- A new approach for MRI-based automatic ASD detection via deep learning,
- An explainable deep neural network-based approach for ASD decision support system,
- Investigate local brain regions based high-level descriptors for ASD detection,
- A comparative analysis of three deep neural networks for ASD detection,
- Study of the importance of data augmentation in the proposed framework,
- Our proposed achieves very promising results on ABIDE dataset.

4   Proposed Approach

As shown in Fig. 1, our proposed approach is constituted of four steps. After a preprocessing step, local Regions of Interest (ROI) are extracted and concatenated into one image. Then, data augmentation is performed to overcome over-fitting issue related to training Deep Neural Networks. Finally, the augmented data are fed a LeNet-5 based deep neural network. More details about the proposed approach are given in the following.

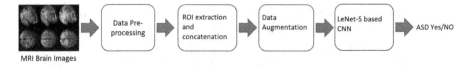

MRI Brain Images

Fig. 1. The proposed approach for ASD detection

4.1 Preprocessing

The Preprocessed Connectomes Project (PCP) published preprocessed versions of the ABIDE dataset with several pipelines [21] using: (1) the NeuroImaging Analysis Kit, (2) the Data Processing Assistant for Resting-State fMRI (DPARSF), (3) the Configurable Pipeline for the Analysis of Connectomes (CPAC) and (4) the Connectome Computation System (CCS). In this work, We used the data processed through Configurable Pipeline for Analysis of Connectomes(C-PAC). The used C-PAC pipeline[2] is constituted of

- a resampling to RPI orientation,
- a slice timing correction,
- a motion correction,
- a global mean intensity normalization and standardization of functional data
- extraction of ROI time series.

In our work, the version that consider a data extraction with global signal regression and a band-pass filtering (0.01–10 Hz) is used.

4.2 Regions of Interest (ROI) Selection

It has been demonstrated that four brain areas are significant in the diagnosis of ASD subjects based on the CC400 functional parcellation atlas of the brain [3]. In the CC400 atlas, the whole brain is parcellated into 400 regions. These regions are called C326, C115, C247 and C188 with the centers of mass equal to (−22.5; −85.5; 31.0), (61.9; −36.3; 34.4), (−2.1; −43.0; −40.7) and (−27.6; −40.2; −17.6), respectively. The four ROI (See Fig. 2) quoted above are the regions of the brain with the most information to detect ASD. In this work, we extracted the four brain areas, We concatenated them into 2D images and then resized them to fit the input size of our deep neural network of 156 * 32.

4.3 Data Augmentation

Data augmentation is an essential step to overcome over-fitting and data scarcity problems when training deep neural networks architectures, it also improve the robustness of the proposed architecture against noise. A transformation-based technique is performed to generate new images. Five transformation functions are considered which rescale, zoom, shift and shear an original image.

---

[2] https://fcp-indi.github.io/docs/latest/user/quick.html#default-pipeline.

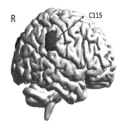 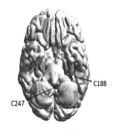 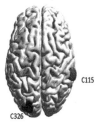

Fig. 2. The most discriminant and important regions of Interest for ASD classification, that are extracted, then concatenated and fed to the LeNet-5 based CNN. These regions are called C326, C115, C247 and C188 with the centers of mass equal to $(-22.5; -85.5; 31.0)$, $(61.9; -36.3; 34.4)$, $(-2.1; -43.0; -40.7)$ and $(-27.6; -40.2; -17.6)$, respectively.

Three expanded and balanced datasets are generated: **Dataset1** of 10k images, **Dataset2** of 30k images and **Dataset3** of 100k images. The performances of the proposed approach are evaluated in the three augmented datasets (refer to Sect. 5.3).

4.4   LeNet-5 Based Deep Neural Network for ASD Detection

The resulting 2D image from the previous steps are fed to LeNet-5 based deep neural network [22]. LeNet-5 is a CNN. It is one of the earliest CNNs, it was firstly implemented for digit images classification on MNIST dataset [22]. Afterwords, it has been applied to solve several problems and it has been demonstrated its high performances in classifying images like for example, for the classification of Alzheimer's disease using fMRI data [23], sleep apnea detection from a single-lead ECG signal [24], hyperspectral images classification or for the classification of pulmonary nodules of thoracic CT images [25] and also for efficient brain tumor segmentation in MRI images [26]. It has been shown that LeNet-5 can deal with small size datasets [22,27] and it requires small size of the input image like in our work. We have compared three famous and popular CNNs (VGG16, LeNet-5 and ResNet) and we found the LeNet-5 is the best performing CNN among them as described in Sect. 5.3.

The LeNet-5 architecture used in this work has 6 layers, not counting the input, all of which contain trainable parameters (weights) as shown in Fig. 3. The six layers are two convolution layers followed by two average pooling layers, and two fully connected layers. Although the LeNet architecture is firstly designed for training a 28×28 MNIST dataset, our input is a 150×32 pixel image. The output layer of the LeNet-5 is a dense layer of size 2 for binary ASD detection with a sigmoid activation function. The bias and the weight matrices are learned through a training process. In our work, the classification is learned by optimizing the cross-entropy between the classification outcome (predicted labels) and the ground truth (true labels), instead of learning the gaussian connection as described in the original paper of [22], using the function defined by:

$$L = 1/N \sum_{i=1}^{n} (Y_i - \hat{Y}_i)^2 \tag{1}$$

where L is the average loss for all the training samples, $\hat{Y}_i$ is the predicted ASD label and Y_i is the real ASD label.

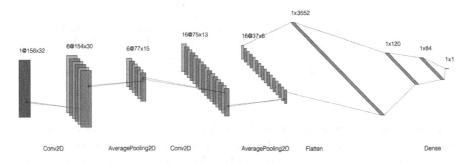

Fig. 3. Our Lenet-5 architecture used as final model

5 Results and Experiments

5.1 Dataset

The rs-fMRI images from Autism Brain Imaging Data Exchange (ABIDE-I) dataset [17] are used to evaluate the performances of the proposed approach. ABIDE is a collaborative consortium that provides neuroimaging data of control and ASD subjects with their phenotypic information. It is born from the collaboration between universities and laboratories around the world. It was built to have an easiest access to a large dataset of MRI images in order to have a better understanding of the disease. These images were collected and annotated across more than 24 brain imaging laboratories around the world. In this work, we use ABIDE-I dataset collected from 17 different imaging sites. It contains of 1112 subjects (539 autism subjects and 573 healthy control subjects).

5.2 Implementation Details

In this work, the choice of the optimal hyperparameters was done thanks to the model selection algorithm GridSearchCV[3] on 3, 4 and 5 fold cross-validations. A batch size of 32 is considered in all the experiments. The range of values that have been explored are: (1) Adam and Rmsprop for the optimizer, and 5, 10, 15, 25 and 40 for the number of epochs.

---

[3] GridSearchCV.

GridsearchCV uses an exhaustive search over specified parameter values for an estimator (the LeNet5 model for this work). The parameters of the estimator are optimized by cross-validated grid-search over a parameter grid. All the possible combinations of parameter values are evaluated and the best combination is retained.

The parameters of the final model are set to Adam for the optimizer, 25 for the number of epochs, 32 for batch-size, a momentum equal to 0.9 and a learning rate equal to 0.001. No fine-tuning is performed and three deep neural networks are trained from scratch as described in Sect. 4 using the three expanded datasets. For all experiments, the dataset is randomly divided into 80% for training, 20% for testing. In order to keep a balanced ratio between the labels, autistic and non-autistic subjects are first separated before performing the random split.

5.3   Performances

Performance Comparison of the LeNet-5 and Other Deep Neural Networks: The performances of the proposed approach have been evalutated using three popular deep neural networks (LeNet5, VGG16 and ResNet50). LeNet5 is a simple and an early convolutional neural network consisting of seven layers: 2 convolutional layers, 2 subsampling layers and 2 fully connected layers. VGG16 [28] is more deeper than LeNet5, it is formed of 13 convolutional layers, and 3 top fully connected layers. While ResNet50 is a deep residual neural network [29] designed to train deep networks with lower complexity. It consists of blocks of convolutional layers and residual shortcut connections.

As shown in Table 1, LeNet5 outperforms surprisingly VGG16 and ResNet50 with an accuracy of 65% on Dataset1. LeNet5 is the more shallow CNN among the tested ones. However, it outperforms the other ones. This is due to the small size of the input image (156 * 32) which represent the concatenation of the four significant CC400 functional brain parcellations. VGG16 and ResNet50 have close performances and they achieved the accuracy of 55% and 56% in MRI images classification for ASD diagnosis.

Importance of Data Augmentation. In order to overcome the lack of labeled datasets required to train deep neural networks, a data augmentation step is performed for MRI images generation as described in Sect. 4.3. The best performing deep neural network (LeNet5 according to our experiment in the previous section), is evaluated on three augmented datasets (see Table 1).

The data augmentation step is a crucial step in our proposed approach and without it an over-fitting problem is shown. To overcome it, the size of the training dataset must be increased. When increasing the size of the original dataset, the proposed LeNet5 based framework reaches an accuracy of 80% on Dataset2 and 95% on Dataset3. The more data is used for the training, the most accurate the LeNet5-based framework becomes. The best performing LeNet5-based framework has an F1-score equal to 0.95, a precision equal to 0.95 and a recall equal to 0.95.

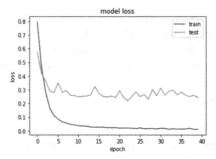

Fig. 4. Training and test loss in terms of training epochs of the LeNet-5 based CNN on Dataset 3.

The train and the validation sets in terms of number epochs of the proposed LeNet-5 based framework for binary ASD classification, is shown in Fig. 4. The proposed framework is not overfitting and training stops after 40 epochs when model performance stops improving.

The proposed method achieves significantly good performance on the augmented ABIDE dataset. Even with simple technique of expanding the training labels, the proposed deep neural network learns how to differentiate accurately between MRI images of control and ASD samples. Thus, the expansion of the labeled training dataset by generating new MRI images could significantly improves the performances of our approach and the achieved performance confirm the possibility of deploying the LeNet5 in a decision support system for ASD diagnosis.

Explainability of Our Proposed Approach: In addition to the high performances of our proposed approach, the output of DL can be explained by the different and the discriminant structure of the CC400 functional brain parcellations between healthy controls and ASD subjects. Only four brain areas are considered and features are learned from these regions of interest. By using our ASD decision support system, the clinician can justify his diagnosis by a disfunctioning in the C115, C188, C247, and C326 brain areas. More quantitative analysis of these brain regions could be performed.

Table 1. Proposed deep neural networks performances for ASD detection in term of accuracy based on different CNNs, and different dataset sizes

Dataset	Number images	VGG16	ResNet-50	LeNet-5
Dataset1	10 K	55%	56%	65%
Dataset2	30 K	–	–	80%
Dataset3	100 K	–	–	95%

Table 2. Comparison of different Deep learning approaches for autism detection disorder in terms of Accuracy

Method	Accuracy
Li et al. [1]	70.4%
Craddock et al. [30]	70%
Sherkatghanad et al. [3]	70.22%
Thomas et al. [15]	66%
Huang et al. [31]	76.4%
Ingalhalikar et al. [32]	71.35%
Jha et al. [33]	77.4%
Our proposed approach	95%

5.4 Comparison with State of Art Methods

Table 2 compares the performances of our LeNet5-based framework with existing state-of-the-art methods for ASD detection in terms of accuracy. Our proposed approach outperforms all existing approaches due to: (1) our data augmentation step, (2) the selection of the significant functional brain parcellations relevant in recognizing ASD and (3) the robustness of deep learning of ASD discriminating features.

6 Conclusion and Future Work

In this paper, a new deep learning based approach for ASD detection from MRI images is proposed. Four significant CC400 functional brain parcellations are extracted and concatenanted into one new input image. Then, the generated input image is fed to a LeNet5-based convolutional neural network. Promising results are achieved on ABIDE dataset that confirm the deployability of the proposed approach into an ASD decision support system. The proposed approach has the advantage of being interpretable and very accurate. The proposed deep learning solution will open new avenues in ASD detection from MRI images and it enables researchers and physicians to develop interpretable computer-aided diagnosis system. We demonstrated the importance of data augmentation on the performances of the framework. We plan for future works to evaluate our approach on others datasets and with different strategies of training.

References

1. Li, H., Parikh, N.A., He, L.: A novel transfer learning approach to enhance deep neural network classification of brain functional connectomes. Front. Neurosci. **12**, 491 (2018)
2. Dekhil, O., et al.: Using resting state functional MRI to build a personalized autism diagnosis system. PloS ONE **13**(10), e020635 (2018)

3. Sherkatghanad, Z., et al.: Automated detection of autism spectrum disorder using a convolutional neural network. Front. Neurosci. Annalen der Physik **13**, 1325 (2020)
4. Bullmore, E., Sporns, O.: Complex brain networks: graph theoretical analysis of structural and functional systems. Nat. Rev. Neurosci. **10**, 186 (2009)
5. Yang, X., Schrader, P.T., Zhang, N.: A deep neural network study of the ABIDE repository on autism spectrum classification. Int. J. Adv. Comput. Sci. Appl. (IJACSA) **11**(4) (2020). https://doi.org/10.14569/IJACSA.2020.0110401
6. Bellak, L.: The schizophrenic syndrome and attention deficit disorder: thesis, antithesis, and synthesis?? Am. Psychol. **49**(1), 25 (1994)
7. Just, M.A., Cherkassky, V.L., Buchweitz, A., Keller, T.A., Mitchell, T.M.: Identifying autism from neural representations of social interactions: neurocognitive markers of autism. PloS ONE **9**(12), e113879 (2014)
8. Sabuncu, M.R., Konukoglu, E.: Clinical prediction from structural brain MRI scans: a large-scale empirical study. Neuroinformatics **13**(1), 31–46 (2014). https://doi.org/10.1007/s12021-014-9238-1
9. Vapnik, V.: The Nature of Statistical Learning Theory. Springer, New York (2013)
10. Konukoglu, E., Glocker, B., Zikic, D., Criminisi, A.: Neighbourhood approximation forests. In: Ayache, N., Delingette, H., Golland, P., Mori, K. (eds.) MICCAI 2012. LNCS, vol. 7512, pp. 75–82. Springer, Heidelberg (2012). https://doi.org/10.1007/978-3-642-33454-2_10
11. Tipping, M.E.: Sparse Bayesian learning and the relevance vector machine. J. Mach. Learn. Res. **1**, 211–244 (2001)
12. Sherkatghanad, Z., et al.: Automated detection of autism spectrum disorder using a convolutional neural network. Front. Neurosci. **13**, 1325 (2020)
13. Huang, Z.A., Zhu, Z., Yau, C.H., Tan, K.C.: Identifying autism spectrum disorder from resting-state fMRI using deep belief network. IEEE Trans. Neural Netw. Learn. Syst. **32**, 847–2861 (2020)
14. Hinton, G.E.: Deep belief networks. Scholarpedia **4**(5), 5947 (2009). Revision #91189
15. Thomas, R.M., Gallo, S., Cerliani, L., Zhutovsky, P., El-Gazzar, A., van Wingen, G.: Classifying autism spectrum disorder using the temporal statistics of resting-state functional MRI data with 3D convolutional neural networks. Front. Psychiatry **11**, 440 (2020)
16. Dvornek, N.C., Ventola, P., Pelphrey, K.A., Duncan, J.S.: Identifying autism from resting-state fMRI using long short-term memory networks. In: Wang, Q., Shi, Y., Suk, H.-I., Suzuki, K. (eds.) MLMI 2017. LNCS, vol. 10541, pp. 362–370. Springer, Cham (2017). https://doi.org/10.1007/978-3-319-67389-9_42
17. Di Martino, A., et al.: The autism brain imaging data exchange: towards a large-scale evaluation of the intrinsic brain architecture in autism. Mol. Psychiatry **19**(6), 659–667 (2014)
18. Dvornek, N.C., Ventola, P., Duncan, J.S.: Combining phenotypic and resting-state fMRI data for autism classification with recurrent neural networks. In: Proceedings of the IEEE 15th International Symposium on Biomedical Imaging (ISBI 2018), pp. 725–728. IEEE (2018)
19. Eslami, T., Mirjalili, V., Fong, A., Laird, A.R., Saeed, F.: ASD-DiagNet: a hybrid learning approach for detection of autism spectrum disorder using fMRI data. Front. Neuroinform. **13**, 70 (2019)
20. Wang, Y., Wang, J., Wu, F.X., Hayrat, R., Liu, J.: AIMAFE: autism spectrum disorder identification with multi-atlas deep feature representation and ensemble learning. J. Neurosci. Methods **343**, 108840 (2020)

21. Craddock, C., et al.: The neuro bureau preprocessing initiative: open sharing of preprocessed neuroimaging data and derivatives. Front. Neuroinform. **7**, 27 (2013)
22. LeCun, Y., Bottou, L., Bengio, Y., Haffner, P.: Gradient-based learning applied to document recognition. Proc. IEEE **86**(11), 2278–2324 (1998)
23. Sarraf, S., Tofighi, G.: Classification of Alzheimer's disease using fMRI data and deep learning convolutional neural networks. arXiv preprint arXiv:1603.08631 (2016)
24. Wang, T., Lu, C., Shen, G., Hong, F.: Sleep apnea detection from a single-lead ECG signal with automatic feature-extraction through a modified LeNet-5 convolutional neural network. PeerJ **7**, e7731 (2019)
25. Zhang, S., et al.: Computer-aided diagnosis (CAD) of pulmonary nodule of thoracic CT image using transfer learning. J. Digit. Imaging **32**(6), 995–1007 (2019)
26. Walsh, J., Othmani, A., Jain, M., Dev, S.: Using U-net network for efficient brain tumor segmentation in MRI images. Healthc. Anal. **2**, 100098 (2022). https://www.sciencedirect.com/science/article/pii/S2772442522000429
27. Hu, W., Huang, Y., Wei, L., Zhang, F., Li, H.: Deep convolutional neural networks for hyperspectral image classification. J. Sens. **2015**, 12 p., 258619 (2015). https://doi.org/10.1155/2015/258619
28. Simonyan, K., Zisserman, A.: Very deep convolutional networks for large-scale image recognition. arXiv preprint arXiv:1409.1556 (2014)
29. He, K., Zhang, X., Ren, S., Sun, J.: Deep residual learning for image recognition. In: Proceedings of the IEEE Conference on Computer Vision and Pattern Recognition, pp. 770–778 (2016)
30. Heinsfeld, A.S., Franco, A.R., Craddock, R.C., Buchweitz, A., Meneguzzi, F.: Identification of autism spectrum disorder using deep learning and the abide dataset. NeuroImage Clin. **17**, 16–23 (2018)
31. Huang, Z.A., Zhu, Z., Yau, C.H., Tan, K.C.: Identifying autism spectrum disorder from resting-state fMRI using deep belief network. IEEE Trans. Neural Netw. Learn. Syst. **32**, 2847–2861 (2020)
32. Ingalhalikar, M., Shinde, S., Karmarkar, A., Rajan, A., Rangaprakash, D., Deshpande, G.: Functional connectivity-based prediction of autism on site harmonized abide dataset. IEEE Trans. Biomed. Eng. **68**(12), 3628–3637 (2021)
33. Jha, R.R., Bhardwaj, A., Garg, D., Bhavsar, A., Nigam, A.: MHATC: autism spectrum disorder identification utilizing multi-head attention encoder along with temporal consolidation modules. In: 2022 44th Annual International Conference of the IEEE Engineering in Medicine and Biology Society (EMBC), pp. 337–341. IEEE (2022)

2D Respiratory Sound Analysis to Detect Lung Abnormalities

Rafia Sharmin Alice[1,2(✉)], Laurent Wendling[2], and KC Santosh[1,2]

[1] 2AI: Applied Artificial Intelligence Research Lab, Computer Science,
University of South Dakota, Vermillion, SD 57069, USA
rafia.alice@coyotes.usd.edu, santosh.kc@usd.edu
[2] SIP - Systèmes Intelligents de Perception, Université de Paris,
45, rue des Saints-Pères, 75270 Paris Cedex 06, France
laurent.wendling@u-paris.fr

Abstract. In this paper, we analyze deep visual features from 2D data representation(s) of the respiratory sound to detect evidence of lung abnormalities. The primary motivation behind this is that visual cues are more important in decision-making than raw data (lung sound). Early detection and prompt treatments are essential for any future possible respiratory disorders, and respiratory sound is proven to be one of the biomarkers. In contrast to state-of-the-art approaches, we aim at understanding/analyzing visual features using our Convolutional Neural Networks (CNN) tailored Deep Learning Models, where we consider all possible 2D data such as Spectrogram, Mel-frequency Cepstral Coefficients (MFCC), spectral centroid, and spectral roll-off. In our experiments, using the publicly available respiratory sound database named ICBHI 2017 (5.5 h of recordings containing 6898 respiratory cycles from 126 subjects), we received the highest performance with the area under the curve of 0.79 from Spectrogram as opposed to 0.48 AUC from the raw data from a pre-trained deep learning model: VGG16. Our study proved that 2D data representation could help better understand/analyze lung abnormalities as compared to 1D data. In addition, our results can be compared with previous works.

Keywords: Lung abnormality · Respiratory sound · 2D data Representation · Deep visual features

1 Introduction

Assistive solutions to problems in the medical arena have been made possible thanks in large part to technologies like machine learning and deep learning. Medical imaging informatics increase the predictive accuracy of early and timely disease identification. Due to the lack of skilled human resources, medical professionals are grateful for such technical support because it enables them to handle more patients. Aside from serious illnesses like cancer and diabetes, the prevalence of respiratory conditions is gradually increasing and posing a life-threatening threat to society. Since early detection and prompt treatment are

KC Santosh et al. (Eds.): RTIP2R 2022, CCIS 1704, pp. 46–58, 2023.
https://doi.org/10.1007/978-3-031-23599-3_5

essential for respiratory disorders, the audio of the respiratory sounds has been proven to be highly helpful.

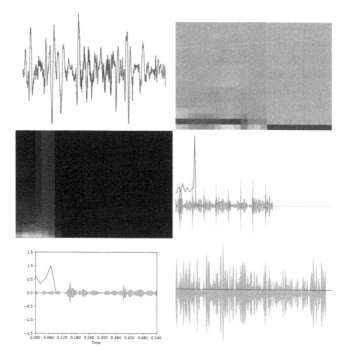

Fig. 1. Qualitative output: raw data (upper-left), MFCC (upper-right), spectrogram (middle-left), spectral centroid (middle-right), spectral roll off (lower-left), and zero crossing rate (lower-right)

In machine learning domain, understanding how data is used is crucial since it facilitates its analysis. Visualization is an effective technique for understanding and improving deep learning models. The use of visual encodings to convert abstract data into useful representations allows data visualization and visual analytics to effectively convey information and uncover insights. Deep learning is a particular set of techniques that, when given a dataset, learns what features are relevant to the task [1]. As an example, we have demonstrated different data formats (in different space) in Fig. 1: raw data, MFCC, Spectrogram, Spectral centroid, Spectral roll-off, and zero-crossing rate. This contrasts with typical machine learning approaches, which employ a dataset with known features such as a collection of autos where the collection of automobiles represents a dataset, with known makes, models, and colors, these represent features. This is helpful for datasets that do not explicitly have tabular elements, such as a collection of pictures, a collection of texts, or an audio library. Deep artificial neural networks are the preferred model architecture for these kinds of models. As complicated deep learning models are difficult to train and comprehend, interactive interfaces and visualizations have been built and developed to assist individuals in understanding what models have learned and how they make predictions. A crucial step in studying and discovering relationships between various entities is feature extraction [2]. To transform the provided audio data into a format that the models can understand, feature extraction is used. It is a method that provides a clear explanation for the majority of the data. For classification, prediction, and recommendation algorithms, feature extraction is necessary.

In the seminal work by Zeiler and Fergus on deep learning visualization [3], a method known as deconvolutional networks allowed projection from a model's learned feature space back to the pixel space, or, to put it another way, gave us a glimpse at what neural networks were seeing in large sets of images. Their method and findings provide a debugging tool for developing a model and shed light on the kinds of properties deep neural networks are learning at particular layers in the model. This study is frequently credited with popularizing visualization in the computer vision and deep learning areas in recent years by demonstrating visualization as a potent tool for understanding and enhancing deep models.

2   Related Works

Integrating speech/audio signal processing is the must when it comes to smart healthcare, where we take multimodal learning and representation into account [4].

For this project, we divide earlier research into the following categories: Aykanat et al. [5] provided a convolutional network as well as a support vector machine-based solution for lung sound classification. The two feature extraction techniques are Spectrogram production utilizing the short-time Fourier transform and mel frequency cepstral coefficient (MFCC) feature extraction (STFT). The mel frequency cepstrum (MFC), used in sound processing, is a representation of a sound's short-term power spectrum based on a linear cosine transform of a log power spectrum on a non-linear mel scale of frequency. MFCC features are also employed in [6,7], where clips are first preprocessed by windowing and framing, and then MFCC features are extracted. A Spectrogram is a graphic depiction of the frequency spectrum in a sound or other signal as it varies over time or in response to other factors. Since MFCC features are frequently employed in audio detection systems, the experiments that were conducted using these features allowed for the establishment of a baseline value for each of the following characteristics: accuracy, precision, recall, sensitivity, and specificity. Audio detection also uses Spectrogram images. They were never put to the test using CNNs for respiratory audio, though. SciPy was used to build the MFCC datasets. They processed these datasets utilizing support vector machines. The open-source Pylab graph creation library and numerous open-source image processing packages were combined to create the Sspectrogram dataset. They reported an accuracy of 86% for classifying healthy-pathological conditions using both SVM and CNN.

Acharya et al. [8] demonstrated a deep learning-based method for classifying lung sounds. They employed multiple data augmentation approaches to expand the dataset because it is very modest for training a deep learning model. They employed a mel-frequency Spectrogram with a window size of 60 ms and 50% overlap for feature extraction. Then, each breathing cycle is transformed into a 2D image, where each value represents the log amplitude value of the signal corresponding to that frequency and time window, and rows correspond to frequencies in mel scale and columns to time (window). They used training samples to train the three-stage network in their proposed hybrid CNN RNN model. According to their research, the hybrid CNN-RNN model produced a score of 66.31% on an 80–20 split for the classification of the four classes of the respiratory cycle. To identify unhealthy patients, they then proposed a patient screening and model tuning strategy. They then developed patient-specific retraining models, which significantly improved the reliability of the results for the original train-test split, achieving a score of 71.81% for leave-one-out cross-validation on the ICBHI17 dataset. The authors suggested feature extraction of lung sounds using wavelet coefficients and their classification by neural network and support vector machines in their work, [9] "Classification Of Normal and Abnormal Lung Sounds Using Neural Network and Support Vector Machines." The study employed a total of 48 samples for the train and test. Lung sounds were divided into six groups. SVMs are an extremely good classifier for categorizing lung sounds, with an accuracy range of 93.51 to 100.

On a dataset of 38 recordings, Pramono et al. [10] examined many characteristics to categorize wheezes and typical respiratory sounds. The dataset used in this study, which tested the discriminatory power of several feature types used in analogous studies in the past, included 38 recordings from various sources. There were 425 incidents total, 223 of which were wheezes, with the remaining events being typical. They showed that specific individual features, such as the tonality index and the MFCC, are far more effective at detecting wheezes. The outcomes of their experiments with various attributes are shown.

Rao et al. [11] using acoustic methods to analyze the lungs. They discussed the acoustic features of various lung conditions. The physical makeup of the human thorax and methods for detecting breathing noises are also covered. Along with several classifiers, the authors have also covered in detail the various signal processing methods needed to examine these noises. Bahoura and Pelletier [12] used cepstral features to distinguish normal and wheezing sounds. They worked with 12 instances from each class and reported the highest true positive value of 76.6% for wheezing sounds. They also reported 90.6% true positives for normal sounds with fourier transform-based features.

Demir et al. [13] employed a CNN-based method to classify lung sounds from the ICBHI 2017 dataset. For the extraction of deep features, they presented a new pretrained Convolutional Neural Network (CNN) model like VGG16 and AlexNet. They reported an overall accuracy of 71.1% and a maximum accuracy of 83.2% for the healthy class (Table 1).

Table 1. Sate-of-the-art works and their performances.

Author	Dataset	Performance (ACC, AUC, SEN, SPEC)
Aykanat et al. [5]	Electronically recorded (17,930)	86%, –, 86%, 86%
Acharya et al. [8]	ICBHI'17 dataset (920)	96%, –, 48.63%, 84.14%
Pramono et al. [10]	Multiple repositories (38)	–, 89.19%, 83.86%, 81.19%
Mukherjee et al. [6]	Electronically recorded (17,930)	86%, –, –, –
Rao et al. [11]	Multiple sources	93%–95%, –, –, –
Demir et al. [13]	ICBHI'17 dataset (920)	71.15%, –, –, –
Ma et al. [14]	ICBHI'17 dataset (920)	–, –, 41.32%, 63.2%

Ma et al. [14] developed a method to differentiate respiratory sounds using the non-local block in the ResNet architecture. In order to attain the best state-of-the-art accuracy, they suggested a LungRBN model, which combines wavelet feature extraction and short-time Fourier transform (STFT) with a product of two ResNet models through a fully linked layer. Discovering strategies to automatically supplement current data, however, has received less focus than finding techniques to improve detection accuracy significantly. They introduced LungRN+NL, an enhanced adventitious lung sound classification, which combines a mixup data augmentation method with a non-local layer of the ResNet neural network to address this issue. In order to extract features from lung sounds, we opt for the time-frequency analysis technique known as short-time Fourier Transform (STFT), taking into account the crucial differentiation between various categories. Following their experiments, on the ICBHI 2017 dataset, they have received an accuracy of 52.26%.

3   Experiments

This section includes dataset collection, evaluation metrics, experiment, results and analysis.

3.1   Dataset

It is crucial to employ a dataset that is comparable to the real-world situation in order to design a resilient system that meets the real-world requirement. Our system was trained using a respiratory sound database that is openly accessible and connected to the International Conference on Biomedical and Health Informatics (ICBHI) [7,15].

In Table 2, we provide a complete dataset. The majority of the database is made up of audio samples that were captured by the School of Health Sciences, University of Aveiro (ESSUA) research team at the Hospital Infante D. Pedro in Aveiro, Portugal, and the Respiratory Research and Rehabilitation Laboratory (Lab3R), ESSUA. At the Papanikolaou General Hospital in Thessaloniki and the

Table 2. Respiratory sound database [15]

Clip type	Number of clips
Healthy	3642
Non-healthy	3256

General Hospital of Imathia (Health), members of the second research team from the Aristotle University of Thessaloniki (AUTH) and the University of Coimbra (UC) recorded respiratory sounds at the Papanikolaou General Hospital, Thessaloniki and at the General Hospital of Imathia (Health Unit of Naousa), Greece. The Respiratory Sound Database includes audio recordings that were separately gathered over several years by two study teams in two distinct nations. The database includes 920 annotated audio samples from 126 participants and a total of 5.5 h of recordings with 6898 breathing cycles, of which 1864 have crackles, 886 have wheezes, and 506 have both [16]. Different stethoscopes and microphones were utilized to gather data. The trachea and six other places on the chest-left and right posterior, anterior, and lateral-were used to record the audio. Adult participants of various ages provided the audio in both clinical and non-clinical contexts. Participants included people with cystic fibrosis, pneumonia, bronchiolitis, COPD, upper and lower respiratory tract infections, asthma, and bronchiectasis. There are 920 audio samples from 126 different people in the ICBHI database. These have annotations from respiratory specialists and are considered a standard in the industry. The dataset includes annotations for each respiratory cycle in 4 classes. The annotations mostly distinguish between two categories: healthy and unhealthy. In the unhealthy category, wheeze and crackle are further broken down, with some cycles having both problems. 1864 of the 6898 cycles, or 5.5 h, have crackles, whereas 886 have wheezes. Wheezes and crackles can be heard during the 506 cycles.

3.2   Model Architecture and Implementation

Resent50: He et al. [7] proposed the ResNet 50, a Residual Network with 50 layers. This model's input size is fixed at 224×224, and its convolutional layers are the same size as those in VGG networks, which follow some straightforward designs like. The outcome is the same for layers with the same amount of filters. If the convolved output size is cut in half while maintaining the time complexity per layer, the number of filters is increased by a factor of two. The model's final layers are a 1000-way fully connected layer with softmax and an average pooling layer. In comparison to VGG nets, this model has fewer filters and is less complex, albeit there are other variations like ResNet101 and ResNet152. The ResNet50 configuration layers are shown in Fig. 2. A network can accept an image as input if its height, width, and channel width are all multiples of 32. Size of the input is $224 \times 224 \times 3$. Using 77 and 33 kernel sizes, respectively, each ResNet architecture conducts the first convolution and max-pooling. The network's Stage 1 then begins, and it consists of 3 Residual blocks with a total

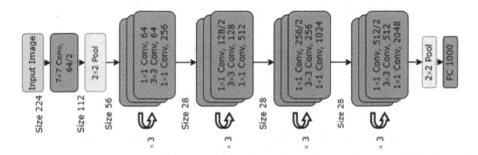

Fig. 2. ResNet50 architecture

of 6 layers. All 3 layers of the block in stage 1's first stage were constructed using kernels that were 64, 64, and 128 in size, respectively.

The identity relationship is represented by the curved arrows. The size of the input will be cut in half in terms of height and width but doubled in terms of channel width since the convolution operation in the residual block is carried out with stride 2. The channel width doubles and the input size is cut in half as it moves from one step to the next. Bottleneck design is applied to deeper networks like ResNet50, ResNet152, etc. A total of three layers are piled on top of one another for each residual function F. Convolutions (1, 3, and 1) make up the three levels. The reduction and subsequent restoration of the dimensions are accomplished by the 11 convolution layers. With lower input and output dimensions, the 33 layer is left as a bottleneck. The network's final layer is an average pooling layer, which is followed by a layer of 1000 neurons that is fully connected (ImageNet class output).

VGG16: VGG Architecture [7]: A dimensioned image Fig. 3 serves as the network's input (224, 224, 3). The first two layers include the same padding and 64 channels with a 3 × 3 filter size. Following a max pool layer of stride (2, 2), two layers have convolution layers of 128 filter size and filter size (3, 3). A max-pooling stride (2, 2) layer that is the same as the layer preceding it comes next. Then, 256 filters with filter widths of 3 and 3 are distributed over 2 convolution layers. After that, there are two sets of three convolution layers, and then a max pool layer comes next. Each filter contains 512 filters and the same padding (3, 3).

This image is then applied to the stack of two convolution layers. These convolution and max-pooling layers both use 3 × 3-sized filters. In order to change the number of input channels, it additionally uses 1 × 1 pixels in some of the layers. After each convolution layer, 1 pixel (the same padding) is inserted to prevent the image's spatial characteristic. After adding a convolution and max-pooling layer to the stack, we got a (7, 7, 512) feature map. In order to construct a (1, 16384) feature vector, this output is flattened. The following three layers are all fully interconnected; the first layer outputs a (1, 256) vector using the most recent feature vector as input, the second layer also generates a (1, 128)

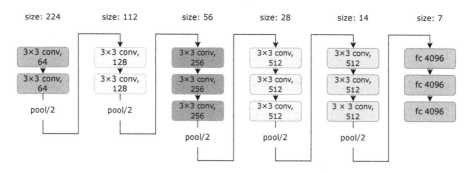

Fig. 3. VGG16 architecture

vector, and the third layer generates 1000 channels for two classes. Every hidden layer uses ReLU [16] as its activation function. ReLU is more computationally effective since it results in speedier learning and lowers the possibility of vanishing gradient problems. The list of VGG topologies in Fig. 3 is extensive. VGG-16 has two unique versions, as can be shown (C and D).

We obtained a (7, 7, 512) feature map after adding a convolution and max-pooling layer to the stack. This output is flattened to create a (1, 16384) feature vector. The next three layers are all completely connected; the first layer uses the most recent feature vector as input and outputs a (1, 256) vector, the second layer also produces a (1, 128) vector, and the third layer produces 1000 channels for two classes. The only difference between them is the use of the (3, 3) filter size convolution in place of some convolution layers (1, 1). These two have, respectively, 134 million and 138 million attributes.

MobileNet: Initially, MobileNet uses a simple 2D convolution layer. Then, a set of convolution layers with varying strides and filter counts known as Depthwise Separable are attached one after the other. In Fig. 4 following the input, each convolutional block proceeds in the following order: BatchNormalization, ReLU activation, and then it is passed to the following block. 32 filters with a stride of 2 and a kernel size of 3×3 make up the first convolution block. As previously stated, a BatchNormalization layer and a ReLU activation come next. Then comes the Depth-wise Separable convolution layer, which is the foundational building component of the MobileNet design. Depth-wise convolution and then pointwise convolution make up this procedure. Unlike depth-wise convolution, which applies a kernel to each channel, normal convolution applies a block of the same channel as the picture to all of the channels. Then, a pointwise convolution 1×1 conv is applied to the stacked output layers. The depth-wise convolution and point-wise convolution functions are referred to collectively through a combination layer function. The point-wise convolution is applied n times and is computationally less expensive than performing n transformations on images. For an n-filter number, depth-wise convolution with a stride of 2 reduces the size first, then stride 1 is used for depth-wise convolution. With each combination

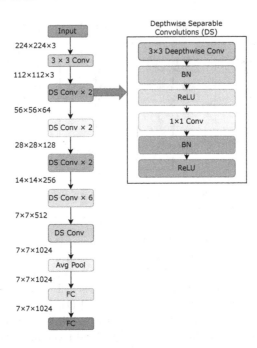

Fig. 4. MobileNet architecture

layer, the number of channels gradually increases from 32 to 1024. Iteratively, the block is called five times at channel output 512. GlobalAveragePooling comes last, followed by the final output layer. The classes are to be listed in the output layer, which is a dense layer. It must be dense if the classes are 3. Softmax is the activation method employed.

3.3   Inception-V3 Architecture

Szegedy et al. [17,18] introduced the Inception-v3 convolutional neural network type as GoogLeNet. This network has 48 layers and can classify photos into 1000 different categories. This model's fixed input size is 299×299 pixels. This model is built on a multi-scale method that combines various classifier structures with different backpropagation sources. The Inception-v3 model expands the network's span and depth without imposing costs. To enable generating more complex decisions, this model applies many Inception layers in convolution on the input feature map at various sizes. The architecture of Inception-v3 is shown in Fig. 5. Convolutions like 5×5, which significantly reduce the input dimensions, were occasionally used in Inception V1. The neural network's accuracy suffers as a result of this. This is because if the input dimension is reduced too much, the neural network is vulnerable to information loss. Additionally, compared to 33, the complexity decreases when larger convolutions like 55 are used. An asymmetric 13 convolution followed by a 31 convolution can be used to factorize

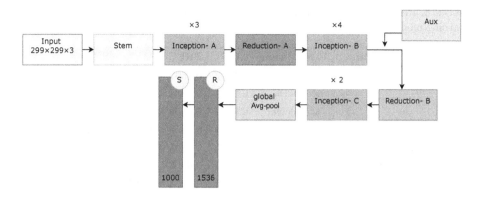

Fig. 5. Inceptionnet-V3 architecture

a 33 convolution. This is the same as sliding a two-layer network with a 33 convolution's receptive field, but it is 33% less expensive.

Only when the input size is m × m does this factorization function well for early layers when input dimensions are large (m is between 12 and 20). The auxiliary classifier enhances the network's convergence, per the Inception V1 architecture. in the architecture of Inception V2. The two 33 convolutions take the place of the 55 convolution. Due to the fact that a 55 convolution is 2.78 more expensive than a 33 convolution, this also reduces calculation time and hence boosts computation speed. Therefore, using two 3 × 3 layers rather than five 5 × 5 layers improves architecture performance. Use of RMSprop optimizer, batch normalization in the fully connected layer of the auxiliary classifier, and Use of 7 × 7 factorized are all additional characteristics of Inception V3, which is identical to and includes all the features of Inception V2. Another technique for regularizing the classifier is label smoothing regularization, which calculates the impact of label-dropout during training. It stops the classifier from making excessively confident predictions about a class. The addition of label smoothing improves the error rate by 0.2%.

3.4 Results and Analysis

To measure the performance, we computed Accuracy (ACC), Precision (PREC) Sensitivity (SEN), and Area Under the Curve (AUC). ACC, PREC, and SEN are computed as follows:

$$ACC = \frac{TP + TN}{TP + FP + TN + FN},$$

$$Precision\ (PREC) = \frac{TP}{TP + FP},\ and$$

$$Sensitivity\ (SEN) = \frac{TP}{TP + FN},$$

Table 3. Performance evaluation on ICBHI 2017 dataset using four pre-trained deep learning models.

Types of data	Model name	ACC	PREC	AUC	SEN
Wave	VGG16	0.4697	0.4697	0.4828	0.4697
	ResNet50	0.5877	0.5882	0.5637	0.7207
	MobileNet	0.5450	0.5659	0.54554	0.6460
	InceptionV3	0.5355	0.5355	0.5000	1.0000
MFCC	VGG16	0.4545	0.4545	0.5315	0.4545
	ResNet50	0.6090	0.6900	0.7700	0.7500
	MobileNet	0.5308	0.5288	0.5150	0.9910
	InceptionV3	0.5261	0.5261	0.5000	1.0000
Spectrogram	**VGG16**	**0.7232**	**0.7486**	**0.7930**	**0.6248**
	Resnet50	0.6558	0.6236	0.7168	0.6876
	MobileNet	0.5592	0.5581	0.5421	0.8496
	InceptionV3	0.5355	0.5355	0.5000	1.000
Spectral centroid	VGG16	0.5655	0.5455	0.6233	0.5500
	Resnet50	0.5735	0.5533	0.7700	0.9820
	MobileNet	0.5592	0.5581	0.5421	0.8496
	InceptionV3	0.5355	0.5355	0.5000	1.0000
Spectral roll-off	VGG16	0.4091	0.4091	0.3836	0.4091
	Resnet50	0.4787	0.5031	0.4680	0.7387
	MobileNet	0.5355	0.5355	0.5000	0.1000
	InceptionV3	0.4882	0.5163	0.3673	0.6991
Zero-crossing rate	VGG16	0.4697	0.4697	0.4828	0.4697
	Resnet50	0.5261	0.5261	0.3973	1.000
	MobileNet	0.3886	0.3749	0.3749	0.1150
	InceptionV3	0.5355	0.5355	0.5000	1.0000

where TP, FP, TN and FN refer to true positive, false positive, true negative and false negative, respectively.

In Table 3, we provide a comprehensive results in terms of aforementioned evaluation metrics (ACC, PREC, AUC, and SEN). In Table 3, we observed that 2D data representations worked better as compared to 1D data representation, which we call raw respiratory sound (wave). Of all 2D data representations, Spectrogram performed better and VGG16 provided an accuracy of 0.7232, a precision of 0.7486, an AUC of 0.7930, and a sensitivity of 0.6248.

We compared our findings with previous works that used exact same dataset. Since they have used different metrics, we aimed at looking whether they can be compared. In their works, they used an additional score - an average score of specificity and sensitivity. On the whole, the proposed work still performs better (Table 4).

Table 4. Performance comparison

Authors	PREC	AUC	SEN	SPEC	Score
Ma et al. (2020) [14]	–	–	0.4132	0.6320	0.5226
Jakovljevic and car-Turukalo (2018) [19]	–	–	–	–	0.3956
Chambres et al. (2018) [20]	–	–	0.2081	0.7805	0.4943
Serbes et al. (2018) [21]	–	–	–	–	0.4986
Kochetov et al. (2018) [22]	–	–	0.5843	0.7300	0.6570
Acharya and Basu (2020) [8]	–	–	0.4863	0.8414	0.66.38
Ma et al. (2019) [23]	–	–	0.3112	0.6920	0.5016
Proposed work	**0.7486**	**0.7930**	**0.6248**	–	–

4   Conclusion

In this paper, we have analyzed deep visual features from 2D data representation of the respiratory sound to detect evidence of lung abnormalities. The primary motivation behind this was to study how well 2D representation and/or visual cues work in decision-making as opposed to 1D raw data. In our work, we have analyzed deep visual features using our Convolutional Neural Networks (CNN) tailored Deep Learning Models, where 2D data in different formats such as Spectrogram, Mel-frequency Cepstral Coefficients (MFCC), spectral centroid, and spectral roll-off were considered. Our experiments on the publicly available respiratory sound database named ICBHI 2017 (5.5 h of recordings containing 6898 respiratory cycles from 126 subjects) have proved that 2D data representation could help better understand/analyze lung abnormalities as compared to 1D data. Using the pre-trained deep learning model (VGG16), we achieved an AUC of 0.79 from Spectrogram as opposed to 0.48 AUC from the raw data.

References

1. Hohman, F.: Visualization in deep learning, March 2019
2. Doshi, S.: Extract features of music, April 2019
3. Zeiler, M.D., Fergus, R.: Visualizing and understanding convolutional networks. In: Fleet, D., Pajdla, T., Schiele, B., Tuytelaars, T. (eds.) ECCV 2014. LNCS, vol. 8689, pp. 818–833. Springer, Cham (2014). https://doi.org/10.1007/978-3-319-10590-1_53
4. Santosh, K.C.: Speech processing in healthcare: can we integrate? In: Dey, N. (ed.) Intelligent Speech Signal Processing, pp. 1–4. Academic Press, Cambridge (2019)
5. Aykanat, M., Kılıç, Ö., Kurt, B., Saryal, S.: Classification of lung sounds using convolutional neural networks. EURASIP J. Image Video Process. **2017**(1), 1–9 (2017)
6. Mukherjee, H., Obaidullah, S.M., Santosh, K.C., Phadikar, S., Roy, K.: A lazy learning-based language identification from speech using MFCC-2 features. Int. J. Mach. Learn. Cyberne. **11**(1), 1–14 (2020)

7. Mukherjee, H., et al.: Automatic lung health screening using respiratory sounds. J. Med. Syst. **45**(2), 19 (2021)
8. Acharya, J., Basu, A.: Deep neural network for respiratory sound classification in wearable devices enabled by patient specific model tuning. IEEE Trans. Biomed. Circuits Syst. **14**(3), 535–544 (2020)
9. Abbasi, S., Derakhshanfar, R., Abbasi, A., Sarbaz, Y.: Classification of normal and abnormal lung sounds using neural network and support vector machines. In: 2013 21st Iranian Conference on Electrical Engineering (ICEE), pp. 1–4. IEEE (2013)
10. Pramono, R.X.A., Imtiaz, S.A., Rodriguez-Villegas, E.: Evaluation of features for classification of wheezes and normal respiratory sounds. PloS ONE **14**(3), e0213659 (2019)
11. Rao, A., Huynh, E., Royston, T.J., Kornblith, A., Roy, S.: Acoustic methods for pulmonary diagnosis. IEEE Rev. Biomed. Eng. **12**, 221–239 (2018)
12. Bahoura, M., Pelletier, C.: New parameters for respiratory sound classification. In: CCECE 2003-Canadian Conference on Electrical and Computer Engineering. Toward a Caring and Humane Technology (Cat. No. 03CH37436), vol. 3, pp. 1457–1460. IEEE (2003)
13. Demir, F., Ismael, A.M., Sengur, A.: Classification of lung sounds with CNN model using parallel pooling structure. IEEE Access **8**, 105376–105383 (2020)
14. Ma, Y., Xu, X., Li, Y.: LungRN+NL: an improved adventitious lung sound classification using non-local block ResNet neural network with mixup data augmentation. In: Interspeech, pp. 2902–2906 (2020)
15. Rocha, B.M., et al.: An open access database for the evaluation of respiratory sound classification algorithms. Physiol. Meas. **40**(3), 035001 (2019)
16. ICBHI 2017 challenge
17. He, K., Zhang, X., Ren, S., Sun, J.: Deep residual learning for image recognition. arXiv preprint arxiv:1512.03385 (2015)
18. Szegedy, C., et al.: Going deeper with convolutions. In: Proceedings of the IEEE Conference on Computer Vision and Pattern Recognition, pp. 1–9 (2015)
19. Jakovljević, N., Lončar-Turukalo, T.: Hidden Markov model based respiratory sound classification. In: Maglaveras, N., Chouvarda, I., de Carvalho, P. (eds.) Precision Medicine Powered by pHealth and Connected Health. IP, vol. 66, pp. 39–43. Springer, Singapore (2018). https://doi.org/10.1007/978-981-10-7419-6_7
20. Chambres, G., Hanna, P., Desainte-Catherine, M.: Automatic detection of patient with respiratory diseases using lung sound analysis. In: 2018 International Conference on Content-Based Multimedia Indexing (CBMI), pp. 1–6. IEEE (2018)
21. Serbes, G., Ulukaya, S., Kahya, Y.P.: An automated lung sound preprocessing and classification system based onspectral analysis methods. In: Maglaveras, N., Chouvarda, I., de Carvalho, P. (eds.) Precision Medicine Powered by pHealth and Connected Health, pp. 45–49. Springer, Singapore (2018). https://doi.org/10.1007/978-981-10-7419-6_8
22. Kochetov, K., Putin, E., Balashov, M., Filchenkov, A., Shalyto, A.: Noise masking recurrent neural network for respiratory sound classification. In: Kůrková, V., Manolopoulos, Y., Hammer, B., Iliadis, L., Maglogiannis, I. (eds.) ICANN 2018. LNCS, vol. 11141, pp. 208–217. Springer, Cham (2018). https://doi.org/10.1007/978-3-030-01424-7_21
23. Ma, Y., et al.: LungBRN: a smart digital stethoscope for detecting respiratory disease using bi-resnet deep learning algorithm. In: 2019 IEEE Biomedical Circuits and Systems Conference (BioCAS), pp. 1–4. IEEE (2019)

Analyzing Chest X-Ray to Detect the Evidence of Lung Abnormality Due to Infectious Disease

Joshua Henderson$^{(\boxtimes)}$ and KC Santosh

Applied AI Research Lab, Computer Science Department,
University of South Dakota, Vermillion, SD 57069, USA
josh.e.henderson@coyotes.usd.edu, santosh.kc@usd.edu

Abstract. Analyzing chest X-ray is the must especially when are required to deal of infectious disease outbreak, and COVID-19. The COVID-19 pandemic has had a large effect on almost every facet of life. As COVID-19 was a disease only discovered in recent history, there is comparatively little data on the disease, how it is detected, and how it is cured. Deep learning is a powerful tool that can be used to learn to classify information in ways that humans might not be able to. This allows computers to learn on relatively little data and provide exceptional results. This paper proposes a customized convolutional neural network (CNN) for the detection of COVID-19 from chest X-rays called basic-Conv. This network consists of five sets of convolution and pooling layers, a flatten layer, and two dense layers with a total of approximately 9 million parameters. This network achieves an accuracy of 95.8%, which is comparable to other high-performing image classification networks. This provides a promising launching point for future research and developing a network that achieves an accuracy higher than that of the leading classification networks. It also demonstrates the incredible power of convolution. This paper is an extension of a 2022 Honors Thesis (Henderson, Joshua Elliot, "Convolutional Neural Network for COVID-19 Detection in Chest X-Rays" (2022). Honors Thesis. 254. https://red.library.usd.edu/honors-thesis/254).

Keywords: Convolutional Neural Network · Binary image classification · COVID-19 · Chest X-rays

1 Introduction

The COVID-19 pandemic has been incredibly influential on the global population over the last 2 years. As of March 4, 2022, there have been over 440 million cases of COVID-19 and almost 6 million deaths [1]. A lot of the reason that it has been so influential is that the discovery of COVID-19 and the ensuing pandemic was an unprecedented event that had little to no available solutions for how to diagnose, treat, or deal with infected individuals. However, the world has

KC Santosh et al. (Eds.): RTIP2R 2022, CCIS 1704, pp. 59–77, 2023.
https://doi.org/10.1007/978-3-031-23599-3_6

adapted rapidly over the past 2 years and is now starting to get back to life as it was before the pandemic. However, it is still essential to have the tools to diagnose diseases like COVID-19 effectively so that researchers and medical experts can adapt quickly to any new diseases that might surface in the future.

"Deep learning is a particular kind of machine learning that achieves great power and flexibility" [2]. There are ample applications for deep learning, many of which can help humans deal with a large pandemic, such as the COVID-19 pandemic. For example, "AI-driven tools can be used to identify novel coronavirus outbreaks as well as forecast their nature of spread across the globe" [3]. One of the most relevant applications of deep learning is image classification. By using deep learning, a computer can be trained to recognize distinctions between two or more classifications of images. This is an incredibly useful tool, especially when dealing with a relatively new disease.

The primary motivation behind this project is to be able to effectively use deep learning for image classification. This will enable advocacy for its use and continued work on some of the world's most difficult problems. Additionally, the work presented here can be used as a cornerstone for additional groundbreaking research in image classification. Not many people get the ability to work on a project that can have a direct, positive impact on society. This research is an example of such a project. By building on this in the future, research in binary image classification could one day be used in a real-world scenario to directly affect the lives of people all over the world.

This paper provides an in-depth description of deep learning as well as the process of designing an architecture for deep learning. This can be used as a reference in the future as well as a foundation for future research. The network defined in this paper also provides excellent performance with low enough memory requirements to be run on a laptop computer. Additionally, this paper provides a comparison of data handling techniques that demonstrates the importance of ensuring a balanced dataset is used.

This paper will begin with a review of related work. Then, an in-depth methodology of the development of the convolutional neural network, followed by the implementation will be provided. Next, this paper discusses the results from the model and how they compare to existing models in the field. Finally, this paper will provide an overview of ways in which the model can be improved upon, to be used as a basis for future research.

2 Related Work

Several different architectures have been established through the work of other researchers. Each one was designed with a specific goal in mind and each one was developed for the classification of images. One key feature of many new architectures used for image classification is an inception module.

The inception module is an innovation that helps to identify features better, specifically in medical images. In traditional CNN models, each layer sends its output to one layer as input. This continues in a pipeline-like procedure until the output layer is reached. In an inception module, the output from one layer is used as input for multiple layers. This allows layers with different filter sizes to be used concurrently to extract features of different sizes [4]. "The extracted parallel features are then stacked depth-wise to form the output of the inception module" [4].

When programming an inception module, padding should be implemented so that the width and height of the output are the same for each of the concurrent layers. Additionally, inception modules can use a lot of memory as the outputs of multiple concurrent layers are being combined. This paper will now discuss three models that use an inception module and two models that do not.

2.1   Inception-v1

Also known as GoogLeNet, this was the first architecture to implement an inception module. The writers' goal was to capture features of varying sizes and complexities by adding concurrent convolutions with different filter sizes, as mentioned above. They attempted to make the computation slightly more efficient and more feasible for training by "judiciously applying dimension reductions and projects wherever the computational requirements would increase too much otherwise" [5]. This model succeeds at its goal and manages to provide exceptional performance for image classification (achieving a top-5 error of just 6.67% in the ILSVRC 2014 classification challenge). However, the computational power required for this network is still very large. It took a few high-end GPUs under a week to train the model, with most limitations due to memory [5].

2.2   Inception-v3

Also known as Inception Net v3, this improves upon Inception-v1 in many ways, including adding factorized 7×7 convolutions. This allows features that are larger to be captured but also increases computation. Batch normalization and label smoothing were also introduced to try to improve the performance of the model [6]. However, this model suffers from overfitting when using it for binary image classification with a small dataset [4]. This is mostly because it was designed to be used on the ImageNet database [4] - a very large database of more than 100,000 classifications and an average of 1000 images per classification [7]. However, there is not a database with this size available of Chest X-rays with COVID-19.

2.3   Truncated Inception Net

Truncated Inception Net is a truncation of Inception Net V3 "to reduce the model complexity and eventually the number of trainable parameters to prevent the model from overfitting issues" [4]. It achieves its goal, providing exceptional performance when performing binary classification of a small dataset of X-rays.

2.4   ResNet-50

ResNet-50 is an implementation of a residual network with 50 layers. Unlike the aforementioned models, ResNet-50 does not typically use an inception module. The key feature of a residual network is that it takes the output from one layer and gives it a shortcut to a few layers later in the model. Then, a residual function is applied to that layer and the output from a few layers later in the model, stored for the same use later, and used as input for the next layer in the model [8]. This provides a top-5 error rate of 5.71% on ImageNet validation [8]. Top-5 error rate is a performance metric used for multiclass image classification. In multiclass image classification, each classification is given a prediction percentage. Top-5 error rate measures the error based on the actual classification being one of the 5 classifications with the highest prediction percentages.

2.5   CT Scan and Chest X-Ray Architecture

CT Scan and Chest X-ray architecture is an architecture designed to be trained on both chest X-rays and CT scans. The architecture proposed in this paper [9] also does not use an inception module but instead uses a sequential convolutional neural network. It begins with a 100×100 input layer. It then performs a three sets of convolution layers without padding, each followed by a max pooling layer. The first convolution has 32 filters, the second convolution has 16 filters, and the final convolution has 8 filters. This is then followed by a dense layer with 256 nodes, another dense layer with 50 nodes, and a final dense layer with 2 nodes. This achieved an accuracy of 96.13% on chest X-rays and 95.83% on CT scans [9]. These results are very impressive, especially considering there were only 672 images used in total (336 chest X-rays and 336 CT scans).

3   Contribution

It has been shown that having big data can be helpful by introducing new manifestations [10]. In this paper, the model was trained on a dataset consisting of 4,187 COVID-19 positive images and 3,916 COVID-19 negative images. This allows the custom-tailored CNN to be accurately trained with the model being given different manifestations. This paper avoids using any pre-trained models as that would introduce a level of uncertainty, especially regarding the data previously used in training the models. As a result, the model presented in this paper, basicConv, was able to produce an accuracy of 95.8%. The results section of this paper will discuss these results in further detail, in addition to a comparison with other high-performing image classification networks.

4   Methodology

Neural networks are a way of deriving meaning from a set of data. To do this, they "process information in a similar way the human brain does" [11]. Neural networks have neurons and different processing layers that work together to extract additional information that may not be immediately visible. Neural networks learn how to classify data by looking at examples of each classification. In this way, they learn very similarly to the way humans learn. However, since computers can process a lot more information than a human in a given time frame, they learn a lot faster than humans. Neural networks can also detect minute details that humans might not immediately notice. This allows them to provide very accurate predictions after a relatively short amount of training time. Various types of neural networks exist today.

4.1   Basics: Network Types

Artificial Neural Networks (ANNs) are the first type of neural network. "An Artificial Neural Network (ANN) is an information or signal processing system composed of a large number of simple processing elements which are interconnected by direct links, and which cooperate to perform parallel distributed processing in order to solve a desired computational task" [11]. ANNs are also called multi-layer perceptrons. They are a combination of dense layers (which will be discussed later) that are good at extracting relationships from sets of data. However, dense layers are very parameter-intensive, and thus very memory- and time-intensive. Even though they are computationally expensive, ANNs have a lot of uses including facial recognition, stock market prediction, and social media [12].

Recurrent Neural Networks (RNNs) are the next type of neural network. "A recurrent neural network (RNN) is a [parallel distributed processing] model that implements temporal processing through feedback connections" [13]. Each state is a function of previous states, and this "is an example of a dynamical recognizer" [13]. RNNs are still being developed today and can be very useful for many things. Some examples of uses for RNNs are sound analysis and CAPTCHA image recognition.

Convolutional Neural Networks (CNNs) are the last type of neural network that this paper will discuss. This is the type of network used in this research and will be expanded upon in great detail. The reason that a CNN was used is that it is the most effective network for binary image classification. Additionally, there are a lot of CNN architectures available, producing a strong starting place for developing a network. A CNN is a neural network whose core layers are convolution layers and pooling layers. These layers will be discussed in detail later. However, they work in combination to identify similarities in areas of arrays of numbers within the same category and differences between different categories. By analyzing portions of an array instead of individual cells, better results can be obtained from arrays where cells located near each other are more closely related than cells that are farther apart.

CNNs are exceptional at identifying patterns, or features, in an array of numbers, which makes them excellent at classification. CNNs can classify a lot of different types of data, as long as the data can be converted to an array of numbers. There can be many dimensions to the array. However, the order of the columns and rows must be of importance for a CNN to be useful. This implies that the columns next to each other are more closely related to one another than columns and rows that are further away. An example of something other than an image that a CNN can classify well is an audio clip (where columns represent time and rows represent the value of each frequency) [14].

4.2 Definitions

There are many terms that are used in deep learning and must be understood to create the best network possible. Keras was used to create this network, but an understanding of all the layers and how they function was developed before they were used in the network. This allowed for a greater understanding of why the network performs as well as it does and allows for more informed decisions when building the network.

Layer. A layer is a function that is applied to an input of a matrix of numbers to gain further understanding from an array of numbers, providing some form of output. There are different types of layers, each of which is designed to do different things. Many of these types will be discussed later.

Architecture. An architecture is a series of layers with specific parameters designed to gain understanding from some input. It is the framework for a neural network. In this project, the goal of the architecture is to predict whether or not COVID-19 is present in an image of a chest X-ray.

Model. A model is an instance of an architecture. It has the layers from the architecture, in addition to several parameters. Each number in a filter is considered a parameter in addition to the weight given to the output of each filter. These weights are calculated through optimization. To understand optimization, one must first understand the concept of loss in the context of a CNN.

Loss. Loss is calculated using backpropagation through training. There are several different loss functions. The loss function used in this study is called binary cross-entropy loss. The equation for binary cross-entropy loss is:

$$-\frac{1}{N} \sum_{i=1}^{N} y_i \cdot \log(p(y_i)) + (1 - y_i) \cdot \log(1 - p(y_i)), \tag{1}$$

where y_i is the actual value (0 or 1), $p(y_i)$ is the predicted probability of the image being classified as positive (a value of 1), and N is the number of images in the test set [15]. This formula enables the same formula to be run over every test image and calculate the binary cross-entropy loss for the entire test set. This is because when $y_i = 1$, the calculation performed will be $\log(p(y_i))$, or the log of the probability that the image should be classified as 1, and when $y_i = 0$, the log of the probability that the image should be classified as 0 (which is $1 - p(y_i)$) is taken [15]. Additionally, using the log values penalizes bad choices more severely, encouraging the model to work toward the correct choice.

Training. Training is the minimization of loss in a model by optimizing the parameters. This is done using an optimizer function. Although there are different functions available, the one used by many research papers, including this one, is the Adam optimizer. The Adam optimizer uses stochastic gradient descent to update parameters. A moving average of the gradient of the loss function for all the parameters is taken at each moment and then the parameters are updated accordingly. This is repeated until the model converges. Unlike regular gradient descent, Adam "computes individual adaptive learning rates for different parameters from estimates of first and second moments of the gradients" [16]. This allows different parameters to learn at different rates and allows for a more efficient convergence of the model. A model is said to have converged when there is no longer a substantial decrease in the loss calculated by the loss function. An untrained model will have an accuracy approximately equal to picking a classification at random. As such, training is a core aspect of model development and is essential to producing a model that performs well.

Testing. Testing calculates the loss and accuracy of the model on testing data, which is not available to the model during training. This provides a method for examining how well the model is performing and is also used to provide final statistics on model performance.

Data. In this implementation, images are inputted as three arrays of numbers, each representing the amount of a primary color (red, green, and blue) present. These arrays are normalized to reduce the chance of bias towards any individual component and to reduce the amount of time it takes the model to converge. For this study, every number was divided by 255, as that is the maximum value for any individual component of color. The data is split into test and train data, with the industry-standard being that 20% of the data is reserved for testing and 80% is used for training. This is the same ratio that was used in this research.

Filter. A filter is an array of numbers (typically between 1 and 0) used to scan an image for a specific feature. These filters are used in a convolution layer to scan an image for features and to classify images with different features. Filters are generated by the model and evolve over the duration of the training. The initial filter is based on the size of the filter and numbers from a normal distribution [14]. These values are not very important and will change as the model is trained.

4.3 Layers

There are many types of layers, several of which will be discussed here. Recall, a layer is a function that is applied to input of an array of numbers to gain further understanding from that array, providing some output in the form of another array of numbers.

Input. An input layer takes input in the model as an array that can have up to three dimensions.

Convolution (2D). In a convolution layer, a filter is passed over the image from left to right and top to bottom. The numbers in a filter are multiplied by the numbers in an area of the input array that is the same size as the filter. Then, the resulting array containing the multiplication of those numbers is averaged and put in the output array in the location of the pixel in the middle of the area where the filter was. As such, filters should be square and should have an odd number of pixels as the length of the sides. This produces an array of numbers indicating the correlation of a filter to the area around each pixel. This convolution is then performed over each of the arrays inputted to the convolution layer. The number of arrays inputted to the layer is equal to the depth of the input. The results from the convolution of each input array are averaged into the final output array. Since most filters are bigger than one pixel, they cannot detect features that may be on the edge of the array. Padding aims to fix this by adding one or more layers of zeros on the exterior of the array. The number of layers of zeros added in padding is equal to $\frac{n-1}{2}$ where n is the length of the side of the filter given that the filter has an odd side length. The output of a convolution layer is called a feature map. If padding is used correctly, the output width and height will be the same as the input width and height. There will be one output array for each filter. As such, the depth of the output will be equal to the number of filters in the layer.

Flatten. The flatten layer takes the numbers from the input array and outputs them into a one-dimensional vector. This makes it easier to create dense layers to arrive at a final probability for prediction. There are no calculations performed on numbers in a flatten layer. It simply takes a multi-dimensional input and transforms it into a one-dimensional output.

Dense. The dense layer is also known as a fully connected layer. In a dense layer, every neuron in the input is connected to every neuron in the output, where a neuron is one of the numbers in a vector. The number of neurons in the output is specified when creating the architecture. A number in the output vector is a combination of all the other numbers in the previous vector, each having a certain weight. A weight is the influence that one neuron in the input has on one neuron in the output. Each of these weights, in addition to a bias parameter, is a trainable parameter and will be optimized during the model training.

Max Pool (2D). A square window of a specified dimension passes over an array of numbers from left-to-right and top-to-bottom. The size of the stride (the number of pixels the window moves by on each iteration) can also be set. The maximum from each window is taken and put into an output array. For a max pool layer with a dimension size of two and a stride of two, the output array will be half of the length and half of the width of the input array. There are no weights or filters used in a max pool layer. It exists to downsize the arrays, condensing the features to allow for more analysis to take place.

Average Pooling (2D). Average pooling is similar to max-pooling. However, instead of taking the maximum from each window, the average is taken.

Concatenate. Concatenate takes several arrays of inputs concatenates them into one set of arrays so that they can be passed into future layers. These arrays will be stacked depth-wise. All of the inputs must have the same width and height dimensions for them to be concatenated. Concatenate layers are commonly used in networks containing inception modules.

Global Average Pooling (2D). Global average pooling takes the average of every number in each of the feature maps. This gives an output of a vector that has a length equal to the number of feature maps. Global average pooling can be used to attempt to reduce overfitting.

Softmax. Softmax takes an input vector, calculates the exponential values of each item, and normalizes those values. This ensures that they sum to 1 so that they can be converted into probabilities. The equation for Softmax is as follows:

$$\sigma(\vec{z})_i = \frac{e^{z_i}}{\sum_{i=1}^{K} e^{z_j}},\tag{2}$$

where $\vec{z}$ is the input vector, $\sigma(z)_i$ is the output number for element i, e^{z_i} is the value of element i in $\vec{z}$, and e^{z_j} is the value of element j in $\vec{z}$ [17].

Sigmoid. Sigmoid takes a vector and fits a sigmoid function to the data. This allows a vector to be transformed into a confidence prediction between two classifications. The equation for the sigmoid function is:

$$S(x) = \frac{1}{1 + e^{-x}},\tag{3}$$

where x is a value in the array [17].

Dropout. Dropout takes several arrays and gets rid of a random number of those arrays. This can be used to prevent overfitting in large neural networks.

4.4   Model Types

There are two ways of implementing a model. A functional model stores the results from each layer in a variable and then feeds those results into the next layer as input. A sequential model, as implemented by Keras, takes input in the first layer, and organizes every other layer as a pipeline. This allows for a simpler implementation of a model that can work as a pipeline. However, models with concurrent layers such as those containing inception modules, cannot be implemented using the sequential method.

All of these layers and types of networks are important to understand when designing a CNN. All of these layers were examined in addition to considering computational limitations when creating the basicConv neural network. This paper will now discuss the implementation of these layers in combination with one another to produce the CNN.

5   Implementation

The model was trained and evaluated the a Hp Spectre x360 with an Intel Core i7-8770U processor, 16 GB of RAM, and a Nvidia MX-150 GPU with 2 GB of usable memory. The Nvidia MX-150 GPU was used to train the model and the GPU RAM (the most limiting computational factor) was almost fully in use the entire duration of training. It took approximately 2 min per epoch to train the model with a batch size of 32 and 203 steps per epoch. The result that achieved the lowest validation loss was achieved on epoch 35 with a validation accuracy of 0.958024. Although higher validation accuracy was achieved (as high as 0.964198), the training was concluded following epoch 45 as no further improvement had been made on the validation loss within 10 epochs.

5.1   Model Architecture

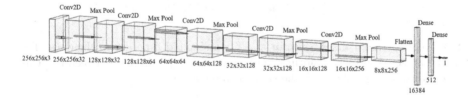

Fig. 1. BasicConv architecture with log scaling

The architecture created is called basicConv. This is because it is a basic convolutional neural network. However, it is perhaps the simplicity of the model that makes it effective. A visualization of the architecture is seen in Fig. 1. The model is sequential, meaning there are no concurrent layers, and it is implemented using the Sequential class from the Keras library. There are a total of five convolution layers, five max-pooling layers, a flatten layer, and two dense layers with a total of 8,925,633 parameters. All of the convolution layers use the rectified linear unit (relu) activation function. This function changes any negative values to 0 during training, allowing for faster convergence and an increase in the performance of the model. Additionally, all of the convolution layers use padding so that the output array is the same width and height as the input array for each convolution layer. This allows for more control over the dimensions of the data throughout the model. All of the max-pooling layers have a window size of 2 and a stride of 2. This implies that the output width and height are half of the input width and height for each max-pooling layer. Additionally, all of the filters used in the convolution layers are of size 3×3.

The first layer is a convolution layer with 32 filters. This takes the input array for the model as well, with the input size being $256 \times 256 \times 3$. 256 was chosen as the input width and height because $256 = 2^8$, which allows the image dimensions to be evenly halved up to 8 times by using max-pooling layers. The second layer is a max-pooling layer. Then, there is a convolution layer with 64 filters followed by a max-pooling layer. The next set of layers consists of two groups, each group containing a convolution layer with 128 filters and a max-pooling layer. The last convolution layer has 256 filters and is followed by a final max-pooling layer. After the convolution and pooling layers are completed, the shape of the data is $8 \times 8 \times 256$. This is then flattened to form a vector of size $16384 = 2^{14}$. Then, there is a fully connected, or dense, layer that outputs a vector of size $512 = 2^9$. This layer alone has 8,389,120 parameters, about 94% of the total parameters. Then, there is another dense layer, using the sigmoid activation function, that outputs a vector of size 1, which will be the prediction of whether or not the array passed into the first layer represents an X-ray that is positive for COVID-19. The model was then compiled using the Adam optimizer and the binary cross-entropy loss function. The accuracy, loss, and area under the roc curve were all calculated throughout training.

Table 1. Dataset composition

Unbalanced dataset

	Positive	Negative	Total
Train	3350	24155	27505
Test	837	6131	6968
Total	4187	30286	34473

Balanced dataset

	Positive	Negative	Total
Train	3350	3133	6483
Test	837	783	1620
Total	4187	3916	8103

One of the biggest challenges of deep learning research is finding data, and successful deep learning research is reliant on having enough data [10]. If there is not enough data used to train the model, the issue of overfitting can arise. This is where the model learns too much about the data and any image that does not resemble the positive training data extremely well could be identified as false or vice versa. This can have drastic effects on the results of a model. Finding data is especially challenging when researching ways to predict COVID-19 as it is a relatively new disease with little data in existence, let alone available to researchers. However, through looking at various papers and open-source GitHub pages that have done similar research, five sources for X-ray images [18–22] were discovered. These were then merged into a joint dataset, adapting the data collection script from the COVID-Net Open-Source Initiative [23]. This produced a total of 34,473 images.

However, as Table 1 shows, the number of negative X-rays in the initial (unbalanced) dataset is approximately 723% of the number of positive X-rays. This is considered a biased dataset. It is important to minimize bias to increase the integrity of results - the effect of the biased dataset on this model will be discussed in greater detail in the results section. As such, a random sample of images was taken from the negative images and in an attempt to make the datasets as equal as possible. There was a data loss of approximately 6.5% when copying random negative images. Manual intervention was avoided as that would introduce another potential source of bias in the dataset. As such, there are approximately 6.5% fewer negative X-rays than positive X-rays in the balanced dataset. This is still significantly less biased than the unbalanced dataset. As the X-rays gathered were anonymous and the only information obtained and stored was whether or not there was COVID-19 present in each X-ray, there are other potential sources of bias [24]. Potential examples of bias could be differing image quality and demographics, but these are not confirmed sources of bias.

5.2   Code Development

There were four scripts developed to implement the CNN, as seen in Fig. 2. The first script was created to read data from the five different sources, number them sequentially, and save them all as .png files in the same directory so that they have a standardized system for being referenced and accessed. This was adapted from the COVID-Net Open-Source Initiative [23]. The images were split into four categories: positive train, negative train, positive test, and negative test. The images were split using random index generation to put 20% of both the negative and positive images into their respective test folders and the rest into their respective train folders.

The second script took the dataset created in the first step and balanced the dataset. This was achieved by first finding whether there were fewer positive or negative images. In the case of the development of basicConv, there were fewer positive images. Because of this, all the images were copied from the positive train and positive test folders to their respective place in the balanced dataset folder. Then, random indexes were selected from the negative train set to make a subset of images equal in size to the positive train set and copied those images to the negative train folder within the balanced dataset folder. The same thing was then done with the test images. As mentioned earlier, there was a data

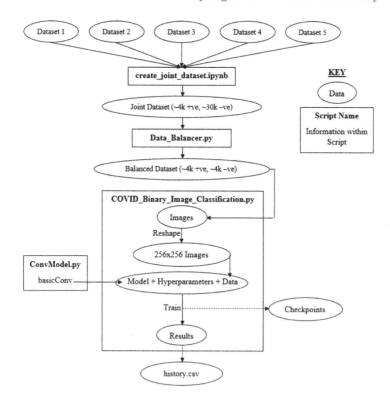

Fig. 2. Flowchart of the four scripts

loss of approximately 6.5% when copying the negative images to the balanced dataset folder.

The third script defines different architectures. It contains implementations of the basicConv architecture as well as a further truncated version of Truncated Inception Net (containing only one inception module), and a small test architecture for ensuring that the rest of the program is working without doing very intensive training. The Truncated Inception Net is too memory-intensive to be run on the GPU used in this paper. However, there will be other options investigated in the future for training architectures with inception modules, as the paper will discuss in the future work section. This third script makes it very easy to define new architectures, so in the future, new architectures can be added to the script to facilitate architecture development.

The final script is the control script. After the imports, this script is divided into six sections: user inputs, data generation, model creation, checkpoint initialization, model fitting, and history write-out. The user input section takes input on batch size, number of epochs, architecture to be run, and a series of Boolean variables for using a GPU, using a checkpoint, using the balanced dataset, and training (if training is set to false, it will just provide a model summary and evaluation). The user also inputs the location of the datasets.

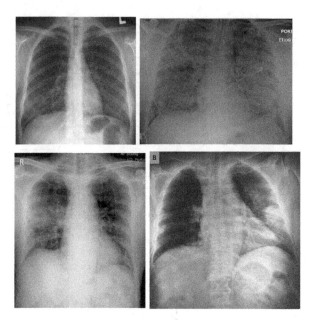

Fig. 3. Chest X-rays of patients that were negative for COVID-19 (top row) and positive for COVID-19 (bottom row) from the training dataset.

The data generation section takes the X-ray images and converts them into usable data. It uses the Keras ImageDataGenerator class to generate a stream of data for use with the model's fit function (discussed later). The image data generator reads in the X-rays from the appropriate folder, splits them into two classes (positive and negative), normalizes the pixels (dividing by 255 because that is the maximum pixel value), groups the images into batches, and resizes the images to the target size. As seen in Fig. 3, X-rays have different dimensions when they are read in, making resizing the images essential. The image with the minimum resolution is of size 156×157 and the image with the maximum resolution is of size 4757×5623 The resizing process is important to be understood, as this is the data that is being given to the model. It is also important to know if the images are being distorted at all.

When images are read in, they are first cropped to the same aspect ratio as the target size, leaving one of the dimensions the same [25]. With a target size of (256, 256), that would mean that the image would be cropped along the larger dimension, taking the middle segment of that dimension. For example, a (300×350) image would get cropped to (300×300) with 25 pixels being cropped from the left and right sides of the image. Then, the image is resized to match the target size [25]. Interpolation is the default method used for resizing [25].

The model creation section first tests for GPU availability. If there is no GPU available, this will set the script to be run without a GPU. This will also alert the user if they inputted that they want to use a GPU but there is not one available. Then, an evaluation function is defined. This runs the model's built-in evaluation function over the test dataset and collects the loss, accuracy, area under the receiver operating characteristic (ROC) curve, and the number of true positives (TP), true negatives (TN), false positives (FP), and false negatives (FN). It then prints out a confusion matrix. Finally, the model is initialized from the architecture chosen in the input section and a summary of the model is printed out.

The checkpoint initialization section first defines a checkpoint path for the selected model. It does this by taking a default directory and appending the model architecture's checkpoint extension, creating directories as needed. If the model is being run using a balanced dataset, it adds "_balanced" to the path. If the directory for the current model's checkpoint is empty and the user inputted that they want to use a checkpoint, the script affirms whether or not the user would like to continue without a checkpoint. If not, an exception is raised, and the script stops. The callback functions are then initialized. These give the model additional features that it would not otherwise have. There is one callback function for handling checkpoints and another callback function for halting training early if the loss has not improved in 10 epochs. An image representation of the model is then saved to the checkpoint file. Finally, the model weights are loaded if the script is using a checkpoint and a pre-training evaluation is performed if the script is going to do training. One issue that will be explored further in the future is that when training from a checkpoint, the model's fit function still initializes the loss to infinity meaning that the first epoch of the training could result in saving a checkpoint that has a higher loss than the loss from the loaded weights.

The model fitting section is where all the training happens. It first defines a fitModel function which takes the following hyperparameters: batch size, steps, model, and number of epochs (initialized to 10 if not specified). Then, the model tries training with the given hyperparameters. If there is an error indicating that there is not enough memory to train (thrown as a resource exhausted error), the function halves the batch size, doubles the step size, and tries to run the model again. If the resource exhausted error is thrown with a batch size of 1, the function raises the error. This function is then called with the given user inputs. Finally, a post-training evaluation is performed, using the evaluation function defined above.

The final section of the control script is the history write-out section. This section only runs if training has been performed. It first defines a path for the model history, stored as a .csv file. If this model has been trained in the past and there is an existing history file, the script will try to read that file and append the history from the current training run to that file. If an exception is raised while trying to read the file, the script will affirm whether the user wants to continue and overwrite the file. In the case of an overwrite or no file present, a blank pandas DataFrame will be created. The history from the current training run will then be appended to the DataFrame whether it is blank or contains existing history. Then, the script will reset the indices in the DataFrame so that

Table 2. Performance metrics for BasicConv by DataSet used. Note: the better performing metric is accented in bold text.

Dataset	Balanced	Unbalanced
Accuracy	0.9580	**0.9859**
Precision	**0.9649**	0.9567
Recall	**0.9534**	0.9247
F-1	**0.9591**	0.9405
AUC	**0.9896**	0.9781

the indexes in the history file are monotonically increasing sequentially. The script will then try to get rid of any useless columns created in concatenation or in resetting the indices. Finally, the DataFrame will be written out to the appropriate location.

6   Results

The measures collected during model training were binary cross-entropy loss, accuracy, the area under ROC, TP, TN, FP, and FN. The binary cross-entropy loss was described earlier, in the methodology section. TP is the number of correct positive predictions that were made. TN is the number of correct negative predictions that were made. FP is the number of predictions that were predicted as positive but were actually negative. FN is the number of predictions that were predicted as negative but were actually positive. A confusion matrix combines TP, TN, FP, and FN into one chart to make them easily comparable, as seen below in Table 3. Accuracy is calculated as the total number of correct predictions the model makes divided by the total number of predictions made. Using the confusion matrix, this formula is $\frac{TP+TN}{TP+TN+FP+FN}$. The ROC curve is a curve plotting TP against FP. The area under the ROC curve is a good indicator of how well the model is predicting positive cases.

After training, precision, recall, and the F-1 score were calculated as well. Precision is the percentage of predictions that were correct out of all the positive predictions. Using the confusion matrix, the formula for precision is $\frac{TP}{TP+FP}$. Recall is the percentage of positive images the model detected and predicted as positive. Using the confusion matrix, the formula for recall is $\frac{TP}{TP+FN}$. The F-1 score is a combined measure of precision and recall, providing a metric for how well the model can predict positive cases. The formula for the F-1 score is $\frac{2 \cdot P \cdot R}{P+R}$ where P is precision and R is recall.

The results from this study in Table 2 and Table 3 show that a seemingly simple CNN can still be very effective. However, the results also show the importance of ensuring data integrity. The model had a higher accuracy when it was running on a biased (unbalanced) dataset. This is because it had a very high number of negative cases, so it learned how to predict negative cases very well. This skewed

Table 3. Confusion matrices for BasicConv

		Unbalanced dataset		
		Predicted		
		Positive	Negative	Total
Actual	Positive	774	63	837
	Negative	35	6096	6131
	Total	809	6159	**6968**
		Balanced dataset		
		Predicted		
		Positive	Negative	Total
Actual	Positive	798	39	837
	Negative	29	754	783
	Total	827	793	**1620**

Table 4. Comparison

Architecture	BasicConv	Inception-v3	TIN	ResNet-50
Accuracy	0.9580	0.9700	**0.9877**	0.9800
Precision	0.9649	**1.0000**	0.9900	**1.0000**
Recall	0.9534	–	–	–
F-1	0.9591	0.9600	0.9700	**0.9800**
AUC	0.9896	–	**0.9900**	–

Notes:
TIN represents Truncated Inception Net.
The best-performing metric is accented in bold text.
Additionally, results are from a different dataset [4], however, the datasets are balanced and are the best available comparative results.

the results and any shortcomings in positive predictions were masked by the negative predictions. Looking at the other metrics, however, it is apparent that the model trained on the balanced dataset performs much better, especially when detecting positive cases.

It is evident in Table 4 that although basicConv performed well, it still underperforms when compared to other networks that use inception modules, such as Inception-v3 and Truncated Inception Net. However, the results are very close for many of the metrics. More layers and parameters in addition to using inception modules could help to improve the results of the architecture in the future. Using residual layers is also something that will be explored, as the ResNet-50 architecture had the best F-1 score in addition to the best precision score.

7   Conclusion and Future Work

COVID-19 has been one of the biggest changes to the lives of many in the last two years. Chest X-rays are one of the ways COVID-19 and other diseases can be detected. Many deep neural networks have been created to try to do that. The CNN proposed in this paper manages to achieve a 95.8% accuracy with an AUC of 0.9896, indicating that positive cases are very well handled. While this is not yet a model that can be used clinically for diagnosis purposes, future work may get closer to that goal.

The primary weakness of this study is the computational limitation. This can be improved upon in the future by using a high performance computing cluster or another system with an increased GPU limit. Another area for improvement is increased pre-processing of data to eliminate noise. This study included very little pre-processing, so using foreign object detection is a possibility in the future. Another form of pre-processing that will be investigated is using border detection to crop images to only include the lungs before reshaping the images to be uniform.

There are many potential future expansions to this research. The first expansion is implementing more architectures. Options for model training that allow an increased GPU memory limit will be explored so that more complex architectures can be trained. This would allow inception modules to be used in addition to multiple dense layers. The next future area of research is the classification of multiple diseases. This would allow an exploration of if different architectures are optimal for different diseases. If so, further research could provide insight into why there are performance differences between different diseases. Different data splitting techniques, such as k-fold data splitting, could also be implemented. This would validate the results further and would provide more insight into the effects of data bias on effectively training a model.

References

1. World Health Organization: WHO Coronavirus (COVID-19) Dashboard. World Health Organization (2020). https://covid19.who.int/. Accessed 5 Mar 2022
2. Bengio, Y., Goodfellow, I., Courville, A.: Deep Learning. MIT Press, Cambridge (2017)
3. Santosh, K.C.: AI-driven tools for coronavirus outbreak: need of active learning and cross-population train/test models on multitudinal/multimodal data. J. Med. Syst. **44**(5) (2020). https://doi.org/10.1007/s10916-020-01562-1
4. Das, D., Santosh, K.C., Pal, U.: Truncated inception net: COVID-19 outbreak screening using chest X-rays. Phys. Eng. Sci. Med. **43**(3), 915–925 (2020). https://doi.org/10.1007/s13246-020-00888-x
5. Szegedy, C., et al.: Going deeper with convolutions. In: 2015 IEEE Conference on Computer Vision and Pattern Recognition (CVPR) (2015). https://doi.org/10.1109/cvpr.2015.7298594
6. Raj, B.: A simple guide to the versions of the inception network. Medium, 31 July 2020. https://towardsdatascience.com/a-simple-guide-to-the-versions-of-the-inception-network-7fc52b863202. Accessed 18 Feb 2022

7. Fei-Fei, L., Deng, J., Russakovsky, O., Berg, A., Li, K.: About ImageNet. ImageNet (2020). https://www.image-net.org/about.php. Accessed 18 Feb 2022
8. He, K., Zhang, X., Ren, S., Sun, J.: Deep residual learning for image recognition. In: 2016 IEEE Conference on Computer Vision and Pattern Recognition (CVPR) (2016). https://doi.org/10.1109/cvpr.2016.90
9. Mukherjee, H., Ghosh, S., Dhar, A., Obaidullah, S.M., Santosh, K.C., Roy, K.: Deep neural network to detect COVID-19: one architecture for both CT scans and chest X-rays. Appl. Intell. **51**(5), 2777–2789 (2020). https://doi.org/10.1007/s10489-020-01943-6
10. Santosh, K.C., Ghosh, S.: COVID-19 imaging tools: how big data is big? J. Med. Syst. **45**(7) (2021). https://doi.org/10.1007/s10916-021-01747-2
11. Macukow, B.: Neural networks – state of art, brief history, basic models and architecture. In: Saeed, K., Homenda, W. (eds.) CISIM 2016. LNCS, vol. 9842, pp. 3–14. Springer, Cham (2016). https://doi.org/10.1007/978-3-319-45378-1_1
12. Kaushik, V.: 8 Applications of Neural Networks. Analytics Steps, 26 August 2021. https://www.analyticssteps.com/blogs/8-applications-neural-networks. Accessed 19 Feb 2022
13. Rodriguez, P., Wiles, J., Elman, J.L.: A recurrent neural network that learns to count. Connect. Sci. **11**(1), 5–40 (1999). https://doi.org/10.1080/095400999116340
14. Rohrer, B.: How do Convolutional Neural Networks work? E2LML.school, 18 August 2016. https://e2eml.school/how_convolutional_neural_networks_work.html. Accessed 16 Feb 2022
15. Godoy, D.: Understanding binary cross-entropy/log loss: a visual explanation. Medium7 February 2019. https://towardsdatascience.com/understanding-binary-cross-entropy-log-loss-a-visual-explanation-a3ac6025181a. Accessed 18 Feb 2022
16. Kingma, D.P., Ba, J.: Adam: a method for stochastic optimization. arXiv preprint arXiv:1412.6980 (2014)
17. Wood, T.: Softmax Function. DeepAI, 17 May 2019. https://deepai.org/machine-learning-glossary-and-terms/softmax-layer. Accessed 18 Feb 2022
18. https://github.com/ieee8023/covid-chestxray-dataset
19. https://github.com/agchung/Figure1-COVID-chestxray-dataset
20. https://github.com/agchung/Actualmed-COVID-chestxray-dataset
21. https://www.kaggle.com/tawsifurrahman/covid19-radiography-database
22. https://www.kaggle.com/c/rsna-pneumonia-detection-challenge
23. Wang, L.: COVID-net open source initiative. GitHub (2021). https://github.com/lindawangg/COVID-Net. Accessed 21 Feb 2022
24. Santosh, K.C.: COVID-19 prediction models and unexploited data. J. Med. Syst. **44**(9) (2020). https://doi.org/10.1007/s10916-020-01645-z
25. https://github.com/keras-team/keras/blob/master/keras/preprocessing/image.py

Chest X-ray Image Super-Resolution via Deep Contrast Consistent Feature Network

M. S. Greeshma$^{(\boxtimes)}$ and V. R. Bindu

School of Computer Sciences, Mahatma Gandhi University, Kottayam, Kerala, India
{greeshmams,binduvr}@mgu.ac.in

Abstract. This paper proposes a chest X-ray image super-resolution reconstruction method - Deep Contrast Consistent Feature Network, which articulates the contrast consistency as a task to learn spatial contrast enhancement curve followed by a depth contrast network. The proposed method trains a network with visual quality measures through learning non-reference loss - Contrast Consistency Loss, which aims to overcome contrast overstretching and contrastive variation. Specifically, this network does not need to reference images at the time of loss formulation. We evaluated the proposed method for chest X-ray 5K datasets over several benchmarks metrics and models for quantitative and qualitative analysis. The extensive experiments report that the proposed model outperforms other approaches.

Keywords: Super resolution · Chest X-ray image · Deep network · Contrast enhancement

1 Introduction

The vital image modality of chest X-rays (CXR) have been widely used to diagnose respiratory diseases, especially with the advent of Covid-19 [5, 18, 19]. In clinical imaging analysis, high-resolution (HR) images with good perceptual characteristics offer better characterization and decision making. Cost-effective techniques such as X-ray, ultrasound, MRI and CT generate medical images; when dealing with them, it is significant to handle images free of distortion and low contrast details [4, 13, 16, 17]. Specifically, CXR resolution enhancement aims to recover the HR images by improving the contrast details. The contrast is a key feature in the subjective evaluation of CXR visual quality. Even though some contrast enhancement methods have been proposed to produce visually pleasing images, they are usually applied for generic images while challenging to maintain the contrast variation of chest X-ray images [19].

The reconstruction of low-dose to high-quality CXR from ionizing radiation and tolerance environment is still challenging and affects information loss and structural disorder. To address these problems of preserving the rib structure and white spots in the super-resolution reconstruction of chest X-rays, certain approaches have reconstructed and analyzed this CXR super-resolution problem such as SNSR-GAN [12], DRCN [10, 11] and CXR SR reconstruction via recursive neural network. This work is an extended version of super-resolution using deep networks for chest x-ray images by the same authors

KC Santosh et al. (Eds.): RTIP2R 2022, CCIS 1704, pp. 78–90, 2023.
https://doi.org/10.1007/978-3-031-23599-3_7

[20]. But most of these methods reconstructed the CXR without concern for resolution characteristics such as contrast, spatial constancy, etc.

In this work, we propose a deep contrast consistent feature to learn spatial contrast consistency followed by a depth contrast network. The spatial contrast consistent curve is introduced to adjust the spatial coherence between the contrastive pixels. And also, the non-reference loss function, which formulates the contrast consistency loss, does not require the reference images during loss evaluation; it overcomes the contrast overstretching and contrastive variation.

The remaining part of this text is structured as follows. Section 2 discusses the background information on contrast enhancement techniques and relevant related works. Deep Contrast Consistent Feature network is depicted in Sect. 3. Experimental discussion and analysis are demonstrated in Sect. 4. Finally, the paper concludes in Sect. 5.

2   Background Study and Related Works

2.1   Preliminaries of Super-Resolution Algorithms

The super-resolution (SR) algorithms aim to reconstruct high-resolution (HR) features from low-resolution (LR) features. This work will be centred on clinical super-resolution imaging; the medical CXR SR images can be precisely diagnosed with an enhanced high-resolution image. Primarily, there are three groups of super-resolution approaches: I) Interpolation-based, II) Reconstruction-based and III) Learning–based [3, 6]. The interpolation-based algorithms can enhance the resolution by the simplest methods but, most of the time, fail in visual quality. The reconstruction-based algorithms can effectively optimize the reconstruction according to the prior information of the data. Therefore, the abovementioned approaches can generate the SR CXR images but loses some high-frequency details. Recently, researchers have focused on learning-based SR algorithms to learn the high-frequency information from HR-LR image pairs. The rapid improvement of machine learning algorithms and hardware performance started the research on SR using deep learning [7]. Generally, a convolutional neural network (CNN) having the building block for formulating deep learning can be expressed as:

$$min \frac{1}{2} \sum_{k=1}^{k} \left(\left\| I_k^{LR} - H_k I_k^{HR} \right\| \right)^2 + \lambda A I_K^{HR} + \beta \left\| I^{HR} - fcnn(I^{LR}|\theta) \right\|_2^2 \quad (1)$$

in which β regularizes the reconstruction from I^{LR} through the forward propagation $fcnn$ of data parametrized by θ. This SR image generates from the downsampled one, which can be computed by $H_k I_k^{HR}$. Dong and their team first proposed the super-resolution using the convolutional neural network, SRCNN [7]. This network is operated through three convolutional layers: 1) patch extraction, 2) non-linear mapping and 3) reconstruction. Moreover, the different variants of deep learning have been reconstructed for the SR images [1, 2, 7–9, 15]. For CXR super-resolution, Zhao et al. employed the CXR images super-resolution reconstruction via recursive neural network [11]. In this network, the Leaky ReLU module is used to extract the rich texture details and correlation between CXR pixels; it is learned through the light-weight recursive layer. Low-dose chest X-ray image super-resolution using generative adversarial nets with spectral normalization is employed in Xu et al. [12], which discusses the use of conditional GAN and spectral normalization to generate the CXR SR image. Rahman et al. explored COVID-19 detection from CXR images using image enhancement techniques by U-Net architecture [19]. In other medical image modalities, Hou et al. used CT images for quality enhancement using dual-channel network SR [17]. Ashwini and Sujatha employed Ultrasound image enhancement using super-resolution [16]. Chen et al. discussed the MRI super-resolution using a generative adversarial network and 3D multi-level densely connected network [13].

This work is the extended version of super-resolution using deep networks for chest x-ray images employed in Greeshma and Bindu [20]. They also discuss the CNN architecture with edge feature extraction, edge reinforcement, and image reconstruction layers. This light-weight network reinforces the edge structures factorized by 3×3 convolutions, enhancing the resolution of CXR with an effective rib structure. But, texture contrast preservation is more challenging in this network. However, contrast consistency is valuable for CXR image visual quality and decision-making. Therefore, we extend the network above to learn the contrast consistency feature and generate the CXR SR images.

2.2   Review of Contrast Enhancement Techniques

Contrast is a focal feature descriptor in medical CXR images. Many contrast enhancement approaches improve the contrast details and identification of perceptual quality in CXR images. According to tone mapping, local contrast enhancement is achieved through various techniques such as a) histogram equalization (HE), b) adaptive histogram equalization (AHE), c) image invert, d) Gamma correction, e) contrast limited adaptive histogram equalization (CLAHE) etc.

In the histogram equalization technique, using histogram characterization to distribute intensity levels of an image in the dynamic range $[0, L - 1]$ is expressed as follows:

$$h_k = T(n_k) \tag{2}$$

in which transformation $T(n_k)$ for the number of pixels n_k with respect to the inte sity value, k [21]. In contrast, the basic histogram equalization is adapted to extend the equalization in small patches; the approach called adaptive histogram equalization. Applying HE and AHE to chest X-ray images, it is perceived that they over amplify the noise and are not distinguished. CLAHE algorithm is operationally the same as the AHE, but the clip limit parameter characterises the selected region [22].

Another alternative approach is image inversion, where the dark spots become lighter and the lighter become darker, mathematically computed as $255 - x$, the difference between the high intensity value 255 and original intensity value x. When dealing with non-linear operations, gamma correction enhances the contrast of the CXR image according to the internal map with respect to the value of the pixel and gamma [19]. The approaches above are simple to enhance the contrast but have difficulty comprising the visual quality and global contrast features such as depth, texture etc. Therefore, chest X-rays suffer from low resolution and contrast consistency in super-resolution imaging.

So we propose the spatial contrast consistency curve to enhance the contrast and retain the saturated regions.

3 Deep Contrast Consistent Feature SR

Given a CXR image, the process is to reconstruct the low-resolution CXR into a high-resolution CXR image and, at the same time, maintain the contrast consistency. This section will discuss Deep Contrast Consistent Feature Network (DCCFN) and its formulations. The detailed deep architecture is shown in Fig. 1. The DCCFN network consists of three functional modules: the feature extractor and non-linear mapping, the depth contrast sub-network and the PixelShuffle layer. The feature extractor and non-linear mapping extract and map to a set of feature maps. The depth contrast subnetwork refines the features with spatial contrast consistency curve maps. Finally, the CXR SR images are reconstructed through the PixelShuffle layer [24].

3.1 DCCFN Model

The DCCFN model aims to optimize the loss between the CXR generated I^{HR} and ground truth HR I^{GT} images and can be formulated as:

$$argmin L_{CCL}\left(I^{HR}, G\left(I^{LR}, \Theta\right)\right) \tag{3}$$

where L_{CCL} is a loss function, and G represents the function learn with parameter Θ to devise the deep model. Firstly, given I^{LR} image, the feature extractor and non-linear mapping layers extract the feature maps over the nonlinear convolutions, which can be formulated as:

$$f^1\left(I^{LR}; W_1, b_1\right) = \phi\left(W_1 * I^{LR} + b_1\right) \tag{4}$$

$$f^l\left(I^{LR}; W_{1:l}, b_{1:l}\right) = \phi\left(W_l * f^1\left(I^{LR}\right) + b_l\right) \tag{5}$$

in which the smaller filters W_l and bias b_l learn through the nonlinearity function ϕ in low-resolution space. The two filters of size 5×5 and 3×3 convolutions were used as the initial feature extractor. After this operation, the I^{LR} become 64 tensor feature map. The inputs from the feature extractor module are passed into the depth contrast network. The depth contrast net is a sub-network with seven convolutional layers with 32 filters of 3×3 size. So we can effectively use the symmetrical concatenation along with these convolutional layers while preserving the contextual contrast details. Tanh activation function is used in the last convolution layer, which generates the 24 feature maps. So, Tanh is easier to optimize and learn curve parameters for accurately designating the contrast of regions. The mathematical formulation can be expressed as:

$$f_2(I^{LR}; W, b) = \sigma Tanh(w_6 \sigma_{ReLU}(w_5 \sigma_{ReLU}(w_4 \sigma_{ReLU}(w_3 \sigma_{ReLU}(w_2 \sigma_{ReLU}(w_1 f^{l-1}(I^{LR})$$
$$+b1) + b2) + b3) + b4) + b5) + b6 \tag{6}$$

where $F_1(Y)$ passes through the first layer and generates feature maps to the remaining five layers with the ReLU activation and finally the seventh layer with Tanh activation to preserve the monotonous functions of the difference between the neighbouring pixels. We present the spatial contrast consistency curve (SCC-curve) which can adjust the contrast information of the image within the dynamic range. Specifically, the quadratic curve can be expressed as:

$$SCC(I(x)) = scc\_I(x) + \alpha(scc\_I(x)(1 - scc\_I(x))) \tag{7}$$

where x indicates the pixel values and α represents the trainable fitting parameter with the Tanh function $[-1, 1]$, preserving from contrast overstretching and brightening the contrast details. So, this net maps all the low-contrast pixels by applying a spatial contrast consistency curve iteratively to retain the contrast consistency. Finally, reconstruction is achieved through the sub-pixel convolutional operation called the PixelShuffle layer [24]. The input image feature for this layer is preprocessed using 3×3 convolutional filters. In fact, upscaling is done through this layer, so not using an upscaled I^{LR} directly as input to the network, and can be described as:

$$f^{l-2}\left(I^{LR}; W_{2:l}, b_{2:l}\right) = \phi\left(W_l * f_2\left(I^{LR}\right) + b_l\right) \tag{8}$$

$$I^{CXR-SR} = F^L(I_{LR}) = PS(W_L * f^{l-2}\left(I^{LR}\right) + b_L) \tag{9}$$

where PS is a periodic shuffling operator that reshuffles the input I^{LR} tensor $\left(h.w.c.r^2\right)$ to HR tensor $(rh.rw.c)$ and r indicates the scale factor. The alternative ways to upsurge the resolution of the input image by convolution with the stride $\frac{1}{r}$ [23]. The activation patterns are periodically triggered at the sub-pixel location: $mod(x, r)$ and $mod(y, r)$ of the convolutional process. It can be expressed as:

$$PS(T)_{x,y,c} = T_{[x/r],[y/r],C.r.mod(y,r)+C.mod(x,r)+c} \tag{10}$$

Thus, the last layer generates the high-resolution CXR from low-resolution CXR through the sub-pixel convolution of a single upscaling filter.

3.2 Training

To facilitate the non-reference loss function in DCCFN, we propose the contrast consistency loss (CCL) that evaluates the perceptual quality of super-resolved images. The contrast consistency loss L_{CCL} preserves the spatial contrast quality information and reduces the noise during training. Spatial consistency is correlated with the differences in neighbouring pixels. The L_{CCL} can be defined as:

$$L_{1CCL} = \frac{1}{k} \sum_{i=1}^{k} \sum_{j\in\Omega} \left|Y_{i_{max}} - Y_{j_{min}}\right| \tag{11}$$

where Ω is the regions (top, down, left, right) that are decomposed from local region k and centred at i. Y denotes the difference between the maximum and minimum intensity values of the local region in the super-resolved image. Routinely, the pixel-based MSE loss (reference loss) function defines the super-resolution learning process [7], which can be expressed as:

$$L_{2MSE} = \frac{1}{r^2 WH} \sum_{x=1}^{rW} \sum_{y=1}^{rH} \left(I_{x,y}^{HR} - F_{x,y}^{L}(I_{LR}) \right)^2 \tag{12}$$

The *total loss* is considered as the (L_{1CCL}; L_{2MSE}) and explicitly evaluated, the above-mentioned *PS* can reduce the training time.

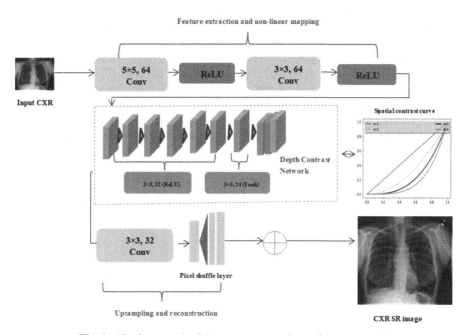

Fig. 1. The framework of deep contrast consistent feature network

4 Experimental Evaluation and Discussion

4.1 Implementation Analysis

In this section, we demonstrate the experimental results of the proposed DCCFN generated by python on ubuntu 20.04 with P100 GPU and 32 GB memory. We utilize the Chest X-Ray Images as a training dataset for CXR image super-resolution collected from: https://www.kaggle.com/datasets/paultimothymooney, which has 4265 CXR images, 3000 training images, 875 validation images and 390 for testing. We directly input the LR CXR images into the DCCFN, and the following sections will discuss the detailed evaluations and results.

For the DCCFN training, to extract the non-overlapping patches from the ground-truth images, $h.r \times w.r$ ($16r \times 16r$). We set 64 filters with 5×5 and 3×3 convolutional filter sizes for the first two convolutional layers to extract the initial features maps. The DCCFN network specification, which includes the framework used, epoch, batch size, learning rate, regularization, loss function and optimizer, has been tabulated in Table 1. In depth contrast sub-network, we set *layers* $= 7$, (f,n) $= (32,3)$ and $(24,3)$ with stride 1, and the last layer normalizes with the tanh activation function of the 24 feature maps. So this sub-network has 13848 trainable parameters due to the selection of the smallest convolutional filter of size 3×3. The reconstruction is done through the PixelShuffle layer of 3×3 convolution. Compared with SRCNN, the computation time is $\log_2 r^2$ faster than in the sub-pixel activation, and can avoid over training time. To train this network, non-reference loss *contrast consistency loss* and pixel-based *MSE* [7] is used. For *CCL* measures the spatial contrast of the local region of 4×4 size and empirically sets the four neighbouring region; L $= \{[0, 0, 0], [-1, 1, 0], [0, 0, 0]\}$, R $= \{[0, 0, 0], [0, 1, -1], [0, 0, 0]\}$, U $= \{[0, -1, 0], [0, 1, 0], [0, 0, 0]\}$, D $= \{[0,0, 0], [0, 1, 0], [0, -1, 0]\}$, and max-pooling of kernel size 4×4 with four stride is used. Thus, the network can learn the HR and contrast consistent parameters; thus, the weights are updated through the Adam optimizer. As shown in Table 4, on comparison of training parameters of different SR models; after the training, this network has 143,676 trainable parameters generated.

Table 1. The DCCFN network specifications

Parameters	Values
Framework	TensorFlow
Epoch	100
Batch size	8
Learning rate	0.001
Regularization	Dropout
Loss-function	Pixel-based MSE and contrast consistency loss
Optimizer	Adam

4.2 Qualitative and Quantitative Comparison

We conduct the qualitative and quantitative comparison of the DCCFN with other state-of-the-art (SOTA) SR methods, including Bicubic, SRCNN [8], ESPCN [24], DRCN-2021 [11], and CXR-SR [20] methods. For the subjective and objective evaluations, we have seleted to demonstare the few SR images reconstructed using the $\times 2$, $\times 3$, *and* $\times 4$ scale factors. Firstly, we qualitatively evaluate the reconstructed SR images via different SR methods, as shown in Fig. 2, Fig. 3 and Fig. 4. From Fig. 2 and Fig. 3, DCCFN achieves better visual performance for $\times 2$ scaling. Some key details are clearer than the SRCNN, ESPCN and DRCN-2021, explicitly, white spots and spine structures. Moreover, the quantitative comparison of DCCFN with other SOTA methods using the benchmark metrics PSNR and SSIM is tabulated in Table 2 and Table 3. The tables show that the

DCCFN has good quantitative values; it significantly expresses the DCCFN execution well. The average PSNR gain of DCCFN is 0.1876 dB for ×3 scaling on the chest-Xray dataset.

To enable the evaluation of the selected region, the image is enlarged by a ×4 scaling as demonstrated in Fig. 4. Though, the DCCFN generated super-resolved image outperforms with a notable gain of PSNR and SSIM. The experimental evaluations show that the DCCFN generated the CXR SR with more pleasant details.

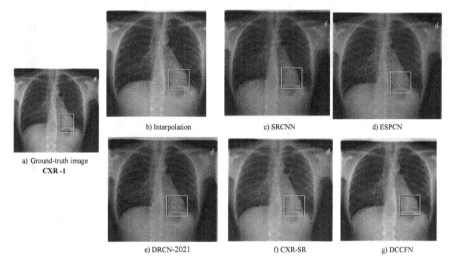

Fig. 2. Subjective qualitative comparison of various SR models for ×2 upscaling on chest X-ray images

Table 2. Quantitative comparison of various SR methods for ×2 upscaling

SR methods	CXR1		CXR2	
	PSNR (dB)	SSIM	PSNR (dB)	SSIM
Bicubic	39.67	0.942	39.54	0.918
SRCNN	41.24	0.934	41.87	0.928
ESPCN	42.65	0.945	42.03	0.939
DRCN-2021	42.57	0.941	42.01	0.952
CXR-SR	42.87	0.948	**43.41**	**0.968**
DCCFN	**43.00**	**0.962**	43.39	0.965

The average PSNR of the chest X-ray image dataset for ×2 upscaling with the interpolation method is 39.30, SRCNN is 40.22, ESPCN is 40.760, DRCN is 40.99, and DCCFN is 41.30. Likewise, the average PSNR of chest X-ray image dataset for ×3 upscaling with the interpolation method is 37.20, SRCNN is 38.33, ESPCN is 38.80, DRCN is 38.91, and DCCFN is 39.16.

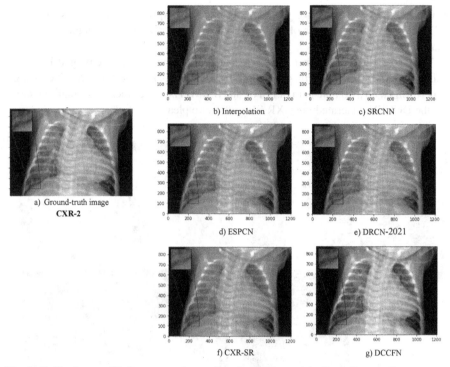

a) Ground-truth image
CXR-2

b) Interpolation

c) SRCNN

d) ESPCN

e) DRCN-2021

f) CXR-SR

g) DCCFN

Fig. 3. Subjective qualitative comparison of various SR models for ×2 upscaling on person_86_bacteria_428.jpg

Table 3. Quantitative Comparison of various SR methods for ×3 upscaling on person1673_virus_2889.jpeg (CXR1), person173_bacteria_831.ipeg (CXR2) and person172_bacteria_827.jpeg (CXR3)

SR methods	CXR1		CXR2		CXR3	
	PSNR (dB)	SSIM	PSNR (dB)	SSIM	PSNR (dB)	SSIM
Bicubic	36.78	0.786	36.89	0.787	36.98	0.790
SRCNN	39.43	0.702	38.47	0.708	38.99	0.701
ESPCN	39.86	0.711	39.63	0.719	39.43	0.709
DRCN-2021	39.44	0.790	39.92	0.784	39.44	0.794
CXR-SR	40.39	0.823	**40.87**	0.856	40.88	0.848
DCCFN	**40.67**	**0.889**	40.75	**0.898**	**40.94**	**0.901**

4.3   Ablation Analysis

We evaluated our algorithm thoroughly, and we conducted a few ablation experiments. Firstly, we train a DCCFN without the contrast consistency loss to recover the SR CXR

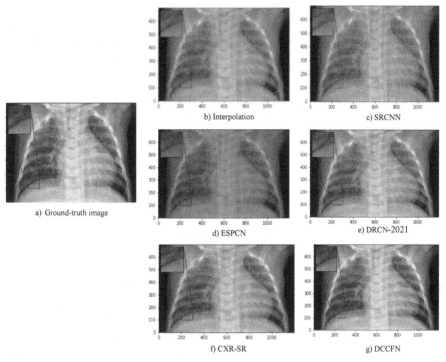

Fig. 4. Subjective qualitative comparison of various SR models for ×4 upscaling on person17_virus_48.jpeg: (a) HR image (PSNR/SSIM), (b) Bicubic (34.56/0.854), (c) SRCNN (36.08/0.874), (d) ESPCN (36.82/0.872), (e) DRCN-2021 (37.80/0.875), (f) CXR-SR (37.79/0.877) and DCCFN (38.01/0.882).

Table 4. Comparison of trainable parameters with different SR models

SR algorithm	Trainable parameters
EPSCN	58,212
DRCN	304,420
CXR-SR	65,29
DCCFN	143,676

image from low-resolution one. Table 5 tabulated the quantitative comparison of DCCFN and DCCFN without CCL; the quantitative analysis observed that the DCCFN network surpassed the metric score without CCL. Secondly, we evaluate the effectiveness of the depth contrast network (DCN), DCN with small filters and proper activation can generate HR counterparts with proper contrast and details. We also demonstrate the visual comparison of DCCFN and without DCN and CCL in Fig. 5.

We can see that removing the CCL loss and DCN fails to recover adequate contrast, edge, and texture information. In Fig. 6, we show the performance of DCCFN with the help of training loss plot; it has a notable learning capability than the model without CCL and DCN modules. The DCCFN model can effectively maintain the consistency of contrast and spatial information for the reconstructed CXR image and recover the ribs and structural details.

Table 5. Quantitative comparison of DCCFN and DCCFN without CCL for ×2 scaling

CXR images	Metric	Without CCL and DCN	DCCFN
person1673_virus_2889.jpeg	PSNR(dB)	39.29	40.73
	SSIM	0.923	0.939
person173_bacteria_831.ipeg	PSNR(dB)	39.87	40.92
	SSIM	0.919	0.931
person172_bacteria_827.jpeg	PSNR(dB)	39.21	40.71
	SSIM	0.922	0.946

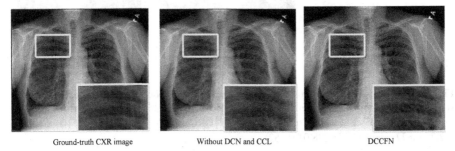

Ground-truth CXR image   Without DCN and CCL   DCCFN

Fig. 5. Visual comparison of DCCFN without CCL and DCN and DCCFN(baseline) for ×4 SR images.

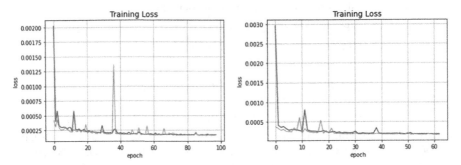

Fig. 6. Training loss graph of 1) DCCFN without CCL and 2) DCCFN. The Blue indicates the training loss and Orange indicates validation loss (Color figure online)

5 Conclusion

We proposed a Deep Contrast Consistent Feature Network for chest X-ray image super-resolution. The depth contrast network is trained with contrast consistency loss. The significance of this network is a non-reference loss function for end-to-end training. The contrast consistency loss is used to preserve the contrastive perceptual information and, at the same time, reduce the artefacts. In general, the proposed DCCFN is a good trade-off between model and reconstruction capability. Experimental evaluations demonstrate that the DCCFN outperforms the other SOTA algorithms quantitatively and qualitatively. In addition, the ablation study shows the significance of each part of the model for CXR image reconstruction.

References

1. Kim, J., Lee, J.K., Lee, K.M.: Deeply-recursive convolutional network for image super-resolution. In: Proceedings of the 2016 IEEE Conference on Computer Vision Pattern Recognition, Las Vegas, NV, USA, pp. 1637–1645 (2016)
2. Tai, Y., Yang, J., Liu, X.: Image super-resolution via deep recursiveresidual network. In: Proceedings of the IEEE Conference on ComputerVision and Pattern Recognition, pp. 3147–3155 (2017)
3. Bevilacqua, M., Roumy, A., Guillemot, C., Morel, M.A.: Single-image super-resolution via linear mapping of interpolated self-examples. IEEE Trans. Image Process. **23**(12), 5334–5347 (2014)
4. Ai, T., et al.: Correlation of chest CT and RT-PCR testing in coronavirus disease 2019 (COVID-19) in China: a report of 1014 cases (2020)
5. Kanne, J.P., Little, B.P., Chung, J.H., Brett, M.E., Ketai, L.H.: Essentials for radiologists on COVID-19: an update - radiology scientific expert panel (2020)
6. Tsai, R.Y., Huang, T.S.: Multiframe image restoration and registration. In: Advances in Computer Vision, Image Process, vol. 1, pp. 317–339 (1984)
7. Dong, C., Loy, C.C., He, K., Tang, X.: Learning a deep convolutional network for image super-resolution. In: Fleet, D., Pajdla, T., Schiele, B., Tuytelaars, T. (eds.) ECCV 2014. LNCS, vol. 8692, pp. 184–199. Springer, Cham (2014). https://doi.org/10.1007/978-3-319-10593-2_13
8. Dong, C., Loy, C.C., He, K.: Image super-resolution using deep convolutional networks. IEEE Trans. Pattern Anal. Mach. Intell. **38**, 295–307 (2016)
9. Dong, C., Loy, C.C., Tang, X.: Accelerating the super-resolution convolutional neural network. In: Leibe, B., Matas, J., Sebe, N., Welling, M. (eds.) ECCV 2016. LNCS, vol. 9906, pp. 391–407. Springer, Cham (2016). https://doi.org/10.1007/978-3-319-46475-6_25
10. Shimizu, M., Kariya, H., Goto, T., Hirano, S., Sakurai, M.: Superresolution for X-ray images. In: 2015 IEEE 4th Global Conference on Consumer Electronics (GCCE), pp. 246–247 (2015)
11. Zhao, C.Y., Jia, R.S., Liu, Q.M., et al.: Chest X-ray images superresolution reconstruction via recursive neural network. Multimed Tools Appl. **80**, 263–277 (2021)
12. Xu, L., Zeng, X., Huang, Z., Li, W., Zhang, H.: Low-dose chest X-ray image super-resolution using generative adversarial nets with spectral normalization. Biomed. Signal Process. Control **55**, 101600 (2020)
13. Chen, Y., Shi, F., Christodoulou, A.G., Xie, Y., Zhou, Z., Li, D.: Efficient and accurate MRI super-resolution using a generative adversarial network and 3D multi-level densely connected network. In: Frangi, A.F., Schnabel, J.A., Davatzikos, C., Alberola-López, C., Fichtinger, G. (eds.) MICCAI 2018. LNCS, vol. 11070, pp. 91–99. Springer, Cham (2018). https://doi.org/10.1007/978-3-030-00928-1_11

14. Wang, Z., Bovik, A.C., Sheikh, H.R., Simoncelli, E.P.: Image quality assessment: from error visibility to structural similarity. IEEE Trans. Image Process. **13**(4), 600–612 (2004)
15. Reid, E.J., Drummy, L.F., Bouman, C.A., Buzzard, G.T.: Multi-resolution data fusion for super resolution imaging. IEEE Trans. Comput. Imaging **8**, 81–95 (2022)
16. Sawant, A., Kulkarni, S.: Ultrasound image enhancement using super resolution. Biomed. Eng. Adv. **3**, 100039 (2022). https://doi.org/10.1016/j.bea.2022.100039
17. Hou, H., Jin, Q., Zhang, G., Li, Z.: CT image quality enhancement via a dual-channel neural network with jointing denoising and super-resolution. Neurocomputing **492**, 343–352 (2022)
18. Barshooi, A.H., Amirkhani, A.: A novel data augmentation based on Gabor filter and convolutional deep learning for improving the classification of COVID-19 chest X-Ray images. Biomed. Signal Process. Control. **72**, 103326 (2022)
19. Rahman, T., et al.: Exploring the effect of image enhancement techniques on COVID-19 detection using chest X-ray images. Comput. Biol. Med. **132**, 104319 (2021)
20. Greeshma, M.S., Bindu, V.R.: Super-resolution using deep networks for chest X-ray images. In: 2021 Sixth International Conference on Image Information Processing (ICIIP), pp. 198–201 (2021). https://doi.org/10.1109/ICIIP53038.2021.9702582
21. Veluchamy, M., Subramani, B.: Image contrast and color enhancement using adaptive gamma correction and histogram equalization. Optik **183**, 329–337 (2019)
22. Zimmerman, J.B., Pizer, S.M., Staab, E.V., Perry, J.R., McCartney, W., Brenton, B.C.: An evaluation of the effectiveness of adaptive histogram equalization for contrast enhancement. IEEE Trans. Med. Imag. **7**(4), 304–312 (1988)
23. Long, J., Shelhamer, E., Darrell, T.: Fully convolutional networks for semantic segmentation. arXiv preprint arXiv:1411.4038 (2014)
24. Shi, W., et al.: Real-time single image and video super-resolution using an efficient sub-pixel convolutional neural network. In: 2016 IEEE Conference on Computer Vision and Pattern Recognition (CVPR), pp. 1874–1883 (2016)

A Novel Approach to Enhance Effectiveness of Image Segmentation Techniques on Extremely Noisy Medical Images

Anuja Deshpande[✉][ORCID]

Department of Electronics, LAD College, Seminary Hills Campus,
Nagpur 440006, Maharashtra, India
anuja_1978@yahoo.com

Abstract. Through this study, I contribute towards segmentation of liver areas and have proposed additional improvements, which positively influence image segmentation. In this study, I have subjected medical images from LiTS - Liver Tumour Segmentation Challenge, which are extremely noisy, to various image segmentation techniques belonging to fully automatic and semi-automatic categories. These varied techniques implement different approaches towards image segmentation problem. All the techniques had initially failed to segment the images with very poor results. Commonly used filters for pre-processing, such as median filter, top hat filter, wiener filter, etc., were ineffective in reducing the noise effectively. Through this study, I have introduced a new combinatorial approach which not only is easier to implement but also much faster as well and resulted in much more enhanced input image quality that significantly improved the segmentation outcomes. Our approach has reduced noise, sharpened the edges, "localized" the segmentation problem before subjecting to various segmentation techniques. The techniques which had failed previously now could segment the images with improved speed of execution, efficiency and accuracy. I have studied our approach on 10 well known image segmentation techniques. Accuracy of these segmentation techniques was determined by computing Jaccard Index, Dice Coefficient and Hausdorff Distance.

Keywords: Noise removal · Segmentation accuracy · Image filtering · Effectiveness · De-convolution

1 Introduction

Images are an inherent part of our daily routine, be it hobby or professional photography (Natural Images), medical images (CT, MRI, Sonography, PET, etc.) for diagnosis and numerous others applications. Each of these employ different imaging technology suitable for the specific purpose. Newer modern imaging equipment offer high-resolution images with minute details offer a great help to

© The Author(s), under exclusive license to Springer Nature Switzerland AG 2023
KC Santosh et al. (Eds.): RTIP2R 2022, CCIS 1704, pp. 91–119, 2023.
https://doi.org/10.1007/978-3-031-23599-3_8

the doctors and the fraternity can make use of these multi-dimensional images with different orientations for diagnosing the problem and subsequently deciding the treatment. People are conscious and attentive towards Liver disorders or tumours today, due to its severity and high impact. These disorders if diagnosed and treated early can improve the patient survival rate and make people live longer. High variations in shape and very close proximity to other organs makes liver segmentation a very difficult task. Various liver conditions viz. fatty liver, iron deposits, fibrosis, tumours, further complicate this segmentation process. Intensity inhomogeneity, complex anatomical structure and organ interconnectivity along with presence of noise, makes medical image segmentation an extremely difficult task to perform on medical images. We continue to seek an effective segmentation technique for this task even today.

Extracting meaningful information from the images is the fundamental activity performed through image segmentation and the accuracy of the segmentation techniques decides if the segmented image is acceptable enough for subsequent applications to consume it for further analysis/processing. Image segmentation algorithms and approaches developed over last many decades have orientation to solve a specific image segmentation problem and are either specific to the image type and/or application area. Each image type has different composition and peculiarities and hence there is no single algorithm that exists today, that can successfully segment all types of images.

Most of these techniques can segment images, which have low to moderate complexity. Very complex images require different handling and in almost all situations require pre-processing step introduced before the segmentation step for the techniques to yield effective segmented image. Complexities can be in terms of colour mixture, texture, overlap, indistinct object boundaries similarity in foreground and background, intensity levels and so on. We can categorize the image segmentation algorithms broadly into fully automatic, semi-automatic and manual segmentation techniques [1]; interactive techniques (semi-automatic) seem to be more effective over others. Various approaches belonging to each of these categories are in existence today [2] with the aim to achieve an effective image segmentation. Each approach or method differs from the other in some or the other form. Table 1 shows major methods as described in [3–5]; viz. threshold, boundary, region,clustering and hybrid (consider boundary and region criteria) and some of the algorithms belonging to each of those methods for quick reference.

2   Methods

The Table 2 lists the interactive image segmentation techniques, which I have experimented on LiTS - Liver Tumour Segmentation Challenge [6] image dataset. The dataset also includes ground truth as a reference for comparison to assess the accuracy of the segmented images.

2.1 Accuracy Measures

There exist various evaluation methods, which have been developed over last several decades to assess accuracy [17,18], such as F1 Score, True Positive Ratio, Similarity Ratio, False Positive Ratio, etc. These however require additional computation of worst case for sensitivity and specificity. Some examples for this

Table 1. Image segmentation approaches

Thresholding	– Otsu's – Histogram
Boundary	– Gray histogram – Gradient (Sobel, Prewitt, Roberts) – Laplacian (Laplacian of Gaussian) – Gradient descent
Region	– Region growing – Split and merge – Watershed – Level set – Active contour models – Live-wire
Clustering	– K-means – Fuzzy C-means – Expectation maximization – Mean-shift – Gaussian mixture model
Hybrid	– Graph cuts – Grab cut – One cut – Random walks

Table 2. Image segmentation techniques

Sr. no.	Techniques
1	Graph Cuts [7]
2	Kernel Graph Cut [8]
3	Grab Cut [9]
4	Active Contour [10]
5	Center of Mass [11,12]
6	Statistical Region Merging [13]
7	Seeded Region Growing [2]
8	GMM-HMRF [14]
9	Random Walks [15]
10	Lazy Snapping [16]

are Average Hausdorff Error and Average Mean Error. Mean Squared Error is another evaluation method but has a drawback that due to squaring function weighs the outliers very heavily. ROC Curve is another such method, but requires computation of TPR and FPR to establish the evaluation. These evaluation methods are significant and quite widely used but require additional steps to achieve conclusive results. For our study, I have used Jaccard Index, Dice Coefficient and Hausdorff Distance as accuracy measures. These evaluation methods not only are computationally inexpensive but also yield conclusive results.

Jaccard Index (JI). The Jaccard Index method evaluates similarity as well as diversity between two data sets A and B and expressed in Eq. (1) and (2) below.

$$J(A, B) = \frac{|A \cap B|}{|A \cup B|} = \frac{|A \cap B|}{|A| + |B| - |A \cup B|} \tag{1}$$

By subtracting Jaccard Index from 1 we get the Jaccard Distance and expressed as

$$d_{\mathrm{J}}(A, B) = 1 - J(A, B) = \frac{|A \cup B| - |A \cap B|}{|A \cup B|} \tag{2}$$

Dice Coefficient (DC). The Dice Coefficient is an effective method to determine the similarity between two sample sets A and B; expressed in Eq. (3) below, where QS represents quotient of similarity.

$$QS = \frac{2 A \cup B|}{|A| + |B|} \tag{3}$$

Hausdorff Distance (HD). The Hausdorff Distance measures spatial distance between two sample sets. It indicates how different the two data sets are from each other; expressed in Eq. (4) and (5) below.

$$d_{\mathrm{H}}(X, Y) = inf\{\epsilon \geq 0; \ X \subseteq Y_\epsilon \ and \ Y \subseteq X_\epsilon\} \tag{4}$$

where,

$$X_\epsilon := \bigcup_{x \epsilon X} \{Z \epsilon M\}; d(Z, X) \leq \epsilon\} \tag{5}$$

2.2 LiTS Dataset

Let us review in Fig. 1, the LiTS - Liver Tumour Segmentation Challenge image dataset that I have used for this study.

As can be seen from the below images, the original images have too much of brightness and very low contrast, a combination, which poses a very difficult challenge for the segmentation techniques to yield good quality segmentation. In most of the images, the object boundaries are not quite distinct as well.

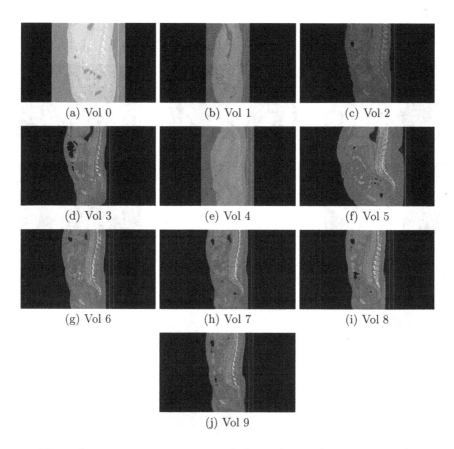

(a) Vol 0   (b) Vol 1   (c) Vol 2

(d) Vol 3   (e) Vol 4   (f) Vol 5

(g) Vol 6   (h) Vol 7   (i) Vol 8

(j) Vol 9

Fig. 1. Liver tumour segmentation challenge dataset (select 10 images)

3 Experiments

When I subjected these images to the segmentation techniques, the results were far from being acceptable. The techniques just failed to segment the images correctly due to excessive noise present in the images. Barring Graph Cut, which is completely interactive, all other techniques failed to produce correct segmentation. Even for Graph Cut technique, I needed many more scribbles to mark foreground and background to get the decent results.

3.1   Initial Results

The below Fig. 2, Fig. 3 and Fig. 4 show output of the discussed image segmentation techniques, which have largely failed to segment correctly. I have shown performance of image segmentation techniques on only three images as an example. Boarder has been added to represent blank white image output of Seeded Region Growing technique.

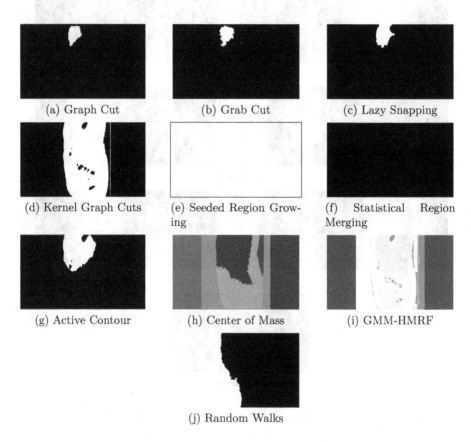

(a) Graph Cut   (b) Grab Cut   (c) Lazy Snapping

(d) Kernel Graph Cuts   (e) Seeded Region Growing   (f)   Statistical   Region Merging

(g) Active Contour   (h) Center of Mass   (i) GMM-HMRF

(j) Random Walks

Fig. 2. Segmentation results - (Vol0)

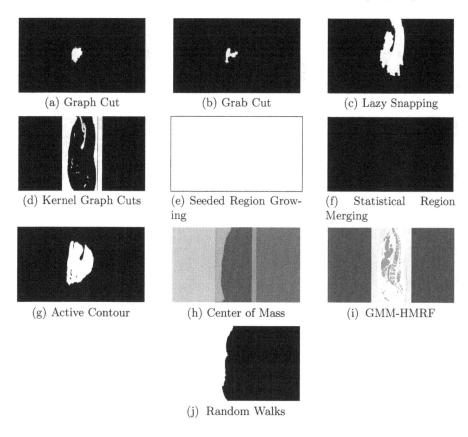

(a) Graph Cut   (b) Grab Cut   (c) Lazy Snapping

(d) Kernel Graph Cuts   (e) Seeded Region Grow-   (f)   Statistical   Region
                          ing   Merging

(g) Active Contour   (h) Center of Mass   (i) GMM-HMRF

(j) Random Walks

Fig. 3. Segmentation results - (Vol1)

As is evident from the three sample sets, the discussed techniques have failed to segment the images correctly, the output is not really acceptable for further processing.

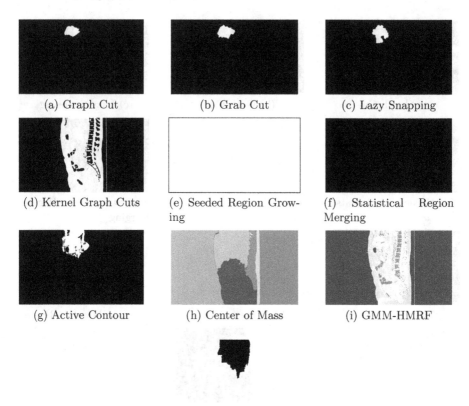

(a) Graph Cut   (b) Grab Cut   (c) Lazy Snapping

(d) Kernel Graph Cuts   (e) Seeded Region Grow-   (f)   Statistical   Region
                          ing   Merging

(g) Active Contour   (h) Center of Mass   (i) GMM-HMRF

(j) Random Walks

Fig. 4. Segmentation results - (Vol2)

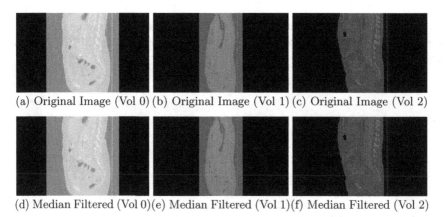

(a) Original Image (Vol 0)(b) Original Image (Vol 1)(c) Original Image (Vol 2)

(d) Median Filtered (Vol 0)(e) Median Filtered (Vol 1)(f) Median Filtered (Vol 2)

Fig. 5. Mediam filtered images

3.2 Image Preprocessing

To overcome the challenges posed by the complex image dataset, I then applied a different approach and introduced the pre-processing step. I have tried out quite a few known filtering techniques, viz. median filtering, top hat filtering, wiener filter and regular expression based filter. However, none of these proved to be effective as can be seen from the three sample images shown in Fig. 5, Fig. 6 and Fig. 7. Top Hat filtering technique resulted in too much loss of information while the others just did not have any visible impact in removing the noise from the images.

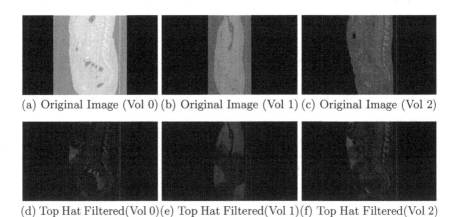

(a) Original Image (Vol 0) (b) Original Image (Vol 1) (c) Original Image (Vol 2)

(d) Top Hat Filtered(Vol 0)(e) Top Hat Filtered(Vol 1)(f) Top Hat Filtered(Vol 2)

Fig. 6. Top hat filtered images

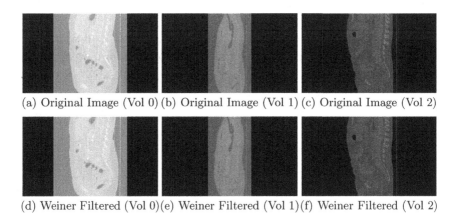

(a) Original Image (Vol 0) (b) Original Image (Vol 1) (c) Original Image (Vol 2)

(d) Weiner Filtered (Vol 0)(e) Weiner Filtered (Vol 1)(f) Weiner Filtered (Vol 2)

Fig. 7. Weiner filtered images

3.3   Our Approach

Since the known image filtering techniques were unsuccessful, I then came up with new idea that employed a combinatorial approach, which significantly reduced the noise and improved the accuracy of the segmentation techniques. In my approach, I have applied contrast enhancement and sharpness improvement techniques, then extracted the ROI incorporating foreground. I then subjected this extracted ROI to the segmentation techniques.

The Steps. Our approach involved implementing below steps sequentially to reduce the noise.

1. Load the image
2. Improve contrast using Adaptive Histogram Equalization algorithm
   (a) Number of tiles - 16 × 16
   (b) Clip Limit - 0.02
3. Improve edges using Lucy-Richardson Deconvolution Technique
   (a) Point Spread Function - Gaussian
   (b) Number of Iterations - 5
4. Remove excess information
   (a) Compute column vector containing mean of each row. Subtract this from the original image
5. Extract polygonal region
   (a) Draw polygon around foreground object
   (b) Extract polygonal region, mark remaining pixels in the image as background
6. Subject extracted polygonal region to segmentation technique for further segmentation

The Process. The end to end process that I have followed for our experiments is described below in Fig. 8.

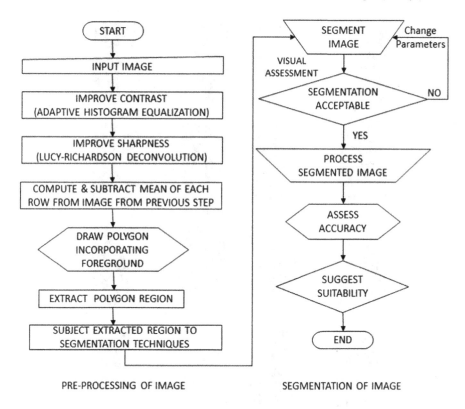

Fig. 8. Pre-processing and segmentation process

3.4   Pre-processed Images

The Fig. 9 shows the original images and preprocessed images obtained using our approach. Our combinatorial approach has significantly reduced the noise while retaining most of the information.

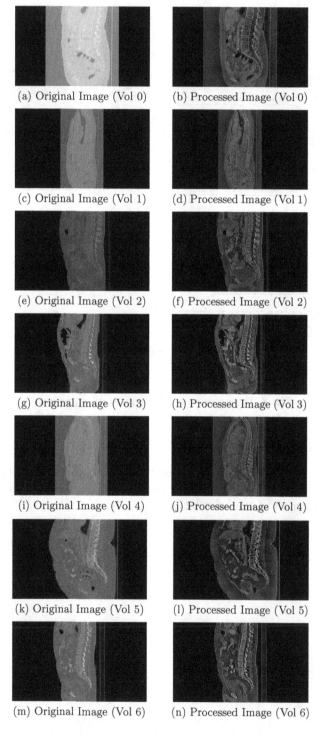

Fig. 9. Original and pre-processed images (Vol 0 to Vol 9)

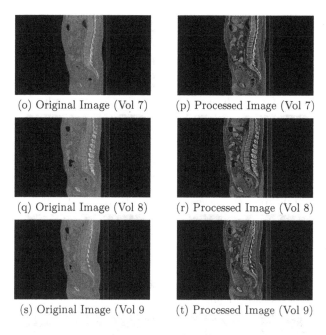

(o) Original Image (Vol 7)   (p) Processed Image (Vol 7)

(q) Original Image (Vol 8)   (r) Processed Image (Vol 8)

(s) Original Image (Vol 9   (t) Processed Image (Vol 9)

Fig. 9. (*continued*)

4   Results

I have performed this experiment using Matlab 2019b on 64-bit Windows PC. This section illustrates our findings of performance of all the earlier discussed image segmentation techniques on LiTS - Liver Tumour Segmentation Challenge dataset (Fig. 1). I have picked up 10 images from the dataset and subjected those images to the various image segmentation techniques. For certain techniques, where initial seed placement plays vital role, we have performed multiple segmentation runs and only the best results are included in this study. I have modified the parameters, which influence segmentation outcome and configured those for different values, had multiple runs and have selected only the best results. The segmented images were compared with the ground truth to understand the effectiveness and hence accuracy. Figures 10, 11, 12, 13, 14, 15, 16, 17, 18 and 19 shows the segmentation sets 1, 2, 3, 4, 5, 6, 7, 8, 9 and 10 respectively, each comprising of original image, pre-processed image, extracted ROI and segmented images. I have also computed the accuracy measures used for this experiment, viz. Jaccard Index, Dice Coefficient and Hausdorff Distance for each of the segmentation results.

5   Observations

The image dataset is extremely complex, as it has excessive brightness, very low contrast especially around foreground object, and overlap with other objects

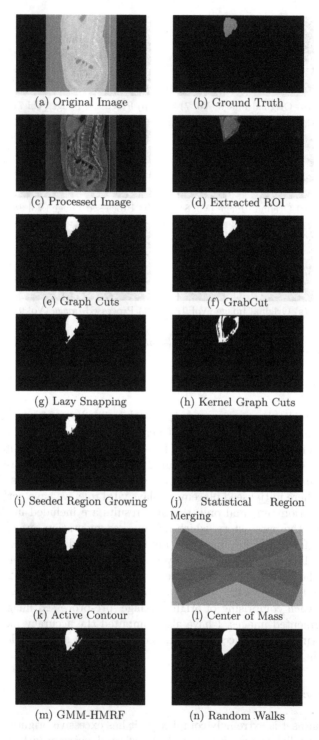

(a) Original Image (b) Ground Truth

(c) Processed Image (d) Extracted ROI

(e) Graph Cuts (f) GrabCut

(g) Lazy Snapping (h) Kernel Graph Cuts

(i) Seeded Region Growing (j) Statistical Region Merging

(k) Active Contour (l) Center of Mass

(m) GMM-HMRF (n) Random Walks

Fig. 10. Segmentation set 1 (image - Vol0)

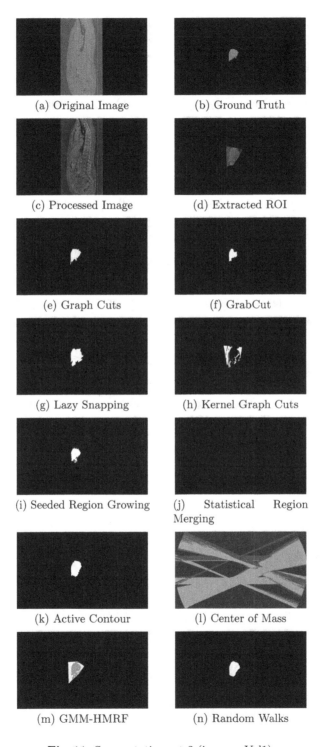

(a) Original Image

(b) Ground Truth

(c) Processed Image

(d) Extracted ROI

(e) Graph Cuts

(f) GrabCut

(g) Lazy Snapping

(h) Kernel Graph Cuts

(i) Seeded Region Growing

(j)   Statistical   Region Merging

(k) Active Contour

(l) Center of Mass

(m) GMM-HMRF

(n) Random Walks

Fig. 11. Segmentation set 2 (image - Vol1)

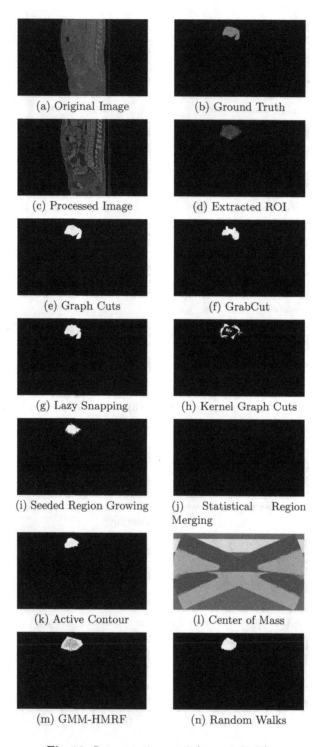

(a) Original Image

(b) Ground Truth

(c) Processed Image

(d) Extracted ROI

(e) Graph Cuts

(f) GrabCut

(g) Lazy Snapping

(h) Kernel Graph Cuts

(i) Seeded Region Growing

(j)   Statistical   Region
Merging

(k) Active Contour

(l) Center of Mass

(m) GMM-HMRF

(n) Random Walks

Fig. 12. Segmentation set 3 (image - Vol2)

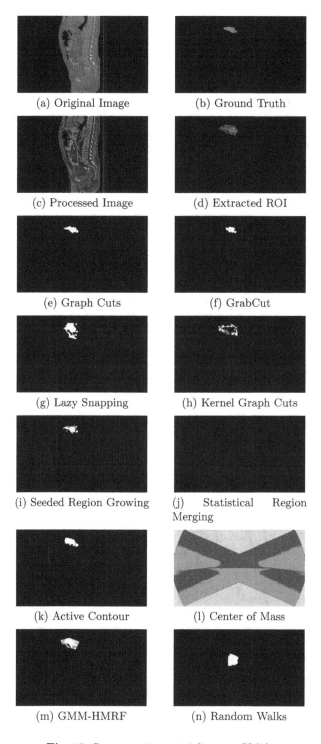

(a) Original Image

(b) Ground Truth

(c) Processed Image

(d) Extracted ROI

(e) Graph Cuts

(f) GrabCut

(g) Lazy Snapping

(h) Kernel Graph Cuts

(i) Seeded Region Growing

(j)   Statistical   Region Merging

(k) Active Contour

(l) Center of Mass

(m) GMM-HMRF

(n) Random Walks

Fig. 13. Segmentation set 4 (image - Vol3)

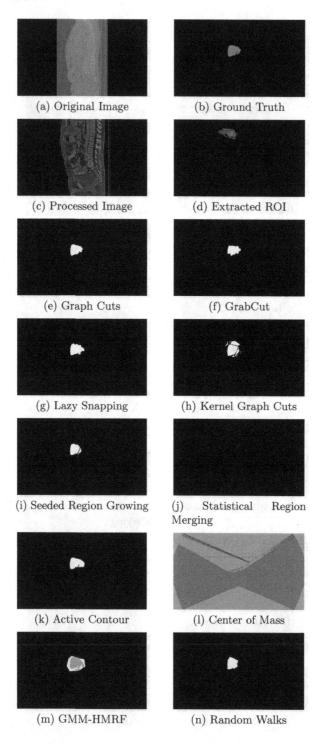

(a) Original Image

(b) Ground Truth

(c) Processed Image

(d) Extracted ROI

(e) Graph Cuts

(f) GrabCut

(g) Lazy Snapping

(h) Kernel Graph Cuts

(i) Seeded Region Growing

(j)   Statistical   Region Merging

(k) Active Contour

(l) Center of Mass

(m) GMM-HMRF

(n) Random Walks

Fig. 14. Segmentation set 5 (image - Vol4)

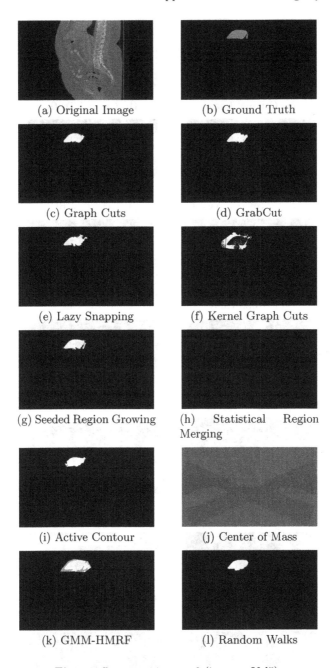

(a) Original Image   (b) Ground Truth

(c) Graph Cuts   (d) GrabCut

(e) Lazy Snapping   (f) Kernel Graph Cuts

(g) Seeded Region Growing   (h) Statistical Region Merging

(i) Active Contour   (j) Center of Mass

(k) GMM-HMRF   (l) Random Walks

Fig. 15. Segmentation set 6 (image - Vol5)

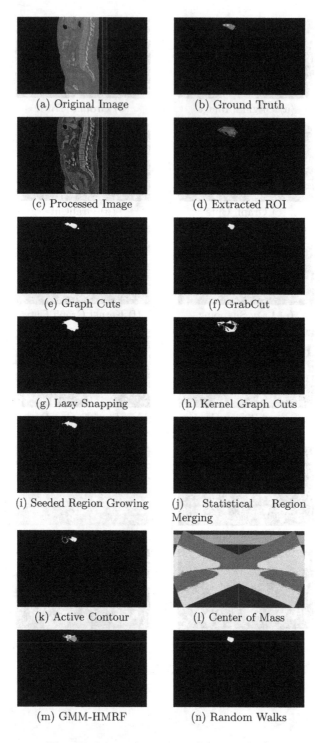

(a) Original Image

(b) Ground Truth

(c) Processed Image

(d) Extracted ROI

(e) Graph Cuts

(f) GrabCut

(g) Lazy Snapping

(h) Kernel Graph Cuts

(i) Seeded Region Growing

(j) Statistical Region Merging

(k) Active Contour

(l) Center of Mass

(m) GMM-HMRF

(n) Random Walks

Fig. 16. Segmentation set 7 (image - Vol6)

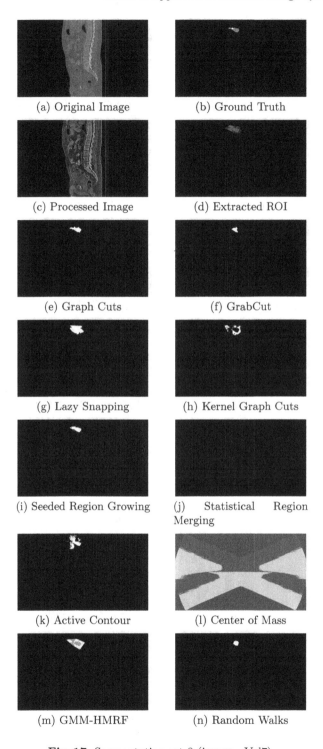

(a) Original Image

(b) Ground Truth

(c) Processed Image

(d) Extracted ROI

(e) Graph Cuts

(f) GrabCut

(g) Lazy Snapping

(h) Kernel Graph Cuts

(i) Seeded Region Growing

(j) Statistical Region Merging

(k) Active Contour

(l) Center of Mass

(m) GMM-HMRF

(n) Random Walks

Fig. 17. Segmentation set 8 (image - Vol7)

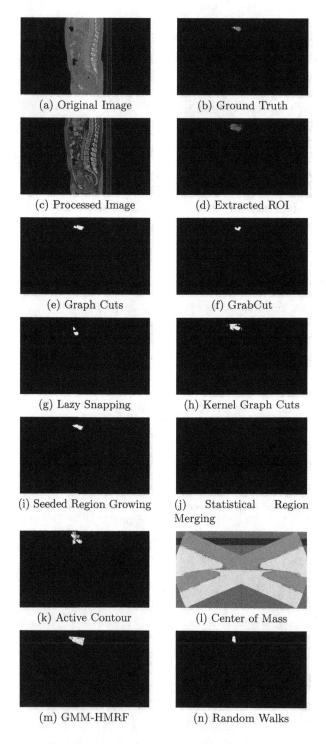

(a) Original Image

(b) Ground Truth

(c) Processed Image

(d) Extracted ROI

(e) Graph Cuts

(f) GrabCut

(g) Lazy Snapping

(h) Kernel Graph Cuts

(i) Seeded Region Growing

(j) Statistical Region Merging

(k) Active Contour

(l) Center of Mass

(m) GMM-HMRF

(n) Random Walks

Fig. 18. Segmentation set 9 (image - Vol8)

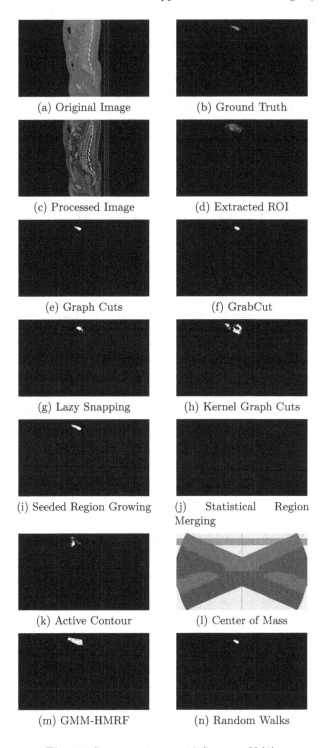

(a) Original Image

(b) Ground Truth

(c) Processed Image

(d) Extracted ROI

(e) Graph Cuts

(f) GrabCut

(g) Lazy Snapping

(h) Kernel Graph Cuts

(i) Seeded Region Growing

(j)   Statistical   Region Merging

(k) Active Contour

(l) Center of Mass

(m) GMM-HMRF

(n) Random Walks

Fig. 19. Segmentation set 10 (image - Vol9)

leading to indistinct object boundary and other high intensity areas elsewhere in the image. As is evident from the Fig. 2, Fig. 3 and Fig. 4, when I subjected these images to various segmentation techniques, I have observed failed results owing to various reasons, viz. segmentation technique having orientation towards solving segmentation problems on Natural images, complexity of the images, and lower inherent interactivity of the techniques with segmentation process itself, etc. Barring Graph Cut and Seeded Region Growing, most of the techniques failed to detect the object boundary correctly leading to failed results.

As is evident from Fig. 5, Fig. 6 and Fig. 7 the known image filters could not successfully remove the noise from the images. Our approach, which has been very effective in removing the noise, is also very evident from the contents in Fig. 9.

Statistical Region Merging and Center of Mass, which are fully automatic segmentation techniques have completely failed on all the images I subjected these to. The primary reason behind this failed segmentation is inhomogeneity, lower intensities and contrast. Center of Mass was the slowest of the studied techniques and it took approximately 40 min for each segmentation that too failed one.

Through the critical analysis, we find that on Vol0 (Fig. 1), Vol4 (Fig. 1) and Vol5 (Fig. 1), Graph Cut, Grab Cut, Seeded Region Growing, Lazy Snapping and active contour were quite effective, and the accuracy was 90–95%. Vol0 (Fig. 1) has marginal overlap, relatively distinct object boundary as compared with other images. Other techniques however, had accuracy quite lower, ranging from 60–80% only. Low contrast and close proximity of other objects with similar intensities seems to have affected these techniques resulting in lower accuracy.

Table 3. Segmentation techniques - set 1

Features	Graph Cut	GrabCut	Lazy Snapping	Kernel Graph Cut	Seeded Region Growing
Orientation	Natural/medical images	Natural images	Natural images	SAR/medical images	Medical images
Execution speed	Faster	Slower	Faster	Faster	Slower
Noisy edge detection	Weak	Weak	Weak	Good	Weak
Multi-object segmentation capability	Yes	Yes	Yes	Yes	No
Foreground & background markers	Many scribbles	Rectangle	Many scribbles	Many scribbles	One pixel as foreground
Effectiveness on	Medium complexity image	Low complexity image	Low complexity image	Medium complexity image	Low complexity image

As to Vol1 (Fig. 1), besides Graph Cut and Seeded Region Growing, Grab Cut has performed equally well, barring the overlap region. In this case, the foreground object is contiguous with homogenous intensities, smooth and marginal overlap. Other techniques could not effectively capture the variations in the intensities leading to very low segmentation accuracy.

Although Vol2 (Fig. 1) does not have very homogeneous intensities, Graph Cut and Lazy Snapping techniques have done well. There are multiple overlap regions having similar intensities with proximity objects, which seems to have interfered with other segmentation techniques resulting in very low segmentation accuracy.

Vol3 (Fig. 1) is a classic case, in which visually, the foreground objects appears to be disconnected, however those are not as can be verified with ground truth. The object boundary also is quite blur and considerable overlap with nearby objects exist. Other techniques could not really detect the object boundary accurately.

Except Graph Cut and Seeded Region Growing, other techniques could not yield effective segmentation for Vol6 (Fig. 1), Vol7 (Fig. 1), Vol8 (Fig. 1) and Vol9 (Fig. 1). These images are quite similar to each other and have blurred object boundary and similar intensity as that of nearby object. The surface are is quite homogeneous though.

5.1   Comparison

For a quick comparison, I have summarized five techniques comprising of Set-1 in the Table 3, and the remaining 5 as Set-2 in Table 4.

Table 4. Segmentation techniques - set 2

Features	Statistical Region Merging	Active Contour	Center of Mass	GMM-HMRF	Random Walks
Orientation	Medical images	Natural images	Medical images	Natural images	Medical images
Execution speed	Slower	Slower	Extremely Slow	Slower	Slower
Noisy edge detection	Weak	Weak	Poor	Weak	Good
Multi-object segmentation capability	No	No	Yes	No	Yes
Foreground & background markers	Many scribbles	Bounding box	None	Polygon	One pixel each
Effectiveness on	Low complexity image	Low complexity image	Low complexity image	Medium complexity image	Medium complexity image

6   Conclusion

It also comes out clearly through this study that pre-processing is essential to segment complex medical images to achieve an acceptable segmentation. It also implies that approach towards edge detection in complex images also needs to be different from that of simpler images and must incorporate low intensity, low contrast, blurred object boundaries, noise, etc. to yield effective and acceptable image segmentation.

This study has brought out that existing known methods for image filtering, viz. median filter, wiener filter, top hat filter, and other regular expression based methods failed to remove the noise across the entire dataset. Such methods, which implement specific function, may not be suitable for removal of noise when the images are extremely complex like the dataset I have used here.

Figure 9 illustrates how our combinatorial approach has been effective to reduce the nose significantly and achieve much clearer image. Our approach is quite simpler to implement, faster, customizable and proved very effective on these image datasets. Without this approach, none of the discussed algorithms could successfully segment the images.

With the new approach that I have introduced here, not only we got a cleaner image to segment but also, the techniques, which failed previously, succeeded in segmenting the foreground although with varying degree of accuracy inherent to the techniques. While the techniques employ global view of the segmentation problem, our approach made it look like a combination of global and local. Algorithms, which allow complete interactivity throughout the segmentation process, e.g. Graph Cut, etc. yield better segmentation results, however, may demand more scribbles for foreground and background marking. Even then, there are situations where performance of such techniques may be limited owing to complexities of the image.

After implementing our approach, Graph Cut and Seeded Region Growing have outperformed all other techniques, across the entire dataset. These techniques have been able to achieve 90% accuracy and in some cases more than 95%. GrabCut has performed better, where the image complexity is relatively low, however could not achieve greater accuracy in general. Statistical Region Merging could not segment the images; failed completely. All other techniques, which are either semi-automatic or fully automatic have generally had low accuracy outcome. Although Center of Mass has orientation towards medical imaging, it has failed completely on these images, similar to Statistical Region Merging.

7   Discussion

Whether interactive or automatic, successful delineation with very high accuracy is only achievable when the edge detection is accurate even in complex image compositions. Complexities in the image hinder with standard approaches towards edge detection, which may be good fit in non-complex scenarios. Edge detection plays very vital role especially when the images have very complex composition. There have been various novel approaches towards this [19]; and these have been very widely used over last many decades, but it looks like we continue to seek better approaches for a better outcome.

Noise could exist in an image in various forms making images more complex to segment and such images require pre-processing step to filter the noise and prepare the image for segmentation step. Without this step, as evident through this study, it is almost certain that segmentation would fail.

Although automated segmentation is the preferred option due to varying shape, size, location, blurred bounday and number of tumors, etc., the accuracy of such segmentation techniques still needs improvement as is demonstrated through various approaches in the recent times [20] including works on the same LiTS database [21,22] very recently. In this study I have demonstrated through my approach that a simple combination of steps, which is faster, in speed and lighter on processing power, can yield a very effective means for noise filtration, thus aiding the segmentation process.

This study also reveals that the discussed techniques, which otherwise fail completely on complex images, can still yield decent segmentation upon introduction of the pre-processing step that I have proposed. Every segmentation technique has inherent advantages and areas of application; introduction of pre-processing step shall further improve the outcome of these segmentation techniques, thereby allowing much wider use in image segmentation related applications. It also implies that combinatorial approach, which I have used to handle the complexities, can be a better choice in segmenting extremely complex images, successfully.

Recently, researchers have turned to Random Walkers for segmentation of medical images. However, native Random Walk technique, particularly for larger images appears to be slower and needs more memory as well. Authors in [23] have proposed an improved Random Walker with Bayes model, called RW Bayes algorithm for medical image segmentation and yields much better accuracy. In this approach, Bayes model integrates in Random Walker sparse system to give an automated segmentation for the adjacent slice. While CT has robustness, higher resolution, shorter acquisition time and greater accessibility makes CT a preferred choice; avoidance of radiation exposure, multiple contrast options, vascular, access to biliary anatomy, parenchymal pathology and minimization of nephrotoxicity risk are benefits of MRI.

Although quite widely in use, the MRI image segmentation is quite complex as the usable information details/features in the image is quite less. On the other hand, CT images usually have excessive noise and very low usable information about soft tissues, particularly the spatial resolution details. PET (Positron Emission Tomography - [24], which uses small amounts of radioactive material, has come up as an excellent choice to evaluate organ and tissue functions in last few years. PET is particularly helpful in tumour detection where there exists large variation in organ shapes making it a challenging process.

8 Applications

Disorders such as Liver cirrhosis or Liver tumours are on rise today globally and the fact that detecting it at an early stage with accurate diagnosis and early treatment instils confidence that the person will have higher survival rate. Accurate diagnosis would require accurate segmentation and hence has motivated us to take up this study. Medical imaging is the crucial first step towards better diagnosis and patient care. This article puts forth a novel approach and an easier one to implement on variety of images such as CT, MRI, X-ray, etc. in the field of cardiac, brain, liver and many other diagnoses.

Acknowledgements. The author would like to acknowledge the organizing committee of LiTS - Liver Tumor Segmentation Challenge (https://competitions.codalab.org/competitions/17094) for making dataset along with ground truth publicly available for research purposes.

Funding. This research did not receive any specific grant from funding agencies in the public, commercial, or not-for-profit sectors.**Declaration of Competing Interest**

The authors declare that they have no known competing financial interests or personal relationships that could have appeared to influence the work reported in this paper.

References

1. Kaur, D., Kaur, Y.: Various image segmentation techniques: a review. Int. J. Comput. Sci. Mob. Comput. **3**, 809–814 (2014)
2. Adams, R., Bischof, L.: Seeded region growing. IEEE Trans. Pattern Anal. Mach. Intell. **16**(6), 641–647 (1994). https://doi.org/10.1109/34.295913
3. Besl, P.J., Jain, R.C.: Segmentation through variable-order surface fitting. IEEE Trans. Pattern Anal. Mach. Intell. **10**(2), 167–192 (1988)
4. Haralick, R.M., Shapiro, L.G.: Image segmentation techniques. Comput. Vis. Graph. Image Process. **29**(1), 100–132 (1985). https://doi.org/10.1016/S0734-189X(85)90153-7
5. Sahoo, P., Soltani, S., Wong, A.: A survey of thresholding techniques. Comput. Vis. Graph. Image Process. **41**(2), 233–260 (1988). https://doi.org/10.1016/0734-189X(88)90022-9
6. CodaLab Competition. https://competitions.codalab.org/competitions/17094
7. Boykov, Y., Jolly, M.P.: Interactive graph cuts for optimal boundary & region segmentation of objects in N-D images. In: Proceedings of the Eighth IEEE International Conference on Computer Vision, vol. 1, pp. 105–112 (2001). https://doi.org/10.1109/ICCV.2001.937505
8. Ben Salah, M., Mitiche, A., Ben Ayed, I.: Multiregion image segmentation by parametric kernel graph cuts. IEEE Trans. Image Process. **20**, 545–w557 (2011). https://doi.org/10.1109/TIP.2010.2066982
9. Blake, A., Rother, C., Brown, M., Perez, P., Torr, P.: Interactive image segmentation using an adaptive GMMRF model. In: Pajdla, T., Matas, J. (eds.) ECCV 2004. LNCS, vol. 3021, pp. 428–441. Springer, Heidelberg (2004). https://doi.org/10.1007/978-3-540-24670-1_33

10. Kass, M., Witkin, A., Terzopoulos, D.: Snakes: active contour models. Int. J. Comput. Vis. **1**(4), 321–331 (1988). https://doi.org/10.1007/BF00133570
11. Aganj, I.: Image Segmentation Based on the Local Center of Mass, January 2019. https://in.mathworks.com/matlabcentral/fileexchange/68561-imagesegmentation-based-on-the-local-center-of-mass
12. Aganj, I., Harisinghani, M.G., Weissleder, R., Fischl, B.: Unsupervised medical image segmentation based on the local center of mass. Sci. Rep. **8**(1), 13012 (2018). https://doi.org/10.1038/s41598-018-31333-5
13. Nock, R., Nielsen, F.: Statistical region merging. IEEE Trans. Pattern Anal. Mach. Intell. **26**(11), 1452–1458 (2004). https://doi.org/10.1109/TPAMI.2004.110
14. Rother, C., Kolmogorov, V., Blake, A.: GrabCut - interactive foreground extraction using iterated graph cuts. In: ACM Transactions on Graphics (SIGGRAPH), August 2004
15. Grady, L.: Random walks for image segmentation. IEEE Trans. Pattern Anal. Mach. IntelL. **28**(11), 1768–1783 (2006). https://doi.org/10.1109/TPAMI.2006.233
16. Li, Y., Sun, J., Tang, C.K., Shum, H.Y.: Lazy snapping. In: ACM SIGGRAPH 2004 Papers on - SIGGRAPH 2004, Los Angeles, California, p. 303. ACM Press (2004). https://doi.org/10.1145/1186562.1015719
17. Powers, D.M.W.: Evaluation: from precision, recall and f-measure to ROC, informedness, markedness & correlation. J. Mach. Learn. Technol. **2**(1), 37–63 (2011)
18. Fawcett, T.: An introduction to ROC analysis. Pattern Recogn. Lett. **27**(8), 861–874 (2006). https://doi.org/10.1016/j.patrec.2005.10.010
19. Davis, L.S.: A survey of edge detection techniques. Comput. Graph. Image Process. **4**(3), 248–270 (1975). https://doi.org/10.1016/0146-664X(75)90012-X
20. Oulhaj, H., Amine, A., Rziza, M., Aboutajdine, D.: Noise reduction in medical images - comparison of noise removal algorithms -. In: 2012 International Conference on Multimedia Computing and Systems, pp. 344–349 (2012)
21. Chen, L., Song, H., Wang, C., et al.: Liver tumor segmentation in CT volumes using an adversarial densely connected network. BMC Bioinform. **20**(Suppl. 16), 587 (2019). https://doi.org/10.1186/s12859-019-3069-x
22. Ayalew, Y.A., Fante, K.A., Mohammed, M.: Modified U-Net for liver cancer segmentation from computed tomography images with a new class balancing method. BMC Biomed. Eng. **3**, 4 (2021). https://doi.org/10.1186/s42490-021-00050-y
23. Dong, C., et al.: An improved random walker with Bayes model for volumetric medical image segmentation. J. Healthc. Eng. **2017**, 1–11 (2017). https://doi.org/10.1155/2017/6506049
24. Bailey, D.L. (ed.): Positron Emission Tomography: Basic Sciences. Springer, New York (2005). https://doi.org/10.1007/b136169

Federated Learning for Lung Sound Analysis

Afia Farjana[1(✉)] and Aaisha Makkar[2]

[1] Applied AI Research Lab – Department of Computer Science, University of South Dakota, 414 E Clark St, Vermillion, SD 57069, USA
afia.farjana@coyotes.usd.edu
[2] College of Science and Engineering, University of Derby, Kedleston Road, Derby DE22 1GB, UK

Abstract. Despite the general success of employing artificial intelligence (AI) to help radiologists perform computer-aided patient diagnosis, creating good models with tiny datasets at different sites is still tough. Medical image analysis is crucial for the quick and precise detection of lung disease and helps clinicians treat patients effectively while averting more fatalities. This is why real-time medical data management is becoming essential in the healthcare industry, especially for systems that monitor patients from a distance. To overcome this challenge, we propose a different approach by utilizing a relatively new learning framework. Individual sites may jointly train a global model using this approach, referred to as federated learning. Without explicitly sharing datasets, federated learning combines training results from various sites to produce a global model. This makes sure that patient confidentiality is upheld across all sites. Additionally, the additional supervision gained from partner sites' results enhances the global model's overall detection capabilities. This study's primary goal is to determine how the federated learning (FL) approach may offer a machine learning average model that is robust, accurate, and unbiased in detecting lung disorders. For this aim, we analyze 325 Lung Sound audio recordings collected from https://data.mendeley.com/ and, transform this audio signal into Melspectrograms. Once the labeling and preprocessing steps were carried out, a Convolutional Neural Network (CNN)(FederatedNet) model was used to classify the respiratory sounds into healthy and unhealthy. We achieved the result of almost 88% validation accuracy. Furthermore, this paper discusses the application of FL and its overview. Lastly, we discuss the main challenges to federated learning adoption and potential future benefits.

Keywords: Federated learning · Lung sound · Machine learning

1 Introduction

'Federated learning' is not a brand-new concept. The Federated Learning Community (FLC), first created in 1976 by philosophy professor Patrick Hill to bring

KC Santosh et al. (Eds.): RTIP2R 2022, CCIS 1704, pp. 120–134, 2023.
https://doi.org/10.1007/978-3-031-23599-3_9

individuals together to learn, assisted students in escaping the isolation and anonymity of huge research universities [1]. Healthcare data analytics holds much promise for federated learning. Sensitive patient data can remain either in local institutions or with individual consumers without going outside during the federated model learning process for both provider-based applications (e.g., building a model for predicting the hospital readmission risk with patient Electronic Health Records (EHR) [2]) and consumer (patient)-based applications (e.g., screening atrial fibrillation with electrocardiograms captured by smartwatch [3]).

Combining machine learning (ML) with electronic health records (EHR) to extract knowledge that can enhance healthcare decision-making is becoming more common. Due to the sensitive nature of patient medical data, these methods necessitate the training of high-quality learning models based on broad and extensive data sets, which are challenging to acquire. In this context, federated learning (FL) is an approach that permits the distributed training of machine learning models with remotely hosted datasets without the need to compile and, thus, compromise data. FL is a promising method for enhancing ML-based systems, integrating them with legal requirements, trustworthiness, and data sovereignty.

Because the healthcare system is complicated, healthcare data are frequently fragmented. For instance, various hospitals could only be allowed to view the clinical records of the patients who belong to their particular patient groups. The protected health information (PHI) of the people contained in these records is extremely sensitive. To control the process of obtaining and analyzing such data, certain laws, including the Health Insurance Portability and Accountability Act (HIPAA) [4], have been devised. A crucial problem is data privacy. Respecting current privacy laws is essential if you want to protect patients' privacy, especially in industries like medicine. This poses a significant barrier for current data mining and machine learning (ML) methods, such as deep learning [5], which normally needs a lot of training data. However, data is necessary for research and training machine learning models that could aid in gaining insight into complex relationships or customized treatments that could otherwise go undiscovered. Therefore, it would be advantageous to be able to integrate comparable or related data from other sites throughout the world while yet protecting data privacy. Federated learning has been suggested as a solution since it depends on sharing machine learning models rather than the actual raw data. Thus, private information is never transferred from the site or device it was collected on. Numerous topics have been discovered for applying these techniques in the developing field of federated learning. This is where the phrase "Federated Learning" enters the conversation. This paradigm has recently gained prominence due to its enormous potential for learning from sensitive material that has been fragmented. It permits training a shared global model using a central server while preserving the data in local institutions where they originated instead of aggregating data from several sources wholly or depending on the conventional discovery and replication method.

Figure 1 shows the third most significant cause of death worldwide, chronic obstructive pulmonary disease (COPD), which affects 65 million individuals and

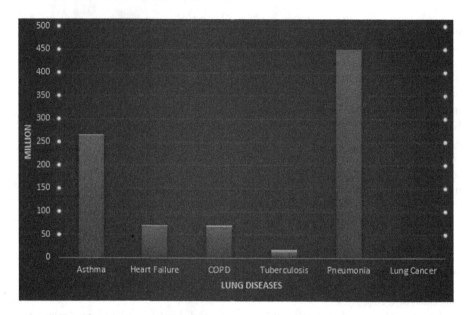

Fig. 1. Trend of lung diseases

results in 3 million deaths annually. Asthma affects 262 million people worldwide. More than 150,000 Americans die of COPD yearly - one every 4 min! The most prevalent chronic illness in children is asthma, which affects 14% of kids worldwide and is becoming worse. A global pandemic, heart failure (HF), affects at least 63.34 million individuals globally and is becoming more common. Although HF is a critical risk for patient survival, other co-existing physiological conditions can pose a significant threat to patient survival [6]. Malignant lung tumors, known as lung cancers, are created when lung cells grow out of control and are distributed to several bodily regions, where they can be fatal [7]. A prevalent respiratory infection affecting 450 million people worldwide each year, pneumonia affects all body regions [8]

In this paper, we illustrated the potential of federated learning methods in healthcare by describing the successful recent research in Sect. 2, after a formal overview of federated learning is represented in Sect. 3. Then, the proposed scheme is elaborated in Sect. 4. Section 5 and Sect. 6 present results and main challenges in this field. Finally, In Sect. 7, the paper is concluded.

2   Systematic Review and Challenges

2.1   Systematic Review

In 2018, Intel evaluated the application of federated learning for brain-image segmentation in collaboration with the Centre for Biomedical Image Computing and Analytics at the University of Pennsylvania [9]. The brain tumor segmentation (BraTS) competition 2018's publicly accessible dataset was utilized [10–13].

The information was a compilation of glioma patients' brain images from several institutions using various MRI models. As many as four radiologists manually annotated each aberrant finding on the MRI scans using one of three labels: peritumoral edematous/invaded tissue, non-enhancing/solid, necrotic/cystic tumor core, or enhancing tumor. The server-client federated learning technique was implemented for the system environment, and the authors selected the U-Net deep convolutional neural networks model for the task. The most recent model version was delivered from the central server to several clients throughout the installation. The server's central model was updated by utilizing federated aggregation and a few suitable models chosen from various clients. Theoretically, this upgrade should improve the central model's responsiveness and precision and benefit clients who receive the revised model from the server in the upcoming round. The BraTS studies ultimately showed that the performance scores of the federated semantic segmentation models on the brain MRI scans were compared to those obtained from models trained on the entire dataset [14].

Healthcare federated learning environments have been used to study a variety of tasks, including phenotyping [16,17], patient representation learning [15,16], patient similarity learning [15], and predictive modeling [18–20]. In particular, Lee et al. [15] established a privacy-preserving framework for patient similarity learning across institutions in a federated scenario. Without revealing patient-level data, their technology could identify comparable patients between hospitals.

Huang and Liu et al. [18] carried out patient clustering with the intention of training numerous more capable and focused NNs instead of just one general one. Community-based federated learning (CBFL) algorithm consists of three steps. First, a denoising autoencoder model was learned and shared with the server by each hospital in the dataset (there is 50 total, each having 560 patients in need of critical care). Each client received the final model after all encoders had been combined. A k-means clustering algorithm was used in the second stage, receiving the average encoded features from each hospital using the previously trained global encoder model as input. As a final step, the FL method was used by all clients to initialize and train k-NN models concurrently. One significant difference was that clients assigned each local data sample to one of the k clusters, and the number of samples in each cluster defined which factor a client's weight updates would affect in the kth NN. Patient mortality and hospital stay length were the article's ultimate forecasts.

Brisimi, T. et al. [19] developed a federated learning technique to forecast hospitalizations for patients with heart illnesses during a target year (EHRs). They gathered patient records for heart-related disorders from the Boston Medical Center. They created a federated learning optimization strategy to address the sparse Support Vector Machine problem using the cluster Primal-Dual Splitting (cPDS) method. SVM were taken into consideration since they work well as classifiers [20] and predict hospitalizations effectively. Scalability and the avoidance of raw data exchanges, which is crucial in the healthcare industry, are advantages. Compared to other centralized and distributed solutions, they also showed that cPDS had a higher convergence rate and more favorable communication costs.

The EXAM (electronic medical record (EMR) chest X-ray AI model) FL model, developed by Dayan, I. et al. [21], predicts how much oxygen symptomatic COVID-19 patients will need in the future,utilizing inputs of vital signs, laboratory data, and chest X-rays. When compared to models trained at a single site using that site's data, EXAM was able to accurately predict outcomes at 24 and 72 h after the patient's initial emergency room visit with an average area under the curve (AUC) > 0.92. It also provided a 16% improvement in average AUC measured across all participating sites and an average increase in the generalizability of 38%. EXAM attained a sensitivity of 0.950 and a specificity of 0.882 for the prediction of mechanical ventilation treatment or death at 24 h at the largest independent test site. In this study, FL enabled quick data science collaboration without data exchange and produced a model for clinical outcome prediction in patients with COVID-19 that generalized across diverse, unharmonized datasets, setting the stage for FL's expanded usage in healthcare.

In 2021, J. H. Yoo et al. [22] developed a hierarchical clustering-based FL approach to predict the severity of Major Depressive Disorder from Heart Rate Variability. They called it Personalized Federated Cluster Models. They addressed issues brought on by non-IID data and demonstrated an improvement in severity prediction accuracy by enabling clients to receive more customized models. This improvement in performance might be enough to enable the deployment of Personalized Federated Cluster Models in many Federated Learning applications that now exist.

2.2 Challenges

Updating weights is the first obstacle to federated learning success. This difficulty arises when the deep learning model for medical image analysis uses backpropagation for optimization during the training phase. The fair distribution of grant money is the second difficulty in federated learning. When several hospitals work together, the larger hospitals typically produce more images, have radiologists with more experience labeling the images, and have superior training facilities. These partners should ideally increase their joint learning contributions and generate higher-quality datasets for improved training feedback. However, doing so is expensive, therefore it makes sense for larger hospitals to anticipate more financing for research grants.

3 Overview of Federated Learning

Multiple institutions or organizations collaborate to solve a machine-learning problem using federated learning, all under the direction of a central server or service provider. As a result, a deep-learning model is updated and maintained by a central server. The model is trained by dispersing itself to distant silo data centers, like hospitals or other healthcare facilities, allowing these sites to maintain the locality of their data. During training, no data from each collaborator is

Table 1. Summary of literature review.

Authors	Data source	Domain	ML techniques
Intel [2018] [14]	Publicly available dataset (multi-institutional)	Federated learning for brain-image segmentation	U-Net deep convolutional neural networks
Lee et al. [2018] [15]	Cross-institution	Without-revealing patient-level data, their technology could identify comparable patients between hospitals through a federated scenario	k-nearest neighbor with k = 3
Li Huang et al. [2019] [18]	Hospitals	Community-based federated learning (CBFL) for Patient mortality and hospital stay length were the article's ultimate forecasts	k-NN
Brisimi, T. et al. [2018] [19]	Boston Medical Center	Federated Learning technique to forecast hospitalizations for patients with heart illnesses	Support vector machine
Dayan, I. et al. [2021] [21]	20 different global institutes	Main objective to train an FL model, called EXAM (electronic medical record (EMR) chest X-ray AI model), that predicts the future oxygen requirements of symptomatic patients with COVID-19 using inputs of vital signs, laboratory data and chest X-rays	EXAM (electronic medical record (EMR) chest X-ray AI model)
J. H. Yoo et al. [2021] [22]	Online	A hierarchical clustering-based FL approach to predict the severity of Major Depressive Disorder from Heart Rate Variability	Personalized federated cluster models

ever sent or exchanged. As in traditional deep learning, the central server maintains a global shared model that is shared among all institutions rather than having the data brought to it. Then, depending on its own patient data, each entity keeps a unique model. Then, based on its uniquely trained model- either by its weight or the error gradient of the model-each center gives feedback to the server. The central server compiles all participant feedback and, using predetermined standards, updates the overall model. By using the predetermined criteria, the model is able to assess the quality of the input and only consider that which adds value. Thus, feedback from centers that produced unfavorable or odd findings can be disregarded. Federated learning is formed by this procedure, which is repeated until the world model is trained. See Fig. 2 (Table 1).

Figure 2 illustrates the federated learning process,

$$global\,model\,parameters = \theta$$

$$the\,data\,size\,of\,client = nk$$

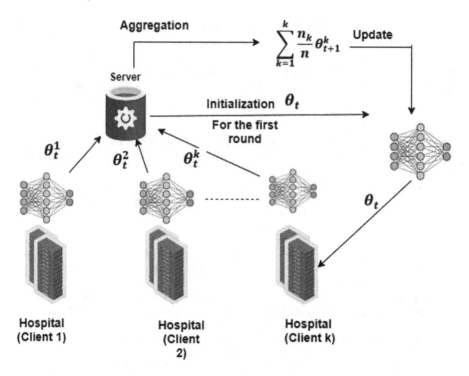

Fig. 2. An overview of federated learning

$$the\,total\,number\,of\,clients = k$$

$$and\,the\,communication\,round\,in\,federated\,learning = t$$

Figure 3 summarizes the learning framework procedures. Without central-izing the data in one location, federated learning enables individual hospitals to gain access to the rich datasets of numerous non-affiliated hospitals. Impor-tant problems like data privacy, data security, data access rights, and access to heterogeneous data are all solved by this method. Consequently, federated learn-ing enables numerous contributors to create a reliable machine-learning model utilizing a substantial dataset [14].

4   Proposed Scheme

The proposed Scheme contains 7 stages in our proposed scheme that helps us to find an avg model. Those are the following stages we added in our implementa-tion part. Data collection and pre-processing. Dataset split, initialize a number of clients, and other methods Initialize global model and proposed workflow of federated learning-Aggregation.

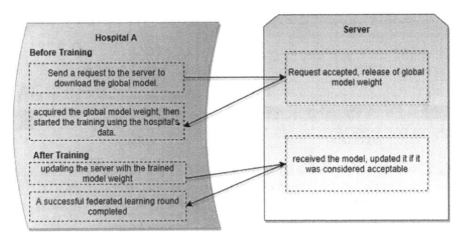

Fig. 3. Summary of one complete round of federated learning

4.1   Data Collection and Pre-processing

In the proposed work, we did data preprocessing and tested a machine-learning model using a publicly available dataset from Mendeley.com. In order to identify the suspected pulmonary disease from the lung sound, we used 336 recordings of lung sounds. The conditions depicted by these recordings were lung fibrosis, chronic obstructive pulmonary disease (COPD), pneumonia, bronchitis, and heart failure. The information reported in this research includes audio recordings taken while various angles of the chest wall were being examined. The spot on the chest wall where the recording was made using a stethoscope (Posterior: P Lower: L Left: L Right R, UPPER: U, ANTERIOR: A, MIDDLE: M). The names of the audio files are encoded: 1. The type of filter is B: BELL 20–200 Hz, Diaphragm 100–500 Hz, and Extended range 50–500 Hz. 2. P1-P112. Patient number. Three copies of each recording were made, each time using a different frequency filter to accentuate a different physiological sound. The dataset can be used to identify the proper type of lung sound or to identify pulmonary disorders from lung sounds. We divided the whole dataset into two categories Healthy and Unhealthy. We turned our audio signal recordings into Mel-spectrograms for the analysis phase. To explore the use of federated learning (FL), we then split the dataset into different clients [24]. We used librosa library for Mel-spectrogram feature extraction purpose.

4.2   Dataset Split and Initialize Number of Clients, and Other Methods

After pre-processing the dataset, we split the data into 5 clients. After creating 2 to 5 clients we processed and batched the training data for each client. In this part, we initialized the number of clients, and other methods which "return: a dictionary with keys clients' names and value as data shards - tuple of images

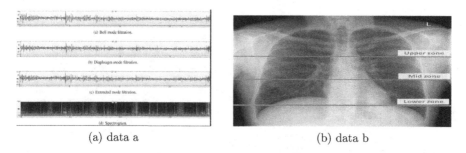

    (a) data a   (b) data b

Fig. 4. Two images with some important information about dataset. (a) A 19-second recording of respiratory lung sound using the three filters and the spectrogram and (b) The location of chest zones used to record lung sound

Table 2. Dataset summary

Cases	Dataset size
Asthma	96
Heart failure	53
Pneumonia	15
Bronchitis	9
N (healthy)	12
Lung fibrosis	105
COPD	27
Pleura effusion	6

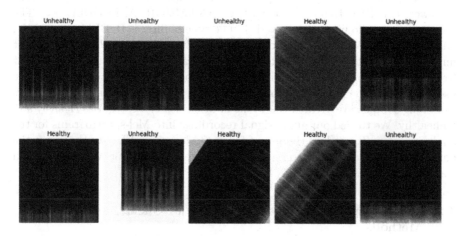

Fig. 5. Dataset mel-spectrogram

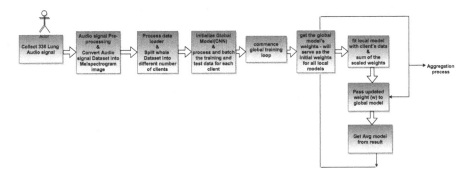

Fig. 6. Proposed scheme

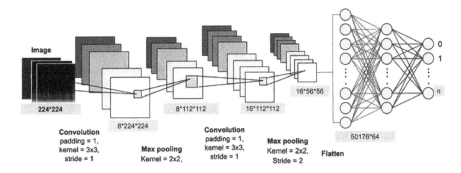

Fig. 7. CNN Architecture (FederatedNet)

and label lists." Function for scaling a model's weights. Return the sum of the listed scaled weights. This is equivalent to the scaled avg of the weights (see Fig. 6) (Table 2 and Fig. 4, Fig. 5 and Fig. 7).

4.3   Initialize Global Model (CNN Architecture - FederatedNet)

The CNN architecture is composed of two primary components. Feature extraction is a procedure used in convolution that separates and identifies the distinct aspects of the image for analysis. The feature extraction network consists of multiple pairs of pooling or convolutional layers. A fully connected layer that classifies the image with the aid of previously recovered features utilizing the results of the convolutional procedure. To lessen the number of features in a dataset, this CNN applies a feature extraction model. It generates new features that condense an initial set of features' existing features. The CNN architecture diagram illustrates the numerous CNN layers. Then preprocessed data was fed into the global deep learning algorithm, convolution neural networks (CNN). The architecture of CNN is represented in Fig. 8 (Table 3).

Table 3. Layers used in pre-trained CNN (FederatedNet) model

Layers	Input layer	Output size	Activation/loss_function
Input Layer	224 * 224 * 3	224,224,8	Activation ("relu") Loss_function: sparse_categorical_crossentropy
Conv2D_1 Maxpooling	224 * 224 * 8, 2 * 2	112,112,8	Activation ("relu") Loss_function: sparse_categorical_crossentropy
Conv2D_2	112 * 112 * 8	112,112,16	Activation ("relu") Loss_function: sparse_categorical_crossentropy
Conv2D_3 Maxpooling	112 * 112 * 16 2 * 2	56,56,16	Activation ("relu") Loss_function: sparse_categorical_crossentropy
Conv2D_4	56 * 56 * 16	56,56,64	Activation ("relu") Loss_function: sparse_categorical_crossentropy
Flatten Dense		(None, 50176) (None, 32)	33211264
Linear_1	186624	(None, 2)	Activation ("softmax") Loss_function: sparse_categorical_crossentropy

Input image: Binarized; size 224×224. Two layers: convolutional and max pooling, are used in a sequence, which is followed by a fully connected layer.

Filter used: 18, 16, 64

Connected layer: For an output layer with a sigmoid activation function, the Convolutional layer consists of 32 output channels (with a kernel size of 3×3), where ReLu is used as an activation function.

Max pooling layer: Flatten layer connects convolution and dense layers. Dense laver serves as an output, where SoftMax action torchon is used and Stochastic Gradient Descent (SGD) optimizer is used to learn (lowering the learning error_rate). We applied sparse_categorical_crossentropy as a loss function where momentum is 0.5.

Classes = 2
input_dim = 50176
num_clients = 5
rounds = 20
batch_size = 32
epochs_per_client = 3
learning_rate = $2e - 2$

4.4 Proposed Workflow of Federated Learning (FL)

After incorporating a Convolutional Neural Network (CNN) based on the deep learning model as a global model, these global models have been distributed to all the datasets (client1 to client100) to train and then collect the updated weights from that local dataset. After getting the updated parameters, our global model compared and aggregated the results using a federated learning algorithm (Federated average Algorithm). Afterward, it built a common, robust machine learning (average) model to find a better result. We randomly initialized global model parameters at the beginning of the communication round and used updated model parameters afterward.

Commence global training loop got the global model's weights - which will serve as the initial weights. For all local models, the initial list is to collect local model weights after scaling randomized client data. Used keys loop through each client and create a new local model. Set the local model weight to the weight of the global model. We Fitted the local model with the client's data scaled the model weights, and add to the list print ('scaling factor', scaling factor). We cleared the session to free memory after each communication round to get the average over all the local models, we simply took the sum of the scaled weights to update the global model, test the global model and printed out metrics after each communications round.

5   Results and Discussion

We employ a total of 325 datasets among them 172 for training and 43 for validation and 110 for testing.20 common rounds were given to 5 clients. After round 20, we achieved train_loss = 3.0452, validation_loss = 2.0735, and validation_acc = 0.875. We achieved an accuracy of 88% and a loss of 2.0735. One of the limitations of our paper is that we applied the CNN deep learning model because our dataset is too tiny for federated learning. We ran tests on our client number between 2 to 5. When we utilized fewer clients, the outcome was not satisfactory, which led us to add additional clients. More communication rounds, hidden layers, and clients are suggested as potential improvements (Table 4).

Table 4. Results (CNN): Avg_Train_loss, Avg_Validation_loss, Avg_Validation_Accuracy

Round No	Avg_Train_loss	Avg_Validation_loss	Avg_Validation_acc%
1/20	6.2006	29.43	17.05%
2/20	4.041	4.102	82.95%
3/20	40.03	4.045	82.96%
4/20	77.39	2.689	82.95%
5/20	3.927	33.64	82.95%
Continued	Continued	Continued	Continued
17/20	3.243	3.029	82.95%
18/20	3.2275	3.027	82.95%
19/20	3.292	1.923	87.5%
20/20	3.8452	19.23	88.0%

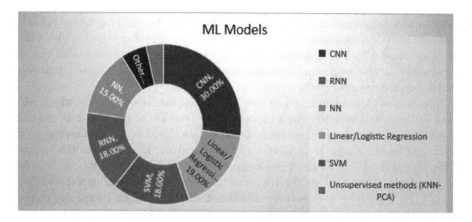

Fig. 8. Frequency of ML model types. The most prevalent neural network types are CNNs, RNNs, and NNs

We also want to summarize the ML models that the publications employed for testing and assessing their FL techniques. Convolutional neural networks (CNNs) are the most widely used models, but neural networks (NNs) and recurrent neural networks (RNNs) are also extremely widespread, as the results of the study are shown in Fig. 8. Support vector machines (SVMs) and regression models have received little research. Tree-boosting systems and collaborative filters are some of the additional model kinds [23]. In our paper we used CNN and compare to other paper our proposed method (CNN) find out almost 100% accuracy in some common round For IID dataset (see Fig. 8).

6   Conclusion

To sum up, developing AI models for patient diagnosis on a small scale is quite challenging for individual sites. This is because the patient population on which the model is built is often extremely small, which in turn, greatly reduces the model's external validity. Federated learning eliminates this hurdle. Through collaboration, many institutions can pool their data to train a global model that gives improved accuracy over a bigger range of patients. In our paper, we implemented the CNN network to analyze 325 lung sound datasets, and our result showed almost 88% accuracy and 2.0735 loss by using a federated learning approach. Since federated learning prioritizes the protection of patient data, there was no direct data sharing in this collaborative effort. Instead, an overall model can be created via the federated aggregating method based on continuous updates from various sources.

Federated learning provides simple scalability, flexible training scheduling, and large training datasets via multi-site cooperation-all requirements for the successful implementation of an AI solution. Significant challenges still need to be fixed before federated learning can effectively be used to build AI models.

Additionally, the novelty of federated learning in medical imaging AI makes this topic attractive to academics, whose work will be crucial to improve the area. The primary objective of this paper was to identify a reliable global FL model that can accurately predict lung diseases. Our proposed method will be highly beneficial to both the medical field and those dealing with lung diseases. Two of the limitation of our study were the small dataset and the time constraints. If we can gather more data for federated learning in the future, there will be a ton of room for additional study. Additionally, we have plans to use several machine learning models with various features for different healthcare regions in the near future (thyroid cancer diagnosis, heart disease prediction etc.). FL will continue to be a topic of active research over the next ten years because not all technological concerns have yet been resolved. Despite this, we firmly believe that it has a highly promising future in terms of its potential impact on precision medicine and eventually enhancing medical treatment.

References

1. Hill, P.: The rationale for learning communities and learning community models (1985)
2. Min, X., Bin, Yu., Wang, F.: Predictive modeling of the hospital readmission risk from patients' claims data using machine learning: a case study on COPD. Sci. Rep. **9**(1), 1–10 (2019)
3. Perez, M.V., et al.: Large-scale assessment of a smartwatch to identify atrial fibrillation. N. Engl. J. Med. **381**(20), 1909–1917 (2019)
4. Gostin, L.O.: National health information privacy: regulations under the Health Insurance Portability and Accountability Act. JAMA **285**(23), 3015–3021 (2001)
5. LeCun, Y., Bengio, Y., Hinton, G.: Deep learning. Nature **521**(7553), 436–444 (2015)
6. Mamun, M., et al.: Heart failure survival prediction using machine learning algorithm: am I safe from heart failure? In: 2022 IEEE World AI IoT Congress (AIIoT). IEEE (2022)
7. Mamun, M., et al.: Lung cancer prediction model using ensemble learning techniques and a systematic review analysis. In: 2022 IEEE World AI IoT Congress (AIIoT). IEEE (2022)
8. https://www.cdc.gov/copd/data.html
9. Bakas, S., et al.: Advancing the cancer genome atlas glioma MRI collections with expert segmentation labels and radiomic features. Sci. Data **4**(1), 1–13 (2017)
10. Antunes, R.S., et al.: Federated learning for healthcare: systematic review and architecture proposal. ACM Trans. Intell. Syst. Technol. (TIST) **13**(4), 1–23 (2022)
11. Li, W., et al.: Privacy-preserving federated brain tumour segmentation. In: Suk, H.-I., Liu, M., Yan, P., Lian, C. (eds.) MLMI 2019. LNCS, vol. 11861, pp. 133–141. Springer, Cham (2019). https://doi.org/10.1007/978-3-030-32692-0_16
12. Konečný, J., et al.: Federated learning: strategies for improving communication efficiency. arXiv preprint arXiv:1610.05492 (2016)
13. Li, X., et al.: Diagnosis of thyroid cancer using deep convolutional neural network models applied to sonographic images: a retrospective, multicohort, diagnostic study. Lancet Oncol. **20**(2), 193–201 (2019)

14. Ng, D., et al.: Federated learning: a collaborative effort to achieve better medical imaging models for individual sites that have small labelled datasets. Quant. Imaging Med. Surg. **11**(2), 852 (2021)
15. Lee, J., et al.: Privacy-preserving patient similarity learning in a federated environment: development and analysis. JMIR Med. Inform. **6**(2), e7744 (2018)
16. Kim, Y., et al.: Federated tensor factorization for computational phenotyping. In: Proceedings of the 23rd ACM SIGKDD International Conference on Knowledge Discovery and Data Mining (2017)
17. Liu, D., Dligach, D., Miller, T.: Two-stage federated phenotyping and patient representation learning. In: Proceedings of the Conference. Association for Computational Linguistics. Meeting, vol. 2019. NIH Public Access (2019)
18. Huang, L., et al.: Patient clustering improves efficiency of federated machine learning to predict mortality and hospital stay time using distributed electronic medical records. J. Biomed. Inform. **99**, 103291 (2019)
19. Brisimi, T.S., et al.: Federated learning of predictive models from federated electronic health records. Int. J. Med. Inform. **112**, 59–67 (2018)
20. Cortes, C., Vapnik, V.: Support-vector networks. Mach. Learn. **20**(3), 273–297 (1995)
21. Dayan, I., et al.: Federated learning for predicting clinical outcomes in patients with COVID-19. Nat. Med. **27**(10), 1735–1743 (2021)
22. Yoo, J.H., et al.: Personalized federated learning with clustering: non-IID heart rate variability data application. In: 2021 International Conference on Information and Communication Technology Convergence (ICTC). IEEE (2021)
23. Pfitzner, B., Steckhan, N., Arnrich, B.: Federated learning in a medical context: a systematic literature review. ACM Trans. Internet Technol. (TOIT) **21**(2), 1–31 (2021)
24. Fraiwan, M., et al.: A dataset of lung sounds recorded from the chest wall using an electronic stethoscope. Data Brief **35**, 106913 (2021)

Performance Analysis of CNN and Quantized CNN Model for Rheumatoid Arthritis Identification Using Thermal Image

A. S. Mahesh Kumar[1]($^{(\boxtimes)}$), M. S. Mallikarjunaswamy[2], and S. Chandrashekara[3]

[1] JSS Science and Technology University, Mysuru, India
as.mahesh.ec@gmail.com

[2] Sri Jayachamarajendra Colleges of Engineering, JSS Science and Technology University, Mysuru, India
msm@sjce.ac.in

[3] ChanRe Rheumatology and Immunology Center and Research, Bengaluru, India

Abstract. Rheumatoid Arthritis (RA) is distinguished by antibody-mediated inflammation. The most prevalent indications of RA are inflammatory, swollen ankles, tightness, and severe joint discomfort. Finally, RA affects function, impairment, and morbidity by damaging neighboring connective tissues like ligaments, tendons, and cartilages. A range of techniques, comprising radiography, Computed Tomography (CT), ultrasonic, Magnetic resonance imaging (MRI), and thermal imaging, are used to identify and RA diagnose. Infrared (IR) thermal imaging is a non-invasive, fast, and effective approach for assessing early RA. IR-based examinations are a common imaging modality since it is radiation-free and non-invasive. In this study, the required dataset is collected using the IR thermal camera. The collected dataset consists of normal and arthritis-affected thermal images. The dataset is then prepared to be compatible with the Convolution Neural Network (CNN) of the Deep Learning (DL) model and statistical parameters such as mean, mode, mode, kurtosis, etc. are derived and the correlation between the parameters is drawn using the covariance matrix. The dataset is then visualized using graphical plots to view the distribution of the statistical parameters. The dataset is then pre-processed using the normalization method and then analyzed using the CNN model. To find the efficiency of the DL model performance metrics such as accuracy, precision, loss, F-1 score, recall, etc. are calculated. To reduce the complexity and to reduce the computational time, the dataset is quantized using the optimization method and a comparison between the trained model and the quantized model is drawn.

Keywords: Arthritis · Thermal image · Data · Pre-process · Optimization · Neural network

1 Introduction

RA symptoms include inflammation, edema, tightness, and joint discomfort. To begin, RA appears in the smaller joints of the body. As the disease advances, RA affects the

KC Santosh et al. (Eds.): RTIP2R 2022, CCIS 1704, pp. 135–150, 2023.
https://doi.org/10.1007/978-3-031-23599-3_10

knees, ankles, and hip joints. The synovium and lining membrane whichfixes the body's joints is where RA disease begins. As a result of joint inflammation, the synovium thickens and the cartilage and bone surrounding it are damaged, causing ligaments to weaken and elasticity. The ligaments of the body play a vital role in joint stabilization [1–3]. These joints gradually lose their original shape and alignment in an RA-infected joint. The key effects on RA are gender, age, and heredity. The likelihood of a woman is similar toa mangetting RA. RA can strike at any age, but it is most frequent in the middle years. Because RA is a chronic ailment, it can be handed down via a person's family tree. Tobacco, exposure to toxic chemicals, overweight, allergies, fractures, changing body balance, carpel tunnel, dryness in the eyes and mouth, heart problems, and lung sickness are all factors that affect the performance of RA indirectly. Figure 1 RA affected hand joints with different temperature values.

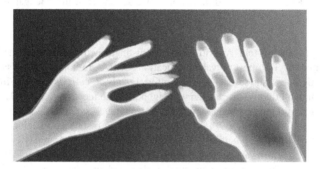

Fig. 1. RA affected hand joints with different temperature values.

RA disease has no recognized cure or long-term treatment. By initiating therapy immediately, it is possible to prevent disease and probable impairment. Disease-Modifying Antirheumatic medicines (DMARDs), Anti-TNF drugs, B-cell treatment, and T-cell therapy are pharmaceuticals used to treat RA [4, 5]. Two international organizations provided diagnostic criteria and methods for RA illness. The European League Against Rheumatism and the American College of Rheumatology [6–8] are the two most well-known worldwide organizations for RA classification. Various imaging modalities are utilized to diagnose RA. X-rays are the most reliable method for identifying joint degeneration and displacement in RA patients [9–11]. MRI gives 3D images of the RA-affected joints, whereas radiography produces only 2D images. MRIs and ultrasounds, for instance, can be utilized to determine the severity of RA [12]. Thermal imaging is regarded as a quick and premature detection method for RA disease assessment. Numerous benefits accompany the needfor thermal imaging approaches in the early detection of RA issues. These are non-invasive, radiation-free, non-contact, and non-invasive. Few researchers focused on employing thermal imaging to monitor and diagnose RA. This IR thermography imaging method [13] is entirely risk-free.

2   Related Works

Depending on the severity of the symptoms, rheumatologists may advise a combination of a modality validation and a blood validation to accurately diagnose RA. Radiographs provide a two-dimensional (2D) image of RA-affected joints, whereas MRI and ultrasonography provide a more accurate three-dimensional (3D) imaging of the sick joints. Wasilewska et al. [14] hypothesized that heat patterns from ROIs could be used as an indicator of inflammation in patients with RA. These photographs were captured with a thermal scanning camera in the IR band (FLIR E60bx Systems Inc., USA). Three minutes of foot thermal recovery were recorded and analysed. Snekhalatha et al. [15] created thermal imaging by employing IR thermograms to describe temperature variations in locations of interest exhibiting anomalous behaviour. It is necessary to measure and compare the skin temperatures of RA patients and healthy individuals to see whether the differences are statistically significant. Use the fuzzy-c-means and the Expectation-Maximization (EM) methodology, which are highly beneficial for arthritis patients, to automatically separate the aberrant regions of the hand. Nouri Ali [16] observed that inflammation alters the distribution of heat throughout the joint. Heat distribution analysis on the skin is an excellent method for finding abnormal areas of the body. Mutual information permits the comparison of two random variables. It is also possible to estimate the joint histogram and mutual information between images using non-parametric windows. Majumdar et al. [17] created Medical IR Thermography (MIT) to detect minute temperature changes and provide statistical quantification for a reliable evaluation of inflammation. Evaluation of inflammation facilitates early treatment planning and provides information on the condition's severity. Utilizing Fuzzy-C-Mean clustering and region-growing, the ROI is extracted from a thermal image.

Frize et al. [18] captured thermal pictures of the hand joints, palms, wrists, and knees of patients. To identify regions of interest, each subject is manually screened. Variance, Max, Min, Mode, and Mean were determined for each participant. The initial evaluation of patient joints by Lasanen et al. [19] used a combination of clinical examination and ultrasound imaging. Later in the procedure, scans of the ankle and knee were performed. In the knee and ankle, clinical evaluations are connected to thermal imaging data. There had been a substantial temperature difference betweeninflamed ankle joints and uninflamed knee joints (P = 0.044, P = 0.001). Using the k-means algorithm, Anburajan et al. [20] outlined the autonomous segmentation of hot spot locations using thermographs. Using surface temperatures, the thermal distribution measure, and thermographic examination, a thermal image of RA patients was created. The Gray-Level Co-occurrence Matrix (GLCM) approach is employed to extract features from the segmented output image using the k-means algorithm. Suma et al. [21] evaluate manual, colour, and k-means picture segmentation and conclude that the latter is the best technique for segmentation. The hot spot area is retrieved using three unique image segmentation methods and compared to a standard thermograph to establish the best effective segmentation technique for early-stage RA detection. Snekhalatha et al. [22] utilizing a fuzzy c means technique, aberrant regions of thermal images are segmented, and statistical characteristics are extracted to compare the patient's data to those of a control subject. Statistics such as standard deviation (SD), mean, skewness, and kurtosis are taken into account during the production of the statistical characteristic. The article

[23] proposes a method for automatically segmenting knee X-ray images and feature extraction using the GLCM technique and programmatically segmenting the image of the knee by deploying the RGB segmentation process, and using the conventional biochemical approach to analyze the extracted features from the knee area of segmented medical images in RA patients.

Gopikrishna et al. [24] automate the segmentation of knee modules using fuzzy c-means techniques. Lastly, compare the two imaging modalities by extracting and correlating features using a biochemical technique. During thermal imaging of the knee, the skin surface temperature of RA and control patients was assessed. The thermal imaging segmentation approach was superior to the x-ray image segmentation procedure. It was discovered that the standard parameters and the medical imaging features had a strong correlation. Gizinska et al. [25] evaluate RA in the arthritic foot using thermal imaging. The average foot temperatures were significantly different in the education and controller groups. Mercieca et al. [26] reported that patients in remission from RA have on average warmer feet and more distinctive thermographic patterns. It is evidence of the symmetry of the RA feet that there is no variation in the mean temperatures of any of the components. As a clinical and self-monitoring tool, thermal imaging may benefit RA patients whose feet demonstrate asymmetrical temperature variations. Using Weka, Sharon et al. [27] evaluated numerous classification strategies, including bagging, AdaBoost, and random subspace, using basic classifiers including random forest and support vector machine (SVM). In terms of classification accuracy, the study revealed that bagging is superior to the other methods. Compared to the actual situation, Bardhan et al. [28] developed a modified multi-seeded region growing method with a 98.6% accuracy rate. Accuracy-based feature selection achieves a RA classification rate of 73%, whereas classic SVMrecursive feature elimination (SVM-RFE) and RELIEF approaches achieve RA classification rates of 67% and 71%, respectively. The AUCs for RA classification are 0.72, 0.65, and 0.67 for SVM-RFE, RELIEF, and accuracy-based feature selection, respectively, indicating that accuracy-based feature selection yields superior classification results. Pauket al. [29] study whether RA patients' cold provocation and rewarming validate ($23 °C$ for 180 s) may be used more consistently to identify inflammation and enhance diagnostic accuracy by employing IR thermography and temperature profiles along with the hand fingers. After cooling and rewarming, it was revealed that the human partswere statistically significant. The area under the receiver operating characteristics (ROC) curve for the human parts after cooling was statistically substantially ($p = 0.05$; p 0.05) different between the two groups. GATT [26] studied the thermal characteristics of RA patients' feet during clinical and radiographic remission is compared with healthy controls. The literature has proven that thermal imaging is a non-invasive techniquefor analysing physiological functions connected with changes in body temperature. Thermal imaging is a non-invasive, radiation-free approachto detecting early signs of RA by monitoring variations in skin temperature. Thermal imaging has the potential to be utilized in the development of formidable instruments. Analysis based on thermal imaging is less expensive than MRI.

3 Materials and Methods

In this study, the required dataset for this work is collected in real-time rather than collecting it from an online repository. To collect the dataset a method called IR imaging is used. Using an IR camera module, the thermal images of the ankle joints are captured. The dataset contains both normal and arthritis-affected thermal images. The collected images are then prepared to make them compatible with the DL model. Significant statistical parameters such as mean, median, mode, etc. for the temperature value are calculated. The prepared data is then visualized to graphically view the distribution of statistical parameters. Then the covariance matrix for the variables is derived. The dataset is then pre-processed using the normalization methods. The pre-processed dataset is then divided into two parts: The training set which is 85% of the total dataset and the validation set which is 15% of the total dataset. The CNN model is then trained using the training dataset and then validated using the validation dataset. The performance metrics such as accuracy, precision, etc. are calculated for the DL model to analyse its efficiency. The dataset is then quantized to reduce complexity and to reduce computation time and the dataset is again validated using the CNN model. The whole process will be given in flow chart in Fig. 2.

3.1 Image Dataset

The image dataset required for this study is collected in real-time using the IR imaging technique rather than collecting it from some repository available on the internet. The temperature of a specimen is measured using IR imaging methods. Most things emit electromagnetic radiation, especially in the IR range of wavelength, that is invisible to the human eye. IR rays, on the other hand, could be sensed as heat on the epidermis. The more the IR radiation a thing radiates, the warmer it is. There are numerous IR imaging implications in the world of medicine, both for man and livestock. IR thermography is now being employed in thermal imaging to make a diagnosis sooner, identify the root of arthritis, and sometimes even discover circulatory abnormalities before they get too serious. In this study, the IR imaging technique is used to evaluate variations in joint temperature. Using an IR camera thermal images are captured which helps in detecting heat patterns to detect the variation of heat in the joints and may also pinpoint the area of inflammation in the joints.

3.2 Preparation of the Dataset

Figure 3 given shows the steps involved in the preparation of the image dataset. The thermal images acquired from the thermal camera are then prepared to make them compatible with the CNN model. Each pixel in that thermal image indicates the temperature at that corresponding point. For each image in the dataset value of the attributes such as maximum, minimum mean, median, skewness, mode, kurtosis, and SD of the temperature are evaluated. The parameters that have been processed are saved in Comma-Separated Values (CSV) files, which enables data to be retained in a tabulated manner. The dataset collected contains both normal thermal images and arthritis-affected thermal images. Each entry is labelled 1 for arthritis-affected thermal images and 0 for the normal thermal images.

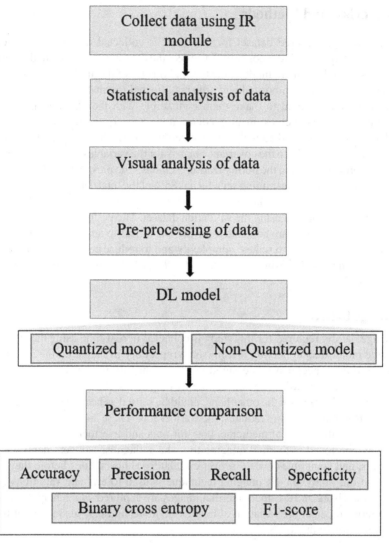

Fig. 2. Work flow of the research

3.3 Data Visualization

It is a common term for visual representations of statistical data. To make it easier to see and understand statistics and variances in the form of graphs, charts, or maps, visualization tools are used. Each attribute calculated in this study is distributed in a graphical representation in Fig. 4, which can see below.

Figure 4 given above shows the graphical representation of the distribution of the statistical parameters calculated such as mean, median, mode, etc. in this study. Figure 4a shows the graph of Maximum temperature shown by both normal thermal images and arthritis-affected thermal images. Figure 4b indicates the minimum temperature shown

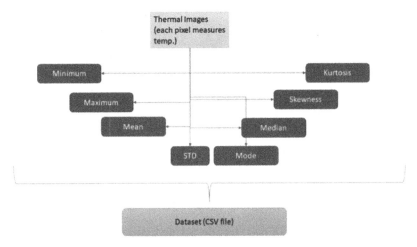

Fig. 3. Image preparation steps

by both normal thermal images and arthritis-affected thermal images. Figure 4c indicates the mean of the temperature shown by both normal and arthritis-affected thermal images. Figure 4d depicts the graphical distribution of the mode of the temperature of both normal and arthritis-affected thermal images. Figure 4e indicatesthe median temperature of both normal and arthritis-affected thermal images. Figure 4f illustrates the SD of the temperature of both normal and arthritis-affected thermal images. Figure 4g represents the distribution of Skewness of the temperature of both normal and arthritis-affected thermal images. Figure 4h represents the distribution of Kurtosis of the temperature of both normal and arthritis affected thermal images.

Figure 5 given above shows the covariance matrix derived for the statistical parameters to find the correlation between the parameters. A covariance matrix is a square matrix that represents the correlation amongst each set of elements in a random vector. It is observed that the variables mean, median, mode, min, and max are highly correlated to each other.

3.4   Data Pre-processing

Normalization is the process of reorganizing data from a database so that it fulfils two fundamental requirements. There is no replication; each piece of data resides in a centralized location. Data dependencies are rational in the sense that all relevant data are maintained collectively. In this study, mean normalization is done on the dataset so that the mean and SD become 0 and 1 correspondingly for every attribute. This leads to a smooth loss curve making it easier for convergence. It also counters the problems like vanishing gradient and exploding gradient.

Mean Normalization is given by,

$$x_i = \frac{x_i - \mu_i}{s_i} \tag{1}$$

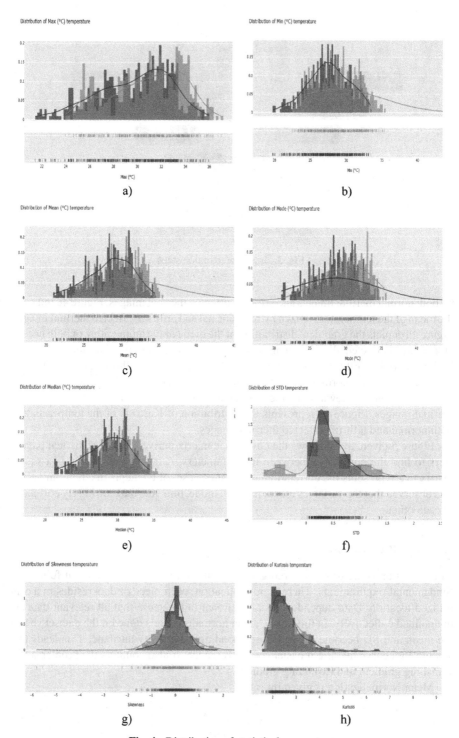

Fig. 4. Distribution of statistical parameter

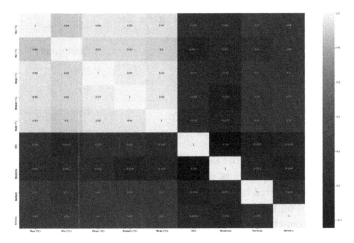

Fig. 5. Covariance matrix

where $\mu(i) \rightarrow$ average values for a feature and $s(i) \rightarrow$ minimum and maximum range of values.

3.5 DL Model

As the name implies, Neural Networks (NN) are a collection of algorithms that handle enormous amounts of data in a manner comparable to that of the brain. A "NN" is a group of neurons that might be biological or synthetic. DL is a form of intelligent approach that employs interconnected networks of neurons in a layered architecture that imitates the operation of the brain. Using NN, which imitates human brain behaviour, computer algorithms may recognize patterns and solve complex problems in AI, computer vision, and DL. A basic NN is divided and distinguished by an Input layer (IL), hidden layers (HL), and output layers (OL). The various layers are linked together via a "network" of nodes. The CNN design, which includes IL, HL, and OL, is used in this work. Images are presented at the IL, and relevant features are taught to HL, with the results obtained at the output layers. The CNN design consists of many Convolution Layers (CL), a Pooling Layer (PL), and an Activation Layer (AL). The CNN's CL is crucial in the feature extraction process. Convolution filters may recognize various features by altering the kernel size of various filters on the images. PL lower the complexity of the following layers, resulting in a reduction in network parameters. The pooling layer is implemented using nonlinear pooling functions such as average and max pool. In a ReLU, all values lower than zero are mapped to zero, but all values greater than zero are maintained.

From Table 1, it is shown that the number of parameters available in the first dense layer is about 216. The number of parameters present in the second dense layer is about 300 and the number of parameters in the third layer is about 13. The total number of parameters present in this study is about 529 and the number of trainable parameters is about 529 which makes the non-trainable parameters 0.

The dataset has been split into training and validationsamples. 85% were used for training purposes and the remaining 15% were used for validation purposes. Mean

Table 1. CNN architecture

Layer (type)	Output structure	Parameters
dense_93	(None, 24)	216
dense_93	(None, 12)	300
dense_93	(None, 1)	13

normalization is performed on the dataset based on the mean and SD of the training dataset. The normalized dataset is used as a training dataset. To Counter, the class imbalance problem weighted binary cross-entropy is used. Where the loss, is weighted for each class based on their ratio in the training dataset. This helped in reducing the loss by a certain amount helping to avoid misclassifications of positive examples. Adam optimizer is used in training and trained for different epochs until the optimal loss and accuracy are obtained. Figures 6 and 7 given below shows the accuracy and loss percentage plot of both the training and validation set.

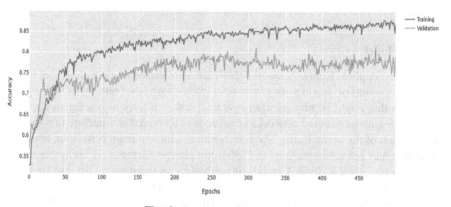

Fig. 6. Accuracy percentage plot

Figure 6 given above shows the accuracy percentage plot of both the training sampleand the validation samplefor the first 500 epochs. The accuracy percentage of both the training and validation samplegradually increases through each epoch and the accuracy percentage of the training set remains higher than the validation set. During these epochs' duration, the training dataset was given a batch size of 32. In later stages of training, to get better accuracy dataset was trained further with different batch sizes (16, 64,128) and learning rates.

Figure 7 given above shows the loss percentage plot of both the training and validation samplefor the first 500 epochs. The loss percentage of both the training set and validation set gradually decreases through each epoch and the loss percentage of the training set remains lower than the validation set.

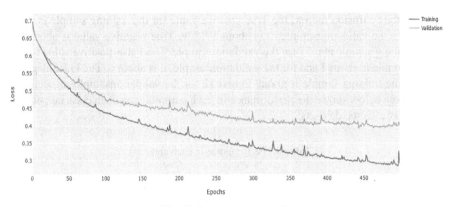

Fig. 7. Loss percentage plot

4 Results and Discussion

This study aims to predict the presence of arthritis in IR thermal images using DL such as CNN. The dataset required for this work is collected in real-time using IR thermal camera. The collected image dataset consists of both normal and RA images. The dataset was split into two parts the training sample (85% of the total sample) and the validating sample (15% of the total sample). The dataset is then normalized and prepared to be analysed by the CNN model. The DL model is first trained using the training dataset and then validated using the validating dataset. Table 2 given below tabulates the performance analysis of the training and validation set.

Table 2. Performance analysis of training and validating set

Matrix	Training set	Validate set
Loss	0.14155	0.44490
Accuracy	0.95558	0.87838
F1 Score	0.94829	0.87453
Precision	0.98920	0.90417
Recall	0.91307	0.85162
Specificity	0.95439	0.92071

From Table 1, the loss percentage of the training set is given as about 1.4% and for the validating set, it is about 4.4%. The accuracy of the training set is about 95.5% and for the validation set, it is about 87.8%. The F1score of the training set is about94.8% and the validation set is about 87.4%. The precision percentage of the training set is about 98.9% whereas the value of the validating set is about 90.4%. The recall value for the training set is about 91.3% and for the validation set, it is about 85.1%. The specificity value for the training set is about 95.4% and for the validation set, it is about 92%.

From the confusion matrix, the True positive value for the training sample is about 339 and for the validationsample, it is about 59. The True negative value is about 457 for the training sample and 71 for the validationsample. The False-positive value for the training sample is about 4 and for the validationsample, it is about 6. The False-negative value for the training sample is about 33 and 12 for the validationsample respectively. Table 3 given below shows the performance of each parameter on each class i.e., normal and arthritis-affected datasets.

Table 3. Performance in each class

Class	Precision	Recall	F1-score	Support
Normal	0.86	0.92	0.89	77
Arthritis	0.91	0.83	0.87	71

Table 3 given above shows the parametric values of both the Normal and Arthritis affected image dataset. The precision value for the Normal image dataset was about to 86% and for the Arthritis affected image dataset, it was about 91%. The recall value for the normal image dataset was about 92% and for the Arthritis affected image dataset, it was about 83%. The F1score for the normal image dataset was about 89% and for the Arthritis affected image dataset, it was about 87%. The support value for the normal image dataset was about 77% and for the Arthritis affected image dataset, it was about 71%.

5   Optimization

The trained model requires very high memory and computation power. This is quantized to reduce memory and computation power using TensorFlow lite. The trained model is 38720 bytes which are very hard to fit into microcontrollers such as ARM Cortex M3 which generally have 64 Kilobytes of RAM. As a result, all N weights' floating-point precision has been lowered from 64 bits to 16/32 bits. The typical dataset is being used to prune parameters throughout model optimization, i.e., to reduce the dimensionality by systematic pruning. TensorFlow lite convertsthe model to Flat buffer format (tflite), the flat buffer is converted into a C byte array in the form of a simple C file. The converted ".h" format file could be used in the embedded C program. The "tflite" model can be deployed on Raspberry pi as well. This model can use additional computational resources like a Neural compute stick if present in Raspberry pi.

After Quantization the model size was reduced to 3832 bytes whichare approximately 9.89% of the initial size. The size could be still reduced if the floating-point weights are converted to an integer, but the accuracy of the model becomes less in that case. Though the dataset is quantized and analysed using the DL model there is not much change in the output performance metrics. The loss percentage of the quantized model is higher compared to the trained model but the loss percentage is negligibly low and so it does not impact the performance metrics value much. Figure 8 given below shows the performance of the optimized model and raw model using the training set.

Performance on Training Set

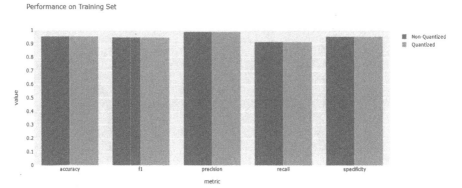

Fig. 8. Performance of the optimized model and raw model using the training set

Variation of training set loss on Quantization

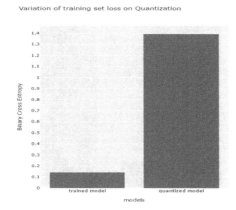

Fig. 9. Variation of training set loss on quantization

Figure 9 given above shows the variation of loss percentage on the training set after quantization. It is given that the loss is less for the trained model and relatively for the quantized model. There is only an increase in the loss but the other matrices like F1, Accuracy, precision, recall, and specificity remain unchanged.

Figure 10 given above shows the performance of the optimized model andraw model using the validating set. There is only an increase in the loss but the other matrices like F1, Accuracy, precision, recall, and specificity remain unchanged.

Figure 11 given above shows the variation of loss percentage on the validation set after quantization. It is given that the loss is less for the trained model and relatively for the quantized model.

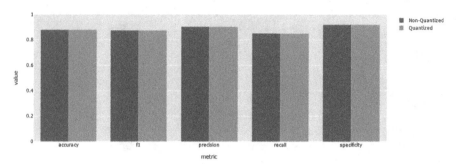

Fig. 10. Performance of the optimized model and raw model using validating set

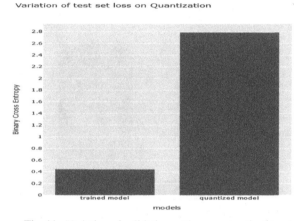

Fig. 11. Variation of validating set loss on quantization

6 Conclusion

Pain, soreness, rigidity, and inflammation in and around one or many joints are common symptoms of rheumatic conditions. There are several methods available to detect and diagnose arthritis such as CT, Ultrasound, MRI, Radiography, etc., but IR imagining is considered one of the most efficient and non-invasive methods. In this study, the dataset is collected using an IR camera in real-time. The collected dataset contains thermal images of both normal and arthritis-affected images. After that, the images are processed to make them compliant with the DL model. For the temperature value, statistically relevant metrics such as mean, median, mode, and so on are computed. The prepared data is then visualized to see the statistical parameter distributions graphically. The covariance matrix for the parameters is then calculated. After that, the data is pre-processed using the normalization method. The pre-processed dataset is then separated into two parts: the training set, which accounts for 85% of the total dataset, and the validation set, which accounts for 15%. The CNN model is then trained and evaluated using the training and validation datasets, respectively. To analyse the efficiency of the model performance metrics of the model such as accuracy, precision, etc. are calculated. The accuracy of the model trained using the dataset is about 95.5%, which makes the model better and more efficient than the pre-existing models. The model is then quantized using the optimization method to reduce the complexity and computational time. A comparison between the loss percentage of the trained model and the quantized model is drawn. The loss percentage is slightly higher in the quantized model than in the trained model but the loss value is negligible hence it does not affect the models.

References

1. Silman, A.J., Pearson, J.E.: Epidemiology and genetics of RA. Arthritis Res. Ther. **4**(S3), S265 (2002)
2. Kourilovitch, M., Galarza-Maldonado, C., Ortiz-Prado, E.: Diagnosis and classification of RA. J. Autoimmun. **48**, 26–30 (2014)
3. Gabriel, S.E.: The epidemiology of RA. Rheum. Dis. Clin. North Am. **27**(2), 269–281 (2001)
4. Burmester, G.R., Pope, J.E.: Novel treatment strategies in RA. The Lancet **389**(10086), 2338–2348 (2017)
5. Calabrò, A., et al.: One year in review 2016: novelties in the treatment of RA. Clin. Exp. Rheumatol. **34**(3), 357–372 (2016)
6. Kim, Y., et al.: Diagnosis and treatment of inflammatory joint disease. Hip Pelvis **29**(4), 211–222 (2017)
7. Smolen, J.S., et al.: EULAR recommendations for the management of RA with synthetic and biological disease-modifying antirheumatic drugs: 2013 update. Ann. Rheum. Dis. **73**(3), 492–509 (2014)
8. Brinkmann, G.H., et al.: Role of erosions typical of RA in the 2010 ACR/EULAR RA classification criteria: results from a very early arthritis cohort. Ann. Rheum. Dis. **76**(11), 1911–1914 (2017)
9. Tins, B.J., Butler, R.: Imaging in rheumatology: reconciling radiology and rheumatology. Insights Imaging **4**(6), 799–810 (2013). https://doi.org/10.1007/s13244-013-0293-1
10. Patil, P., Dasgupta, B.: Role of diagnostic ultrasound in the assessment of musculoskeletal diseases. Ther. Adv. Musculoskelet. Dis. **4**(5), 341–355 (2012)
11. Narvaez, J.A., Narváez, J., De Lama, E., De Albert, M.: MR imaging of early RA. Radiographics **30**(1), 143–163 (2010)
12. Van der Heijde, D.M.: Assessment of radiographs in longitudinal observational studies. J. Rheumatol. Suppl. **69**, 46–47 (2004)
13. Snekhalatha, U., Anburajan, M., Teena, T., Venkatraman, B., Menaka, M., Raj, B.: Thermal image analysis and segmentation of hand in evaluation of RA. In: 2012 International Conference on Computer Communication and Informatics, pp. 1–6. IEEE (2012)
14. Wasilewska, A., Pauk, J., Ihnatouski, M.: Image processing techniques for ROI identification in RA patients from thermal images. Acta Mechanica et Automatica **12**(1), 49–53 (2018)
15. Snekhalatha, U., Anburajan, M., Teena, T., Venkatraman, B., Menaka, M., Raj, B.: Thermal image analysis and segmentation of hand in evaluation of RA. In: 2012 International Conference on Computer Communication and Informatics (ICCCI), Coimbatore, pp. 1–6. IEEE (2012)
16. Nouri, A., Amirfattahi, R., Moussavi, H.: Mutual information-based detection of thermal profile in hand joints of RA patients using non-parametric windows. In: 2016 IEEE Canadian Conference on Electrical and Computer Engineering (CCECE), pp. 1–4. IEEE 2016

17. Majumdar, P., Das, K., Nath, N., Bhowmik, M.K.: Detection of Inflammation from temperature profile using Arthritis knee joint Datasets. In: 2018 IEEE International Conference on Healthcare Informatics (ICHI), pp. 409–411. IEEE (2018)
18. Frize, M., Adéa, C., Payeur, P., Gina Di Primio, M. D., Karsh, J., Ogungbemile, A.: Detection of RA using IR imaging. In: Medical Imaging 2011: Image Processing, International Society for Optics and Photonics, vol. 7962, pp. 79620M (2011)
19. Lasanen, R., et al.: Thermal imaging in screening of joint inflammation and RA in children. Physiol. Meas. **36**(2), 273 (2015)
20. Snekhalatha, U., Anburajan, M., Sowmiya, V., Venkatraman, B., Menaka, M.: Automated hand thermal image segmentation and feature extraction in the evaluation of RA. Proc. Inst. Mech. Eng. [H] **229**(4), 319–331 (2015)
21. Suma, A.B., Snekhalatha, U., Rajalakshmi, T.: Automated thermal image segmentation of knee RA. In: 2016 International Conference on Communication and Signal Processing (ICCSP), pp. 0535–0539. IEEE (2016)
22. Umapathy, S., Vasu, S., Gupta, N.: Computer aided diagnosis-based hand thermal image analysis: a potential tool for the evaluation of RA. J. Med. Biol. Eng. **38**(4), 666–677 (2018)
23. Snekhalatha, U., Rajalakshmi, T., Gopikrishnan, M., Gupta, N.: Computer-based automated analysis of X-ray and thermal imaging of knee region in evaluation of RA. Proc. Inst. Mech. Eng. Part H **231**(12), 1178–1187 (2017)
24. Snekhalatha, U., Rajalakshmi, T., Gopikrishna, M.: Automated segmentation of knee thermal imaging and x-ray in evaluation of RA. Int. J. Eng. Technol. (UAE) **7**, 326–330 (2018)
25. Gizińska, M., Rutkowski, R., Szymczak-Bartz, L., Romanowski, W., Straburzyńska-Lupa, A.: Thermal imaging for detecting temperature changes within the rheumatoid foot. J. Therm. Anal. Calorim. **145**(1), 77–85 (2020). https://doi.org/10.1007/s10973-020-09665-0
26. Gatt, A., et al.: Thermal characteristics of rheumatoid feet in remission: Baseline data. PLoS ONE **15**(12), e0243078 (2020)
27. Sharon, H., Elamvazuthi, I., Lu, C.K., Parasuraman, S., Natarajan, E.: Classification of RA using machine learning algorithms. In: 2019 IEEE Student Conference on Research and Development (SCOReD), pp. 245–250. IEEE (2019)
28. Bardhan, S., Bhowmik, M.K.: 2-Stage classification of knee joint thermograms for RA prediction in subclinical inflammation. Australas. Phys. Eng. Sci. Med. **42**(1), 259–277 (2019)
29. Pauk, J., Ihnatouski, M., Wasilewska, A.: Detection of inflammation from finger temperature profile in RA. Med. Biol. Eng. Comput. **57**(12), 2629–2639 (2019)

Image Processing and Pattern Recognition of Micropores of Polysulfone Membrane for the Bio-separation of Viruses from Whole Blood

Shamima Khatoon$^{(\boxtimes)}$ and Gufran Ahmad ⓘ

Dayalbagh Educational Institute (Deemed-to-Be-University), Dayalbagh, Agra, U.P., India
{baigshamimakhatoon,gufranahmad}@dei.ac.in

Abstract. The VIVID™ GX membrane, is having great significance in clinical testing applications as well as the Lab-on-Chip Plasma Extraction. The designing and optimization of membrane-based devices is still an ongoing challenge for the researchers and direct fabrication and testing is the only option. The VIVID™ GX is the commercially available flat Polysulfone (PS) Plasma Membrane having asymmetric microporous structure, and clear demarcation of the pore boundaries is the key challenge to model the exact morphological details. The earlier modeling techniques still lacks the realization of the random distribution of micropores of this membrane including all possible variability in pore sizes from sub-micron to micron level. In this work we have proposed the procedure for Image Processing and Pattern Recognition of a microporous polymer membrane using MATLAB and COMSOL Multiphysics. We have traced the pore perimeter (contour) for the 'front', 'back' and 'cross-section' of the membrane employing the morphological operations for image processing. The retrieved perimeter pixelart is then employed for modeling the membrane structure in two domains viz. 'solid content' and 'porous content', for their clear demarcation. The proposed modeling strategy has a great potential in the field of optimization of Plasma Separators and other Microfluidics Lab-On-Chip Devices. We have successfully retrieved the pore range from approx.0.2 μm to 14 μm for the back-side and approx. upto 118 μm for the front-side for the samples under study. The proposed study has illustrated to the point processing and modeling strategy for the randomly distributed pores across the surfaces.

Keywords: Asymmetric pores · VIVID™ plasma membrane · On-chip plasma separators · Morphological operations

1 Introduction

A point of care testing (POCT) or field testing is becoming an ultimate need for rapid and equipment-free diagnosis, especially during pandemics like COVID-19. Such techniques not only necessitate a microliter of blood sample but also make handling and disposal of the sample easier. Microfluidic-based approaches [1–12] are self-driven and can process

© The Author(s), under exclusive license to Springer Nature Switzerland AG 2023
KC Santosh et al. (Eds.): RTIP2R 2022, CCIS 1704, pp. 151–163, 2023.
https://doi.org/10.1007/978-3-031-23599-3_11

samples without centrifugal rotation, which likely necessitates a longer operation time due to slower flow rates (0.19 L/min to 0.85 L/min).Therefore, membrane-based POC (Point of Care) devices, which are either pump-based [13] or self-driven [14–16], are gaining attention due to their less operating time (up to a few minutes) and maximum plasma output with an extraction efficiency ranging from 20–95%. Moreover, pump-based devices suffer from the problem of RBC hemolysis, while pump-free devices are in an improving stage to get more extraction efficiency with minimum applied pressure drops and membrane fouling.

The working principle of 'Membrane Based Plasma Separators' can be generalised by the size selection microfiltration of the blood cells. The cells above 500 nm, like RBCs, WBCs, etc., and bacteria, act as retentates, while the cells below 500 nm, such as viruses, RNA, proteins, etc., are extracted along with plasma into some collection conduit as a permeate. Some research groups also developed and tested membrane-based devices based on gravitational-assisted sedimentation [17], de-wetting super-hydrophobicity [14], immunocapture and size-filtration [16] methods, which outperformed previously, reported similar types of POC devices [13, 18–21].

Optimization is required to improve the plasma extraction efficiency for such types of biomedical devices like On-Chip-Plasma Separators. The recreation of an exact membrane structure can help the researchers and the modeling engineers to simulate the approximate outcome, which is ultimately quite challenging. In general, a homogeneous continuous pore structure model is used by researchers due to its modeling simplicity [22], to simulate models containing porous materials.

The membrane morphology supports continuous operation without membrane clogging and fowling, by size selection, trapping of various cells of random dimensions present in the whole blood, and passing on the target species like viruses, proteins, RNA, etc., through the membrane cross-section.

Any kind of "Membrane based-Plasma Separator" that has been developed and tested so far incorporates a commercially available Vivid™ plasma membrane due to its supporting features for such applications. This membrane is highly superhydrophobic at the upstream (front) and super hydrophilic at the downstream (back). Maïwenn et al. have reported a highly asymmetric pore morphology [16], with a size ranges from 7 μm to 29 μm with a mean of 21.12 μm at the front side, whereas 1 μm to 9 μm with a mean of 2.84 μm at the Back-side of the membrane [16]. The variation in the pore size and pore density throughout the membrane volume is basically due to the underlying chemical methods used for casting the membrane [24, 25]. The Vivid™ Plasma membrane is also considered as a reference to optimise other engineered membranes under study [26]. Conclusively, it can be said that this membrane is very asymmetric in terms of its structure, taking into account various morphological characteristics like its pore sizes, pore distribution, pore shape, tortuosity, etc.

The presented paper is broadly divided into two major sections; first section covers the image processing of the FESEM Images of three samples of the membrane, viz 'Front' (sample no. 01), 'Back' (sample no. 02) and 'Cross-section' (sample no. 03). In this section the pattern recognition for demarcation of the pore boundaries has been covered in detail. The next section is the extension of the processed images obtained from the first section, in order to model the microporous structure as 'porous content' and 'solid content' through COMSOL simulation for application part. In the experimental section we have also highlighted the need and flow chart of the proposed work. While the key findings can be better visualized through the morphological operations on FESEM Images of the Membrane and the 2D models for all three samples under study.

2 Experimental Section

2.1 Methodology

We have prepared three samples from an A4 sized sheet of Vivid™ GX-Plasma Membrane by using an 80W CO_2 Laser Cutting Machine. These samples were subsequently observed in a JEOL JSM-7610F PLUS Field Emission Scanning Electron Microscope (FESEM) at accelerating voltages of 2–5 kV under different magnifications to observe all the features reported in this study. These samples were first attached to the stub using carbon tabs, then coated with platinum in a JEOL JEC-3000FC autofine platinum coater for 40–60 s. We have assumed that the shinier surface is the back-side of the Vivid Membrane (sample no. 02), or the plasma outlet side. The pore dimension observed for the back side is from '0.247 μm × 0.226 μm', with a mean diameter of 0.363 μm, to '13.569 μm × 11.201 μm', with a mean diameter of 17.595 μm. The other side of the membrane is comparatively less shiny, so we assume it the front-side or the Plasma Inlet side of Vivid® membrane (sample no. 01). The minimum-sized pore with a circular shape is observed at the front-side having a diameter of 7.639 μm and the maximum-sized pore having dimension '81.597 μm × 117.708 μm', with a mean diameter of 143.225 μm. The morphological characteristics of the membrane are depicted in Fig. 1 and the measurements of the pores from sub-micro to millipore size ranges are listed in Table 1, illustrating the random and variable nature of pores within the sample.

Table 1. Pore morphological characteristics of porous polymer membrane.

Pore size (μm)	Samples under study	
	Front	Back
Min	7.639	0.247
Max	117.708	13.569
Mean (max)	143.225	17.595

With COMSOL Multiphysics, one can define the material properties such as porosity and permeability for porous structures, but their software interpretation is best in the case of uniform structures. Also, when material properties are unknown and only structural details like pore size are available for modeling then, under such conditions, a unit cell, which is a fraction of the actual cell, is assumed.

To make things easier to understand, such a unit cell has a hexagonally packed few spherical pores with solid content in the spaces between them [23]. Thus, with just software-based inbuilt functions, the minute morphological variations cannot be

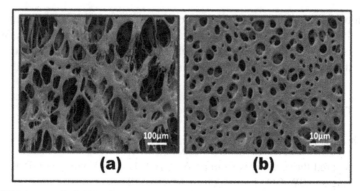

Fig. 1. SEM Image of Vivid® Plasma Membrane. (a) Front-Side (Sample no. 01) and (b) Back-Side (Sample no. 03)

mapped. Another popular method for modelling realistic pore structures is to obtain a binary image of a porous material sample, convert it to the "DXF" file format, and then import it into the COMSOL 2D geometry model. However, two problems are associated with this approach. The first problem is that a grayscale image of a heterogeneous porous structure can result in poor morphological recreation, especially for the front side of the membrane, and the second one is that it is not possible to separately select porous content as an explicit domain from the COMSOL Geometry.

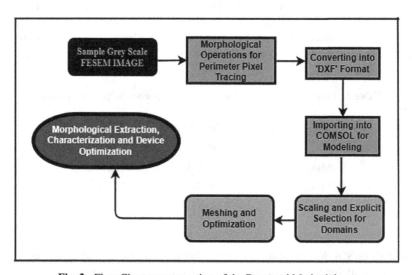

Fig. 2. Flow Chart representation of the Proposed Methodology

The proposed work presented an effective method to eliminate these problems successfully, by retrieving the 100% structural details without any loss of the sub-micro level pores. This can be achieved by prior image processing using selective morphological operations in a required sequence, followed by the proper choice of edge detection technique, before actually importing the "DXF" image file into COMSOL for post processing. Figure 2 depicts the flow chart of our methodology.

3   Image Processing Using MATLAB

In order to separate the porous content from the solid part of the porous material, various techniques like edge detection methods, morphological closing and opening, image dilation, sterile operator, impose, complement, etc. are used. The presented work utilised a number of techniques in the proper sequence on the SEM image using MATLAB 2021b licenced software. The front-side and cross-section of the SEM image need more processing steps as compared to the back side, as the underlying smaller pore network is visible through the larger pores. The histograms shown in Fig. 3 represent larger variations in the grayscale intensity for all 0 to 256 levels. Conclusively, we employ a series of Morphological Reconstructions using Adaptive Thresholding for SEM Images in Fig. 1.

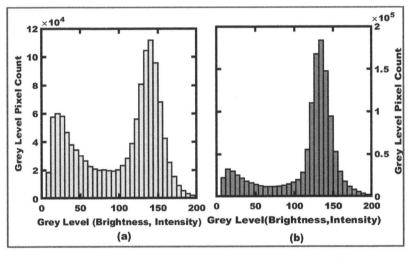

Fig. 3. Histogram of Vivid Plasma Membrane. (a) Front-Side (Sample no. 01) and (b) Back-Side (Sample no. 02)

3.1   Morphological Reconstruction by Adaptive Thresholding and Morphological Operations

For SEM images of our samples shown in Fig. 1, there are a lot of variations in the foreground intensity and contrast, as observed in their respective histograms also (Fig. 3). Hence, the retrieval of pore structure just by edge detection can result in almost all open pores and loss of morphological details at the sub-micron level. For such images, we have followed the image processing methodology by first opting for binarization with "Adaptive thresholding," followed by a series of morphological operations in the proper sequence and with the proper choice of parameters, such as "disk radius" for "Sterile" and "fill" operators, depending upon the pore structure to be reconstructed. Table 2 summarises the choice of operations and parameters used for image processing. The processed images after the implementation of these techniques for the front and back sides of the membrane samples (Sample nos. 01 & 02) are shown in Fig. 4 and Fig. 5, respectively. Figures 4(c) and 5(c) depict bi-level (1's and 0's) pixel art or bitmap images that distinguish porous and solid contents as "Black" and "White" respectively.

Table 2. MATLAB Commands, Operations and choice of parameters for Polymer Membrane Sample no. 01, 02 and 03

Image processing methodology			Polysulfone membrane sample no. 01 and 02 (front and back-side)	Polysulfone membrane sample no. 03	
Operation	Command	Parameter		Upper band	Lower band
Binarization	>>image binarize 'Adaptive Thresholding'		Adaptive Thresholding		Forground Polarity 'Dark' Sensitivity = 0.5
Dilation and closing	>>sterile >> image close	Disk radius	10	3	1
Morphological erosion for pores			>>Image fill 'holes'		
Perimeter pixel tracing	>>bwperim	Pixel connectivity		8	
Dilating the perimeter pixel	>>sterile	Disk radius	2	1	2

The grey scale images as shown in Fig. 4(a) and 5(a), lacks in the clear demarcation of the pore boundaries. After binarization there is a lot of false recreation in the solid contents of the porous structure as black patches as shown in Fig. 4(b) and 5(b). The patches are dilated and eroded, as shown in Figs. 4(C) and 5(C), to obtain a true realisation of the front and back sides of the membrane sample respectively. The high pixel connectivity followed with the dilation of the pore perimeter results in high contrast pore boundaries and clear demarcation of pore contours at all submicron levels for both the front and back sides of the membrane, as shown in Figs. 4(g) and 5(g).

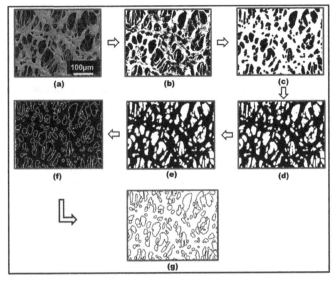

Fig. 4. (a) Original SEM Sample no. 01 (Front-Side), (b) Binary Image using Adaptive Thresholding, (c) Dilation of solid content and closing of pore Boundaries, (d) Dilated Image complement, (e) Morphological Erosion by filling up the pores, (f) Perimeter Pixel Tracing and Dilating pore boundaries. (g) Complement of the Edge Detection

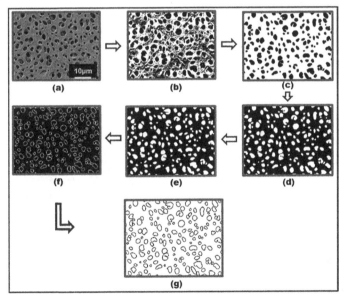

Fig. 5. (a) Membrane SEM Image Sample no. 02 (Back-Side), (b) Binary Image using Adaptive Thresholding, (c) Dilation of Solid content and closing of pore Boundaries, (d) Dilated Image complement, (e) Morphological Erosion by filling up the pores, (f) Perimeter pixel tracing and dilating pore boundaries, (g) Complement image of the Edge Detection

3.2 Morphological Recognition for Membrane Cross-Section

Figure 6(a) depicts a complete cross-sectional view of membrane sample no. 03. After observation of the pores, we have realised that the area with higher pore density, i.e., smaller pores, is the cross-section, near the back side of the membrane (top view as per the orientation in the Imaging Stub) while the area consisting of larger pores represents the front side of the membrane. The cross-sectional thickness of membrane is approximately 300 μm, as observed under FESSEM.

We again followed the Image Processing Methodology, which had been chosen for Sample No. 01 and Sample No. 02, but separately on two bands, i.e., the "upper band" with smaller pores and the "lower bands" with larger pores. After close observation of the cross-sectional SEM image of sample no. 03 and some prior image processing, we have concluded that the cross-section clearly reflects two different regions with greater variation in pore morphology. Furthermore, we realised that, for much more realistic detection of the target boundaries, it would be better to process each band separately with a different set of parameters and then finally concatenate both the processed images to get the full image depicting the perimeter pixel of pores for the whole cross-section. Figure 6(b)

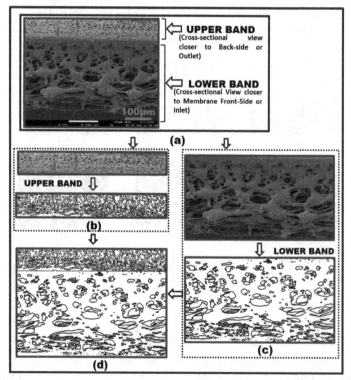

Fig. 6. (a) Complete Cross-Sectional SEM Image of Polymer Membrane (Sample no. 03) (b) Upper Band Closer to the Front-side and its processed Image after Morphological Operations, (c) Lower Band Closer to the Back-side and its processed Image after Morphological Operations, (e) Morphological Operations on the Lower Band of SEM Cross-Section, (f) Combining the upper and the lower band by concatenation to reconstruct the complete cross-section

and (c) show the processed images for the upper and lower bands, respectively, and Fig. 6(d) shows the combined concatenated image.

For the lower part of the SEM cross section, adaptive thresholding, along with keeping the foreground polarity "dark" than the background with a sensitivity of "0.5", results in better recognition of cross-sectional porous structures.

4   Modeling of Polymer Structure Using COMSOL Multiphysics

4.1   2D Modeling

COMSOL Multiphysics is used to model the Auto CAD Exchange File Format ('DXF' File) of the respective 'tiff' images as described in Image Processing section. The length scale unit of 2D Geometry is set to μm and the DXF file for front, back and cross-section of the membrane is imported simultaneously as 2D Geometry 1, 2 and 3 respectively. These imported file reveals real size in μm scale range which is clearly visible by Figs. 7, 8 and 9 respectively.

The 2D COMSOL Model of the Front Side (Sample no. 01) of the membrane, created with the help of 'DXF' image of Fig. 4(g) is shown in Fig. 7. Similarly, Fig. 8 depicts the 2D Model of the Back Side (Sample no. 02) of the membrane, obtained from the 'DXF' image of Fig. 5(g). In the same manner, the Cross-Sectional 2D Model of the membrane shown in Fig. 9 is generated from the 'DXF' version of the processed image of Membrane Cross-Section (Sample no. 03) shown in Fig. 6(d). In all the COMSOL Models of the membrane samples in the xy plane 2D geometry, the blue shade depicts

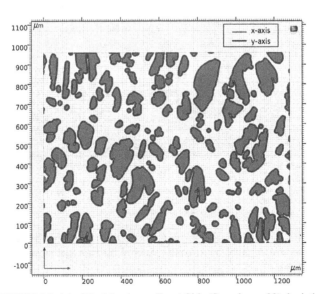

Fig. 7. 2D COMSOL Model of the Membrane Front-Side (Sample no. 02) depicting Micropores of random sizes ranging from about 7 μm to 118 μm

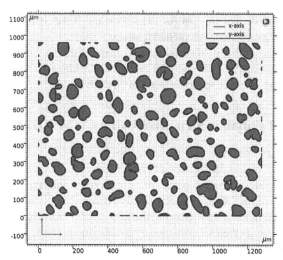

Fig. 8. 2D COMSOL Model of the Membrane Back-Side (Sample no. 02) depicting variation in pore size range from about 0.2 μm to 14 μm

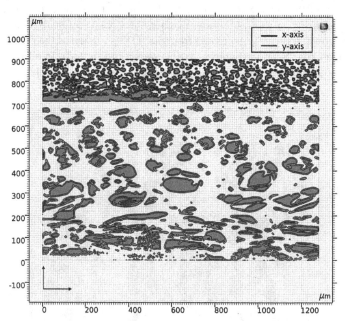

Fig. 9. 2D COMSOL model of the Membrane Cross-Section (Sample no. 03) depicting the variation in the pore density, from the upper band (nearer to the back-side) towards the lower-band (nearer to the front side)

the 'Porous Contents', while the 'Grey Shades' depicts the 'Solid Contents'. The demarcation between the solid and porous contents can be easily seen through the darker blue contours, depicting the pore perimeter pixelart.

The close observations of the pores shown in Fig. 9 gives a clear understanding of the pore distribution and also about the gradual variations in the pore sizes and pore density. The Model is successfully revealing the asymmetric porous structure of the VIVID™ Plasma Membrane, with the gradual increase in the pore density from the front towards the back side of the membrane.

5   Conclusion

In this work, image processing for grey scale FESEM Images of an asymmetric flat microporous polysulfone polymer membrane is presented. Random shape patterns of the micropores of the Plasma GX-Membrane are recognized successfully for a wide range of pore sizes, covering from 0.247 μm to 117.708 μm. The recognized pore perimeter pixelart can be employed for generating the 2D Geometric Model with explicit selection between 'Porous' and 'Solid Content'. Also one can easily observe the reduction in the pore sizes from the front towards the back side of the membrane with the help of the 2D Model, this shows gradual reduction in porosity also. With the help of just modeling of such microporous structure we can easily study the nature of the pores that can be helpful is designing various types of Microfiltration Applications. Thus, we can conclude that the 2D Model can be utilized for the characterization of the membrane, study of pores, optimization of the microfluidic and Lab-on-Chip Devices based on the fluid dynamic study or flow study of the devices such as Plasma Separator, Biomixers and other Bioseparators. The method presented here is significantly useful, quick and easy-to-use, as well as free from many variables, parameters, and complex coding techniques.

Acknowledgement. The research work is funded by the DST, Ministry of Science & Technology, Govt. of India, under the Women Scientist-B KIRAN Project Grant (DST/WOS-B/HN-17/2021). The authors express their gratitude to Pall Corporation, Mumbai, India for timely providing Vivid® GX-Membrane. The authors are also thankful to Prof. Sahab Das, Head, Department of Chemistry, Faculty of Science, Dayalbagh Educational Institute (DEI), for providing the FESSEM Lab Facilities and to Dr. Manju Srivastav for assisting with SEM Imaging.

References

1. Shim, J.S., Ahn, C.H.: An on-chip whole blood/plasma separator using hetero-packed beads at the inlet of a microchannel. Lab Chip **12**, 863–866 (2012). https://doi.org/10.1039/C2L C21009F
2. Lee, K.K., Ahn, C.H.: A new on-chip whole blood/plasma separator driven by asymmetric capillary forces. Lab Chip (2013). https://doi.org/10.1039/C3LC50370D
3. Woo, S.O., Oh, M., Nietfeld, K., Boehler, B., Choi, Y.: Molecular diffusion analysis of dynamic blood flow and plasma separation driven by self-powered microfluidic devices. Biomicrofluidics **15**(3), 034106 (2021). https://doi.org/10.1063/5.005136
4. Dimov, I.K., Basabe-Desmonts, L., Garcia-Cordero, J.L., Ross, B.M., Park, Y., Ricco, A.J., Lee, L.P.: Stand-alone self-powered integrated microfluidic blood analysis system (SIMBAS). Lab Chip **11**, 845–850 (2011). https://doi.org/10.1039/C0LC00403K

5. Chen, X., Cui, D.F., Liu, C.C., Li, H.: Microfluidic chip for blood cell separation and collection based on crossflow filtration. Sens. Actuators B Chem. **130**(1), 216–221 (2008). https://doi.org/10.1016/j.snb.2007.07.126

6. VanDelinder, V., Groisman, A.: Separation of plasma from whole human blood in a continuous cross-flow in a molded microfluidic device. Anal. Chem. **78**(11), 3765–3771 (2006). https://doi.org/10.1021/ac060042r

7. Tachi, T., Kaji, N., Tokeshi, M., Baba, Y.: Simultaneous separation, metering, and dilution of plasma from human whole blood in a microfluidic system. Anal. Chem. **81**(8), 3194–3198 (2009). https://doi.org/10.1021/ac802434z

8. Amasia, M., Madou, M.: Large volume centrifugal microfluidic device for blood plasma separation. Bioanalysis **2**, 1701–1710 (2010). https://doi.org/10.4155/bio.10.140

9. Gorkin, R., et al.: Centrifugal microfluidics for biomedical applications. Lab Chip **10**, 1758–1773 (2010). https://doi.org/10.1039/B924109D

10. Zhao, C., Cheng, X.: Microfluidic separation of viruses from blood cells based on intrinsic transport processes. Biomicrofluidics **5**(3), 032004-032004-10 (2011). https://doi.org/10.1063/1.3609262

11. Sun, M., Khan, Z.S., Vanapalli, S.A.: Blood plasma separation in a long two-phase plug flowing through disposable tubing. Lab Chip **12**, 5225–5230 (2012). https://doi.org/10.1039/C2LC40544J

12. Panaro, N.J., Lou, X.J., Fortina, P., Kricka, L.J., Wilding, P.: Micropillar array chip for integrated white blood cell isolation and PCR. Biomol. Eng. **21**(6), 157–162 (2005). https://doi.org/10.1016/j.bioeng.2004.11.001

13. Wang, S.Q., et al.: Simple filter microchip for rapid separation of plasma and viruses from whole blood. Int. J. Nanomed. **7**, 5019–5028 (2012). https://doi.org/10.2147/IJN.S32579

14. Liu, C., et al.: A high-efficiency superhydrophobic plasma separator. R. Soc. Chem. Lab Chip **16**, 553–560 (2016). https://doi.org/10.1039/C5LC01235J

15. Su, X., et al.: High-Efficiency Plasma Separator Based on Immunocapture and Filtration. Micromachines **11**(4), 352 (2020). https://doi.org/10.3390/mi11040352

16. Lopresti, F., et al.: Engineered membranes for residual cell trapping on microfluidic blood plasma separation systems: a comparison between porous and nanofibrous membranes. Membranes **11**(9), 680 (2021). https://doi.org/10.3390/membranes11090680

17. Liu, C., et al.: Membrane-based, sedimentation-assisted plasma separator for point-of-care applications. Anal. Chem. **85**(21), 10463–10470 (2013). https://doi.org/10.1021/ac402459h

18. Homsy, A., et al.: Development and validation of a low cost blood filtration element separating plasma from undiluted whole blood. Biomicrofluidics **6**(1), 12804–128049 (2012). https://doi.org/10.1063/1.3672188

19. Yang, X., Forouzan, O., Brown, T.P., Shevkoplyas, S.S.: Integrated separation of blood plasma from whole blood for microfluidic paper-based analytical devices. Lab Chip **12**, 274–280 (2012). https://doi.org/10.1039/C1LC20803A

20. Songjaroen, T., Dungchai, W., Chailapakul, O., Henry, C.S., Laiwattanapaisal, W.: Blood separation on microfluidic paper-based analytical devices. Lab Chip **12**, 3392–3398 (2012). https://doi.org/10.1039/C2LC21299D

21. Thorslund, S., Klett, O., Nikolajeff, F., Markides, K., Bergquist, J.: A hybrid poly (dimethylsiloxane) microsystem for on-chip whole blood filtration optimized for steroid screening. Biomed. Microdevice **8**(1), 73–79 (2006). https://doi.org/10.1007/s10544-006-6385-7

22. Xiong, Q., Baychev, T.G., Jivkov, A.P.: Review of pore network modelling of porous media: experimental characterisations, network constructions and applications to reactive transport. J. Contam. Hydrol. **192**, 101–117 (2016). https://doi.org/10.1016/j.jconhyd.2016.07.002

23. Hu, Y., Wang, Q., Zhao, J., Xie, S., Jiang, H.: A novel porous media permeability model based on fractal theory and ideal particle pore-space geometry assumption. Energies **13**(2), 510 (2020). https://doi.org/10.3390/en13030510

24. Tan, X., Rodrigue, D.: A review on porous polymeric membrane preparation. Part I: production techniques with polysulfone and poly (vinylidene fluoride). Polymers **11**, 1160 (2019). https://doi.org/10.3390/polym11071160

25. Barth, C., Gonçalves, M.C., Pires, A.T.N., Roeder, J., Wolf, B.A.: Asymmetric polysulfone and polyethersulfone membranes: effects of thermodynamic conditions during formation on their performance. J. Membr. Sci. **169**(2), 287–299 (2000). https://doi.org/10.1016/S0376-7388(99)00344-0

26. Sofian, M.S.M., et al.: Effect of solvent concentration on performance of polysulfone membrane for filtration and separation. IOP Conf. Ser.: Mater. Sci. Eng. **226**, 012171 (2017). https://doi.org/10.1088/1757-899x/226/1/012171

An Extreme Learning Machine-Based AutoEncoder (ELM-AE) for Denoising Knee X-ray Images and Grading Knee Osteoarthritis Severity

Sushma Chaugule$^{(\boxtimes)}$ (iD) and V. S. Malemath (iD)

Department of CSE, KLE DR. M. S. Sheshgiri College of Engineering and Technology,
Belagavi, India
vidhu_sun@yahoo.co.in

Abstract. Osteoarthritis (OA) is the most usual form of arthritis. Radiologists assess the OA severity by observing the pieces of evidence on both sides of knee bones, hinged on the Kellgren–Lawrence (KL) grading system. Computer-assisted diagnosis has been a prime field of research for the past few decades as it tends to provide highly accurate performance. In this work, we propose the Knee Osteoarthritis (KOA) classification problem to segregate the severity into five grades. The proposed work can be framed into two-stage, using X-ray images. Stage one deals with preprocessing and denoising, while stage two deals with classification. This work considers, a standard OAI dataset as well as locally collected images as input, and are fed to an Extreme Learning Machine-based AutoEncoder (ELM-AE) to get the denoised images, which are then used for training the Dense Neural Network model DenseNet201 and are later classified, based on KL grades. In experimentation, evaluation of performance is carried out for the model with and without using autoencoders. It is observed that with autoencoders the overall performance is enhanced significantly for standard as well as the local dataset.

Keywords: Extreme learning machine · Denoising autoencoders · Knee OA · X-ray images · DenseNet201 · OAI

1 Introduction

Knee Osteoarthritis (KOA) is a prevailing musculoskeletal disorder and a major cause of unwholesomeness, especially in the elder community. It is estimated to affect approximately 12.5% of patients above the age of 45. KOA commonly affects the medial femorotibial joint compartment with narrowed joint space, subchondral sclerosis, marginal osteophytes, and subchondral cysts, either from interminably high-impact activities or increased load due to obesity, old knee injury, frequent stress, or heredity. Plain radiographs are the main doer of imaging, although there is a weak relationship among radiographic findings, skeletal changes, and clinical symptoms [1]. [2] defines OA as "…a heterogeneous group of conditions that leads to joint symptoms and signs

© The Author(s), under exclusive license to Springer Nature Switzerland AG 2023
KC Santosh et al. (Eds.): RTIP2R 2022, CCIS 1704, pp. 164–175, 2023.
https://doi.org/10.1007/978-3-031-23599-3_12

which are associated with defective integrity of articular cartilage, in addition to related changes in the underlying bone and at the joint margins".

The KL grades are defined as - Grade 0 shows no pathological features; Grade 1 shows doubtful joint space narrowing and probable osteophytic lipping; Grade 2 shows confined osteophytes and probable joint space narrowing; Grade 3 shows moderate multiple osteophytes, definite joint space narrowing, some sclerosis, and probable deformity of bony ends; Grade 4 shows large osteophytes, marked joint space narrowing, severe sclerosis, and definite deformity of bone ends. Figure 1 shows the original grades and the definitions of the Kellgren-Lawrence (KL) Grading Scale [3].

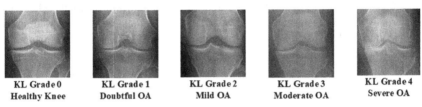

KL Grade 0	KL Grade 1	KL Grade 2	KL Grade 3	KL Grade 4
Healthy Knee	Doubtful OA	Mild OA	Moderate OA	Severe OA

Fig. 1. Knee joint X-Ray samples showing the five KL grades with their corresponding indicators [4]

The several modalities of medical imaging include Radiographs, Magnetic Resonance, Ultrasound, Computed Tomography, Nuclear Medicine, and Optical Methods [5, 6]. It is evident that plain radiographs are mainly used in the diagnosis of KOA, as it is cost-effective, easily available, safe, and have the ability to generate clear images [7]. So, in our study, we worked on knee radiographs. However, in the initial stages of OA, it is highly challenging to detect and predict KOA severity based only on the symptoms and radiographs.

The main disadvantage of X-Ray images is low contrast, which easily gets altered by additive noise. Noise in the X-ray images may be due to the human body liquid content or secondary radiations, this will require denoising. Many times, while denoising, high-frequency components like texture, and borders are difficult to separate from the noise thus losing certain information. It is possible to reduce this noise by applying Gaussian noise to the picture. Thus, the purpose of our work is to address X-image denoising and classifying according to KL grades, to help medical practitioners correctly diagnose KOA severity.

The paper is organized as follows: Sect. 2 presents the related work that briefs various authors' contributions. Data collection, preprocessing, image enhancement, feature extraction, and classification are presented as a part of the proposed methodology in Sect. 3. Section 4 gives the evaluation of the proposed method with results and discussion and finally, the paper is concluded in Sect. 5.

2   Related Work

From the literature it is evident that in the field of medical science, Artificial Intelligence (AI) pays a major role in diagnosing the patients for the severity of the disease. Present works majorly use Convolutional Neural Networks (CNN) that help learn features in the image and precise, faster classification into binary or multiple classes. The gravitating image processing, pattern recognition, and machine learning techniques can be combined to help in diagnosis [8–13].

Many researchers have worked on different imaging modalities to get enhanced medical visualizations. The main focus is on X-ray images [14, 15], MRI [16, 17], and CT images [18, 19], amongst the other modalities. Inputs are usually collected from OAI, MOST or clinical raw data. This input data is pre-processed i.e., denoised – may be using autoencoders [20, 21], or using suitable filters [22, 23] namely circular Fourier Filter [24]. Pre-processing may include techniques like edge detection [25] namely Sobel, Robert, Prewitt, Zero Cross, and Canny Edge detection algorithms [9, 10]. Other forms of pre-processing like histogram equalization, contrast enhancement, thresholding, and edge detection [24] are used. From the literature so far, it is evident that denoising using autoencoders can be explored more. These pre-processed images, can ease the task of building fully automated systems [24, 26] and semi-automated systems [27].

Various researchers have carried out extensive work to diagnose KOA using machine learning (ML) techniques [28]. Researchers have worked on various techniques of feature extraction like Haralick [29], fisher score [30], wavelets [31], different image segmentation [32, 33] like Watershed, Otsu's segmentation [34], ASM [22], pixel segmentation [35], thresholding, region-based, clustering, Markov random field, artificial neural network, deformable and atlas guided method [32]. Some researchers have extensively worked on segmentation techniques [36], morphological techniques [26], DenseNet [23, 37] and classification techniques namely Naive Bayes, random forest classifiers [24], feature-based classification [38], ANN [33, 39, 40], SVM [29], KNN [41, 42].

From the literature it is evident that the authors have worked extensively on varied image processing techniques, all giving their best results. It is observed that the challenge is to recover meaningful information and obtain high-quality images from noisy images. Thus, in this work, we use an extreme learning machine-based autoencoder (ELM-AE) for denoising. Also, it can be inferred from the above studies that detection of OA severity at the correct time and restrict OA progression, is present days demanding task. Thus, advanced machine learning techniques can be explored more to meet present-day challenges. This paper aims to use the newest advancements in neural networks like DenseNet201 for feature extraction, as they are found to give best results for X-ray images [43] and these are used for classifying the KOA severity grade using knee radiographs for intime and precise results.

3 Proposed Methodology

This research aims to develop an enhanced classification model based on feature extraction using the Dense Convolutional Network (DenseNet) for the classification of KOA severity. Amongst the many architectures of DenseNet, we have used DenseNet 201 which comprises a normalized input layer, a fully connected layer, a rectified linear activation unit (ReLU) layer, and a softmax output layer. Figure 2 depicts the flowchart of the proposed approach.

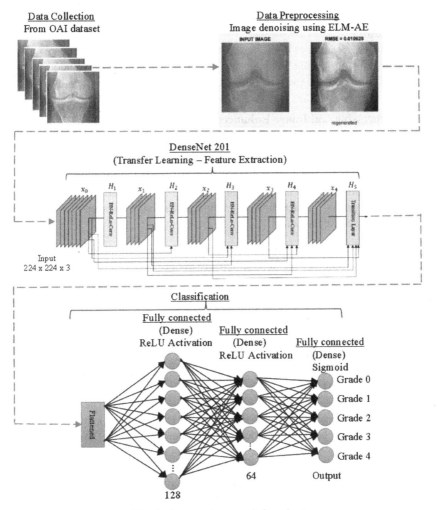

Fig. 2. Proposed approach flowchart

3.1 Data Collection

The input data are the Knee X-ray images and are obtained from OsteoArthritis Initiative (OAI) [44]. It is a longitudinal, multi-center, prospective observational study of KOA, that aims at biomarker identification, onset, and progression, scientific investigation, and development of OA drugs. OAI enrolled 4796 participants including both genders, aged between 45 to 79 years. In our study, images collected include baseline, bilateral, Posterior-Anterior (PA) fixed flexion X-ray images. A total of 5,778 images are used for experimentation, which are broken down into five grades, with Grade 0: 2286 images, Grade 1: 1046 images, Grade 2: 1516 images, Grade 3: 757 images, and Grade 4: 173 images. Of the 5778 images, 170 images are randomly selected and saved in each severity grade. Thus 850 images are further split as 80/20 i.e., 136 images for training and 34 images for testing.

Additionally, 250 images in PA view and PNG format are collected from local medical practitioners considering 50 images in each grade. The split 80/20 randomly selects 40 images for training and the remaining 10 for testing.

3.2 Pre-processing and Image Enhancement

Generally, medical images are subjected to noise. Noise in the X-ray image is mainly due to scattered radiations [45] and the liquid content in the human body. This may cause problems for the medical experts if they get improper information, hence it is predominant to eliminate such components. In this work, as a part of preprocessing the input images are passed through three stages; image denoising based on ELM-AE, image resizing, and image enhancement.

Image Denoising. AutoEncoder (AE) is an unsupervised model, comprising an encoder, which compresses the input into lower dimensions forming a bottleneck layer and a decoder to reconstruct the original data. Thus, in the construction of input data, the count of output units is equal to the count of inputs [46].

ELM (Extreme Learning Machines) is a learning algorithm defined for single-hidden layer feedforward neural networks. ELM sets its weights using Moore-Penrose generalized inverse instead of gradient-based backpropagation. ELM produces good generalization performance and learns at an extreme faster learning speed, thus the name Extreme Learning Machine [47].

ELM-AE constructs an ELM based on a multi-layer perceptron and is used to learn new representations of data. ELM-AE is a unique three-layered neural network, that comprises of an input layer, one-hidden layer, and an output layer. The first layer, generates random input weights and prepares the dataset $D_n = \{x_1, ..., x_n\}$, where x_i is a d-dimensional vector. The second layer, calculates the hidden layer by adding noise (e.g., Gaussian noise) to x_i as shown in Eq. 1, and constructs the pair of original input and noisy input, $T_n = \{(x_1, y_1), ..., (x_n, y_n)\}$, where y_i is the noise added along with x_i. ELM-AE then uses y_i to calculate a function

$$h_i = \sigma(W\, y_i + b) \tag{1}$$

considering $\{W, b\}$ parameters, where h_i gives the latent representation, and σ is an activation function, that may be sine, sigmoid, hard limit, radial basis function, triangular basis function, or ReLU activation function. In the third layer, the latent representation h_i helps in reconstructing the clear output x_i' using Eq. 2, by mapping it in reverse

$$x_i' = \sigma(W'\, h_i + b') \tag{2}$$

considering $\{W', b'\}$ parameters, where W' = WT [48]. This shows that the weights considered for input encoding and latent representation decoding are the same. By minimizing the cost function between x_i and x_i' ($i = 1, ..., n$) in the training set T_n, optimized parameters are obtained. On successful training, ELM-AE constructs a clear output from the noisy input [49].

Image Resizing. The DenseNet model generally requires same sized input. The input image sizes usually differ, resizing the images to a fixed size becomes very important, before passing them to the DenseNet model for feature extraction and classification. In this work, the images are resized to keep the images large so that the features and data patterns of the images are not disturbed.

Image Enhancement. Image enhancement improves the quality of the images and in this work, the histogram equalization technique has been used. Here, the images are processed and contrast adjusted by altering the intensity distribution of the image histogram. This technique effectively spreads out the repeated intensity values by straightening them out, so it is considered one of the pixel brightness transformation techniques. Thus, histogram equalization improves image quality as well as restricts over-enhancement.

3.3 Feature Extraction and Classification Using DenseNet201

The architecture of DenseNet is based on the connection of all layers. Here every layer act on the inputs from the preceding layers, and it passes its output in terms of feature maps to all the leading layers. This arrangement helps to reduce information redundancy and also the number of parameters. DenseNet is known for taking in fewer parameters and gives high accuracy with $N(N + 2)/2$ direct connections, also it lessens the vanishing-gradient problem and reinforces feature propagation [50].

In this work, the KOA features are extracted using DenseNet201 to classify the grades of the disease. DenseNet201 includes automatic extraction of features and computes weights in the training process. The features extracted from the input data are then forwarded to a classifier. The feature extraction process consists of many pairs of convolutional layers and pooling layers. The convolutional layer performs convolution operations on the input data using the digital filters. The pooling layer performs dimensionality reduction and the threshold is calculated. In the backpropagation, a number of parameters are adjusted, which minimizes the number of connections within the DenseNet201 architecture. At the end of the subsampling layer, the fully connected layers perform dimensionality reduction, as in traditional neural networks. DenseNet201 are mainly used in health care applications as time series data and the frequency representation images help in generating features automatically which are later used for classification.

The input layer normalizes the data using Z-score normalization and is flattened which will take input of size $224 \times 224 \times 3$. The densely connected layers are hidden and have 512 neurons forming the first layer, 128 forming the second layer, 64 forming the third layer, and 32 in the last layer. For every hidden layer, there is ReLU as an activation function and softmax activation as the output layer. There are 1,921 trainable parameters. Finally, a fully connected layer performs the classification with an output size corresponding to the number of classes, followed by a softmax layer and a classification layer. This model uses stochastic gradient descent with a momentum (sgdm) optimizer and uses the sparse categorical cross-entropy for the loss function [51]. As the parameters take a long time in the execution process, optimizers train the parameters effectively and help converge faster. This research incorporates a sgdm optimization algorithm for fine-tuning the parameters of DenseNet201, which gives better results even with smaller datasets.

Finally, in the classification, two densely connected layers, one with 128 neurons and the other with 64 neurons, respectively, are added. For classification, the top of DenseNet201 is removed, which is used for feature extraction, this is given to a sigmoid activation function for KOA severity grade classification. The sigmoid activation function replaces the softmax activation function used in the classical DenseNet201 architecture. Each neuron in every layer is fully connected forming dense connections. The input 2D feature maps from fully connected layer 1 are expanded to a 1D feature vector using the Bernoulli function. The dropout strategy randomly blocks certain neurons in the two layers of the fully connected layers depending on specific probability, this prevents over-fitting in deep networks. The sigmoid activation function maps the non-normalized outputs to KOA severity grades [52].

4   Results and Discussion

Here the experimentation is done in two phases i.e., pre-processing and classification. Pre-processing concentrates on denoising of X-ray images using ELM-AE, feature extraction and classification are done using DenseNet201. Experimentation is carried out on 2 different datasets: one being the OAI dataset and the other dataset consists of images collected from a local medical practitioner.

OAI Dataset. From the OAI dataset with 5778 images, randomly 170 images each are selected for every grade of KOA and saved as Grade 0 through Grade 4; i.e., 850 images from 5778 images. The split decision for these images in each grade is 80/20, giving 136 for training and 34 for testing. The training details are mini-batch size to be 10, 40 epochs, 85 iterations/epoch, all of this gives 3,400 iterations. Once the training process is done, a random test image can be chosen to evaluate the performance of the model in predicting KOA severity. The accuracies for each grade are calculated and are shown in Table 1.

Table 1. Performance evaluation in terms of accuracy for the OAI dataset.

KL grades	Images from OAI	Randomly selected images	Randomly selected for training/testing	Without ELM-AE		With ELM-AE	
				Correctly classified images	Accuracy	Correctly classified images	Accuracy
Grade 0	2286	170	136/34	32	94.11%	33	97.05%
Grade 1	1046	170	136/34	30	88.23%	30	88.23%
Grade 2	1516	170	136/34	29	85.29%	29	85.29%
Grade 3	757	170	136/34	32	94.11%	32	94.11%
Grade 4	173	170	136/34	33	97.05%	33	97.05%
Total	5778	850		156	91.75%	157	92.35%

For the OAI dataset, the model with an autoencoder attained the accuracy of 92.34%, which is better as compared to the model without an autoencoder giving the accuracy of 91.75%.

Locally Collected Images. 250 images are collected from local medical practitioners accounting 50 images in each grade. The split 80/20 randomly selected 40 images for training and the rest 10 for testing. With the same training details and the local images, the model is trained once again. Later, testing is carried out for randomly selected test images and the performance is evaluated for the model in predicting KOA severity. The accuracies for each grade are calculated for locally collected images and are shown in Table 2.

Table 2. Performance evaluation in terms of accuracy for locally collected images.

KL grades	Images collected locally	Randomly selected for training/testing	Without ELM-AE		With ELM-AE	
			Correctly classified images	Accuracy	Correctly classified images	Accuracy
Grade 0	50	40/10	9	90.00%	10	100.00%
Grade 1	50	40/10	9	90.00%	9	90.00%
Grade 2	50	40/10	8	80.00%	9	90.00%
Grade 3	50	40/10	9	90.00%	9	90.00%
Grade 4	50	40/10	10	100.00%	10	100.00%
Total	250		45	90.00%	47	94.00%

For locally collected images, the model with an autoencoder attained the accuracy of 94.00%, which is better as compared to the model without an autoencoder giving the accuracy of 90.00%.

OAI dataset and locally collected images are analyzed for precision, recall and F measure considering all KL grades and the results are depicted in Table 3.

Considering OAI images and the model with autoencoder shows the accuracy increase by only 0.59%, this is because of the standard dataset used. As the images in OAI are already preprocessed to a certain level, denoising such images may not affect the accuracy. On the other hand, considering the locally collected images and the model with autoencoder gave an accuracy increase of 4.00%. Thus, it is evident that autoencoders help in building a better-performing model for raw data. After combining both the datasets the overall performance in terms of accuracy is found to be 92.72%.

Table 3. Analysis in terms of precision, recall and F measure

	Precision	Recall	F measure
Grade 0	0.9556	0.9773	0.9663
Grade 1	0.8400	0.8864	0.8625
Grade 2	0.8837	0.8636	0.8735
Grade 3	0.9535	0.9318	0.9425
Grade 4	0.9773	0.9773	0.9773
Total	0.9220	0.9273	0.9244

5   Conclusion

Health care systems are always under increased pressure to give critical performance measures with a high level of accuracy. The main aim of the proposed approach is to get better accuracy levels in diagnosing the grades of KOA severity. This work exhibits a novel KOA severity classification based on denoising and DenseNet201. To enhance the performance at the microlevel, autoencoders are implemented for denoising. Experimentation is carried out on both standard OAI datasets and locally collected images and are presented. Results are compared and it is observed that the use of an autoencoder enhances the overall performance and classification accuracy significantly.

References

1. Hayes, B., Kittelson, A., Loyd, B., Wellsandt, E., Flug, J., Stevens-Lapsley, J.: Assessing radiographic knee osteoarthritis: an online training tutorial for the Kellgren-Lawrence grading scale. MedEdPORTAL (2016). https://doi.org/10.15766/mep_2374-8265.10503
2. Kohn, M.D., Sassoon, A.A., Fernando, N.D.: Classifications in brief: Kellgren-Lawrence classification of osteoarthritis. Clin. Orthop. Relat. Res. **474**(8), 1886–1893 (2016). https://doi.org/10.1007/s11999-016-4732-4
3. Kellgren, J.H., Lawrence, J.S.: Radiological assessment of osteo-arthrosis. Ann. Rheum. Dis. **16**(4), 494–502 (1957). https://doi.org/10.1136/ard.16.4.494
4. Chen, P., Gao, L., Shi, X., Allen, K., Yang, L.: Fully automatic knee osteoarthritis severity grading using deep neural networks with a novel ordinal loss. Comput. Med. Imaging Graph. **75**, 84–92 (2019). https://doi.org/10.1016/j.compmedimag.2019.06.002
5. Dongare, P.P., Gornale, S.S.: Medical Imaging in Clinical Applications Algorithmic and Computer Based.pdf, no. May (2021)
6. Hayashi, D., Roemer, F.W., Guermazi, A.: Imaging of osteoarthritis - recent research developments and future perspective. Br. J. Radiol. **91**(1085), 20170349 (2018). https://doi.org/10.1259/bjr.20170349
7. Tiulpin, A., Thevenot, J., Rahtu, E., Lehenkari, P., Saarakkala, S.: Automatic knee osteoarthritis diagnosis from plain radiographs: a deep learning-based approach. Sci. Rep. **8**(1), 1 (2018). https://doi.org/10.1038/s41598-018-20132-7
8. Gornale, S.S., Patravali, P.U., Manza, R.R.: A survey on exploration and classification of osteoarthritis using image processing techniques. Int. J. Sci. Eng. Res. **7**, 334–355 (2016)

9. Ruikar, D.D., Hegadi, R.S., Santosh, K.C.: A systematic review on orthopedic simulators for psycho-motor skill and surgical procedure training. J. Med. Syst. **42**(9), 1–21 (2018). https://doi.org/10.1007/s10916-018-1019-1

10. Ruikar, D.D., Sawat, D.D., Santosh, K.C.: A systematic review of 3D imaging in biomedical applications. In: Medical Imaging. Boca Raton: Taylor & Francis, a CRC title, part of the Taylor & Francis imprint, a member of the Taylor & Francis Group, the academic division of T&F Informa, plc, 2020, pp. 154–181. CRC Press (2019). https://doi.org/10.1201/9780429029417-8

11. Gornale, S.S., Patravali, P.U., Manza, R.R.: Detection of osteoarthritis using knee X-ray image analyses: a machine vision based approach. Int. J. Comput. Appl. **145**(1), 20–26 (2016). https://doi.org/10.5120/ijca2016910544

12. Sumathi, S., Paneerselvam, S.: Computational intelligence. In: Computational Intelligence Paradigms, pp. 25–52 (2020). https://doi.org/10.1201/9781439809037-6

13. Teoh, Y.X., et al.: Discovering knee osteoarthritis imaging features for diagnosis and prognosis: review of manual imaging grading and machine learning approaches. J. Healthc. Eng. **2022** (2022). https://doi.org/10.1155/2022/4138666

14. Kubakaddi, S., Urs, N.: Detection of knee osteoarthritis by measuring the joint space width in knee X-ray images. Int. J. Electron. Commun. **3**(4), 18–21 (2019)

15. Navale, D.I., Ruikar, D.D., Houde, K.V., Hegadi, R.S.: DWT textural feature-based classification of osteoarthritis using knee X-ray images. In: Santosh, K.C., Gawali, B. (eds.) RTIP2R 2020. CCIS, vol. 1381, pp. 50–59. Springer, Singapore (2021). https://doi.org/10.1007/978-981-16-0493-5_5

16. Guida, C., Zhang, M., Shan, J.: Knee osteoarthritis classification using 3D CNN and MRI. Appl. Sci. **11**(11), 5196 (2021). https://doi.org/10.3390/app11115196

17. Schiratti, J.B., et al.: A deep learning method for predicting knee osteoarthritis radiographic progression from MRI. Arthritis Res. Ther. **23**(1), 1–10 (2021). https://doi.org/10.1186/s13075-021-02634-4

18. Singha, R., Dalai, C.K., Sarkar, D.: A study on evaluation of knee osteoarthritis with MRI and comparing it with CT scan, high resolution USG and conventional radiography. Asian J. Med. Sci. **12**(12), 120–125 (Dec.2021). https://doi.org/10.3126/ajms.v12i12.39174

19. Vashishtha, A., Acharya, A.K.: An overview of medical imaging techniques for knee osteoarthritis disease. Biomed. Pharmacol. J. **14**(2), 903–919 (2021). https://doi.org/10.13005/bpj/2192

20. Gondara, L.: Medical image denoising using convolutional denoising autoencoders. In: IEEE International Conference on Data Mining Workshops, ICDMW, pp. 241–246 (2016). https://doi.org/10.1109/ICDMW.2016.0041

21. Vankayalapati, R., Muddana, A.L.: Denoising of images using deep convolutional autoencoders for brain tumor classification. Rev. d'Intelligence Artif. **35**(6), 489–496 (2021). https://doi.org/10.18280/ria.350607

22. Lee, H.-C., Lee, J.-S., Lin, M.C.-J., Wu, C.-H., Sun, Y.-N.: Automatic assessment of knee osteoarthritis parameters from two-dimensional X-ray image. In: First International Conference on Innovative Computing, Information and Control - Volume I (ICICIC 2006), vol. 2, pp. 673–676 (2006). https://doi.org/10.1109/ICICIC.2006.242

23. Norman, B., Pedoia, V., Noworolski, A., Link, T.M., Majumdar, S.: Applying densely connected convolutional neural networks for staging osteoarthritis severity from plain radiographs. J. Digit. Imaging **32**(3), 471–477 (2018). https://doi.org/10.1007/s10278-018-0098-3

24. Brahim, A., et al.: A decision support tool for early detection of knee OsteoArthritis using X-ray imaging and machine learning: data from the OsteoArthritis Initiative. Comput. Med. Imaging Graph. **73**, 11–18 (2019). https://doi.org/10.1016/j.compmedimag.2019.01.007

25. Zahurul, S., Zahidul, S., Jidin, R.: An adept edge detection algorithm for human knee osteoarthritis images. In: 2010 International Conference on Signal Acquisition and Processing, ICSAP 2010, vol. 2, no. 4, pp. 375–379 (2010). https://doi.org/10.1109/ICSAP.2010.53

26. Anifah, L., Purnama, I.K.E., Hariadi, M., Purnomo, M.H.: Automatic segmentation of impaired joint space area for osteoarthritis knee on X-ray image using Gabor filter based morphology process. IPTEK J. Technol. Sci. **22**(3) (2011). https://doi.org/10.12962/j20882033.v22i3.72

27. Gan, H.S., Sayuti, K.A., Karim, A.H.A., Rosidi, R.A.M., Khaizi, A.S.A.: Analysis on semi-automated knee cartilage segmentation model using inter-observer reproducibility. In: Proceedings of the 7th International Conference on Bioscience, Biochemistry and Bioinformatics - ICBBB 2017, pp. 12–16 (2017). https://doi.org/10.1145/3051166.3051169

28. Suganyadevi, S., Seethalakshmi, V., Balasamy, K.: A review on deep learning in medical image analysis. Int. J. Multimed. Inf. Retr. **11**(1), 19–38 (2022). https://doi.org/10.1007/s13735-021-00218-1

29. Subramoniam, M., Barani, S., Rajini, V.: A non-invasive computer aided diagnosis of osteoarthritis from digital x-ray images. Biomed. Res. **26**(4), 721–729 (2015)

30. Shamir, L., Ling, S.M., Scott, W., Hochberg, M., Ferrucci, L., Goldberg, I.G.: Early detection of radiographic knee osteoarthritis using computer-aided analysis. Osteoarthr. Cartil. **17**(10), 1307–1312 (2009). https://doi.org/10.1016/j.joca.2009.04.010

31. Gornale, S.S., Patravali, P.U., Hiremath, P.S.: Automatic detection and classification of knee osteoarthritis using Hu's invariant moments. Front. Robot. AI **7**, 591827 (2020). https://doi.org/10.3389/frobt.2020.591827

32. Shaikh, M.H., Panbude, S., Joshi, A.: Image segmentation techniques and its applications for knee joints: a survey. IOSR J. Electron. Commun. Eng. **9**(5), 23–28 (2014). https://doi.org/10.9790/2834-09542328

33. Pandey, M.S.: Science & Technology, no. April (2015)

34. Gornale, S.S., Patravali, P.U., Uppin, A.M., Hiremath, P.S.: Study of segmentation techniques for assessment of osteoarthritis in knee X-ray images. Int. J. Image Graph. Signal Process. **11**(2), 48–57 (2019). https://doi.org/10.5815/ijigsp.2019.02.06

35. Ahmed, S.M., Mstafa, R.J.: A comprehensive survey on bone segmentation techniques in knee osteoarthritis research: from conventional methods to deep learning. Diagnostics **12**(3), 611 (2022). https://doi.org/10.3390/diagnostics12030611

36. Shan, L., Zach, C., Charles, C., Niethammer, M.: Automatic atlas-based three-label cartilage segmentation from MR knee images. Med. Image Anal. **18**(7), 1233–1246 (Oct.2014). https://doi.org/10.1016/j.media.2014.05.008

37. Chaugule, S., Malemath, V.S.: Osteoarthritis detection using densely connected neural network. In: Santosh, K., Hegadi, R., Pal, U. (eds.) Recent Trends in Image Processing and Pattern Recognition, pp. 85–92. Springer, Cham (2022). https://doi.org/10.1007/978-3-031-07005-1_9

38. Hegadi, R.S., Navale, D.I., Pawar, T.D., Ruikar, D.D.: Osteoarthritis detection and classification from knee X-ray images based on artificial neural network. In: Santosh, K.C., Hegadi, R.S. (eds.) RTIP2R 2018. CCIS, vol. 1036, pp. 97–105. Springer, Singapore (2019). https://doi.org/10.1007/978-981-13-9184-2_8

39. Gornale, S.S., Patravali, P.U., Hiremath, P.S.: Detection of osteoarthritis in knee radiographic images using artificial neural network. Int. J. Innov. Technol. Explor. Eng. **8**(12), 2429–2434 (2019). https://doi.org/10.35940/ijitee.L3011.1081219

40. Hegadi, R.S., Navale, D.N., Pawar, T.D., Ruikar, D.D.: Multi-feature-based classification of osteoarthritis in knee joint X-ray images. In: Medical Imaging. Boca Raton: Taylor & Francis, a CRC title, part of the Taylor & Francis imprint, a member of the Taylor & Francis Group,

the academic division of T&F Informa, plc, 2020, pp. 74–96. CRC Press (2019). https://doi.org/10.1201/9780429029417-5

41. Jean De Dieu, U., et al.: Diagnosing knee osteoarthritis using artificial neural networks and deep learning. Biomed. Stat. Informatics 2(3), 95–102 (2017). https://doi.org/10.11648/j.bsi.20170203.11

42. Mahum, R., et al.: A novel hybrid approach based on deep CNN features to detect knee osteoarthritis. Sensors 21(18), 6189 (2021). https://doi.org/10.3390/s21186189

43. Karim, M.R., et al.: DeepKneeExplainer: explainable knee osteoarthritis diagnosis from radiographs and magnetic resonance imaging. IEEE Access 9, 39757–39780 (2021). https://doi.org/10.1109/ACCESS.2021.3062493

44. Chen, P.: Knee osteoarthritis severity grading dataset. Mendeley Data, vol. V1 (2018). https://doi.org/10.17632/56rmx5bjcr.1

45. Hammersberg, P., Stenström, M., Hedtjärn, H., Mångård, M.: Image noise in X-ray imaging caused by radiation scattering and source leakage, a qualitative and quantitative analysis. J. Xray. Sci. Technol. 8(1), 19–29 (1998). http://www.ncbi.nlm.nih.gov/pubmed/22388424

46. Sevinc, O., Mehrubeoglu, M., Guzel, M.S., Askerzade, I.: An effective medical image classification: transfer learning enhanced by auto encoder and classified with SVM. Trait. du Signal 39(1), 125–131 (2022). https://doi.org/10.18280/ts.390112

47. Huang, G.B., Zhu, Q.Y., Siew, C.K.: Extreme learning machine: theory and applications. Neurocomputing 70(1–3), 489–501 (2006). https://doi.org/10.1016/j.neucom.2005.12.126

48. Du, J., Vong, C.M., Chen, C., Liu, P., Liu, Z.: Supervised extreme learning machine-based auto-encoder for discriminative feature learning. IEEE Access 8, 11700–11709 (2020). https://doi.org/10.1109/ACCESS.2019.2962067

49. Nishio, M., et al.: Convolutional auto-encoders for image denoising of ultra-low-dose CT. Heliyon 3(8), e00393 (2017). https://doi.org/10.1016/j.heliyon.2017.e00393

50. Huang, G., Liu, Z., Pleiss, G., Van Der Maaten, L., Weinberger, K.: Convolutional networks with dense connectivity. IEEE Trans. Pattern Anal. Mach. Intell. 1 (2019). https://doi.org/10.1109/tpami.2019.2918284

51. Villa-Pulgarin, J.P., et al.: Optimized convolutional neural network models for skin lesion classification. Comput. Mater. Contin. 70(2), 2131–2148 (2022). https://doi.org/10.32604/cmc.2022.019529

52. Jaiswal, A., Gianchandani, N., Singh, D., Kumar, V., Kaur, M.: Classification of the COVID-19 infected patients using DenseNet201 based deep transfer learning. J. Biomol. Struct. Dyn. 39(15), 5682–5689 (2021). https://doi.org/10.1080/07391102.2020.1788642

Computer Vision and Pattern Recognition

Motor Imagery Classification Combining Riemannian Geometry and Artificial Neural Networks

Hubert Cecotti$^{(\boxtimes)}$ (iD) and Girish Tiwale (iD)

Department of Computer Science, California State University, Fresno, CA, USA
hcecotti@csufresno.edu

Abstract. Brain-computer interfaces (BCIs) based on non-invasive electroencephalography provide a means of communication for people with severe disabilities. BCI based on the detection of motor imagery can be used for both communication and rehabilitation purposes [8]. For transferring BCIs outside of the lab to clinical settings, it is necessary to have a high accuracy. The current state of the art techniques includes the use of distance based on the Riemannian geometry. In this paper, we propose a new pattern recognition system for the multiclass classification of brain evoked responses corresponding to motor imagery. The method is based on the combination of features based on Riemannian geometry obtained from 15 frequency bands from 8 24 Hz to cover the mu and beta bands, and a feedforward neural network for the classification. We compare the performance of the multi-layer perceptron (MLP) and the extreme learning machine (ELM) classifiers. The system has been assessed on two publicly available datasets. The kappa value for 4-class is 0.53. The average binary classification across the six pairwise tasks is 80.83%. The results support the conclusion that multi-band classification can be successfully achieved using artificial neural networks and MLPs provide substantially better performance than ELMs approaches.

Keywords: Brain-computer interface · Motor imagery · Classification

1 Introduction

Brain-Computer Interface (BCI) provides a direct communication path for individuals with motor disabilities [3]. The BCI translates the brain activity into commands that are further used to interact with the real world (e.g., to move a pointer on a computer screen or wheelchairs). BCI systems can be used as a new tool for improving the daily life of both physically challenged and normal human beings who are medically fit. BCIs have a lot of applications in the fields where neural prosthetics can be controlled by the signals emerging from them [11]. Non-invasive BCIs are based on electroencephalographic (EEG) activities with

This study was supported by the NIH-R15 NS118581 project.

KC Santosh et al. (Eds.): RTIP2R 2022, CCIS 1704, pp. 179–189, 2023.
https://doi.org/10.1007/978-3-031-23599-3_13

electrodes placed at the surface of the scalp. BCIs identify well defined patterns in EEG activity and classify the signals [3].

Motor Imagery (MI) is one of the most relevant BCI paradigms for people with severe disabilities. MI is the mental execution of an action without any muscle activation. However, it activates the same brain areas as the actual activity [15]. MI results in Event Related Synchronization (ERS) and desynchronization (ERD) [16]. The rhythms related to the activity are enhanced while others are desynchronized. Studies show that EEG related features are mostly present in the mu (8–13 Hz) and beta (13–25 Hz) bands [9,17,19]. Covariance matrices are often considered for the features extraction process. The covariance matrices are Symmetric Positive Definite (SPD). Since the Riemannian Geometry is the native space for the SPD matrices, Riemannian geometry is the optimal geometry to be considered [3]. Studies have shown that Riemannian geometry provides the framework for EEG data manipulation. The covariance matrices can be used and the Riemannian distance between the two covariance matrices can be used for the classification. However, these approaches have very high computational complexity when considering a high dimensional space: a large number of sensors and frequency bands. Thus, the problem becomes computationally expensive when the covariance matrices are very large [3]. For this reason, we extract features based on the covariance matrix for each frequency band. The main contributions of this paper are: 1) We propose to combine a density-based approach using Riemannian geometry with a discriminant approach using artificial neural networks to learn the relationships between frequency bands; 2) We compare feedforward artificial neural networks and extreme learning machines for the classification of the brain evoked responses. The remainder of the paper is organized as follows: The related works are described in the Sect. 2. The descriptions of the datasets and the methods are explained in Sect. 3. The results are presented in Sect. 4. Finally, the main contributions, results and future scope of the project are summarized in Sect. 5.

2   Related Works

The approach to tackle the classification of EEG problems is critical to obtain a robust system that can be deployed in clinical settings. There are many studies that have been carried out for the EEG data classification task.

2.1   Feature Extraction

For the features extraction, a lot of the studies are focused on filter bank approaches with the common spatial patterns (CSP) [1]. CSP detects patterns in the and creates spatial filters that are applied to the signal to compute the features that maximize the variance of 2 classes. Discriminating features can be extracted through a filter banks ranging 4 Hz 24 Hz with 4 Hz bandwidth [18]. Different methods are used by researchers for feature extraction purposes from the pre-processed EEG signals. The most widely used method is Principal component analysis (PCA), Independent Component Analysis (ICA) and Wavelet Transformations(WT) [12].

2.2   Classification

Multiple Riemannian geometry-based approaches have been proposed [4]. The features were extracted using Common Spatial Patterns (CSP). In the first method, the minimum distance to the Riemannian mean was implemented. In the second approach, the covariance matrices were mapped to the tangent space and these matrices were treated as Euclidean objects. The second method provided better results than the first minimum distance to the Riemannian Mean [4]. The most widely used classification approaches are Artificial Neural Networks (ANN), k-nearest neighbors (k-NN), LDA and SVM. The K-nearest neighbors' classifier with the help of cosine distance has also been tested over EEG signals and has performed quite well [7]. Convolutional neural networks (CNN) have been used for feature extraction and classification of MI tasks [21]. The studies have shown that CNN can improve the classification accuracy when combined with other discriminant approaches. However, it is said that the classifiers performance is dependent on the dataset. Thus, the selection of the best classifier depends on the characteristics of the dataset. Classification fusion is being adapted by many researchers for improving BCI performance [10].

The most widely used density-based approach is the use of Riemannian geometry. The Riemannian geometry-based approaches have state-of-the-art results on BCI applications. Though this approach is not one of the most commonly used, it needs to be explored more [13]. In the case of EEG data, a covariance matrix is formed through spatial filters computation. Covariance matrices lie in the Symmetric Positive Definite Matrices (SPD) and hence in the Riemannian geometry domain [3]. Thanks to this property of covariance matrices, we can use distance with Riemannian geometry.

3   Methods

3.1   Database

In this study, we consider two datasets, which are freely available on BNCI Horizon 2020 project website [5,20]. The first dataset was originally released by the Institute for Knowledge Discovery (Laboratory of Brain-Computer Interfaces), Graz University of Technology (Austria) as data set 2a of the BCI Competition IV. The dataset consists of recorded signals from 9 different subjects. It has four different motor imagery tasks: left hand movement (class 1), right hand movement (class 2), both feet movement (class 3) and tongue (class 4). Each session consisted of 6 runs and each run had 12 trials for each class, i.e., 48 trials in total per run. Overall, each session contains 288 trials; some trials are removed using the information corresponding to the presence of artefacts in the signal. The experimental paradigm is described in Fig. 1, with the different events happening at each trial, and the electrode placement.

The dataset contains the data from 22 different EEG channels that were recorded using electrodes sampled at 250–Hz. and band-pass filtered between 0.5–100 Hz. Additional notch filter 50 Hz was enabled [6]. In this study, we considered 17 of the 22 electrodes (FC3, FC1, FCz, FC2, FC4, C5, C3, C1, Cz, C2, C4, C6, CP3, CP1, CPz, CP2 and CP4) that covered the central area of the scalp.

The second dataset contains EEG signals from 14 participants with a motor imagery task (right vs. feet), using 15 sensors including C3, Cz, and C4. The sampling rate 512 Hz. The training has 5 runs of 20 trials; the test has 3 runs of 20 trials. It corresponds to 100 and 60 examples for training and the test, respectively.

We consider a time segment of duration 3 s, after 3 s post-trial onset. Therefore, we have $N_c = 17$ and $N_t = 3 \cdot f_s = 750$. We bandpass the signal in the following 15 frequency bands in 4 groups: 1) 8–10, 10–12, 12–14, 14–16, 16–18, 18–20, 20–22, 22 24; 2) 8–12, 12–16, 16–20, 20–24; 3) 8–16, 16–24; 4) 8–24 Hz.

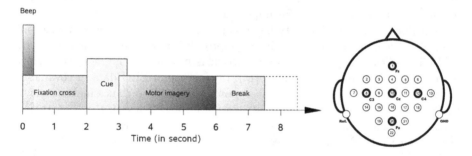

Fig. 1. Experimental paradigm and placement of the electrodes.

Table 1. Kappa values for 4 classes with different sets of frequency bands (dataset 1).

Subject	Set 1	Set 2	Set 3	Set 4
A01	0.28	0.59	0.62	0.69
A02	0.18	0.35	0.38	0.38
A03	0.52	0.78	0.63	0.68
A04	0.18	0.32	0.45	0.43
A05	0.13	0.13	0.11	0.16
A06	0.23	0.13	0.18	0.24
A07	0.52	0.63	0.61	0.55
A08	0.29	0.42	0.59	0.56
A09	0.34	0.53	0.67	0.58
Mean	0.3	0.43	0.47	0.47
SD	0.14	0.22	0.21	0.19

Table 2. Kappa values for 2 classes with different sets of frequency bands (dataset 2).

Subject	Set 1	Set 2	Set 3	Set 4
1	0.32	0.28	0.12	0.17
2	0.65	0.46	0.37	0.34
3	1.00	1.00	1.00	1.00
4	0.64	0.67	0.63	0.63
5	0.06	0.08	0.21	−0.04
6	0.03	0.53	0.60	0.57
7	0.39	0.64	0.72	0.65
8	0.85	0.69	0.73	0.73
9	0.54	0.63	0.63	0.56
10	0.09	0.05	0.12	−0.08
11	0.15	0.10	0.07	0.30
12	0.29	0.28	0.24	0.18
13	0.37	−0.05	0.11	0.05
14	0.17	0.17	0.15	0.04
Mean	0.40	0.40	0.41	0.36
SD	0.30	0.31	0.30	0.33

3.2 Features Extraction

The feature extraction process is based on the Riemannian geometry framework. We consider P_i a tangent vector at Q. $D(t)$ is the geodesic between Q and Q_i [9]. The Riemannian manifold Z is a differentiable manifold. At each point, there lies a tangent space, and it is a finite-dimensional Euclidean space [14]. It contains the Symmetric and Positive Definite matrix i.e., the covariance matrix $Q(N_c)$. The vector space T_Q over the manifold Z contains the tangent space for the derivatives of a covariance matrix Q. The dimension of the tangent space and the manifold is provided by: $d_{ts} = (N_c(N_c + 1))/2$. We consider 2 data points, Q_1 and Q_2 corresponding to 2 covariance matrices. The geodesic distance on the manifold is the minimum length curve joining Q_1 and Q_2. It is defined by:

$$\delta_R(Q_1, Q_2) = \left\| log(Q_1^{-1} Q_2) \right\|_F = \left[\sum_{i=1}^{N_c} log^2 \lambda_i \right]^{1/2} \tag{1}$$

where λ_i, i $= 1,\dots,N_c$ are the real eigenvalues of $Q_1^{-1} Q_2$ and N_c is the number of channels. Each tangent vector P_i is seen as the derivative at $t = 0$ of the geodesic $D_i(t)$ between exponential mapping $Q_i = Exp_Q\,(P_i)$ and Q, Q defined as:

$$Exp_Q(P_i) = Q_i = Q^{1/2} exp(Q^{-1/2} P_i Q^{-1/2}) Q^{1/2} \tag{2}$$

The logarithmic mapping gives the inverse mapping which is defined as,

$$Log_Q(Q_i) = P_i = Q^{1/2} log(Q^{-1/2} Q_i Q^{-1/2}) Q^{1/2} \tag{3}$$

The Riemannian mean of $J \times 1$ SPD matrices in terms of geodesic distance is given by:

$$G(Q_1, \ldots, Q_J) = \underset{Q \in Q(N_c)}{\arg\min} \sum_{i=1}^{J} \delta_R^2(Q, Q_i) \tag{4}$$

Considering 1×1 SPD matrices $y_i > 0_{1 \times J}$, this definition gives:

$$G(y1, \ldots, yJ) = \sqrt[J]{y1, \ldots, yJ} \tag{5}$$

For each MI classification task, we calculated the class-wise covariance matrices $Q_G^{(c)}$, where $= [1: K]$ depicts the class indices. A Riemannian distance algorithm has been used to compute the distance between class-wise covariance matrix $Q_G^{(c)}$ and an unknown test trial.

3.3 Classification

We consider two types of feedforward artificial neural network: the multi-layer perceptron (MLP) and the extreme learning machine (ELM). We have not considered convolutional neural networks because there is no real underlying structure in the input features. With the MLP, weights are learnt between the input and hidden layer, between the hidden layer and the output layer, while with the ELM, random projections are performed between the input layer and the hidden layer, so only the weights between the hidden and last layer are tuned in relation to the data and the ground truth. This comparison allows us to determine the extent to which it is necessary to learn weights between the input layer and the hidden layer. For each classifier, we consider 10 runs to account for the weight initialization. The input layer contains $N_{freq} \times N_{class}$, 60 features for 15 frequency bands and 4 classes. For the multi-class performance, we report the kappa value which is defined by:

$$\kappa = \frac{p_o - p_e}{1 - p_e} \tag{6}$$

where p_o is the accuracy and p_e is the probability of chance agreement, $p_e = 1/N_{class}$.

4   Results

The performances using the Kappa values for the multi-class classification (dataset 1) using the different MLPs across the different participants are presented in Table 3. The performances for the different ELMs are given in Table 4. For the MLP, the best performance is obtained with $nh = 250$ with a Kappa value of 0.53 ± 0.19. The performance with ELMs is substantially inferior, the best performance is obtained with $nh = 100$ with a Kappa value of 0.36 ± 0.20. For the best MLP, we report the binary classification tasks for the 6 possible

Table 3. Kappa values with MLPs for the multiclass classification (dataset 1).

Subject	MLP1 nh=50	MLP2 nh=100	MLP3 nh=150	MLP4 nh=200	MLP5 nh=250	MLP6 nh=300
A01	0.54 ± 0.06	0.54 ± 0.03	0.57 ± 0.05	0.57 ± 0.05	0.58 ± 0.06	0.55 ± 0.05
A02	0.43 ± 0.02	0.44 ± 0.02	0.43 ± 0.02	0.44 ± 0.03	0.43 ± 0.01	0.44 ± 0.02
A03	0.81 ± 0.02	0.81 ± 0.02	0.81 ± 0.02	0.81 ± 0.01	0.81 ± 0.01	0.81 ± 0.01
A04	0.45 ± 0.05	0.42 ± 0.06	0.42 ± 0.04	0.44 ± 0.03	0.42 ± 0.03	0.42 ± 0.04
A05	0.18 ± 0.05	0.17 ± 0.04	0.19 ± 0.02	0.2 ± 0.03	0.17 ± 0.02	0.19 ± 0.02
A06	0.32 ± 0.03	0.34 ± 0.03	0.36 ± 0.03	0.36 ± 0.02	0.36 ± 0.04	0.37 ± 0.04
A07	0.64 ± 0.02	0.65 ± 0.03	0.64 ± 0.01	0.64 ± 0.02	0.64 ± 0.03	0.65 ± 0.01
A08	0.69 ± 0.01	0.69 ± 0.02	0.68 ± 0.03	0.68 ± 0.03	0.68 ± 0.03	0.67 ± 0.02
A09	0.61 ± 0.04	0.62 ± 0.05	0.61 ± 0.06	0.62 ± 0.05	0.61 ± 0.06	0.62 ± 0.04
Mean	0.52 ± 0.03	0.52 ± 0.03	0.52 ± 0.03	0.53 ± 0.03	0.52 ± 0.03	0.52 ± 0.03
SD	0.20 ± 0.02	0.20 ± 0.01	0.19 ± 0.02	0.19 ± 0.01	0.19 ± 0.02	0.19 ± 0.01

Table 4. Kappa values with ELMs for the multiclass classification (dataset 1).

Subject	ELM1 nh = 100	ELM2 nh = 200	ELM3 nh = 500	ELM4 nh = 1000	ELM5 nh = 2000	ELM6 nh = 5000
A01	0.37 ± 0.08	0.18 ± 0.11	0.25 ± 0.05	0.3 ± 0.06	0.33 ± 0.06	0.38 ± 0.03
A02	0.32 ± 0.04	0.21 ± 0.06	0.23 ± 0.05	0.26 ± 0.06	0.27 ± 0.04	0.28 ± 0.02
A03	0.71 ± 0.05	0.47 ± 0.08	0.54 ± 0.07	0.62 ± 0.05	0.65 ± 0.05	0.64 ± 0.04
A04	0.22 ± 0.05	0.12 ± 0.05	0.12 ± 0.06	0.1 ± 0.05	0.1 ± 0.02	0.1 ± 0.03
A05	0.1 ± 0.06	0.04 ± 0.04	0.04 ± 0.03	0.06 ± 0.03	0.05 ± 0.02	0.05 ± 0.02
A06	0.13 ± 0.05	0.06 ± 0.05	0.1 ± 0.05	0.11 ± 0.03	0.1 ± 0.04	0.08 ± 0.03
A07	0.52 ± 0.06	0.38 ± 0.06	0.46 ± 0.05	0.45 ± 0.03	0.49 ± 0.02	0.49 ± 0.03
A08	0.48 ± 0.08	0.25 ± 0.09	0.31 ± 0.08	0.39 ± 0.04	0.38 ± 0.03	0.42 ± 0.04
A09	0.41 ± 0.05	0.25 ± 0.09	0.33 ± 0.06	0.32 ± 0.04	0.36 ± 0.04	0.37 ± 0.04
Mean	0.36 ± 0.06	0.22 ± 0.07	0.26 ± 0.06	0.29 ± 0.04	0.30 ± 0.04	0.31 ± 0.03
SD	0.20 ± 0.01	0.14 ± 0.02	0.17 ± 0.01	0.18 ± 0.01	0.20 ± 0.01	0.20 ± 0.01

combinations in Table 7. The average accuracy for Left vs Right, Left vs Foot, Left vs Tongue, Right vs Feet, Right vs Tongue, Feet vs Tongue is 73.88 ± 16.64, 84.12 ± 13.69, 85.25 ± 10.75, 83.96 ± 11.53, 83.34 ± 12.48, and 74.45 ± 11.63. The four different sets of frequency bands are evaluated separately and presented in Table 1 for dataset 1 and Table 2 for dataset 2. The sets 4 and 3 provide better performances than sets 1 and 2, which contain more bands. The four sets cover the same frequencies but the resolution is different (2, 4, 8, 16 Hz for the sets 1, 2, 3, and 4). The same pattern of performance is observed for the binary classification with dataset 2 (see Tables 5 and 6). It is possible to reach a kappa value with the MLP while the kappa value reaches only 0.43 with the ELM approach. The multi-class performance is compared with key state of the art algorithms from the literature in Table 8. It shows relatively similar results compared to

Table 5. Kappa values with MLPs for the binary classification (dataset 2).

Subject	MLP1 nh = 50	MLP2 nh = 100	MLP3 nh = 150	MLP4 nh = 200	MLP5 nh = 250	MLP6 nh = 300
1	0.43 ± 0.07	0.38 ± 0.06	0.46 ± 0.06	0.45 ± 0.05	0.45 ± 0.09	0.45 ± 0.05
2	0.61 ± 0.04	0.62 ± 0.04	0.65 ± 0.04	0.61 ± 0.04	0.61 ± 0.03	0.63 ± 0.04
3	1.00 ± 0.01	1.00 ± 0.00	1.00 ± 0.00	1.00 ± 0.01	1.00 ± 0.00	1.00 ± 0.00
4	0.73 ± 0.02	0.74 ± 0.03	0.74 ± 0.04	0.76 ± 0.02	0.76 ± 0.02	0.76 ± 0.01
5	0.25 ± 0.14	0.27 ± 0.06	0.28 ± 0.07	0.28 ± 0.11	0.29 ± 0.10	0.34 ± 0.06
6	0.63 ± 0.05	0.61 ± 0.04	0.60 ± 0.05	0.60 ± 0.02	0.61 ± 0.04	0.58 ± 0.04
7	0.67 ± 0.06	0.65 ± 0.03	0.65 ± 0.02	0.67 ± 0.04	0.66 ± 0.04	0.63 ± 0.02
8	0.79 ± 0.02	0.79 ± 0.02	0.78 ± 0.03	0.81 ± 0.03	0.80 ± 0.02	0.80 ± 0.02
9	0.70 ± 0.02	0.74 ± 0.06	0.72 ± 0.04	0.75 ± 0.04	$0.75 \pm .04$	0.74 ± 0.05
10	0.04 ± 0.10	0.09 ± 0.07	0.06 ± 0.05	0.05 ± 0.11	0.07 ± 0.06	0.06 ± 0.07
11	0.21 ± 0.09	0.13 ± 0.04	0.16 ± 0.05	0.17 ± 0.06	0.19 ± 0.06	0.14 ± 0.04
12	0.37 ± 0.10	0.42 ± 0.08	0.36 ± 0.08	0.34 ± 0.07	0.39 ± 0.08	0.34 ± 0.03
13	0.26 ± 0.11	0.23 ± 0.06	0.26 ± 0.09	0.26 ± 0.11	0.32 ± 0.07	0.26 ± 0.10
14	0.20 ± 0.08	0.17 ± 0.05	$0.21 0.08$	0.20 ± 0.10	0.16 ± 0.06	0.17 ± 0.05
Mean	0.49 ± 0.07	0.49 ± 0.05	0.50 ± 0.05	0.50 ± 0.06	0.50 ± 0.05	0.49 ± 0.04
SD	0.28 ± 0.04	0.28 ± 0.02	0.28 ± 0.02	0.29 ± 0.04	0.28 ± 0.03	0.28 ± 0.03

Table 6. Kappa values with ELMs for the binary classification (dataset 2).

Subject	ELM1 nh = 100	ELM2 nh = 200	ELM3 nh = 500	ELM4 nh = 1000	ELM5 nh = 2000	ELM6 nh = 5000
1	0.01 ± 0.14	0.15 ± 0.12	0.30 ± 0.12	0.31 ± 0.09	0.37 ± 0.05	0.35 ± 0.07
2	0.05 ± 0.12	0.37 ± 0.16	0.41 ± 0.14	0.49 ± 0.09	0.50 ± 0.06	0.47 ± 0.08
3	0.40 ± 0.51	0.99 ± 0.01	1.00 ± 0.00	1.00 ± 0.00	1.00 ± 0.00	1.00 ± 0.00
4	0.11 ± 0.19	0.61 ± 0.12	0.70 ± 0.06	0.70 ± 0.06	0.72 ± 0.03	0.71 ± 0.01
5	0.01 ± 0.14	0.06 ± 0.11	0.07 ± 0.14	0.16 ± 0.15	0.15 ± 0.07	0.17 ± 0.11
6	0.13 ± 0.19	0.47 ± 0.13	0.56 ± 0.04	0.60 ± 0.05	0.59 ± 0.04	0.60 ± 0.04
7	0.09 ± 0.16	0.55 ± 0.07	0.66 ± 0.07	0.68 ± 0.05	0.68 ± 0.04	0.69 ± 0.03
8	0.22 ± 0.29	0.75 ± 0.03	0.75 ± 0.04	0.80 ± 0.01	0.79 ± 0.03	0.80 ± 0.02
9	0.17 ± 0.16	0.61 ± 0.05	0.63 ± 0.08	0.70 ± 0.06	0.70 ± 0.05	0.71 ± 0.04
10	-0.02 ± 0.14	-0.02 ± 0.09	0.02 ± 0.06	0.04 ± 0.05	0.03 ± 0.06	0.04 ± 0.06
11	0.07 ± 0.10	0.13 ± 0.11	0.13 ± 0.08	0.10 ± 0.05	0.09 ± 0.04	0.09 ± 0.03
12	0.06 ± 0.16	0.21 ± 0.13	0.16 ± 0.08	0.18 ± 0.04	0.13 ± 0.04	0.15 ± 0.04
13	0.02 ± 0.10	0.06 ± 0.07	0.09 ± 0.06	0.16 ± 0.07	0.16 ± 0.08	0.14 ± 0.08
14	0.00 ± 0.14	0.14 ± 0.06	0.14 ± 0.05	0.12 ± 0.06	0.13 ± 0.04	0.13 ± 0.04
Mean	0.09 ± 0.18	0.36 ± 0.09	0.40 ± 0.07	0.43 ± 0.06	0.43 ± 0.05	0.43 ± 0.05
SD	0.11 ± 0.11	0.30 ± 0.04	0.31 ± 0.04	0.31 ± 0.03	0.32 ± 0.02	0.32 ± 0.03

other approaches. It is worth noting the difference that exists across subjects when comparing approaches.

Table 7. Binary classification accuracy with MLP4.

Subject	LvsR	LvsF	LvsT	RvsF	RvsT	FvsT
A01	81.42	95.29	83.59	85.25	98.94	72.93
A02	52.96	87.5	71.19	86.5	75.17	85.11
A03	94.16	97.63	93.63	99.06	97.54	84.19
A04	74.14	88.05	89.2	94.31	84.45	62.68
A05	54	65.07	69.28	68.18	67.46	56.31
A06	51.57	66.64	75.94	73.21	66.48	71.03
A07	84.29	96.13	93.5	97.36	96.74	65.4
A08	84.63	67.63	92.31	80.66	79.26	82.12
A09	87.77	93.13	98.62	71.12	84	90.3
Mean	73.88	84.12	85.25	83.96	83.34	74.45
SD	16.64	13.69	10.75	11.53	12.48	11.63

Table 8. Comparison with state-of-the-art methods.

Subject	MLP	MDRM [2]	Winner 1	Winner 2	Winner 3
A01	0.57	0.75	0.68	0.69	0.38
A02	0.44	0.37	0.42	0.34	0.18
A03	0.81	0.66	0.75	0.71	0.48
A04	0.44	0.53	0.48	0.44	0.33
A05	0.20	0.29	0.4	0.16	0.07
A06	0.36	0.27	0.27	0.21	0.14
A07	0.64	0.56	0.77	0.66	0.29
A08	0.68	0.58	0.75	0.73	0.49
A09	0.62	0.68	0.61	0.69	0.44
Mean	0.53	0.52	0.57	0.51	0.31
SD	0.19	0.17	0.18	0.23	0.15

5   Discussion and Conclusion

The efficiency of Brain-Computer Interfaces based on motor imagery is directly related to the accuracy of motor imagery detection. The classification of motor imagery is a difficult problem as the features are in the frequency domain and they require some specific processing steps to be enhanced. Such steps typically include temporal and spatial filtering. Contrary to the common spatial pattern approach that first creates spatial filters for enhancing the signal, the proposed approach uses covariance matrices for all the different frequency bands. Therefore, instead of having a single Riemannian distance between two covariance matrices, we obtain multiple distances that can then be used as features for another classifier. In this case, we combine sequentially two types of approaches:

a density-based method using the distance to the mean for each frequency band and each class, and then a discriminant approach for combining the distances to the means into a single decision. We have compared MLP and ELM approaches for the classification of these features and shown that the ELM gives the best kappa value (0.36) in the multi-class problem with 100 hidden units while the MLP gives better results for the same number of hidden units (0.52). The best performance is reached with 200 hidden units but there is no significant difference when comparing the number of hidden units, from 50 to 300.

The response occurring during the time segment is not fixed at a particular time like event-related potentials, but it may fluctuate, and multiple responses could be combined. In this study, we have only focused on a single segment within the time segment of interest. While there are statistical differences across participants between the different methods, it appears that some methods work better for some participants than some others. Further work will include the combination of different approaches to enhance overall accuracy.

We have proposed to combine features extracted from distances to the mean using the Riemannian geometry framework and classifiers based on feedforward artificial neural networks. The MLP provides a better performance compared to the ELM classifier and shows it is necessary to learn the weights between the input and hidden layers, the random projections with the ELM approach do not provide a high level of performance. Finally, we have shown the interest of using different sets of frequency bands with different sizes covering the mu and beta bands.

References

1. Ang, K.K., Chin, Z.Y., Wang, C., Guan, C., Zhang, H.: Filter bank common spatial pattern algorithm on BCI competition iv datasets 2a and 2b. Front. Neurosci. **6**, 39 (2012)
2. Barachant, A., Bonnet, S., Congedo, M., Jutten, C.: Multiclass brain-computer interface classification by riemannian geometry. IEEE Trans. on Biomed. Eng. **59**, 920–928 (2012)
3. Barachant, A., Bonnet, S., Congedo, M., Jutten, C.: Riemannian geometry applied to BCI classification. In: Vigneron, V., Zarzoso, V., Moreau, E., Gribonval, R., Vincent, E. (eds.) LVA/ICA 2010. LNCS, vol. 6365, pp. 629–636. Springer, Heidelberg (2010). https://doi.org/10.1007/978-3-642-15995-4_78
4. Barachant, A., Bonnet, S., Congedo, M., Jutten, C.: Multiclass brain-computer interface classification by riemannian geometry. IEEE Trans. on Biomed. Eng. **59**(4), 920–928 (2011)
5. Brunner, C.: Four class motor imagery (001–2014) (2020). http://bnci-horizon-2020.eu/database/data-sets
6. Brunner, C., Leeb, R., Müller-Putz, G., Schlögl, A., Pfurtscheller, G.: BCI competition 2008-graz data set a. Institute for Knowledge Discovery (Laboratory of Brain-Computer Interfaces), Graz University of Technology, vol. 16, pp. 1–6 (2008)
7. Chatterjee, R., Sanyal, D.K.: Study of different filter bank approaches in motor-imagery EEG. Smart Health. Analy. IoT Enabled Environ. **178**, 173 (2020)

8. Chowdhury, A., et al.: Active physical practice followed by mental practice using bci-driven hand exoskeleton: A pilot trial for clinical effectiveness and usability. IEEE J. Biomed. Health Inform. **22**(6), 1786–1795 (2018). https://doi.org/10.1109/JBHI.2018.2863212

9. Gaur, P., Pachori, R.B., Wang, H., Prasad, G.: A multi-class EEG-based BCI classification using multivariate empirical mode decomposition based filtering and riemannian geometry. Expert Syst. Appl. **95**, 201–211 (2018)

10. Ilyas, M.Z., Saad, P., Ahmad, M.I.: A survey of analysis and classification of EEG signals for brain-computer interfaces. In: 2015 2nd International Conference on Biomedical Engineering (ICoBE), pp. 1–6. IEEE (2015)

11. Khasnobish, A., Bhattacharyya, S., Konar, A., Tibarewala, D.: K-nearest neighbor classification of left-right limb movement using EEG data. In: Oral Presentation In International Conference On Biomedical Engineering And Assistive Technologies, NIT Jalandhar (2010)

12. Lakshmi, M.R., Prasad, T., Prakash, D.V.C.: Survey on EEG signal processing methods. Int. J. Adv. Res. Comput. Sci. Softw. Eng. **4**(1), 195–212 (2014)

13. Lotte, F., Congedo, M., Lécuyer, A., Lamarche, F., Arnaldi, B.: A review of classification algorithms for EEG-based brain-computer interfaces. J. Neural Eng. **4**(2), R1 (2007)

14. Moakher, M.: A differential geometric approach to the geometric mean of symmetric positive-definite matrices. SIAM J. Matrix Anal. Appl. **26**(3), 735–747 (2005)

15. Mulder, T.: Motor imagery and action observation: cognitive tools for rehabilitation. J. Neural Transm. **114**(10), 1265–1278 (2007)

16. Pfurtscheller, G.: Functional brain imaging based on erd/ers. Vision. Res. **41**(10–11), 1257–1260 (2001)

17. Raza, H., Cecotti, H., Li, Y., Prasad, G.: Adaptive learning with covariate shift-detection for motor imagery based brain-computer interface. Soft. Comput. **20**(8), 3085–3096 (2016)

18. Raza, H., Cecotti, H., Prasad, G.: Optimising frequency band selection with forward-addition and backward-elimination algorithms in EEG-based brain-computer interfaces. In: Proceedings of the International Joint Conference on Neural Networks, pp. 1–7 (2015)

19. Raza, H., Rathee, D., Zhou, S.M., Cecotti, H., Prasad, G.: Covariate shift estimation based adaptive ensemble learning for handling non-stationarity in motor imagery related EEG-based brain-computer interface. Neurocomputing **343**, 154–166 (2018)

20. Steyrl, D.: Two class motor imagery (002–2014) (2020). http://bnci-horizon-2020.eu/database/data-sets

21. Tang, Z., Li, C., Sun, S.: Single-trial EEG classification of motor imagery using deep convolutional neural networks. Optik **130**, 11–18 (2017)

Autism Spectrum Disorder Detection Using Transfer Learning with VGG 19, Inception V3 and DenseNet 201

Md. Fazlay Rabbi[1]([✉])[iD], Fatema Tuz Zohra[1][iD], Farhana Hossain[1][iD],
Naznin Nahar Akhi[1][iD], Shakil Khan[1][iD], Kawsher Mahbub[1][iD],
and Milon Biswas[2][iD]

[1] Department of Computer Science and Engineering, Bangladesh University
of Business and Technology, Dhaka, Bangladesh
`fazlay.rabbi7a@gmail.com`
[2] Department of Computer Science, The University of Alabama at Birmingham,
Birmingham, AL, USA

Abstract. A person with autism or autism spectrum disorder (ASD)
has trouble recognizing, socializing, and communicating with others.
ASD is not only about one situation. In fact, it has numerous groups
of situations. Although it cannot be fully recovered, the right treatments
and services can help a person's symptoms and daily activities. Deep
learning has achieved outstanding results in pattern recognition tasks
in the current times. CNN-based methods are widely suggested for the
research. By taking proper care, children can improve easily. For this,
we decided to work on autism in children through image classification
for early detection. Early detection can help children provide strength
and capability for a better life. It can lessen children's symptoms and
can improve their normal development by assisting them to analyze new
capabilities as a way to allow them to be independent for the rest of
their lives. To deal with these difficulties, the right guidelines and strategies can help a lot. To provide the necessary guidelines in time, early
detection is very important. We employed deep learning techniques to
conduct our research utilizing the image dataset. We tried to implement
a method that can detect autism in children through facial expressions.
In this research, we use VGG 19, Inception V3, and DenseNet 201.

Keywords: Autism · ASD · Facial image · Transfer learning · Binary
classification · Deep learning · Confusion matrix · VGG 19 · Inception
V3 · DenseNet 201 · CNN · Preprocessing · Recall · Precision · F1
score

1 Introduction

Almost we all heard the word "Autism" in our life. But we aren't fully aware
of the fact that what it is unless someone in our own family is suffering from

KC Santosh et al. (Eds.): RTIP2R 2022, CCIS 1704, pp. 190–204, 2023.
https://doi.org/10.1007/978-3-031-23599-3_14

it. "The world health organization (WHO) estimates that one in 100 children [30] worldwide have ASD." Autism signs are typically easy to spot before the age of five. The conduct and interpersonal communication of the person being diagnosed with ASD are the key areas of focus. It is unknown how common autism is in many low- and middle-income nations. In the past, screening equipment was used to catch instances earlier and began therapy as soon as possible which sometimes gave the most successful outcomes. It is found in research that approximately 30% of children with autism have less extreme signs and symptoms at age 6 years than at 3 years. It is far surprising to see that some children appear to get better dramatically while others do not. But it is an encouraging sign that seems to indicate that autism doesn't worsen with age and can get much better with time in some cases. Deep learning has demonstrated incredible performance in the area of pattern recognition in recent times. Numerous CNN-based methodologies are being suggested for evaluation. Neuro images in ASD patients can be interpreted using CNN techniques. The researchers discovered that 2.53% of the eligible individuals had been identified with ASD between 2014 and 2019. The current rate of autism worldwide shows that the common occurrence of ASD around the world is growing day by day. Today, it is crucial to identify ASD in children as soon as possible. Due to the lack of a conventional medical testing system for ASD, diagnosing it may be difficult. In fact, diagnosis is completed by searching the child's developmental records and behavior. 'Deep Learning' models have advanced tremendously as a consequence of years of study by numerous scientists and researchers. There are many models of this type that can be used to categorize autism. We can efficiently diagnose autism using a variety of CNN-based techniques.

2   Review of Literature

Over the years, there has been an upsurge in autism. The condition affects people from all races and socioeconomic backgrounds. "Approximately 1.8% of children in the United States have been diagnosed with autism, a figure that has more than doubled over the past 20 years, based on a WHO (World Health Organization) report from 2022. It is estimated that 1 in 160 individuals globally has autism and that 1 in 100 children have ASD [30]." Today, adequate medical care, successful interventions, therapies, and treatments significantly enhance the quality of life for children with autism. "With the use of three pre-trained models-MobileNet (95% accuracy), Xception (94%), and InceptionV3 (89%), Ahmed, Z.A. et al. [3] created a deep learning-based online application for autism detection." "A face-based attention recognition model was suggested by Banire, B. et al. [6] employing two techniques: an SVM classifier and a CNN method for converting time-domain spatial data into 2D spatial images." "Li, G., Liu, et al. [15] suggested a patch-level data-expanding approach to multi-channel CNN and obtained respectable accuracy for an early autism diagnosis." To extract the features from unlabeled videos, Liang, S et al. [16] developed an unsupervised feature-learning technique. The technique can produce results with an accuracy of 98.3%. Khosla, Y et al. [13]

achieved 87% accuracy using pre-trained deep learning models - MobileNet, InceptionV3, and ResNetV2.Facial expressions, AUs, arousal, and valence were used in an end-to-end method for Autism categorization developed by Li, B. et al. [14]. Autism detection ability was enhanced by approximately 7% with 76% f1 score, as evidenced by the use of several facial attribute representations. "A CNN classifier model was suggested by Jahanara, S. et al. [12] to identify autism. The pre-trained ImageNet VGG19 version, ReLU actuation Function, Adam Optimizer, and categorical cross-entropy loss function all have been employed in CNN and have produced results that are significantly more accurate than the conventional method of diagnosis." "A method to diagnose ASD based on anthropometric facial traits that may distinguish between ASD and TD was proposed by Michelassi, G.C. et al. [19], and the best result was obtained by an SVM classifier with 86.2% accuracy." Sumi, A.I. et al. [24] developed a system that gathers information from four distinct sensors (GPS, heart rate, accelerometer, and sound). The system also uses a fuzzy rule-based approach. "Afrin, M. et al. [1] suggested an artificial intelligence (AI)-based solution for autistic kids and demonstrated a recognition performance based on the LDPv descriptor." Taj-Eldin, M. et al. [25] talked on the usefulness of wearable physiological and emotion monitoring equipment for patients with ASD. Additionally, they contrasted their sensing capacities and investigated the literature on cutting-edge prototypes, clinical validity, and clinical viewpoints. Yolcu, G. et al. [31] proposed a deep learning strategy for recognizing facial expressions with four CNN structures and obtained a 5% success rate higher than the face recognition system using raw photos. "Duda, M. et al. [10] employed machine learning to distinguish between autism and ADHD. SVC, LDA, Categorical Lasso, and Logistic Regression performed with an accuracy of 93%, corresponding to a 92% reduction in the number of behaviors recorded with the standard SRS." LeNet, GoogLeNet, AlexNet, VGGNet, and ResNet were utilized by Beary, M. et al. [8] to categorize children as either healthy or autistic. The SVM model is thought to be the most often used technique to acquire ASD classification, according to research and analysis done by Thabtah, F. [26]. Al Banna, M. et al. [5] evaluated emotional state using an AI-based emotion detection system and discovered sensor data for autistic patients. "With an F1 score of 95% and an accuracy of 95%, Lu, A. et al. [17] proposed a feasible ASD screening method that uses face pictures and the VGG16 model to identify children with ASD." "In [32], children with ASD and TD were subjected to eye tracking while talking face-to-face with interviewers. Four ML classifiers - SVM, LDA, DT, and RF-were employed to implement forward feature selection in order to achieve the highest classification accuracy." "In [2], for the classification of ASD, the authors created three AI-based techniques: FFNNs, ANNs, and LBP." "Baranwal, A. et al. [7] employed Artificial Neural Networks (ANN), Random Forest, Logistic Regression, Decision Tree, and SVM as part of a dataset screening technique to detect ASD in adults, kids, and teenagers." "Rani, P. et al. [21] used image processing and machine learning methods to identify emotions in autistic kids by analyzing their facial gestures." "Thabtah, F et al. [27] suggested an AI technique that maintains sensitivity, specificity, and accuracy." "Mazumdar, P. et al. [18] described a method for identifying children with ASD that uses data from both eye-tracking and machine learning." "A CNN-based model may be more helpful than other traditional machine learning classifiers to detect autism, according to Raj, S. et al. [20], who employed a variety of machine learning and deep learning approaches to do so." "In [4], to develop classifiers to identify ASD, authors pre-processed autism datasets and suggested a machine learning approach." "Satu, M.S. et al. [22] discussed autism in Bangladesh's divisional regions and used the J48, Logistic Model Tree, Random Forest, and Reduced Error Pruned Tree. J48 produced the best results." Thomas, M. et al. [28] introduced an original approach for identifying ASD that makes use of ANN. For the diagnosis of ASD, structural and functional MRIs were performed. Buffle, P, et al. [9] offered information to understand the requirements and difficulties faced by pediatric practitioners with the detection of ASD. "In [11], authors applied deep learning algorithms to identify ASD patients using the brain imaging dataset to identify ASD patients, and they reported achieving 70% accuracy." From sparse-array raw EEG signals, authors [29] utilized a CNN model to distinguish between facial emotions seen by people with and without ASD. In order to socially communicate with autistic kids, Silva, V. et al. [23] created an automated system that recognizes emotions from facial features and interacts with them with a robotic platform.

The literature study demonstrates that autism has had a significant negative impact on children's lives and that this impact is growing daily. Doctors and researchers are working constantly to treat the child. Although we have seen some uses of machine learning techniques, we believe there is still much to be done. Therefore, we made the decision to employ transfer learning with the most recent innovations in order to quickly and reasonably identify the autistic child and assist their guardians in improving the child's condition by taking necessary actions.

Table 1. Literature review

Authors Name	ACC (%)	AUC (%)	Sensitivity (%)	Specificity (%)
Raj, S. et al. [20]	98.30	–	96.78	100.0
Zhao, Z. et.al [32]	92.31	92.0	84.21	100.0
Baranwal, A et.al. [7]	96.77	98.96	100.0	93.55
Akter, T et al. [4]	99.32	99.29	99.32	99.27
Li, B et.al [14]	76.0	–	76.0	69.0
Pramit et.al [18]	59.00	–	68.00	50.00
Ahmed, I.A et.al [2]	97.60	97.56	97.00	97.00
Khosla, Y. et.al. [13]	87.0	–	–	–
Beary, M et.al. [8]	94.64	–	–	–
Ahmed, Z.A et.al [3]	95.0	–	97.0	93.0
Banire, B et.al [6]	95.9	96.5	–	–
Silva, V et.al [23]	93.6	99.0	93.5	98.5

3 Dataset

The dataset that has been used in this study is collected from Kaggle. It is an open-source dataset that is available to be used by all. The age range is between 4 to 13. The dataset, entitled 'Autistic Children Facial Dataset' contains a total of 2936 facial images of children, where 1468 images for autistic children and 1468 images for non-autistic children. It is divided into 3 categories: train, test, and valid. Each three of them contains 2 subcategories: autistic and non_autistic. In the training repository, there are 1268 images of the autistic child and 1268 images of the non-autistic child. In the test repository, each of the sub-categories contains 150 images. In the validation repository, each of the sub-categories contains 50 images.

We provide the classifier with the image data, pre-process it to make it trainable and testable, transform it to an array of pixels, and scale all the images to 224×224 pixels so that the machine can analyze them more quickly. In order to normalize the data, we first convert the arrays to NumPy-arrays and then divide those NumPy-arrays by 255 (the image's grayscale range) to obtain values for the NumPy-arrays that fall between 0.0 and 1.0. We sparse these data into two classes by setting 0 for all the 'autistic data' and 1 for all the 'non-autistic data' which are referred to as the predicted outputs. The classifier then uses this data to train the machine. We have shown some sample images below.

Fig. 1. Autistic child 1

Fig. 2. Autistic child 2

Fig. 3. Autistic child 3

Fig. 4. Normal child 1

Fig. 5. Normal child 2

Fig. 6. Normal child 3

4 Methodology

In this section, the steps that have been taken to complete this research have been illustrated. This section includes the methods that are used to perform this classification, how we get them, use them, and which one is preferred.

We will be classifying whether the child is Autistic or Normal. We have used facial images as input data for this classification. To make this classification possible we need to process a huge amount of data. For that, we use deep learning models. Three deep learning models are used up to their latest versions, namely VGG 19, Inception V3, and DenseNet 201. These models are lightweight, have faster processing capability, are easy to use, maintain accuracy, reliability, and so on compared to the other available models. They are more developed than their previous versions. We have measured the performances of these three models individually and compared their accuracy, precision, and recall. The comparisons are given below in Table 2 and Table 3. We have also measured the AUROC value which is shown in Table 4. After all these calculations are done, we get the VGG 19 as our preferred model among the three of them.

At this point, transfer learning is used. We import one of the deep learning models at a time from the 'Keras applications'. We employ 3 fully connected layers, 1 softmax layer, 5 maxpooling layers, and 16 convolutional layers. We use the VGG19 method including the parameters where include_top is false, weight is imagenet and input shape is $224 \times 224 \times 3$. As the layers of the models are already trained using the 'imagenet dataset' there is no need to train the layers again so we create a loop and set the value for layer_trainable as false. Then, flattening is performed and the resulting outputs are sent into the dense layer. In the parameters of the EarlyStopping function, the value of monitor is loss, mode is min, verbose is 1 and patience is 5. The model is compiled where the optimizer used is adam, loss is calculated by sparse categorical cross-entropy and the metric used is accuracy. As an activation we use softmax. We execute the model, where we provide 'input data' in the form of arrays, their 'predicted outputs', epochs is 11, callback is EarlyStopping function, batch size is 32 and shuffle is true, to train the machine. Once the training is completed we can test the machine for unknown data and the machine predicts if the new data belongs to the autistic class or the normal class.

Table 2. Comparing the performances of VGG 19, Inception V3 and DenseNet 201 (**to classify Autistic Child**).

Model name	Accuracy (%)	Precision (%)	Recall (%)	F1 score (%)
VGG 19	85.0	83.0	87.0	85.0
Inception V3	78.0	79.0	77.0	78.0
DenseNet 201	83.0	79.0	91.0	84.0

Table 3. Comparing the performances of VGG 19, Inception V3 and DenseNet 201 (**to classify Normal Child**).

Model name	Accuracy (%)	Precision (%)	Recall(%)	F1 score (%)
VGG 19	85.0	87.0	83.0	85.0
Inception V3	78.0	77.0	80.0	79.0
DenseNet 201	83.0	89.0	76.0	82.0

Table 4. AUROC values of VGG 19, Inception V3 and DenseNet 201

Model name	AUROC value
VGG 19	0.923
Inception V3	0.859
DenseNet 201	0.910

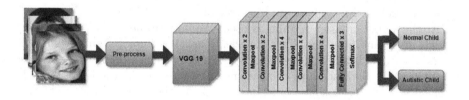

Fig. 7. Proposed methodology

4.1   Classification Algorithms

VGG 19, Inception V3, DenseNet 201

In our system, we have used 3 deep learning models and after comparing their performances we get the VGG 19 as our chosen model.

Significance of Accuracy Curve. We have shown the training accuracy curve of the three models. Training accuracy performs a very critical role in measuring testing accuracy. If we can achieve good training accuracy then we will be able to get good testing accuracy also. When training accuracy is good, it means we have trained our machine well enough to learn how it can recognize unknown data. As we are working with facial data processing so in our case, we tried to teach the machine how to learn the images by recognizing their pixel density. And we have been able to get around 95–99.9% training accuracy for all the models. So it can be said that the machine will recognize the testing data well.

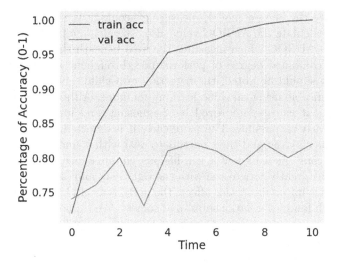

Fig. 8. Accuracy of VGG 19

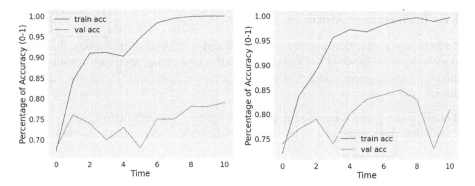

Fig. 9. Accuracy of Inception V3   **Fig. 10.** Accuracy of DenseNet 201

5   Result and Discussion

We have proposed the VGG 19 model for Autism detection. Here, we use VGG 19, Inception V3, and DenseNet 201. The models provide 85% accuracy with VGG 19, 78% accuracy with Inception V3, and 83% accuracy with DenseNet 201. Amongst all of them, we can see that VGG 19 gives more accuracy. The system can be executed using both Google-Colab and Jupyter notebook. We have noticed that the results, these software platforms provide are pretty much reliable, but the results may vary up to the rate of (+–)2%.

To identify the chosen model, measuring accuracy is not well enough, We also need to calculate the AUROC value also. To calculate the factors in a ROC curve, we use AUROC which measures the area beneath the entire ROC curve and offers a combined degree of performance throughout all feasible category thresholds. It should be noted, the detection of a child's situation in autism is simple and suitable using machine learning methods. Although it is not a fully curable thing, it can get improved by diagnosing, and for that, it should be detected as early as possible. The more early it is detected, the more it will be helpful for the children and their parents to deal with it and make the situation easy for everyone. As we know it is a lifelong circumstance but the lifestyles of anyone may be greatly progressed with the right care and aid. It just not affects the child who is infected but also affects the persons around him/her mentally. It varies through families, relationships, and society. We cannot deny the fact that early detection can make many things get better and can be developed when it is not too late. Early intervention stops complex behavior from turning into a dependency. Proper early remedy can reduce children's signs and symptoms and can improve their natural behavior.

5.1   Performance Matrices

Performance evaluation matrices are displayed in this section. Among the three models, we have selected the finest model after evaluating their performances. In the performance evaluation, '0' defines an autistic child, and '1' defines a normal child.

Recall What percentage of true positives were successfully identified?
Precision How many of the positive identifications were actually accurate?

$$Recall = \frac{TP}{TP + FN} \qquad (1) \qquad Precision = \frac{TP}{TP + FP} \qquad (2)$$

F1 Score. It assesses the dataset's accuracy of the model. F1 score is defined as follows:

$$F1score = 2 * \frac{Recall * Precision}{Recall + Precision} \qquad (3)$$

Accuracy. Accuracy is one factor to consider during classification. It is the proportion of predictions that our model successfully predicted.

$$Accuracy = \frac{TP + TN}{TP + FN + FP + TN} \qquad (4)$$

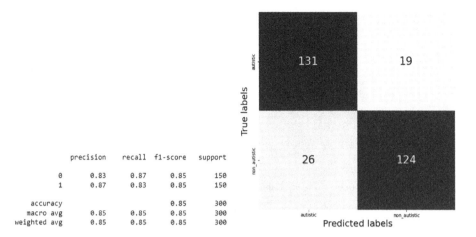

```
              precision    recall  f1-score   support

          0       0.83      0.87      0.85       150
          1       0.87      0.83      0.85       150

   accuracy                          0.85       300
  macro avg       0.85      0.85      0.85       300
weighted avg      0.85      0.85      0.85       300
```

Fig. 11. Performance of VGG 19

Fig. 12. VGG 19 confusion matrix

```
              precision    recall  f1-score   support                  precision    recall  f1-score   support

          0       0.79      0.77      0.78       150              0       0.79      0.91      0.84       150
          1       0.77      0.80      0.79       150              1       0.89      0.76      0.82       150

   accuracy                          0.78       300       accuracy                          0.83       300
  macro avg       0.78      0.78      0.78       300      macro avg       0.84      0.83      0.83       300
weighted avg      0.78      0.78      0.78       300     weighted avg      0.84      0.83      0.83       300
```

Fig. 13. Performance of inception V3   **Fig. 14.** Performance of DenseNet 201

ROC Curve. The total performance of a model with respect to category thresholds is summarized by the ROC curve. The TPR and the FPR are represented by the ROC curve.

– TPR - (True Positive Rate)
– FPR - (False Positive Rate)

$$TPR = \frac{TP}{TP + FN} \qquad (5) \qquad\qquad FPR = \frac{FP}{FP + TN} \qquad (6)$$

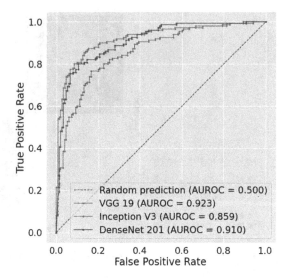

Fig. 15. ROC curve

6   Comparative Study

We know that each work is more individual than the others. Because every author works in their own way and methodology. The methodology and the models that are used in this paper are totally unique. We have used a different amount of data for training, testing and validation, pre-processed them and used different methods. Although every piece is different, comparison with various papers gives us an overall idea about the concept and prepares our minds to think differently. Here, in this section, we will try to make a comparison of different papers with ours. Table 5 displays some comparisons.

Table 5. Performance matrices of our proposed model with the related studies

Authors name	ACC (%)	AUC (%)	Sensitivity (%)	Specificity (%)
Baranwal, A et.al. [7]	96.77	98.96	100.0	93.55
Ahmed, I.A et.al [2]	97.60	97.56	97.00	97.00
Li, B et.al [14]	76.00	–	76.00	69.00
Proposed Model	85.00	92.30	87.00	83.00

Baranwal, A, et al. [7] use ASD screening datasets like binary, integer, and string type data. It is a questionnaire-format dataset. 292 child records are used. They use ANN, RF, LR, DT, and SVM ML models for classifying autism and get 96.77% accuracy. Ahmed, I.A et al. [2] use 547 child image data. They use ANN, FFNN, and CNN models and their proposed model is CNN-based ResNet-18 which provides 97.6% accuracy. Li, B, et al. [14] use a video dataset and get access to 88 children's data. The classifier is trained using four facial attributes: expressions, valence, AUs, and arousal. About 1.2 million samples from 88 kids are included in the dataset. They achieve 76% accuracy using seven binary classifiers utilizing BottleNeck, MobileNet, and EESP approaches. Whereas we've used a facial-image-based dataset which contains 2936 image data. We have used transfer learning techniques which make the classifiers much faster while executing the code. The deep learning techniques used are VGG 19, Inception V3, and DenseNet 201. All these three models are reliable and generate reasonable results. We have got 85.0% accuracy.

7 Contribution

Autism is a life-long situation where one cannot be fully cured but proper remedies and services can improve one's symptoms and everyday activities. There are many treatments available to deal with it because it is not a matter to be ignored. Children with autism are also a part of our society. So it is our responsibility to make them capable enough to live their life healthily. Doctors and researchers have been working on how autism can be detected effectively. Autism can be identified in a number of ways, including eye tracking, brain MRIs, human behavior observation, etc. One of the most effective ways among them to detect autism is to use facial expressions with the help of ML techniques. Deep learning has achieved outstanding results in a wide range of pattern recognition and image analysis in recent times. We decided to work on autism in children through image classification for early detection. We used the dataset of facial images of children which assisted us with preparing, testing, and approving the models to analyze Autism. We made an effort to create a model using deep learning and transfer learning techniques. We used three methods and among all of them, VGG 19 provided the most accurate results in our research. It is able to detect the child's condition pretty accurately and fast. Using this ML model we can help the child by detecting their disease and making their parents conscious of their child's condition which helps them to consult with a specialist as early as possible. We think and hope that early detection can really help and improve a child's life and the child's family members through their life journey.

8 Conclusion

In a few countries, autism no longer gets sufficient interest to work on. In truth, it is overlooked in many countries. Parents of autistic children can learn early on a way to assist their child to enhance mentally, emotionally, and bodily during their developmental degrees with help from specialists and companies. However, it's so vital to diagnose ASD, as without an analysis this can make so many things tough for someone who's affected and for those who are related to them.

In this paper, we carried out some ML models: VGG 19, DenseNet 201, and Inception V3. VGG 19 is taken into consideration to be one of the best computer imaginative and prescient models to this point. Amongst all the classifiers we can see that VGG 19 gives more accuracy.

References

1. Afrin, M., Freeda, S., Elakia, S., Kannan, P.: AI based facial expression recognition for autism children. IJETIE **5**(9), 7 (2019)
2. Ahmed, I.A., et al.: Eye tracking-based diagnosis and early detection of autism spectrum disorder using machine learning and deep learning techniques. Electronics **11**(4), 530 (2022)
3. Ahmed, Z.A., et al.: Facial features detection system to identify children with autism spectrum disorder: Deep learning models. Comput. Math. Methods Med. **2022**, 3941049 (2022)
4. Akter, T., Khan, M.I., Ali, M.H., Satu, M.S., Uddin, M.J., Moni, M.A.: Improved machine learning based classification model for early autism detection. In: 2021 2nd International Conference on Robotics, Electrical and Signal Processing Techniques (ICREST), pp. 742–747. IEEE (2021)
5. Al Banna, M.H., Ghosh, T., Taher, K.A., Kaiser, M.S., Mahmud, M.: A monitoring system for patients of autism spectrum disorder using artificial intelligence. In: Mahmud, M., Vassanelli, S., Kaiser, M.S., Zhong, N. (eds.) BI 2020. LNCS (LNAI), vol. 12241, pp. 251–262. Springer, Cham (2020). https://doi.org/10.1007/978-3-030-59277-6_23
6. Banire, B., Al Thani, D., Qaraqe, M., Mansoor, B.: Face-based attention recognition model for children with autism spectrum disorder. J. Health. Inform. Res. **5**(4), 420–445 (2021)
7. Baranwal, A., Vanitha, M.: Autistic spectrum disorder screening: prediction with machine learning models. In: 2020 International Conference On Emerging Trends In Information Technology and Engineering (IC-ETITE), pp. 1–7. IEEE (2020)
8. Beary, M., Hadsell, A., Messersmith, R., Hosseini, M.P.: Diagnosis of autism in children using facial analysis and deep learning. arXiv preprint arXiv:2008.02890 (2020)
9. Buffle, P., Naranjo, A., Gentaz, E., Vivanti, G.: Experiences and attitudes on early identification practices of autism: A preliminary survey of pediatric professionals in ecuador. Children **9**(2), 123 (2022)
10. Duda, M., Ma, R., Haber, N., Wall, D.: Use of machine learning for behavioral distinction of autism and ADHD. Transl. Psychiatry **6**(2), e732–e732 (2016)
11. Heinsfeld, A.S., Franco, A.R., Craddock, R.C., Buchweitz, A., Meneguzzi, F.: Identification of autism spectrum disorder using deep learning and the abide dataset. NeuroImage Clin. **17**, 16–23 (2018)
12. Jahanara, S., Padmanabhan, S.: Detecting autism from facial image. researchgate (2021)
13. Khosla, Y., Ramachandra, P., Chaitra, N.: Detection of autistic individuals using facial images and deep learning. In: 2021 IEEE International Conference on Computation System and Information Technology for Sustainable Solutions (CSITSS), pp. 1–5. IEEE (2021)
14. Li, B., et al.: A facial affect analysis system for autism spectrum disorder. In: 2019 IEEE International Conference on Image Processing (ICIP), pp. 4549–4553. IEEE (2019)

15. Li, G., Liu, M., Sun, Q., Shen, D., Wang, L.: Early diagnosis of autism disease by multi-channel CNNs. In: Shi, Y., Suk, H.-I., Liu, M. (eds.) MLMI 2018. LNCS, vol. 11046, pp. 303–309. Springer, Cham (2018). https://doi.org/10.1007/978-3-030-00919-9_35

16. Liang, S., Sabri, A.Q.M., Alnajjar, F., Loo, C.K.: Autism spectrum self-stimulatory behaviors classification using explainable temporal coherency deep features and svm classifier. IEEE Access **9**, 34264–34275 (2021)

17. Lu, A., Perkowski, M.: Deep learning approach for screening autism spectrum disorder in children with facial images and analysis of ethnoracial factors in model development and application. Brain Sci. **11**(11), 1446 (2021)

18. Mazumdar, P., Arru, G., Battisti, F.: Early detection of children with autism spectrum disorder based on visual exploration of images. Sig. Process. Image Commun. **94**, 116184 (2021)

19. Michelassi, G.C., et al.: Classification of facial images to assist in the diagnosis of autism spectrum disorder. researchsquare (2021)

20. Raj, S., Masood, S.: Analysis and detection of autism spectrum disorder using machine learning techniques. Proc. Comput. Sci. **167**, 994–1004 (2020)

21. Rani, P.: Emotion detection of autistic children using image processing. In: 2019 Fifth International Conference on Image Information Processing (ICIIP). pp. 532–535. IEEE (2019)

22. Satu, M.S., Sathi, F.F., Arifen, M.S., Ali, M.H., Moni, M.A.: Early detection of autism by extracting features: a case study in bangladesh. In: 2019 International Conference On Robotics, Electrical And Signal Processing Techniques (ICREST), pp. 400–405. IEEE (2019)

23. Silva, V., Soares, F., Esteves, J.S., Santos, C.P., Pereira, A.P.: Fostering emotion recognition in children with autism spectrum disorder. Multimodal Technol. Interact. **5**(10), 57 (2021)

24. Sumi, A.S., et al.: fASSERT: a fuzzy assistive system for children with autism using Internet of Things. In: Wang, S., et al. (eds.) BI 2018. LNCS (LNAI), vol. 11309, pp. 403–412. Springer, Cham (2018). https://doi.org/10.1007/978-3-030-05587-5_38

25. Taj-Eldin, M., Ryan, C., O'Flynn, B., Galvin, P.: A review of wearable solutions for physiological and emotional monitoring for use by people with autism spectrum disorder and their caregivers. Sensors **18**(12), 4271 (2018)

26. Thabtah, F.: Machine learning in autistic spectrum disorder behavioral research: A review and ways forward. Inform. Health Soc. Care **44**(3), 278–297 (2019)

27. Thabtah, F., Kamalov, F., Rajab, K.: A new computational intelligence approach to detect autistic features for autism screening. Int. J. Med. Informatics **117**, 112–124 (2018)

28. Thomas, M., Chandran, A.: Artificial neural network for diagnosing autism spectrum disorder. In: 2018 2nd International Conference on Trends in Electronics and Informatics (ICOEI), pp. 930–933. IEEE (2018)

29. Torres, J.M.M., Clarkson, T., Hauschild, K.M., Luhmann, C.C., Lerner, M.D., Riccardi, G.: Facial emotions are accurately encoded in the neural signal of those with autism spectrum disorder: A deep learning approach. Biol. Psych. Cogn. Neurosci. Neuroimag. **7**(7), 688–695 (2022)

30. WHO: Autism statistics & rates in 2022, world health organization (who) (2022). https://www.elemy.com/studio/autism/statistics-and-rates.elemy.com

31. Yolcu, G., et al.: Facial expression recognition for monitoring neurological disorders based on convolutional neural network. Multimedia Tools Appli. **78**(22), 31581–31603 (2019). https://doi.org/10.1007/s11042-019-07959-6
32. Zhao, Z., et al.: Classification of children with autism and typical development using eye-tracking data from face-to-face conversations: Machine learning model development and performance evaluation. J. Med. Internet Res. **23**(8), e29328 (2021)

Shrimp Shape Analysis by a Chord Length Function Based Methodology

Fernando J. Ramírez-Coronel[1], Oscar M. Rodríguez-Elías[1]($\boxtimes$),
Madaín Pérez-Patricio[2], Edgard Esquer-Miranda[3],
Julio Waissman-Vilanova[4], Mario I. Chacón-Murguía[5],
and Omar Hernández-González[1]

[1] Tecnológico Nacional de México/I.T. de Hermosillo, División de Estudios de Posgrado e Investigación, Hermosillo, Sonora, Mexico
{d09330874,omrodriguez,omar.hernandezg}@hermosillo.tecnm.mx

[2] Tecnológico Nacional de México/I.T. de Tuxtla Gutiérrez, División de Estudios de Posgrado e Investigación, Tuxtla Gutiérrez, Chiapas, Mexico
madain.pp@tuxtla.tecnm.mx

[3] Universidad Estatal de Sonora, Hermosillo, Sonora, Mexico
edgard.esquer@ues.mx

[4] Universidad de Sonora, Departamento de Matemáticas, Hermosillo, Sonora, Mexico
julio.waissman@unison.mx

[5] Tecnológico Nacional de México/I.T. de Chihuahua, División de Estudios de Posgrado e Investigación, Chihuahua, Chihuahua, Mexico

Abstract. The most expensive operational cost in shrimp farming and in every aquaculture system is feeding. To estimate the quantity of food is necessary to know the total biomass of the pond. Traditionally, this is done by taking samples and weighting, which is invasive and stress the animals. Non intrusive methods have been tried to estimate pond biomass using different technologies, being one of them computer vision. Computer vision faces several challenges, such as the problem of how to identify shrimps, count them, estimate their size and their mass. In this work, a chord length function based methodology is proposed as a viable alternative to analyze shrimp's shape and count them, this methodology generates histograms of the shape of the shrimps and therefore, a set of statistical parameters (mean, median, mode, variance, standard deviation, maximun and minimum) to quantify shape and which can be useful to identify shrimps, estimate their sizes, and even find a relationship between morphometric measures with respect to biomass.

Keywords: Shrimp biomass estimation · Shrimp count · Shape analysis · Chord length function

1 Introduction

Automatic feeding and monitoring of aquaculture farms have become a hot topic, given that the industry is growing and has the potential to even support the

KC Santosh et al. (Eds.): RTIP2R 2022, CCIS 1704, pp. 205–219, 2023.
https://doi.org/10.1007/978-3-031-23599-3_15

four pillars of food global security [6]. One of the most important aquaculture cultivated species is shrimp. The traditional way to know how to feed shrimps is using feed trays, but this is inaccurate and very prone to errors. To automatize this process is necessary to be able to estimate the total biomass of the pond which is related to the quantity of food needed. To do this, it is necessary to estimate the average weight and the total number of shrimps [14]. It is also a very important topic in aquaculture since feeding is the most expensive operational cost of aquaculture farms [21].

Traditionally, total biomass estimation is done by taking samples and weighting, which is slow, prone to errors, and can generate stress to the shrimps [14]. Computer vision represents a low-cost non-intrusive alternative to count shrimps and estimate their size, and using these values to estimate the average shrimp mass. Techniques to relate shape parameters and longitude to estimate weight have been applied in [17,22]. But they have based their size (total length) estimation on simple shape descriptors, that is to say, shape parameters such as pixel area, carapace length, and perimeter. In the case of counting techniques, some proposed methodologies have been applied in shrimp farming for shrimp larvae counting using image processing as in [2,11,12]. Others have applied networks-based methodologies to recognize and count shrimps as [9,10,22]. But, to the best of the authors' knowledge, no research has been done in exploring the shape-size relations using advanced image processing descriptor-based methodologies applied to shrimps. This would be of great help in order to count shrimps, estimating with a better aproximation their size and therefore, their mass and even for biology studies of their morphology. This paper is organized as follows, in Sect. 2 a state of the art review of shape analysis methods is done, in Sect. 3, the methodology is presented and is explained, in Sect. 4, a discussion is done about the method, its possible parallelization, and a testing done to assess the feasibility of implementation. Finally, in Sect. 5 the conclusions are presented.

2   Theoretical Background

Every object's form encompasses two components: shape and size; where size is the physical scale of an object determined by comparison with one or more of its spatial dimensions as area, length, perimeter, width, mass, etc. Shape is determined as the remnant component of form that remains after differences in size, position, and rotation between two or more objects have been discarded; and it can be conceptualized by comparing with a reference as a circle, ellipse, mean distance, etc. [15].

Biometrics focus in quantifying and detecting the phenotypic appearance of species, individuals, behaviors and morphological traits [23]. Morphometrics is the quantitative analysis of form and the relation between its components (shape and size) which is almost exclusively focused on land-mark based methods and less in outline methods [15,18,23]. Allometry is the relationship between shape and size [23].

A shape descriptor tries to quantify shape being some set of numbers produced to describe a shape feature. Shape descriptors should meet the following requirements: to be complete, to represent the content of information items, to be compact in representation and storing, and to be simple in order to easily compute distances between them [16].

Shape features and shape descriptors must have some essential properties in order to be efficient: identifiability, transtlation, rotation and scale invariance, affine invariance (preserves straightness and parallelism of lines), noise resistance, occulation invariance, statistically independence, and reliable [16].

Shape descriptors can be classified as shown in Fig. 1, derived from [26]. It can be seen that contour based and region based descriptors can be divided into structural and global descriptors. Figure 1 also indicates that there is a tradeoff between efficacy and accuracy, which apply to all the descriptors.

In the case of shrimps, power models have been used to relate size with weight; for instance, in [8], image processing is used to estimate carapace length from area pixels, which in turn can be used to estimate weight using a power law relation between length and weight. The main points of this methodology are: intensity thresholding of the blue channel, area pixels thresholding and the power law relations.

In [17], multivariate prediction models containing area, perimeter, length, and width are established. The main points of this methodology are: background segmentation by applying histogram threshold segmentation, oppening morphological operation, lenght computed by a new proposed algorithm which encompasses thinning, branch recognition and elimination, and length reconstruction. Width is determined while extracting length. Fitting equations with combinations of weight, area, perimeter, length, and width allow to design and validate multivariate prediction models.

These applications take into account very simple shape parameters to estimate total size of shrimp and are implemented with a focus in post-harvesting production, that is to say, production lines (conveyors). They only use size spatial dimension relationships, but not allometric relations between shape and size.

2.1   Counting and Size Estimation Methods

Being similar to fish, number of shrimps and their mass are directly related to the total biomass of the tank [14], therefore, counting shrimps and estimating their sizes is foundamental to estimate the total pond biomass.

Computer vision allows to estimate size, numbers, and even mass of shrimps as has been done in other contexts. In [20], several works are revisited and finally a general synthesis methodology is established for image sequences which uses a combination of AI techniques to count the fish, compute the biomass using weight-length regression, and predict the trajectory using Kalman filters. In

[23], a review of livestock farming research to estimate body weight is presented. It mentions four modeling aproaches for bodyweight prediction of livestock: 1) Traditional approach, 2) Computer vision approach, 3) Computer vision plus machine learning approach, 4) Computer vision plus deep learning.

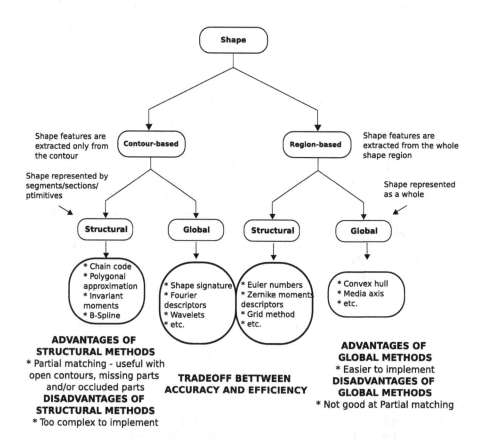

Fig. 1. Classification of shape descriptors derived from [26]

In the case of shrimp farming several image processing methodologies have been used to count shrimps. In [11], a methodology to count baby shrimps (post-larvae) was applied, whose main steps are: adaptive thresholding due to brightness inconsistency, and a blob detection process. The blobs here are the livers of shrimps wich represent them and which can be easily seen, since other parts of shrimps are semitransparent. The error with respect to manual counting was 7%.

In [2], a method to count shrimp larvae is proposed, whose main steps are: a modified Canny edge detector with anisotropic diffusion to enhance larvae characteristics, and blob analysis to analyse three primary features: area, centroid, and boundary. The method presented a root rean square error of less than 6%.

In [12], a methodology based on template matching with co-occurrence color histogram to count shrimp larvae is proposed. This process took one minute to analyse one image. The average error was 3.25%. The accuracy was 97% compared to mannual counting.

In [3], a system to count nursery pacific white shrimp is proposed using color, size, and shape which has the next main image processing stages: creating a region of interest, filtering with a 2D filter, thresholding to remove noise, counting, and storage. It mentions that it is not useful to estimate size since output shrimp pixels may differ from the original.

In [7], an image based shrimp length determination methodology is implemented using OpenCV tools whose main points are: Gaussian blur, thresholding, Canny edge detection, dilation and erosion, and finally contour operations to locate all the contour coordinates, compute the contour area and draw the contour showing the region of interest. The relative percent error compared with manual measurements is 6.23%.

In [22], a methodology to estimate shrimp population, density and size using computer vision is proposed with the next main points: U-net segmentation method and a Marker-controlled watershed segmentation algorithm which is useful to segment overlapping elements. It had a mean absolute error for counting of 0.160 and a root mean square error for estimating shrimp length of 0.293.

In [10], a transfer learning model for CNN real time shrimp recognition was conducted. A CNN Classifier Faster R-CNN Inception V2 was used. The model showed an accuracy as high as 99%. The speed of the model was 58 ms and was trainned during 72 h.

2.2   Other Image Processing Implementations Related with Shrimps

Besides the works done in counting and size estimation mentioned before, there are works in detection and quality assessment of shrimps that are worth to mention since the image processing techniques can be of help in shape analysis for biomass estimation.

In [9], an underwater surveillance system that can recognize shrimps and remanent food is presented. The computer vision part of the system is as follows: lighting and defogging to overcome water turbidity and low visibility and a YOLO algorithm for shrimp recognition.

In [13], a shape analysis methodology using Turn Angle Cross-correlation for shrimp quality evaluation is developed encompassing the next main steps: the H, S and V values obtained from the Blue chanel of RGB image are thresholded; morphological operations, a fast countour trace algorithm, and a set of turning angle functions (shape descriptors) of sample images of the shrimp are used to create a uniform model which is compared with good and broken models to clasify the shrimp. It was shown that the methods applied which focus on the global shape were more effective.

In [19], a method to classify aquatic fauna as dead or live using optical flow to detect movement and shape analysis by extracting borders for body feature analysis is proposed. It uses a classification tree to classify fauna as live or dead depending on motion and shape.

The work done in [13], shows the use of a shape signature applied to quality evaluation. The use of these shape descriptors could be of great help in analysing allometric relations in shrimps.

2.3   Chord Length Function

A better methodology needs to be implemented in the shrimp's case to get advanced shape representations that could help to identify shrimps, count them and help to provide allometric relationships, such a manner better estimations of size and body weight could be made. To the best of the authors' knowledge, one alternative that has not been exploited to analyze shrimps in the context of shape representation and description for biomass estimation is what is called, shape signature, which is also a global shape descriptor.

A shape signature is a one dimensional function derived from a shape contour which captures the perceptual feature of the shape; being some of them the centroid distance function, the complex coordinates, the curvature signature, the cumulative angular function, the area function, the chord length signature, etc. [16, 24–26].

Shape signatures are often used as preprocessing steps for other feature extraction algorithms, such as Fourier descriptors and wavelets [16]. They are usually normallized to be scale and translation invariant, and shift matching is needed to find the best matching between two shapes [26]. In order to increase its robustness and reduce matching load, a shape signature can be simplified by obtaining its signature histogram which is rotationally invariant [26]. One shape signature whose has no reference point (e.g. a centroid used to get the descriptor) is what is called chord length function. This parametric 1D representation of the boundary can be used to compute a histogram and statistical parameters, that could be used for analysing and clasifying shrimps in different's stages of their lives. To the best of the authors' knowledge, the chord length function was proposed by D. Zhang and G. Lu in [25], as a signature function to be used in a Fourier descriptor and no work has been done applying this descriptor alone and getting its histogram to analyse allometric relations of objects.

The chord length signature/function is proposed as follows by [25]:

"For each boundary point p, its $r^*(t)$ is the distance between p and another boundary point p' such that pp' is perpendicular to the tangent vector at p".

Where $r^*(t)$ is the chord length function and t is the arclength parameter.

From the analysis done by [16], the chord length function has the next properties: the original function cannot be reconstructed, it has good invariance of translation, rotation and, scaling; it has bad affine invariance, bad noise, occulation, non-rigid deformation invariance, and low computational complexity

From [25], the chord length function overcomes the problems of biased centroids due to bounday noise and defections of other shape signatures but this non-reference point representation is very sensitive to noise.

Shrimps have a characteristic that could make the use of contour based feature extraction techniques really applicable to infer animal variables. This is that even if their external body is semi-transparent, which could make difficult applying image processing techniques to them, their livers are of black color and have a very characteristic shape [11]. The contour perimeter, area, and other metrics could be used to identify shrimps and estimate their size and mass based on applying image processing to them focusing in their livers form (shape and size).

3   Proposed Methodology

The proposed methodology based on what is called chord length function or chord length signature [25] is shown in Fig. 2 in a simplified way.

3.1   Preprocessing

Having in mind the simplified methodology, a good preprocessing is required to extract the contours of the shrimps and to be able to compute the approximation of the tangent lines. So the requirement would be to have contours of one pixel width. To achieve this, first the gray scale image has to be thresholded, then, impurities removed, and the contours extracted and thinned. Openning can be used to remove impurities in the thresholded image contours and smoothing them recovering approximately their original sizes [4]. Canny edge detector is recommended for border extraction given its good properties of noise inmunity, detecting true edges with minimum error, and getting smoother corners [1]. For getting a one pixel border, an octal thinning algorithm proposed by [5] can be used due to its simplicity and easy parallelization to achieve fast processing time.

3.2   Processing

Once the preprocessing is done, the algorithm will take the border map and begin to search for contours walking through the image from begin to end. If the algorithm finds a contour it will walk through it searching for other contour pixels in the eight neighbors in a specified way (e.g. Look for the right neighbor, then the inferior diagonal, and so on in a counterclockwise) this is important because the way in which the contours are walked through (clockwise or counterclockwise) will affect the process of coding in which directions (quadrants) the perpendicular line segmens are computed since they are contained by the contour. Every contour pixel found is stored in a container (array, tuple, etc.) by saving its coordinates, and the value of that pixel is changed from 255 to other to avoid repeating the cycle; and once the closed contour is walked through by the algorithm, the list of positions of the pixels of the contour are saved in a container of contours and continues searching for contours from the position of the next pixel from the first one of the last contour.

Given that the values of the pixels were changed, the algorithm is going to ignore the pixels of the contours that already has saved. The algorithm is going to continue to do this until it walk through all the image pixels. Once this is done, the container of contours is taken and the process of computing the perpendicular segments to the curvature for each contour in the container is begun. One way to approach this, is approximating the derivative of every point by taking other contour pixel in a near position and computing the slope of the secant line that joints the two points, after this is done the slope of the perpendicular line to the tangent is computed and the perpendicular line is now defined, since the algorithm has the point and the slope. But the algorithm still does not have the perpendicular segment, since it needs to find the other point in the perpendicular line which lies in the border. In [24], the authors menton that the presented definition can cause ambiguities when passing to more than one point and restricting the line inside the contour is needed, but the example they provide in [24] would increase the computational burden since it implicates checking for middle points (a kind of bisection method) to guarantee to be inside the boundary. That can be easily fixed by walking through a discretized line in a way that avoids to go outside the object and jumping rows or columns, to guarantee a boundary point is met, which can be done using the defined direction in which the contour was walked through, as can be seen in Fig. 3, where the segments or vectors whose magnitude want to be computed are shown.

Once the point is found, the distance is computed using the Euclidean form (or maybe another approximation in case of trying to parallelize the algorithm). The distance between the points or longitud of the segment is stored in a container of longitudes. Once the contour is finished the container is stored in a container of contours. This is going to be done for every contour. Finally, every container of longitudes can be used to compute the histogram that represents the shape of the shrimp, and its statistical parameters.

A more detailed methodology block diagram than the one in Fig. 2 is shown in Fig. 4.

4   Methodology, Qualitative Analysis, and Discussion

One important question regarding counting and sizing algorithms is the processing time, which also depends of the application. One way of improving the processing time is parellizing what can be parallelized to divide and distribute the task between several cores working at the same time. The stages of the method that could be parallelized are: the thresholding, opening, Canny edge detector, thinning, finding the perpendicular segment to the tangent line approximation (or vector), the distance storing process, and the statistical measurements generation part. The process stage that could not be parallelized is the search and storing of contours. In the case of tangent line approximation, the algorithm maybe could be parallelized depending of the formula used to compute the distances. This is due to the euclidean distance has a high computational cost for being processed by a GPU core, so if another measurement is to be used for distance computation, the results it would throw should be compared with the sequential methodology result, to know how good the algorithm is.

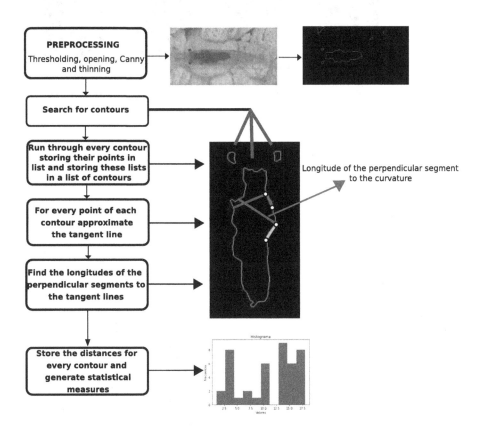

Fig. 2. Simplified methodology.

4.1   Computational Complexity of the Algorithm

The fastest computation time of the algorithm that can be achieved parallelizing its non-preprocessing stages for an image with several contours is the velocity of computing one contour. Asumming an object of the exact size of the image (worst

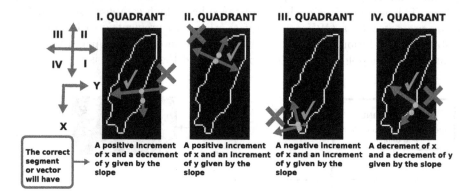

Fig. 3. Finding the perpendicular segments or vectors.

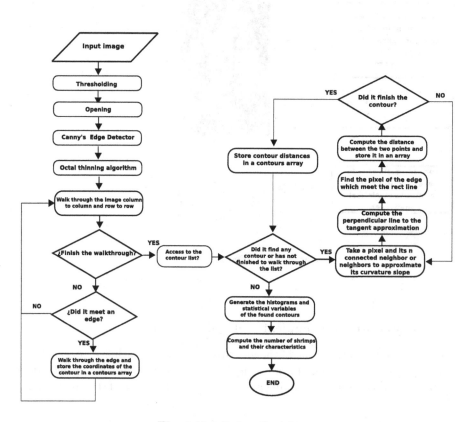

Fig. 4. Detailed methodology.

case scenario), the algorithm is going to run through all the image contours, so it's going to run through the perimeter length given by Eq. 1

$$perimeter = 2row + 2col \qquad (1)$$

and for every contour pixel is going to aproximate a derivative which could be done by taking the slope of the secant line from an 8-neighbor connected pixel at an n distance. So ignoring this calculations and concentrating in the walkthrough, that is, the pixels following the perpendicular line, the number of pixels the algorithm is going to walkthrough ignoring lines of corners is given by Eq. 2

$$totalPixelWalkedthrough = 4(rowxcol) = 4areaImage \qquad (2)$$

Suppose for simplicity of the analysis $row = col$, therefore, the perimeter can be expressed as in Eq. 3 and the walkthrough as in Eq. 4

$$perimeter = 4row \qquad (3)$$

$$totalPixelWalkedthrough = 4(rowxrow) = 4areaImage = 4row^2 \qquad (4)$$

So the number of pixels walked through has a quadratic relation with respect to the rows of the image. As the resolution of the image increment, computational time is going to increment in a quadratic way. If the number of equal contours increment, the computational time is going to increment in a linear way with respect to the number of objects.

The parallelized version which is going to be sequential in the quest of contours and their storing, is going to increment linearly in that step. It is going to be also affected by resolution, but the more objects it has to characterize, the algorithm shines more, since it would take advantage of a greater number of kernels.

Other way to decrement the processing time of both sequential and parallel forms of the algorithm would be to sample the points of the contour that it is going to be used, but this will affect the accuracy of the method and therefore, the resolution of the histogram and the statistical values (tradeoff between efficiency or processing time and accuracy or estimation).

Analysing other characteristics of the algorithm, it can be seen that it is invariant to the rotation of the shrimps; no matter its orientation, the shape it's not going to change, so when the algorithm passes through the same point in different cases of rotation the perpendicular line to the curvature is going to be the same and the container of longitudes is going to have the same longitudes in a different order, which does not affect the computation of the statistical values and the drawing of the histogram.

4.2   Testing the Feasibility of Implementation

To test the proposed idea, a sequential program was developed in Python relying on numpy, PIL, and matplotlib, as libraries to manipulate arrays and images. A few images of freshwater shrimps in an aquarium were used. The results are shown in Fig. 5. To be sure that the program is properly working, the perpendicular lines that the program is computing and whose lengths are stored in each point of the contour are drawn, such a manner, a visual demostration of their computation is shown and which can also help to identify its limitations. The program also gave the next statistical parameters: the mean distance of the contour of the livers of the shrimp is 69.97 *pixels*, the variance of the contour of the livers of shrimp is 1273.14 *pixels*^{2}, the standard deviation of the contour of the livers of the shrimp is 35.68 *pixels*, the maximun distance or longitude of the contour of the livers of the shrimp is 231 *pixels*, the minimun distance or longitud of the contour of the livers of the shrimp is 2 *pixels*, and the mode of the distances or longitudes of the contour of the livers of the shrimp is 61 *pixels*.

The program was tested with a few more images including one with multiple shrimps in one image. The standard deviation was varying from 29.9 to 42.2 pixels. The mean of the standar deviation for six different shrimps of similar size was 34.35 pixels.

From the images with the perpendicular lines shown, it can be seen that the program has limitations when the figure is not a closed one, when it is occluded or when it is only shown partially in the image. But as an advantage to other methods, it gives a characteristic histogram of the form of a shrimp and parameters that clearly show, when compared with other, that the object is a shrimp, since the characteristc form of the livers is traduced in a set of statistical parameters that are similar for different shrimps.

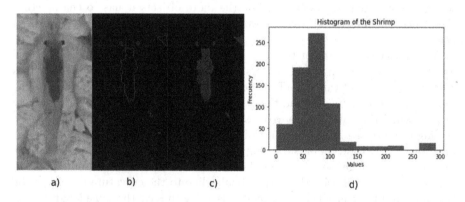

Fig. 5. Chord length function program testing: a) the shrimp, b) the thinned borders of the shrimp, c) the image of the border with the perpendicular lines to the curvature, c) the generated histogram.

4.3   Possible Implementations

As contour pixels are stored, it would be easy to get the perimeter and to use a perimeter-size relationship to estimate mass as it's done by [17]. The output of the methodology could be used as a "preprocessing" step of machine learning methods as is shown in Fig. 6. This goes in accordance with the modelling approaches based on machine learning and deep learning for body weight estimation of livestock mentioned by [23]. The number of shrimps would be the number of contours that meet a predefined criteria given by the statistical parameters. It also could be used to feed the statistical parameters of shrimps in different stages of their life to a machine learning or deep learning model and to be able to predict how the shrimp is growing.

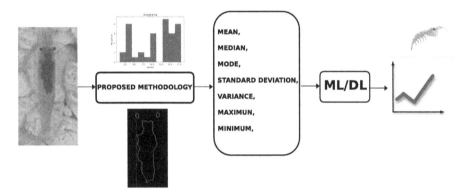

Fig. 6. Proposed methodology as a kind of preprocessing for ML/DL methods derived from [23].

5   Conclusions

A chord length signature based methodology is proposed in this article in order to be able to count shrimps and characterize them by the statistical parameters derived by their histograms. The testing was only done for analysing the feasibility of implementation. To really test the method against other, a greater dataset will be needed. The proposed method can be parallelized in most of its stages having a bottleneck in the contour quest, walkthrough and storing. The algorithm is invariant against traslation, scaling, and rotation. It also gives several statistical parameters which can be used to recognize shrimps and to analize their forms. For further work and given all the analysis done in this paper, the algorithm will be compared with other solutions for a quantitative analysis and tested in a greater dataset. Also the results could be used to define a kind of growth morphology map of shrimps, since there is a relation between shape features and biomass of shrimps. The conclusion is that this represents a novel biomass estimation methodology and a novel methodology for analysing the shape-size relations, at least in shrimp farming.

Acknowledgements. We acknowledge the financial support provided by Conacyt to the first author, with the scholarship 709298, and by the TecNM with the project 15290.22-P

References

1. Acharya, T., Ray, A.K.: Image processing: principles and applications. John Wiley & Sons (2005)
2. Awalludin, E.A., et al.: Combination of canny edge detection and blob processing techniques for shrimp larvae counting. In: Proceedings of the 2019 IEEE International Conference on Signal and Image Processing Applications, ICSIPA 2019 (2011), pp. 308–313 (2019). https://doi.org/10.1109/ICSIPA45851.2019.8977746
3. Boksuwan, S., Panaudomsup, S., Cheypoca, T.: A prototype system to count nursery pacific white shrimp using image processing. In: International Conference on Control, Automation and Systems 2018-Octob(Iccas), pp. 1187–1189 (2018)
4. Burger, W., J. Burge, M.: Principles of Digital Image Processing: Fundamental Techniques (2009)
5. Chin, R.T., Wan, H.-K., Stover, D.L., Iverson, R.D.: A one-pass thinning algorithm and its parallel implementation. Comput. Vis. Graph. Image Process. **40**(1), 30–40 (1987)
6. FAO: The state of world fisheries and aquaculture, vol. 32 (2020). https://doi.org/10.4060/ca9229en
7. Gamara, R.P.C., Baldovino, R.G., Loresco, P.J.M.: Image-based shrimp length determination using OpenCV. In: 2021 IEEE 13th International Conference on Humanoid, Nanotechnology, Information Technology, Communication and Control, Environment, and Management (HNICEM), pp. 1–5. IEEE (2021)
8. Harbitz, A.: Estimation of shrimp (Pandalus borealis) carapace length by image analysis. ICES J. Mar. Sci. **64**(5), 939–944 (2007). https://doi.org/10.1093/icesjms/fsm047
9. Huang, I.J., et al.: The Prototype of a smart underwater surveillance system for shrimp farming. In: Proceedings of the 2018 IEEE International Conference on Advanced Manufacturing, ICAM 2018, pp. 177–180 (2019). https://doi.org/10.1109/AMCON.2018.8614976
10. Isa, I.S., Norzrin, N.N., Sulaiman, S.N., Hamzaid, N.A., Maruzuki, M.I.F.: CNN transfer learning of shrimp detection for underwater vision system. In: Proceeding - 1st International Conference on Information Technology, Advanced Mechanical and Electrical Engineering, ICITAMEE 2020, pp. 226–231 (2020). https://doi.org/10.1109/ICITAMEE50454.2020.9398474
11. Kesvarakul, R., Chianrabutra, C., Chianrabutra, S.: Baby shrimp counting via automated image processing. In: ACM International Conference Proceeding Series Part, vol. F1283, pp. 352–356 (2017). https://doi.org/10.1145/3055635.3056652
12. Khantuwan, W., Khiripet, N.: Live shrimp larvae counting method using co-occurrence color histogram. In: 2012 9th International Conference on Electrical Engineering/Electronics, Computer, Telecommunications and Information Technology, ECTI-CON 2012, pp. 1–4 (2012). https://doi.org/10.1109/ECTICon.2012.6254280
13. Lee, D.J., Xiong, G., Lane, R.M., Zhang, D.: An efficient shape analysis method for shrimp quality evaluation. In: 2012 12th International Conference on Control, Automation, Robotics and Vision, ICARCV 2012, pp. 865–870, Dec 2012. https://doi.org/10.1109/ICARCV.2012.6485271

14. Li, D., Hao, Y., Duan, Y.: Nonintrusive methods for biomass estimation in aquaculture with emphasis on fish: a review. Rev. Aquac. **12**(3), 1390–1411 (2020). https://doi.org/10.1111/raq.12388
15. MacLeod, N.: Morphometrics: history, development methods and prospects. Zoolog. Syst. **42**(1), 4–33 (2017). https://doi.org/10.11865/zs.201702
16. Mingqiang, Y., Kidiyo, K., Joseph, R.: A survey of shape feature extraction techniques. In: Pattern Recognition Techniques, Technology and Applications, vol. 2008 (2008). https://doi.org/10.5772/6237
17. Pan, P.M., Li, J.P., Lv, G.L., Yang, H., Zhu, S.M., Lou, J.Z.: Prediction of shelled shrimp weight by machine vision. J. Zhejiang Univ. Sci. B **10**(8), 589–594 (2009). https://doi.org/10.1631/jzus.B0820364
18. Rahagiyanto, A., Adhyatma, M.: Nurkholis: A review of morphometric measurements techniques on animals using digital image processing. In: Proceedings of the Third International on Food and Agriculture, vol. 3, pp. 67–72 (2020)
19. Ramalakshmi Palani, S., Durairaj, D., Balasubramaniyan, K., Gurusamy, S.: Estimating the survival of aqua fauna by image analysis techniques from the video sequences of pond aquaculture. AgroLife Sci. J. **10**(1), 227–235 (2021)
20. Shortis, M.R., Ravanbakhsh, M.: Progress in the automated identification, measurement, and counting of fish in underwater image sequences. Mar. Technol. Soc. J. **50**(1), 4–16 (2015)
21. Tanveer, M., Balasubramanian, S., Sivakumar, M., Manimehalai, N., Jagan, P.: A technical review on feeders in aquaculture. Int. J. Fisheries Aquatic Stud. **6**(4), 305–309 (2018). www.fisheriesjournal.com
22. Thai, T.T.N., Nguyen, T.S., Pham, V.C.: Computer vision based estimation of shrimp population density and size. In: Proceedings - 2021 International Symposium on Electrical and Electronics Engineering, ISEE 2021, pp. 145–148 (2021). https://doi.org/10.1109/ISEE51682.2021.9418638
23. Wang, Z., Shadpour, S., Chan, E., Rotondo, V., Wood, K.M., Tulpan, D.: ASAS-NANP SYMPOSIUM: Applications of machine learning for livestock body weight prediction from digital images. J. Anim. Sci. **99**(2), 1–15 (2021). https://doi.org/10.1093/jas/skab022
24. Zhang, D., Lu, G.: A comparative study on shape retrieval using fourier descriptors with different shape signatures. In: Proceedings of International Conference On Intelligent Multimedia And Distance Education (ICIMADE 2001), pp. 1–9 (2001)
25. Zhang, D., Lu, G.: A comparative study of fourier descriptors for shape representation and retrieval. In: Proceedings of 5th Asian Conference on Computer Vision (ACCV), pp. 646–651, Jan 2002
26. Zhang, D., Lu, G.: Review of shape representation and description techniques. Pattern Recogn. **37**(1), 1–19 (2004). https://doi.org/10.1016/j.patcog.2003.07.008

Supervised Neural Networks for Fruit Identification

Ahana Bandyopadhyay[1], Sourodip Ghosh[1], Moinak Bose[1(✉)], Louisa Kessi[2], and Loveleen Gaur[3]

[1] Applied AI Research Lab, Vermillion, SD 57069, USA
moinakbose12@gmail.com
[2] ORPALIS - A PSPDFKit Company, Auvergne-Rhone-Alpes, France
louisa.kessi@pspdfkit.com
[3] Amity International Business School, Amity University, Gautam Buddha Nagar, Uttar Pradesh 201313, India
lgaur@amity.edu

Abstract. Thinking about the quick progression of humankind, a critical concern is given to the nourishments that we devour. In the proposed research, we propose a fruit classification system using two popular deep learning frameworks, CNN and ResNet50. With a total data size of $28,283$ fruit images (41 different categories), both the models performed exceptionally well on the network architectures, where the test accuracy achieved by CNN and ResNet50 V2 was 97.48% and 98.89% respectively, therefore obtaining a state of the art results when compared to research findings in accordance to the same dataset. The training directory was augmented, and a validation set of 12% was set to monitor the consistency and reliability of the results achieved. A number of evaluation parameters like Precision, Sensitivity, F-Scores, and ROC were calculated to analyze the results obtained. Furthermore, we took advantage of a predictor model to visualize the results on a test set with $3,615$ images. Our code can be found in the mentioned link: https://github.com/Sourodip-ghosh123/Fruits-360.

Keywords: Fruit classification · Convolutional Neural Networks · Deep neural networks · ResNet

1 Introduction

In addressing human brain perception, images are the most basic strategy. Various procedures have been utilized over the previous years for fruit detection utilizing computer vision technology. One of the most eminent applications is the utilization of deep neural networks to recognize, order, and separate between various types of fruits. When contrasted with customary feature extraction in CNN, the image can be analyzed, by pre-processing and feature extraction process, often followed by a detection/segmentation objective. Parts affected in fruits can be estimated manually which are troublesome, expensive and are conveniently impacted by physical factors, including contrasting evaluation and validation.

KC Santosh et al. (Eds.): RTIP2R 2022, CCIS 1704, pp. 220–230, 2023.
https://doi.org/10.1007/978-3-031-23599-3_16

The computer vision strategies used to identify a fruit rely upon four basic features, which are: (i) power, (ii) concealing, (iii) shape, and (iv) texture [1]. This paper proposes a compelling usage of neural networks through images containing surface features for fruit identification. The validation is done by base discrimination classifiers, reliant on the quantifiable and co-occasion features. While some works focus on the estimation of plant health [2,3], some works actively focus on finding methods for enriching and diagnosing the quality of fruits. Recent findings suggest techniques for localization of fruit identification-based framework for gathering and recognizing fruit types [4].

Bargoti et al. [5] implement a Faster R-CNN framework to classify apples, almonds and mangoes. They achieve an F1-Score, greater than 0.9. Ren et al. [6] discuss quicker Region-based convolutional association. Puttemans et al. [7] designed an ablation on fruits with a technique for recognizing pre-processed images of strawberries and apples. Barth et al. [8] discuss a technique to create a synthetic dataset, by using empirical measurements exploration of images from 3D plant models. Ghosh et al. [9] use a ShuffleNet V2 architecture on the same dataset to achieve a classification accuracy of 96.24% with lowered model computations, as ShuffleNet uses low trainable parameters, hence less training and convergence time.

In the proposed context, we have incorporated the classification of two different fruit recognition-based supervised neural networks, trained/validated on a fruit database consisting of 41 classes of fruit images, utilizing a custom structured convolutional neural network (CNN) architecture and a pre-trained deep neural network (DNN) architecture, ResNet50V2, to predict test images and evaluate overall performance between the techniques. This essentially calls attention to the parameters of distinction while reviewing the designs. The pre-trained classifier outflanks previous research findings on this particular dataset, thereby accomplishing a state-of-the-art accuracy with other deciding assessment parameters.

2 Model Architectures

The dataset, Fruits-360 was evaluated using two different networks. The best model was evaluated on the basis of performance and factors which completely diminish the chances of over-fitting, with accurate precision. The network architectures were evaluated on the same processed images to produce a fair comparison analysis. The CNN model is finally trained on image size 100×100 for 10 epochs. The accuracy and loss curves of the training and validation sets after 10 epochs are shown in Fig. 2.

2.1 Convolutional Neural Networks

Convolutional Neural Networks (CNN) or ConvNets are a sort of Artificial Neural Networks (ANN) that is generally utilized for image classification, object recognition, and neural style transfer. Filters additionally are kernels which are the basic structure blocks of CNN. They help to extract patterns and highlights like edges, corners, shapes, surfaces, and articles from an image. A channel is fundamentally a grid that is generally small in size. This channel performs element-wise multiplication with the image pixel esteems and afterwards slides onto the following window with a specific step and incentive subsequent to including the estimations of each item. This procedure proceeds until the whole image is navigated.

Traditional CNN is manufactured utilizing three fundamental layers; Convolutional layers, Pooling layers, and Fully Connected (FC) layers. Afterwards, unique CNN models were set up by various researchers, by fluctuating profundity and width of layers and furthermore replacing the layers [10–13]. For example, to rearrange the CNN design, for measurement decreases, pooling layers are replaced by the Conventional layer with an expanded number of steps [11].

The custom CNN architecture for our experimentation was developed using an input layer, 15 hidden layers (consisting of conv2d, pooling, dropout, and FC layers containing activation units, passing information, layer by layer), and an output layer, capable of deciding the class of the fruit, using labels. Two dropout layers, each of 0.2 and 0.3 respectively were used. For each FC layer, an activation function, 'ReLU' was used. For the output layer, 'softmax' activation was utilized since there are 41 classes in total. The optimizer, NADAM was used to update weights and biases. Nadam (Nesterov-accelerated Adaptive Moment Estimation) [14] thus combines Adam and NAG. NAG allows us to perform a more accurate step in the gradient direction by updating the parameters with the momentum step before computing the gradient. In this specific dataset, NADAM outperforms all other optimizers, as shown in the equations.

2.2   ResNet50 V2 - Deep Neural Network

ResNet50 V2 is a subclass of Residual Network model [15] (DNN), containing 48 Convolutional Layers, a max-pool and an avg pool layer. This model was utilized to assess this dataset. ResNet50 V2 was considered incredibly valuable at distinguishing low, mid and significant level features from an image. The technique effectively manages the exceptionally eminent vanishing gradient problem in CNNs. By and large including more layers in CNN's expansion train error rate, which is tackled with the recommended strategy. This thought permitted the authors to build quantities of identity layers on a shallow model, therefore, a deep model. This forestalled the new model to surpass the training error rate, just as helped the designers gain MAC training parameters while exceeding 50 layers. ResNet utilizes Batch Normalization at its centre. The Batch Normalization modifies the input layer to expand the presentation of the system. The issue of covariate shift is relieved. ResNet utilizes the Identity Connection, which assists with shielding the system from vanishing gradient issues. Likewise, Deep Residual Network utilizes bottleneck residual blocks to expand the presentation of the system. The contrast between the V1 and V2 renditions is as per the following:

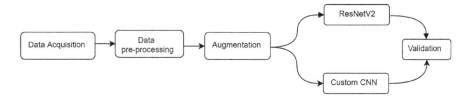

Fig. 1. Workflow for the proposed experiment

1. ResNet V1 includes the second non-linearity after the expansion activity is acted in the middle of the x and $f(x)$. ResNet V2 has evacuated the last non-linearity, subsequently, making the way for the contribution to yield as character association.
2. ResNet V2 applies Batch Normalization and ReLU actuation to the contribution before the augmentation with the weighted network (convolution activity). ResNet V1 plays out the convolution followed by Batch Normalization and ReLU actuation.

With all the component appraisal, the ResNet50 V2 adaptation was thought of. NADAM optimizer was utilized to survey this model. The last 100×100 size images were prepared for 10 epochs.

3 Experiment

The data has been evaluated using a Custom Convolutional Neural Network (CNN) and a pre-trained Deeply Convoluted Neural Network, ResNet50 V2. The inspiration for assessment utilizing the specific structures was a direct result of their superior execution regarding standard error metrics when contrasted with comparable designs previously assessed on this specific dataset. CNN uses $526,709$ parameters, while ResNetV2 uses an increased $23,603,369$ trainable parameters. This provides the pre-trained architecture to assess with MAC access points, therefore determining more trainable points, beneficial for model training. Figure 1 shows the workflow of the proposed experimentation.

3.1 Data: Fruits-360

The dataset utilized for this exploration is the Fruits 360 dataset [16]. This dataset has a high calibre, nitty-gritty component evaluated, portioned images of fruits. The number of classes in the original dataset is 131 altogether, however, we have limited it to 41 classes of fruits to coordinate the extent of the examination. We selected 41 common fruit classes and the class variations between them. The rest was discarded because of their rare occurrence or because they were vegetable classes. The proposed strategy utilizes $28,283$ images altogether. The pictures were obtained from an assortment of points (top-see, side-face) in view of a rotational viewpoint. The images were originally distributed in the Training

Table 1. Number of images for proposed method from the FRUITS 360 dataset.

Class index	Class	Training images	Validation images	Test images
0	Apple Braeburn	492	75	89
1	Apple Crimson Snow	444	66	82
2	Apple Golden 1	480	74	86
3	Apple Golden 2	492	86	78
4	Apple Golden 3	481	73	88
5	Apple Granny Smith	492	80	84
6	Apple Pink Lady	456	80	72
7	Apple Red 1	492	83	81
8	Apple Red 2	492	88	76
9	Apple Red 3	429	80	64
10	Apple Red Delicious	490	75	91
11	Apple Red Yellow 1	492	83	81
12	Apple Red Yellow 2	672	107	112
13	Banana	490	78	88
14	Banana Lady Finger	450	68	86
15	Banana Red	490	84	82
16	Cherry 1	492	83	81
17	Cherry 2	738	120	126
18	Cherry Rainier	738	113	133
19	Cherry Wax Black	492	81	85
20	Cherry Wax Red	492	86	78
21	Cherry Wax Yellow	492	85	79
22	Grape Blue	984	157	171
23	Grape Pink	492	87	77
24	Grape White	490	85	81
25	Grape White 2	490	74	92
26	Grape White 3	492	89	75
27	Grape White 4	471	80	78
28	Grapefruit Pink	490	81	85
29	Grapefruit White	492	83	81
30	Guava	490	71	95
31	Lychee	490	85	81
32	Mango	490	74	92
33	Mango Red	426	69	73
34	Orange	479	78	82
35	Pineapple	490	96	70
36	Pineapple Mini	493	82	81
37	Raspberry	490	77	89
38	Redcurrant	492	90	74
39	Strawberry	492	76	88
40	Strawberry Wedge	738	118	128

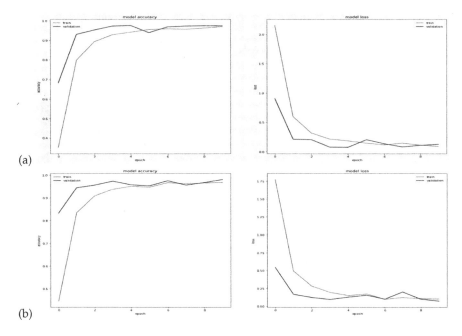

Fig. 2. Accuracy vs Loss graph for training and validation for (a) CNN and (b) ResNet50 V2

and Testing directories. The number of images per class, utilized from the dataset is referenced in Table 1.

3.2   Experimental Setup

The model was processed utilizing the Tensorflow Processing Unit (TPU) to improve ideal execution and experimentation time. This empowered the creators to quicken training time, further handling improved models.

TPUs are generally referred to as hardware accelerators that represent considerable authority in deep learning errands. They are upheld in Tensorflow 2.1 both through the Keras high-level API and, at a lower level, in models utilizing a custom train circle. The overseeing rule is to utilize groups of 128 components for each centre. This relies upon the number of centres for the specific TPU. For the proposed model, the number of cores was 8. At this size, the 128×128 hardware lattice multipliers of the TPU are well on the way to be kept occupied. The speed, in this way, gets amplified at ease. The Cloud TPU is all the more remarkable in execution (180 versus 120 TFLOPS) and multiple times bigger in memory capacity (64 GB versus 16 GB of memory) than NVIDIA's best GPU, Tesla V100. This is the principle purpose behind the framework to have experimented with TPU.

Table 2. Number of images after data augmentation

	Training set	Testing set	Validation set
# of images	22,232	3,615	3,500

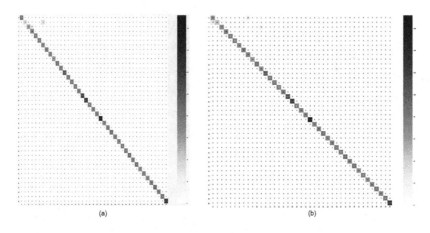

(a)   (b)

Fig. 3. Confusion matrix for (a) CNN and (b) ResNet50 V2

3.3 Data Augmentation

The images were unique in size 100×100 pixels. The size of the images was kept unblemished. The size didn't influence the input layer of the model architectures. The images were of high calibre, hence no pre-treatment of images was done to forestall tampering with the features of the images. Notwithstanding, there was a minor class imbalance in the classes of the dataset. For the issue, Data Augmentation was utilized. The training directory was extended, while the test and validation sets were kept unblemished. Over-sampling of the data had been favoured over under-sampling. The final number of images before model training is demonstrated in Table 2.

4 Result Analysis

The final confusion matrix evaluated after the final training of the dataset using CNN and ResNet50 V2 in Fig. 3(a) and Fig. 3(b) respectively. The proposed CNN architecture was able to classify $3,524$ images against the total set of $3,615$ images whereas ResNet50 V2 was able to classify $3,575$ images against the total test set of $3,615$ images. The test accuracy achieved by the CNN dataset was 97.48% while ResNetV2 achieved a test accuracy of 98.89%.

Table 3 contains the results obtained per class. The comparison analysis has been mentioned with respect to the CNN and ResNet50 V2 model. Aside from

Table 3. Precision and Sensitivity scores of CNN vs ResNet50 V2 model.

Class index	Class	CNN		ResNet50 V2	
		Precision	Sensitivity	Precision	Sensitivity
0	Apple Braeburn	0.85	0.99	0.82	1.00
1	Apple Crimson Snow	1.00	0.79	1.00	0.70
2	Apple Golden 1	1.00	1.00	1.00	1.00
3	Apple Golden 2	1.00	1.00	1.00	1.00
4	Apple Golden 3	1.00	1.00	0.91	1.00
5	Apple Granny Smith	1.00	1.00	1.00	0.89
6	Apple Pink Lady	0.81	0.83	0.92	1.00
7	Apple Red 1	0.86	1.00	1.00	0.80
8	Apple Red 2	0.82	0.80	0.99	0.88
9	Apple Red 3	1.00	1.00	1.00	0.87
10	Apple Red Delicious	1.00	1.00	0.86	1.00
11	Apple Red Yellow 1	1.00	0.96	0.92	0.84
12	Apple Red Yellow 2	1.00	1.00	1.00	1.00
13	Banana	1.00	1.00	0.99	1.00
14	Banana Lady Finger	1.00	1.00	1.00	1.00
15	Banana Red	1.00	1.00	0.99	0.99
16	Cherry 1	1.00	1.00	0.95	1.00
17	Cherry 2	1.00	1.00	1.00	0.95
18	Cherry Rainier	1.00	0.96	1.00	1.00
19	Cherry Wax Black	1.00	1.00	1.00	1.00
20	Cherry Wax Red	1.00	1.00	1.00	1.00
21	Cherry Wax Yellow	1.00	1.00	1.00	1.00
22	Grape Blue	0.99	1.00	1.00	1.00
23	Grape Pink	1.00	1.00	1.00	1.00
24	Grape White	0.96	1.00	1.00	1.00
25	Grape White 2	1.00	1.00	1.00	1.00
26	Grape White 3	1.00	1.00	1.00	1.00
27	Grape White 4	1.00	1.00	1.00	1.00
28	Grapefruit Pink	1.00	1.00	0.91	1.00
29	Grapefruit White	1.00	1.00	1.00	1.00
30	Guava	1.00	1.00	1.00	0.96
31	Lychee	1.00	1.00	1.00	1.00
32	Mango	1.00	1.00	1.00	1.00
33	Mango Red	1.00	1.00	0.75	0.93
34	Orange	1.00	1.00	1.00	1.00
35	Pineapple	1.00	1.00	1.00	1.00
36	Pineapple Mini	1.00	1.00	1.00	1.00
37	Raspberry	1.00	1.00	1.00	1.00
38	Redcurrant	1.00	1.00	1.00	1.00
39	Strawberry	1.00	1.00	1.00	1.00
40	Strawberry Wedge	1.00	0.99	1.00	0.88

the class Apple Pink Lady, all the classes achieved an overall 85 – 100% Precision and Sensitivity. The ROC scores of the CNN model were 98.65% whereas ResNet50 V2 achieved 99.43%. The average Precision and Sensitivity of the CNN model were 0.982 and 0.983, whereas the average precision and Sensitivity of the ResNet50 V2 model were 0.976 and 0.968. The related performance on the Fruits-360 dataset by previous authors are mentioned in Table 4.

$$Precision = \frac{true\ positives}{true\ positives + false\ positives}$$

$$Sensitivity = \frac{true\ positives}{true\ positives + false\ negatives}$$

$$F_{Score} = \frac{2 * Precision \times Sensitivity}{Precision + Sensitivity}$$

Calculating F-Score from the equations as mentioned, CNN has an F-Score of 0.982, while ResNet50 V2 has an F-Score of 0.972.

The performance of the models in predicting correct classes of fruits were estimated, which is demonstrated in Fig. 4. The green labels indicated that the predicted labels were the same as the test labels. The red label in the CNN model prediction demonstrates a wrongly predicted label (see Fig. 4 illustration 1). The fruit was classified as Apple Red 3, despite, the true label being Cherry Rainer. This was a result of the comparatively lesser specificity score of the model in class Cherry Rainer (see class index 18, Table 3). Thus the detection of error prevails for the particular class using custom CNN architecture, which was again balanced using ResNet50 V2 architecture (see class index 18, Table 3).

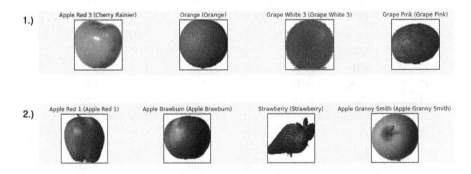

Fig. 4. Predictor model results (green if predicted = true label) 1.) CNN and 2.) ResNet50 V2 (Color figure online)

Table 4. Comparison analysis between the proposed method vs previous methods

Source	Method	Dataset	Accuracy
Ghazanfar et al. [17]	CNN	22,341	92%
Dang et al. [18]	EfficientNet-b0	17,624	95%
Ghosh et al. [9]	ShuffleNet V2	28,283	96.24%
Proposed method	CNN	28,283	97.48%
Proposed method	ResNet50 V2	28,283	98.89%

5   Conclusion

With the progression of deep learning and the immense prospects of training models on enormous image datasets, the extent of the exploration was surveyed and the performance accomplished a state of the art results contrasted with authors already tending to this dataset. The experiments showed that a high performance and recognition analysis can be achieved when blending shallow neural networks with deep neural networks, thus making ResNet50 V2 a noteworthy model design to the extent of this exploration. The CNN and ResNet50 V2 were surveyed on various appraisal parameters and their misclassification esteems were limited to a great extent. Besides, the models have an exceptionally low possibility of over-fitting, in this way concluding the proposed research on the fruit assessment issue.

References

1. Arivazhagan, S., Shebiah, R.N., Nidhyanandhan, S.S., Ganesan, L.: Fruit recognition using color and texture features. J. Emerg. Trends Comput. Inf. Sci. **1**(2), 90–94 (2010)
2. Ghosh, S., Chakraborty, A., Bandyopadhyay, A., Kundu, I., Sabut, S.: Detecting diseased leaves using deep learning. In: Sabut, S.K., Ray, A.K., Pati, B., Acharya, U.R. (eds.) Proceedings of International Conference on Communication, Circuits, and Systems. LNEE, vol. 728, pp. 41–46. Springer, Singapore (2021). https://doi.org/10.1007/978-981-33-4866-0_6
3. Kaur, P., et al.: Recognition of leaf disease using hybrid convolutional neural network by applying feature reduction. Sensors **22**(2), 575 (2022)
4. Zawbaa, H.M., Abbass, M., Hazman, M., Hassenian, A.E.: Automatic fruit image recognition system based on shape and color features. In: Hassanien, A.E., Tolba, M.F., Taher Azar, A. (eds.) AMLTA 2014. CCIS, vol. 488, pp. 278–290. Springer, Cham (2014). https://doi.org/10.1007/978-3-319-13461-1_27
5. Bargoti, S., Underwood, J.: Deep fruit detection in orchards. In: 2017 IEEE International Conference on Robotics and Automation (ICRA), pp. 3626–3633. IEEE (2017)
6. Ren, S., He, K., Girshick, R., Sun, J.: Faster r-cnn: Towards real-time object detection with region proposal networks. In: Advances In Neural Information Processing Systems, pp. 91–99 (2015)

7. Puttemans, S., Vanbrabant, Y., Tits, L., Goedemé, T.: Automated visual fruit detection for harvest estimation and robotic harvesting. In: 2016 Sixth International Conference on Image Processing Theory, Tools and Applications (IPTA), pp. 1–6. IEEE (2016)
8. Barth, R., IJsselmuiden, J., Hemming, J., Van Henten, E.J.: Data synthesis methods for semantic segmentation in agriculture: a capsicum annuum dataset. Comput. Electron. Agricult. **144**, 284–296 (2018)
9. Ghosh, S., Mondal, M.J., Sen, S., Chatterjee, S., Roy, N.K., Patnaik, S.: A novel approach to detect and classify fruits using shufflenet v2. In: 2020 IEEE Applied Signal Processing Conference (ASPCON), pp. 163–167. IEEE (2020)
10. Szegedy, C., et al.: Going deeper with convolutions. In: Proceedings of the IEEE Conference On Computer Vision And Pattern Recognition, pp. 1–9 (2015)
11. Springenberg, J.T., Dosovitskiy, A., Brox, T., Riedmiller, M.: Striving for simplicity: The all convolutional net, arXiv preprint arXiv:1412.6806 (2014)
12. LeCun, Y., Bengio, Y., et al.: Convolutional networks for images, speech, and time series. In: The Handbook of Brain Theory and Neural Networks, vol. 3361(10), 1995 (1995)
13. Lin, M., Chen, Q., Yan, S.: Network in network, arXiv preprint arXiv:1312.4400 (2013)
14. Dozat, T.: Incorporating nesterov momentum into adam (2016)
15. He, K., Zhang, X., Ren, S., Sun, J.: Deep residual learning for image recognition. In: Proceedings of the IEEE Conference On Computer Vision And Pattern Recognition, pp. 770–778 (2016)
16. Mureşan, H., Oltean, M.: Fruit recognition from images using deep learning. Acta Universitatis Sapientiae, Informatica **10**(1), 26–42 (2018)
17. Latif, G., Alsalem, B., Mubarky, W., Mohammad, N., Alghazo, J.: Automatic fruits calories estimation through convolutional neural networks. In: Proceedings of the 2020 6th International Conference on Computer and Technology Applications, pp. 17–21 (2020)
18. Chung, D.T.P., Van Tai, D.: A fruits recognition system based on a modern deep learning technique. J. Phys. Conf. Ser. **1327**, 012050 (2019)

Targeted Clean-Label Poisoning Attacks on Federated Learning

Ayushi Patel$^{(\boxtimes)}$ and Priyanka Singh◉

Dhirubhai Ambani Institute of Information and Communication Technology,
Gandhinagar 382007, Gujarat, India
`201801203@daiict.ac.in`

Abstract. Federated Learning (FL) has become one of the most extensively utilized distributed training approaches since it allows users to access large datasets without really sharing them. Only the updated model parameters are exchanged with the central server after the model has been trained locally on the devices holding the data. Because of the distributed nature of the FL technique, there is a possibility of adversarial attacks that aim to manipulate the behavior of the model. This paper explores targeted clean-label attack in which adversaries inject poisoned images into compromised clients' dataset to alter the behaviour of the model on a specific target image at test time. The standard CIFAR10 dataset is used in this study to conduct various experiments and manipulate the image classifier. This study discovered that the behavior of a FL model can be altered maliciously towards a specific target image without significantly affecting the model's overall accuracy. In addition, the attack's impact grows in direct proportion to the number of injected poisonous images and malicious client (i.e. controlled by adversaries) participating in the FL process.

Keywords: Federated Learning · Targeted attacks · Data poisoning · Clean label

1 Introduction

The artificial intelligence industry is dominated by data-driven machine learning methods. For the model to work well in broader deployments, a large scale diversified dataset is needed, which is not always available due to a variety of factors such as competitive dynamics between different organisations, legal restrictions, user discomfort, privacy concerns, and so on. Because of the aforementioned challenges, there has been an increase in the number of proposals for various distributed training architectures. For example, under the Federated Learning (FL) paradigm, instead of collecting all essential data on a central server, the data remains on numerous edge devices e.g., computers, mobile phones, and IoT devices. Each data holding device is responsible for training the model using local data. Only the 'model parameters' are exchanged with the central server, where the global model is developed by aggregating the local parameters. So Federated

© The Author(s), under exclusive license to Springer Nature Switzerland AG 2023
KC Santosh et al. (Eds.): RTIP2R 2022, CCIS 1704, pp. 231–243, 2023.
https://doi.org/10.1007/978-3-031-23599-3_17

Learning has evolved as a privacy-enhancing technology, allowing the model to be trained locally on data from millions of devices without actually sharing it.

Despite the fact that FL eliminates the need for a centralized database, it remains subject to adversarial attacks that might compromise the model's integrity and endanger data privacy in a situation where an adversary controls a portion of edge devices. By tempering local training data or model parameters, these devices may then be corrupted to achieve adversarial goals. Because there is no central authority to validate data, malicious clients can poison the trained global model. Despite the fact that FL restricts the malicious agent's access to a subset of the data available on a few devices, this can still significantly impair model performance, and they can be reverse-engineered to reveal clients' data.

This study explores vulnerability of FL systems to various adversarial attacks attempting to alter the behaviour of global model. Broadly, the attacks on FL can be classified into two main categories:

- Attacks on the model behaviour: The goal of these attacks is to alter the model's behaviour. There may be one or more malicious clients capable of causing model behaviour to degrade by delivering poisoned updates to the central server. These attacks are difficult to detect owing to the fact that the central server has no knowledge of the client's training data.
- Privacy attacks: The goal of these attacks is to infer sensitive information about the clients/participants in the FL process. They endanger not only the privacy of the data that the clients have, but also the local model parameters that the clients provide to the central server.

This paper concentrates on the first type of attacks: attacks on the model behaviour. Shafahi et al. [1] presented targeted data poisoning attacks on neural networks as part of attacks altering the behaviour of the model, as well as a method to generate 'clean-label poisoned instances' (i.e. poisoned instances are correctly labeled) to alter classifier's behaviour. The attack occurs during training time by carefully introducing poisoned instances into the training data with the purpose of manipulating classifier behaviour on one specific target instance at time. Since the attacks are targeted, the change in overall model accuracy is trivial and hence readily overlooked while accomplishing the intended misclassification.

FL, like machine learning, is vulnerable to adversarial attacks, particularly this type of poisoning attacks, and recent research [5,6,9] has demonstrated that the FL model's functionality can be significantly damaged. So, this research focuses on extending the attack described in [1] in the context of Federated Learning. To create clean-labeled poison instances, the study employs the optimization-based strategy described in [1]. The study looks into the model's behavior using two variables: the number of malicious clients involved in the FL process and the number of poisoned instances injected by them.

The rest of the paper is organized as follows: Sect. 2 gives a brief overview of the possible attacks on FL and discusses about an optimization method that can generate poisoned instances. Section 3 presents the related work and Sect. 4 provides experimental setup, threat model and framework for data poisoning attack on FL. Section 5 contains four different experiments on images from CIFAR-10 dataset followed by a discussion about the results in Sect. 6 and finally, the conclusion.

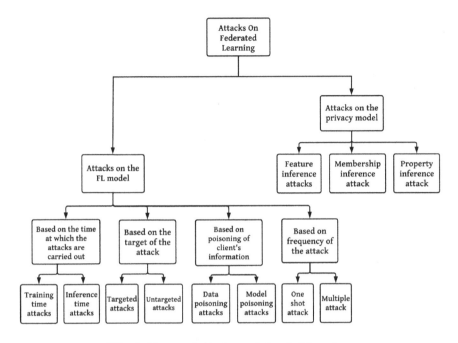

Fig. 1. Types of attacks on federated learning

2 Background Concepts

In this section, we will go through potential attacks that might occur in a federated learning situation. Thereafter, a brief overview of an optimization-based technique for generating poison instances is provided [1].

2.1 Overview of Attacks on FL

The distributed nature of FL can be exploited by the adversaries to influence model behaviour and infer sensitive information about FL participants. Broadly the attacks on FL can be categorized into: Attacks on the FL model and Privacy attacks.

Now, the attacks on the FL model can be classified further according to the four scenarios outlined below.

1. Time at which the attacks are carried out

– Training time attacks: These attacks take place during data gathering, data preparation, and model training processes. The primary purpose of these attacks is to either influence the behaviour of the model getting trained or infer information from the training data.
– Inference time attacks: These attacks occur after the model has been trained. The fundamental goal of these attacks is to obtain information about the model's characteristics.

2. Target of the attack

– Targeted attacks: These attacks are aimed at misclassifying a certain target instance or class as a different class chosen by the adversary. The key goal here is to question the system's integrity rather than to reduce overall model accuracy.
– Untargeted attacks: The primary purpose of these attacks is to change the model in a way that it ends up predicting any of the incorrect classes. These attacks cause a noticeable drop in model performance and are thus clearly detectable.

3. Poisoning of client's information

– Data poisoning attacks: The attacker tampers with the training data of one or more clients involved in the FL process. The primary goal of these attacks is to degrade the performance of the global model.
– Model poisoning attacks: The attacker directly modifies the updated weights sent to the central server by different clients.

4. Frequency of the attack

– One shot attack: These attacks are carried out at one precise moment during the training process.
– Multiple attacks: These attacks occur repeatedly during the training process, either throughout all of the training rounds or just a few of them.

Similarly, the privacy attacks can be classified further into the three categories outlined below.

1. Feature inference attacks

– The major goal of these attacks, as the name implies, is to retrieve the dataset of clients participating in the FL process. Clients either exchange their gradients or local model parameters with the central server during communication rounds, providing surface for the attackers.

2. Membership inference attacks

– Given the training data of clients participating in FL and the local model, these attacks attempt to determine whether or not this data was utilised to train the model.

3. Property inference attack

– These attacks are aimed at identifying whether or not certain properties are possessed by clients participating in FL process. For example, whether a client possesses certain qualities that are not directly related to the FL model's core goal.

2.2 Optimization Based Method to Generate Poisons

Shafahi et al. [1] proposed an optimization-based strategy for creating poisons which, when introduced to the training set, carries a change on the behaviour of the classifier. Let's start by deciphering a few terms.

– **Target instance** is an instance from the test dataset that we intend to misclassify at test time.
– **Base instance** is an instance from the test dataset. The model will misclassify the target instance with the label of base instance at test time.
– **Poison instance** is an instance generated by making imperceptible changes to base instance. It is injected to the training dataset to spur misclassification.

Let $f(x)$ denote feature representation of input x, p poison instance, b base instance and t target instance then Eq. (1) represents how poisons are generated via feature collision.

$$p = argmin_{x} \, ||f(x) - f(t)||_2^2 + \beta ||x - b||_2^2 \qquad (1)$$

The first term in Eq. (1) causes the poison instance to migrate in feature space toward the target instance. The second term in Eq. (1) transforms the poison instance into a base class instance. Shafahi et al. [1] proposes an algorithm to optimize Eq. (1). The forward step is a gradient descent update to reduce the L2 distance between base instance and target instance in feature space, whereas backward step is a proximal update to minimise the Frobenius distance from the base instance in input space [1].

3   Related Work

A variety of targeted attacks with the purpose of injecting a secondary or backdoor task into the model have been proposed in the literature. These are regarded effective as long as they are successful in preserving the overall accuracy of the model. Bagdasaryan et al. proposed a model-poisoning technique where the attacker compromises one or more clients, connects basic patterns in training data with a specific target label and train the model locally using constraint-and-scale technique. The resulting model, thereafter replaces the joint model as a result of federated averaging [2]. They showcased that this type of model-poisoning attack is significantly powerful than data-poisoning attacks. Bhagoji et al. exploited the lack of transparency in the client updates and boosted the malicious client's update to overcome the effect of other clients [3]. Wang et al. trained the model using projected gradient descent (PGD) so that at every training round the attacker's model does not deviate much from the global model [4]. This was more robust than the simple model replacement strategies against a range of defense mechanisms provided in [2] and [3].

Sun et al. implemented data poisoning attacks exploiting the communication protocol and suggested bi-level data poisoning attacks - ATTacks on Federated Learning (AT^2FL) [5]. The extensive experiments carried out by the authors suggest that it can significantly damage performances of real world applications. Tolpegin et al. investigated targeted data poisoning attacks where malicious clients' 'mislabeled' data changes the behaviour of the global model [6]. They suggest a defensive approach for identifying malevolent clients who are engaged in the FL process. The study indicated that as the number of malevolent individuals rises, the detrimental influence on the global model also improves. In addition, increasing the number of malevolent players in later rounds of training can improve the efficacy of these attacks. For CIFAR-10 dataset, the findings show that if 40% of total clients are altered, the number of images correctly classified for the target class drops to 0% and overall model accuracy drops by 3.9%, from 78.3% to 74.4%. Cao et al. investigated the number of poisoned samples and attackers as variables influencing the performance of poisoning attacks [7]. The study found that the attack success rate grows linearly with the number of poisoned samples. When the number of poisoned samples is kept constant, the attack success rate increases with the increased number of attackers. The study also suggested a method called 'sniper' for removing poisoned local models from malevolent players during training.

Generative Adversarial Networks (GANs) have been widely employed in recent years to produce poisoned data since they improve the accuracy of back-door tasks and secure the attack against potential defences. Zhang et al. developed a GAN-based approach for creating poisoned samples as well as a poisoning attack model for the FL framework [8]. It was further extended to an approach where the attacker acts as benign participant in the FL process, sending poisoned updates to the server [9]. Ligeng Zhu et al. showed that private training data can be obtained exploiting publicly shared gradients questioning the safety of gradient exchange [10].

4   Clean-Label Poisoning Attacks on Federated Learning

This paper takes into account attacks on FL models that aim to change the model behaviour during test time. The attacks are also targeted i.e., they intend to manipulate model behaviour on a single test instance. In addition, the attacker is expected to be able to inject poisons into the training set of one or more clients, classifying the attack as targeted data poisoning attacks.

This section will cover the dataset utilized for the attack, as well as the experimental setting, the adversaries' goals, the framework used to produce poisons, and ultimately targeted data poisoning attacks in the case of FL.

4.1   Dataset

This study focuses on a range of experiments about the targeted clean-label attacks for the image classification task utilizing the CIFAR-10 [11] dataset. There are 50,000 training samples in the CIFAR-10 dataset, with 5000 samples in each of the 10 classes, i.e., aeroplane, car, bird, cat, deer, dog, frog, horse, ship, truck. There are also 10,000 test samples on the premises. This study utilizes RESNET18, which is an 18-layer deep convolutional neural network (CNN). Without the introduction of poisoned instances, the model achieved an accuracy of 78.07% in case of FL.

4.2   Experimental Setup

This research utilizes the PyTorch framework to construct a FL scenario in Python. The experiments are conducted by firstly loading the RESNET18 model that was trained on the IMAGENET dataset, but do not use *pretrained* weights and trains the model from scratch on CIFAR-10 dataset. In total, 50 clients were involved in the FL process. By default, 5 of the 50 clients were assumed to be under the control of adversaries. Also, it is assumed that the adversaries can only manipulate the training data on their local device. This study assumes a non-iid (independent and identically distributed) scenario, where each client is randomly assigned 1000 images from the CIFAR-10 dataset. This FL configuration has been trained for a total of 100 global epochs. Federated averaging (fedAvg) is utilized as central aggregator.

4.3   Threat Model

This study takes into consideration a scenario in which a portion of clients is controlled by adversaries who don't have access to training data but can access the model and its parameters. This can be exploited to generate poisoned instances. It is safe to make this assumption as a lot of traditional networks (i.e., RESNET, Inception, etc.) are utilized to extract features. It is also assumed that the federated aggregation operations are not compromised.

4.4   Adversarial Goal

The attack described in this work is targeted, focusing on misclassifying only a specific target instance during testing. It will result in a minor change in overall model accuracy, allowing the attack to go unnoticed while still accomplishing the desired purpose. Targeted attacks are harder to detect than the untargeted attacks as they are more covert.

4.5   Generating Poison Instances

To create the poison instance, the attacker will first select a base instance and a target instance from the test dataset. Thereafter he will make undetectable modifications to the base instance using the optimization-based technique described in [1]. In the experiments, we injected several poisoned instances generated with the watermarking approach mentioned in [1]. These poisoned instances were labeled as base class and seem remarkably similar to the original base instances, resulting in clean-label attacks.

4.6   Data Poisoning Attack on FL

To undertake targeted data poisoning attacks on a FL model with 50 clients, we first pick 5 clients at random to act as adversaries. Thereafter, these malicious clients train the model on poisoned dataset (clean dataset + 50 poison instances) to compromise the behaviour of the model. We consider, (1) 'bird' as our target class, (2) 'dog' as our base class (Figs. 2 and 3).

Fig. 2. Target instance from the class "bird"

Fig. 3. The first row has three random base instances from the class "dog." The second row contains poison instances created from the respective base instances for the target instance depicted in Fig. 2.

5   Experiments and Results

We conducted the experiments on images from CIFAR-10 dataset. We considered an experimental scenario where we evaluate different *target instance - base instance* combinations with varying watermarking opacity. We are presenting results for three such pairs, which are described below.

1. dog vs bird (opacity: 30%)
2. airplane vs frog (opacity: 30%)
3. airplane vs frog (opacity: 20%)

Cao et al., investigated the number of poisonous images and malicious clients as variables influencing attack success rate [7]. The results obtained in this research are similar to the conclusions reached in [7].

5.1   Experiment 1

In the first experiment we have kept number of malicious clients as 5 i.e. constant and we vary number of poisonous images from 0 to 80. Figure 4 shows that the attack success rate grows almost linearly as the number of malicious images injected increases. As we increase the number of poisonous images, Model weights achieved after federated averaging of poisoned weights derives away from the original weights resulting in higher attack success rate.

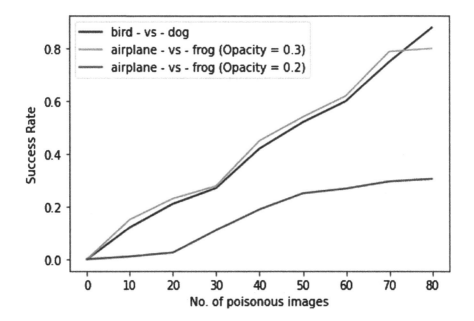

Fig. 4. Experiment 1

5.2   Experiment 2

In the second experiment, we maintained the number of poisonous images constant at 60 and varied the number of malicious clients from 0 to 6. Figure 5 shows that the attack success rate grows almost linearly as the number of malicious clients participating in the FL process increases. As we increase number of malicious clients, poisoned local models involved in the global model aggregation also increases resulting in higher attack success rate.

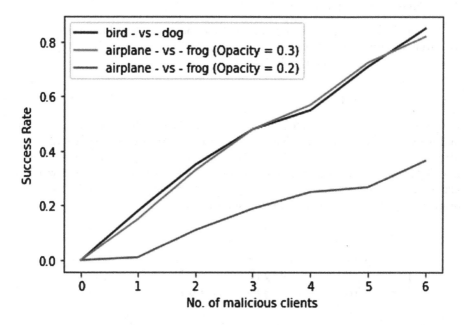

Fig. 5. Experiment 2

5.3   Experiment 3

In the third experiment, we examine overall accuracy of the model under conditions when poison instances are inserted into the dataset vs when they are not. For all cases, we maintained the total number of malicious clients participating in the FL process at 5. We will evaluate the change in overall model accuracy when the number of poisonous images increases from 50 to 70. When we insert 50 poisonous images, the initial 78.07% is reduced by an average of 0.1%. When we raise the number of poisonous images to 70, it reduces by 0.22% on average. This suggests that targeted data poisoning has little effect on the overall model accuracy while achieving the desired misclassification (Fig. 6).

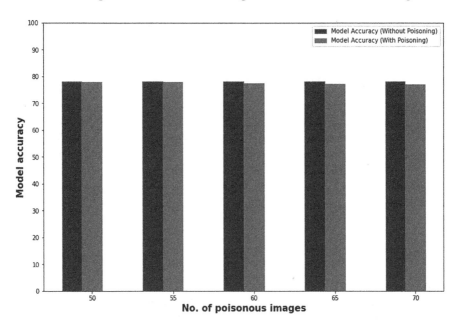

Fig. 6. Experiment 3

5.4   Experiment 4

In the fourth experiment, the study tries to determine minimum number of poisonous images required to incorrectly classify each image of a certain class. We used the CIFAR-10 dataset's 'bird' class as our target class and 'dog' as our base class. The experiment's findings show that if we create more than 80 poison images for each image in the 'bird' class, we can misclassify all of the images present in that class. In this experiment, the overall model accuracy drops significantly to 70% from the original 78.07%. This is due to the fact that in our previous experiments, only one specific image from the target class was incorrectly classified rather than all of the images from that class.

6   Discussion

If M_i^t represents local model parameter of $i^t h$ participant at $t^t h$ epoch then if we have N participants in the FL process then global parameter vector M_G^t

$$M_G^t = 1/N \sum_{i=1}^{N} M_i^t \tag{2}$$

Now, we assume that p out of these N participants are under the control of an adversary then poisoned global parameter vector $M_{G'}^t$

$$M_{G'}^t = 1/N(\sum_{i=1}^{p} M_i^t + \sum_{j=p+1}^{N} M_j^t) \tag{3}$$

The local model parameter vector of clients under an adversary's control is represented by the first term in Eq. (3). It is linearly proportional to the global parameter vector. As a result, when the number of participants under the control of an adversary increases, its contribution in calculating global parameter vector at the central server also increases. We were able to demonstrate the same in experiment 2 when we increased the number of malicious clients and saw an almost linear increase in the attack success rate.

7   Conclusion

In our research, we focused on targeted clean-label data poisoning attacks in FL environment. We were able to show how FL models are susceptible to data poisoning attacks. We demonstrated that the behaviour of a FL model can be altered to misclassify a specific test image, affecting the model's overall accuracy just slightly. We also demonstrated the impact of varied numbers of poisonous instances and malicious clients in the FL process. Based on the experiments, we concluded that the attack success rate increases as we increase the number of poisonous images and clients engaging in the learning process.

In future, we want to validate the scalability of the attack by testing the model on different datasets. In addition, we want to develop a defense mechanism against the targeted clean-label data poisoning attacks.

References

1. Shafahi, A., et al.: Poison frogs! Targeted clean-label poisoning attacks on neural networks. In: NIPS Conference (2018)
2. Bagdasaryan, E., Veit, A., Hua, Y., Estrin, D., Shmatikov, V.: How to backdoor federated learning. In: International Conference on Artificial Intelligence and Statistics, pp. 2938–2948 (2020)
3. Bhagoji, A., Chakraborty, S., Mittal, P., Calo, S.: Analyzing federated learning through an adversarial lens. In: Proceedings of the 36th International Conference on Machine Learning (ICML), vol. 97, pp. 634–643 (2019)
4. Wang, H., et al.: Attack of the tails: yes, you really can backdoor federated learning, In: Advances in Neural Information Processing Systems, vol. 33 (2020)
5. Sun, G., Cong, Y., Dong, J., Wang, Q., Lyu, L., Liu, J.: Data poisoning attacks on federated machine learning. IEEE Internet Things J. 1 (2021)
6. Tolpegin, V., Truex, S., Gursoy, M., Liu, L.: Data poisoning attacks against federated learning systems, pp. 480–501 (2020)
7. Cao, D., Chang, S., Lin, Z., Liu, G., Sun, D.: Understanding distributed poisoning attack in federated learning. In: 2019 IEEE 25th International Conference on Parallel and Distributed Systems (ICPADS), pp. 233–239 (2019)

8. Zhang, J., Chen, B., Cheng, X., Binh, H.T.T., Yu, S.: PoisonGAN: generative poisoning attacks against federated learning in edge computing systems. IEEE Internet Things J. **8**, 3310–3322 (2021)

9. Zhang, J., Chen, J., Wu, D., Chen, B., Yu, S.: Poisoning attack in federated learning using generative adversarial nets. In: 2019 18th IEEE International Conference on Trust, Security and Privacy in Computing and Communications/13th IEEE International Conference on Big Data Science and Engineering (TrustCom/BigDataSE), pp. 374–380 (2019)

10. Zhu, L., Han, S.: Deep leakage from gradients. In: Yang, Q., Fan, L., Yu, H. (eds.) Federated Learning. LNCS (LNAI), vol. 12500, pp. 17–31. Springer, Cham (2020). https://doi.org/10.1007/978-3-030-63076-8_2

11. Krizhevsky, A., Hinton, G., et al.: Learning multiple layers of features from tiny images (2009)

Building Marathi SentiWordNet

Rupali S. Patil[✉][iD] and Satish R. Kolhe[iD]

School of Computer Sciences, Kavayitri Bahinabai Chaudhari North Maharashtra
University, Jalgaon 425001, Maharashtra, India
rupali.patil173@gmail.com
http://nmu.ac.in/

Abstract. Recently, many websites have offered users a platform to
post their reviews and feelings around goods, service quality, strategies,
and current affairs in their native languages. The extensive English lexical resources, like part-of-speech taggers, parsers, and polarity lexicons,
have helped develop sophisticated sentiment analysis applications for
the English language. However, the sentiment lexicon falls short for the
resource-poor language, such as Marathi, in the Sentiment Analysis (SA)
area. In spite of the fact that there have been attempts to create polarity lexicons in Indian dialects, they suffer from many deficiencies, such
as a lack of publicly available sentiment lexicons with a proper scoring
mechanism of opinion words. This research work presents a word-level
translation scheme to create the first comprehensive Marathi polarity
resource: "Marathi SentiWordNet" using a merger of existing linguistic
resources: English SentiWordNet, Hindi SentiWordNet, Marathi Word-
Net, and IndoWordNet. The two polarity scores, positive and negative,
are assigned to each Marathi opinion word. To increase the word coverage, the lexicon is systematically expanded using the Marathi synsets of
IndoWordNet. Manual annotators have evaluated the resource resulting
in a substantial agreement score (0.76 Kappa score). The Comparison
of the proposed Marathi SentiWordNet approach and state-of-art work
building SentiWordNet for Indian languages has been presented. The
generated Marathi SentiWordNet would serve as a tool for sentiment
analysis-related tasks concerning Marathi text.

Keywords: Sentiment analysis · Marathi · SentiWordNet

1 Introduction

The result of today's digital age is the enormous amount of user-generated content. Constantly increasing Internet use and online activities like social media
communications, surveillance, online transactions, e-commerce, online booking,
blogging, and micro-blogging show how to extract, transform, load rapidly, and
analyze massive amounts of structured and unstructured data. Thus, mining
such data and identifying users' sentiments/opinions, wishes, moods, likes, and
dislikes is essential in business decisions. Sentiment Analysis, called Opinion Mining, tries to mine information from various user-generated content like reviews,

© The Author(s), under exclusive license to Springer Nature Switzerland AG 2023
KC Santosh et al. (Eds.): RTIP2R 2022, CCIS 1704, pp. 244–260, 2023.
https://doi.org/10.1007/978-3-031-23599-3_18

news, and blogs and classify them according to their polarity as positive, negative, or neutral.

In recent years, Sentiment Analysis [27] in many Indian dialects has acquired enormous recognition for the inclination to make judgments based on reviews in almost all facets of decision-making. With the rapid growth of accessibility of the massive data on the web, attaining insights from people's thoughts and beliefs improves the perception of their sentiments. KPMG-Google report specifies that India's internet users (234 million) have surpassed English users (175 million) [1]. With an 18% yearly increase rate, it will witness 534 million by 2021, leading the massive Indian regional language data over the air [3]. Sentiment analysis is more difficult in Marathi, a low-resourced Indo-Aryan language, than in Indo-European languages due to the inflections in Marathi words and phrases [28]. The three primary techniques for the creation and annotation of sentiment lexicons specifically (a) manual process, (b) using dictionary, and (c) using corpus [3]. Manual annotation depends on the construction of manual dictionaries by linguists of the target language. This way produces the most reliable resource; however, this approach is time-consuming and annotator biased. The dictionary-based method initiates with the starting seed list and broadens it over the other lexical resources, like WordNet and SentiWordNet [4]. The critical shortcoming of the process is the narrow scope of words necessary for processing domain-specific content. The corpus-based process primarily relies on the labeled corpus of user reviews utilizing positive and negative categories of sentiment terms with maximum coverage of domain-specific words. The dictionary-based method for sentiment lexicon creation is extensively utilized for producing opinion to process English text since extracting and analyzing opinions coming out of words require a rich collection of linguistic resources of that dialect. However, unlike English, Marathi being a resource-scarce dialect, creating a sentiment lexicon for Marathi content is an essential and challenging work. One popular approach for resource-poor languages is to utilize available resources in English to produce a source lexicon. The source lexicon is then translated using a Machine Translation system or a bilingual dictionary to create the resulting target lexicon [14]. In the case of the English-Marathi language pair, a sound Machine Translation system is unavailable. The online bilingual dictionaries possess rare Marathi-English word pairs. The manual translation is costly with regards to human resources and time. A distinct approach is to utilize available collateral corpora for the language pair and a word-alignment tool to acquire a one-to-one mapping among words. Aforementioned process requires a adequately broad corpus to obtain an appropriate number of exclusive word pairs. Such an enormous corpus is unavailable for the English-Marathi language pair. WordNets established under the IndoWordNet framework do not map words directly but match synsets instead [15]. These WordNets for Indian languages serve well in translation from source to target lexicon. The SentiWordNets present for such Indian languages assists to assign polarity to the collection of words from the target language. The proposed procedure is encouraged by the preceding efforts on developing Marathi sentiment lexicons [29]. The preceding modules have integrated morphological notions with corpus-based processes by classifying the words corresponding to their part of speech and synsets using pre-annotated corpora and dictionary-based approaches. Word coverage is one of the fundamental requirements of the lexicon-based sentiment analysis systems. However, their methodology did not contribute sufficient coverage of Marathi sentiment words with sentiment scores as they have created the Marathi lexicons for adjectives and adverbs only. Their studies have not focused on storing and classifying the nouns and verbs into objective (neutral) and subjective (positive or negative) classes. The proposed research is a word-level translation technique using Google Translate to generate a Marathi sentiment lexicon based on different existing lexical resources such as English SentiWordNet, Hindi SentiWordNet, and Marathi WordNet. The research considered all four major word classes - adjectives, adverbs, nouns, and verbs. Moreover, to increase the word coverage, the Marathi SentiWordNet has been expanded using the Indian languages' lexical resource - IndoWordNet. Sentiment lexicon construction by [29] ignored the retention of the part of speech tags and concentrated on classifying the words (Marathi) into positive and negative polarities along with their sentiment scores. However, the lexicon presented in this research work is not only a lexical resource of sentiment words with their polarity class and scores but also the part of speech available. The contributions of the research work are as follows:

- Propose and implement a word-level translation system for building Marathi SentiWordNet.
- Translate English opinion words from English SentiWordNet 3.0 to the target language: Marathi using Google Translate.
- Propose the expansion of Marathi SentiWordNet using Hindi SentiWordNet and Marathi WordNet through the Marathi Hindi WordNet linking, removing the duplicates.
- Propose a novel sentiment expansion scheme using the Marathi synsets from the Indian language resource IndoWordNet.
- Evaluate the lexical resource, Marathi SentiWordNet, generated in this research work.

The remaining paper is arranged as follows; Sect. 2 illustrates the literature study regarding creating lexical resources in Indian dialects. Section 3 shows the proposed methodology, which utilizes diverse linguistic resources to create and extend the Marathi SentiWordNet. Section 4 shows the experiments and the results, and the article concludes in Sec. 5.

2   Related Work

Sentiment Analysis has been a rapidly developing area in Natural Language Processing since its introduction in 1961 by IBM. The most critical research goal is to automatically determine the sentiment orientation or polarity (negative, neutral, positive) of the analyzed text. The analysis is performed on discrete words, phrases, sentences, or paragraphs of the text. Sentiment analysis depends on lexical resources to identify sentiment-bearing words and determine their polarity. Various methods have been used in the literature, such as WordNet-based, Dictionary-based, Corpus-based, and Generative methods for Sentiment lexicon generation in a new target language [4]. General Inquirer dictionary, created at Harvard [16], is a manually created resource often used in sentiment analysis research. [17] used a machine learning approach to construct a lexicon of sentiment terms. Multiple techniques and methods have been proposed for the identification of word polarity [5]: extraction of adjectives [18] [19], nouns [20], and linguistics patterns from subjective expressions [21]. Sentiment Analysis research started in English; however, various tools and resources have been developed for many other dialects with high demand. Different approaches have been experimented for non-English languages such as Chinese [11], Urdu [12]. Marathi, being a resource-poor language, has inadequate tools to perform Sentiment Analysis. Due to the developing stage of Indian languages' linguistic resources such as SentiWordNets, Part-Of-Speech Taggers, Stemmers, and the Annotated Corpora are not adequate to classify the sentiments expressed in Indian texts efficiently. The primary Sentiment Analysis studies have been reported for Hindi, Bengali, Tamil, Malayalam, Urdu, Kannada, and insignificant resource creation for Punjabi, Oriya, Nepali, Marathi, Telugu, Konkani, and Manipuri [6] [13]. The research compares the proposed work with state-of-art work in building SentiWordNet for various Indian languages. The authors [22] presented the lexicon of adjectives and adverbs with polarity scores using Hindi Wordnet and the development of an annotated corpora of Hindi Product Reviews. Hindi subjective lexicon contains 8048 adjectives and 888 adverbs. They achieved 79% accuracy in the classification of reviews and 70.4% agreement with human annotators. The authors [7] proposed the SentiWordNet for the Bengali language based on a bilingual dictionary followed by noise reduction techniques. The authors [23] presented the SentiWordNets for three Indian languages, viz., Hindi, Bengali, and Telugu, based on English SentiWordNet, the Subjectivity List, WordNets, and corpus. An intuitive online game has been developed to create and validate the resulting SentiWordNet(s) by involving the Internet population. The work has been validated using automatic, semi-automatic, and manual methodologies. The authors [26] presented the SentiWordNet for Odia using the existing resources for Indian languages. The WordNets of Bengali, Tamil, Telugu, & Odia languages are used through the common synset identifier. The final target lexicon contains 13,917 tokens (Adjective and adverbs - 4747, Nouns and verbs - 9170) along with their sentiment polarity, part-of-speech tag, and synset ID. The inter-annotator agreement, the Fleiss Kappa score, was calculated for the annotated sample set with a 0.76 score to evaluate the target lexicon. Table 8 compares the proposed work of building a Marathi SentiWordNet with the Indian language SentiWordNet works. The three approaches based on corpus, English SentiWordNet, and Hindi SentiWordNet [29] which incorporates the adjectives and adverbs are experimented to generate the Marathi linguistic resource. The lexicon consists of 43 positive, 29 negative, and 325 neutral entities. If the corpus size is adequate, the coverage can be increased by capturing the language-specific progressions. In the English SentiWordNet-based approach, the Marathi lexicon contains 860 positive, 1069 negative, and 8324 neutral entities. The Hindi SentiWordNet-based method built the lexicon with 220 positive, 397 negative, and 1758 neutral entities.

3 Methodology

The research aims to build the Marathi SentiWordNet using the following resources. The English SentiWordNet 3.0 (SWN) [14], Hindi SentiWordNet (HSWN) [24], Marathi WordNet [25], IndoWordNet (IWN) [8,9], Google Translate [10]. The step-by-step procedure is illustrated in Fig. 1. The process can be adopted for a different target language, which has a WordNet associated with other Indian languages' WordNets.

3.1 SentiWordNet 3.0-Based Approach

The English lexical resource SentiWordNet 3.0 [14] encompasses 117,659 words that come in numerous senses. The word from SentiWordNet has the part-of-speech (POS), unique id, polarity scores as positive and negative, synset terms, and glosses. For example, the word "active" appears with sense#3 as: "a 00038750 0.125 0 active#3". The objective score can be calculated as 1 - (positive score + negative score). The word-by-word nouns, adjectives, adverbs, and verbs from SentiWordNet 3.0 are translated into Marathi using Google Translate, and polarity scores are assigned to corresponding Marathi words. The first sense synsets from SentiWordNet are targeted since they are a word's primary sense. The statistics of different resources are given in Table 1.

Table 1. Statistics of SentiWordNet 3.0, Marathi WordNet, Hindi SentiWordNet, and IndoWordNet

Resource/POS	Noun	Adjective	Adverb	Verb	Total
SentiWordNet 3.0	82,115	18,156	3,621	13,767	117,659
Marathi WordNet	28,162	7,747	1,059	3,529	40,497
Hindi SentiWordNet	1,283	1,298	65	368	3,014
IndoWordNet	23,253	5,263	538	3,147	32,201

Algorithm 1 in Fig. 2 shows the SentiWordNet-based Marathi subjective lexicon generation.

3.2 Hindi SentiWordNet-Based Approach

The Indian language WordNets are associated to Hindi WordNet. With the help of this association, this module gets the polarity scores from Hindi SentiWordNet

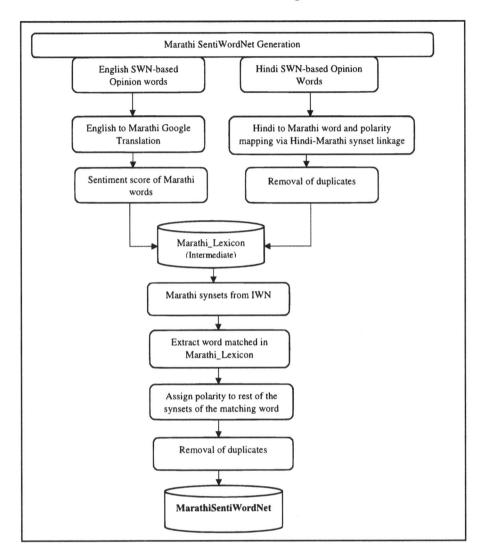

Fig. 1. Block diagram of proposed Marathi SentiWordNet

and assigns them to the Marathi Adjectives/Adverbs/Nouns/Verbs, resulting in a Marathi subjective lexicon. The other Indian languages' SentiWordNets can be used to increase word coverage. Figure 3 shows the Hindi SentiWordNet-based Marathi lexicon.

Algorithm 1: Algorithm for Populating Marathi SentiWordNet using English SWN3.0

```
Main ():
  slc = SubjLexCreator_GoogleTrans_SWNBased()
  swn_file = read(SentiWordNet3.0.0.txt)
  detail_adj_list = slc.extract_adj(swn_file)
  detail_adv_list = slc.extract_adv(swn_file)
  detail_verb_list = slc.extract_verb(swn_file)
  detail_noun_list = slc.extract_noun(swn_file)
  eng_mar_adj_list = slc.eng_to_mar_translate(detail_adj_list, adj_translated.txt)
  eng_mar_adv_list = slc.eng_to_mar_translate(detail_adv_list, adv_translated.txt)
  eng_mar_verb_list = slc.eng_to_mar_translate(detail_verb_list, verb_translated.txt)
  eng_mar_noun_list = slc.eng_to_mar_translate(detail_noun_list, noun_translated.txt)
  //Consider First (primary) sense of a word
  first_sense_adj = slc.get_first_sense_list(detail_adj_list)
  first_sense_adv = slc.get_first_sense_list(detail_adv_list)
  first_sense_verb = slc.get_first_sense_list(detail_verb_list)
  first_sense_noun = slc.get_first_sense_list(detail_noun_list)
  slc.get_senti_score(fisrt_sense_adj, 'a') //Part-of-speeches are retained in the result dictionary
  slc.get_senti_score(fisrt_sense_adv, 'r')
  slc.get_senti_score(fisrt_sense_verb, 'v')
  slc.get_senti_score(fisrt_sense_noun, 'n')
eng_to_mar_translate(detail_src_list, filename):
  while detail_src_list ≠ EmptyList do
      if word sense of s in details_src_list ==1 then
          translator = googgle_translator():
          eng_mar_list.append(s, translator.translate(s, lang_src = 'en', lang_tgt = 'mr'))
      end if
  end for
get_senti_score(first_sense_src, pos):
  while f in first_sense_src do
  //f [0] = id, f [1] = first sense English word from SWN, f [2] = pos_score, f [3] = neg_score
      pos_score = float (f [2])
      neg_score = float (f [3])
      obj_score = 1 - (pos_score + neg_score)
      if ((pos_score > neg_score) and (pos_score > obj_score)) then //Positive words
          if (pos_result_dict.get(mar) == None) then // no duplicates
              pos_result_dict.update({mar:(eng, pos_score, neg_score, obj_score )})
              Write (pos, word, English word, pos_score, neg_score, obj_score) in the 'pos_result_file'
          end if
      else if((neg_score > pos_score) and (neg_score > obj_score)) then //Negative words
          if (neg_result_dict.get(mar) == None) then // no duplicates
              neg_result_dict.update({mar:(eng, pos_score, neg_score, obj_score )})
              Write (pos, word, English word, pos_score, neg_score, obj_score) in the 'neg_result_file'
          end if
      else if (obj_result_dict.get(mar) == None) //Neutral words
          obj_result_dict.update ({mar:(eng, pos_score, neg_score, obj_score )})
          Write (pos, word, English word, pos_score, neg_score, obj_score) in the 'obj_result_file'
          end if
      end if
  end while
```

Fig. 2. Algorithm to generate Marathi SentiWordNet using SentiWordNet3.0

Algorithm 2: Algorithm for Populating Marathi SentiWordNet using Hindi SentiWordNet (HSWN)

```
Main ():
    slc = SubjLexCreator_HSWNBased()
    hswn_file = read (HSWN_WN.txt)


    //Extract Marathi adjective/adverb/verb/noun list from Marathi WordNet
    mar_adj_list = slc.extract_mar_adj(mar_adj_file)
    mar_adv_list = slc.extract_mar_adv(mar_adv_file)
    mar_verb_list = slc.extract_verb(mar_verb_file)
    mar_noun_list = slc.extract_noun(mar_noun_file)


    //Extract Hindi adjective/adverb/verb/noun list from Hindi WordNet
    hindi_adj_list = slc.get_hin_adj(hswn_file)
    hindi_adv_list = slc.get_hin_adv(hswn_file)
    hindi_noun_list = slc.get_hin_noun(hswn_file)
    hindi_verb_list = slc.get_hin_verb(hswn_file)


    adj_lex_dict = slc.get_marathi_lexicon(hindi_adj_list, mar_adj_list)
    adv_lex_dict = slc.get_marathi_lexicon(hindi_adv_list, mar_adv_list)
    noun_lex_dict = slc.get_marathi_lexicon(hindi_noun_list, mar_noun_list)
    verb_lex_dict = slc.get_marathi_lexicon(hindi_verb_list, mar_verb_list)

get_marathi_lexicon(hindi_list, mar_list):
    // mar_list = [ ['अभ्यासी', '00015892'], ['अभ्यासू', '00035660'], ... ]
    // hindi_list = [('10363', '0.0', '0.0'), ('2627', '0.0', '0.75'),(),()......]
    while mar in mar_list do
        Get pos/neg scores from Hindi dictionary and assign to corresponding marathi word
        (use Hindi – Marathi linkage via common synset-id)
        Write the result in mar_lex_dict with pos, positive, negative and objective score
    end while
```

Fig. 3. Algorithm to generate Marathi lexicon using Hindi SentiWordNet

3.3 Expansion Using IndoWordNet (IWN) - Marathi Language Synsets

IndoWordNet [2,8,9] is a linked lexical knowledge base of wordnets of 18 scheduled languages of India, viz., Assamese, Bangla, Bodo, Gujarati, Hindi, Kannada, Kashmiri, Konkani, Malayalam, Meitei (Manipuri), Marathi, Nepali, Odia, Punjabi, Sanskrit, Tamil, Telugu, and Urdu. The Indian language WordNets are getting constructed by the expansion of Hindi WordNet. The wordnets follow the principles of minimality, coverage, and replaceability. The IndoWordNet is highly similar to EuroWordNet; the pivot language is Hindi, linked to English WordNet. It contains synsets for all Marathi words under four classes of Part-Of-Speech - Noun, Adjective, Adverb, and Verb. The statistics of Marathi synsets from IndoWordNet are presented in Table 1. Figure 4 presents the algorithm to expand the Marathi lexicon using IndoWordNet.

Algorithm 3: Algorithm to expand the Marathi SentiWordNet using Hindi SentiWordNet (HSWN) and IndoWordNet (IWN)

```
Expand ():
    lex_dict = {} //To store result of SWN + HSWN + IWN based MarathiSWN without
duplicates
        for all w in SWNBased_Marathi_lexicon
            lext_dict = w
        end for

        for all w in HSWNBased_Marathi_lexicon
            if w not in lex_dict then // remove duplicates
                lext_dict = w
            end if
        end for
        //Use IndoWordNet (IWN) e.g. synsets - 30#योग्य, लायक, समर्थ, सक्षम, पात्र, काबील, पाठाउ#
        for all synsets in mar_synset_list:
            words = synsets.split( '#')
            for word in words:
                if (word in lex_dict) then
                    word_matched = word // Word found
                    values = lex_dict[word]
                    for w in words:
                        if (w ≠ word_matched) then //New word added in result dictionary
                            lex_dict.update({w:values})
                        end if
                    break
                    end for
                end if
            end for
        end for
```

Fig. 4. Expansion of Marathi lexicon using IndoWordNet

4   Experiments and Results

The machine configuration and programming language used for the development is as below -

– Windows 64-bit

- i7 core processor
- 16 GB RAM
- Python Programming Language

4.1 SentiWordNet 3.0-Based Marathi Lexicon

The approach uses the Google Translate tool to translate English first sense synsets to corresponding Marathi words. The tool serves limited requests translation at a time in a given period, due to which the SentiWordNet data is split into 561 files containing 20 KB data each. This takes an average of 80 s of translation time per file, which is a significant amount of time.

The translation errors and the words whose POS are changed due to translation are removed from the resulting Marathi SentiWordNet. Table 2 shows the result of this approach.

Table 2. Statistics of SentiWordNet-based Marathi lexicon

Class/Polarity	POS	NEG	NEU	Total
Noun	390	598	17,001	17,989
Adjective	784	1,017	6,571	8,372
Adverb	63	44	1,753	1,860
Verb	16	15	682	713
Total	1,253	1,674	2,6007	28,934

4.2 Hindi SentiWordNet-Based Marathi Lexicon

Table 3 shows the result of the Hindi SentiWordNet-based approach.

Table 3. Statistics of Hindi SentiWordNet-based Marathi lexicon

Class/Polarity	POS	NEG	NEU	Total
Noun	8	14	1,888	1,910
Adjective	207	393	1,609	2,209
Adverb	13	4	149	166
Verb	3	4	593	600
Total	231	415	4,239	4,885

To increase the word coverage, the above two lexicons, viz., Hindi SentiWordNet-based Marathi lexicon and SentiWordNet-based Marathi lexicon, are ensembled together by removing the duplicates. Table 4 shows the statistics of the Marathi lexicon generated using SentiWordNet and Hindi SentiWordNet.

Table 4. Ensemble of SentiWordNet and Hindi SentiWordNet-based Marathi Lexicons

Class/Polarity	POS	NEG	NEU	Total
Noun	571	759	18,567	19,897
Adjective	1,356	1,725	8,721	11,802
Adverb	143	69	1,814	2,026
Verb	34	46	1,233	1,313
Total	2,104	2,599	30,335	35,038

4.3   Extension of Marathi Lexicon Using IndoWordNet

The words in IndoWordNet are represented as unique synset ID, synsets, and gloss.

For Example – the word 'मूर्ख' {murkha} {silly} is represented as: 27 –> मूर्ख,, बावळा, बावळट, अज्ञानी, मूढ, जड, मंद, निर्बुद्ध, मठ्ठ, बेअक्कल, शंख, बिनडोक, अडाणी, ढ, ठोंब्या, अर्धवट,, बेअक्कली, भोट, खेंदड, खेंदाड (all marathi synonyms of the word 'silly') –> "ज्याला बुद्धी नाही किंवा कमी आहे असा:"मूर्ख माणसाला एखादी गोष्ट पटवून देणे फारच कठीण आहे."

The word has 20 synsets present in the IndoWordNet. The approach uses the comma-separated synsets lists to search into the Marathi lexicon generated using SentiWordNet and Hindi SentiWordNet. The polarity scores of a synset word that exists in the Marathi lexicon are assigned to the rest of the terms from the same synset. The newly created word, polarity scores, and POS are included in the resulting lexicon by removing the duplicates. For Example - the word 'मूर्ख' is searched in the Marathi SentiWordNet. The word polarities of 0.625 and 0.125 are fetched and assigned to all the synsets of 'Silly' बावळा, बावळट,, अज्ञानी, मूढ, जड, मंद, निर्बुद्ध, मठ्ठ, बेअक्कल, शंख, बिनडोक, अडाणी, ढ, ठोंब्या, अर्धवट, बेअक्कली, भोट,, खेंदड, खेंदाड other than बेअक्कल and अडाणी as these words were already present in the resulting lexicon. The word coverage has increased by 6056 new words using this approach. Table 5 shows the statistics of the final resulting Marathi Senti-WordNet using English SentiWordNet, Hindi SentiWordNet, Marathi WordNet, and IndoWordNet.

Table 5. Statistics of Final Marathi SentiWordNet using SentiWordNet, Marathi WordNet, Hindi SentiWordNet, and IndoWordNet

Class/Polarity	POS	NEG	NEU	Total
Noun	857	977	21,169	23,003
Adjective	1,380	2,791	9,118	13,289
Adverb	149	72	1,194	1,415
Verb	45	120	2,000	2,165
Total	2,431	3,960	33,481	39,872

Table 6 presents the words in the resulting Marathi SentiWordNet generated in this work.

Table 6. Marathi SentiWordNet using SentiWordNet, Marathi WordNet, Hindi SentiWordNet, and IndoWordNet

POS	Word	English Translation	pos_score	neg_score
a	जबाबदार	responsible	0.625	0
r	सर्वोत्तम	to the highest degree	0.5	0
a	अस्वस्थ	restless	0	0.75
v	घाबरणे	to be afraid	0.125	0.625
n	वादविवाद	debate	0.25	0.125

4.4 Resource Evaluation

The random sampling of words was created from the target lexicon to evaluate the reliability of the Marathi SentiWordNet generated using Hindi SentiWord-Net, English SentiWordNet, and IndoWordNet. The 2000 random samples from positive and negative polarity lists were selected. These sample sets were made available to two manual raters to annotate the samples as positive or negative independently. The annotators were native Marathi speakers and spoke Marathi on a day-to-day basis. No rater had prior knowledge about the assigned polarity to a word that confirmed impartial annotation of the words. The statistical Cohen's Kappa [30] score is determined for the annotated sample set to measure the interrater agreement on the categorical scales. The Kappa κ is computed as:

$$\kappa = \frac{p_0 - p_e}{1 - p_e} \tag{1}$$

where p_o is the relative observed agreement between annotators, and p_e is the hypothetical probability by chance agreement. If the raters are in complete agreement, then k = 1. If there is no agreement, then k = 0. For m categories, O observations and $o_m i$ is the number of times rater i predicted category m:

$$p_e = \frac{1}{o^2} \sum_m o_{m1} o_{m2} \tag{2}$$

Suppose XX and YY be the number of agreements, XY and YX be the number of disagreements between the two raters -

$$p_0 = \frac{XX + YY}{XX + XY + YX + YY} \tag{3}$$

$$p_e = \left[\left(\frac{XX + XY}{XX + XY + YX + YY} \right) \cdot \left(\frac{XX + YX}{XX + XY + YX + YY} \right) \right] \\ + \left[\left(\frac{YX + YY}{XX + XY + YX + YY} \right) \cdot \left(\frac{XY + YY}{XX + XY + YX + YY} \right) \right] \tag{4}$$

The overall obtained Kappa score κ is presented in Table 7.

Table 7. Evaluation of inter-rater agreement for Marathi SentiWordNet

XX	YY	XY	YX	p_o	p_e	Kappa score (κ)
978	787	104	131	0.8825	0.5045	0.76

Marathi SentiWordNet generated in the research work observed a substantial agreement score. Table 8 shows the comparison of the proposed methodology with an existing state of the art for Indian languages' SentiWordNets.

Table 8. Comparison of the research work with the current state-of-art for Indian languages SentiWordNets

Study	Language	Resources used	Techniques used	Resources created	Result
[22]	Hindi	Hindi WordNet	1. Breadth First Graph traversal by exploring synonyms and antonyms 2. Bi Lingual dictionary using English-Hindi Linking 3. Translated Dictionary using Google Translate	1. Hindi lexicon of adjectives and adverbs with polarity scores 2. Annotated corpora of Hindi product reviews	70.4% Overall agreement with Annotations
[7]	Bangla	1. English SentiWordNet 2. Subjectivity Lexicon 3. English-Bangali dictionary	Word level translation followed by error reduction	SentiWordNet (Bengali)	Polarity-wise Performance Pos – p –56.59%, r –52.89% Neg – p –75.57%, r –65.87%
[23]	Bengali, Hindi, Telugu	1. English SentiWordNet 2. Subjectivity Lexicon 3. English-Hindi dictionaries (SHABDKOSH, Shabdanjali) 4. English-Bengali dictionary 5. English-Telugu dictionary - Aksharmala 6. WordNets for Hindi and Bengali	1. Bi Lingual dictionary based 2. WordNet based lexicon expansion 3. Antonym generation tech. to increase the word coverage 4. Corpus based approach 5. Gaming methodology	Bengali SentiWordNet, Hindi SentiWordNet, Telugu SentiWordNet	Polarity-wise performance 1. Bengali SentiWordNet Pos – p –56.59%, r –52.89% Neg – p –75.57%, r –65.87% 2. Hindi SentiWordNet Pos –88.0%, Neg –91.0% 3. Telugu SentiWordNet Pos – 82.0% Neg –78.0%
[26]	Odia	1. WordNets of Bengali, Tamil, Telugu, & Odia 2. SentiWordNet for Bengali, Tamil, & Telugu	WordNet based approach	SentiWordNet for Odia	Inter-annotator Agreement (Fleiss Kappa) = 0.76
Proposed work	Marathi	1. WordNets of Hindi, Marathi 2. Hindi SentiWordNet 3. English SentiWordNet 4. IndoWordNet	1. Word level translation based on English SentiWordNet 2. Expansion of Marathi SentiWordNet using Hindi SentiWordNet, IndoWordNet	Marathi SentiWordNet	Inter-annotator Agreement (Fleiss Kappa) = 0.76

5   Conclusion

The experiment in this research is the first-ever attempt to produce the Marathi SentiWordNet, which would assist as a guideline. It will emerge as a powerful resource in the Sentiment Analysis of Marathi content. The work presents a word-level translation method for producing a sentiment lexicon in Marathi, a resource-scarce language, by merging the linguistic and lexical resources, such as English SentiWordNet and Hindi SentiWordNet, and IndoWordNet, to expand and increase the word coverage of the resulting lexicon. The corresponding part-of-speeches of the opinion words are also preserved in the resource. The Marathi SentiWordNet contains 23,003 nouns with 857 positive, 977 negative, and 21169 neutral entities, 13,289 adjectives with 1380 positive, 2791 negative, and 9118 neutral entities. The 1415 adverbs with 149 positive, 72 negative, and 1194 negatives, and the 2165 verbs with 45 positive, 120 negative, and 2000 neutral entities. The Marathi SentiWordNet covers 33,816 words using English SentiWordNet and Hindi SentiWordNet. The 6056 new words are included to enrich the lexicon using the IndoWordNet synsets of Marathi, resulting in all 39,872 words with their positive and negative scores and the POS. The proposed Marathi Senti-WordNet provides sufficient coverage of Marathi opinion terms (Table 5). However, machine translation is required for this approach, which increases translation errors.

The main limitation of the method is the incorrect translation of some English words because of the morphological dissimilarities between the source and target languages. Another drawback is that the research focused on the terms with the first sense to translate to the target language since it is a primary sense, resulting in the loss of words other than the primary sense. The methodology could be adopted by any Indian language for which WordNet exists. This resource can be extended in the future by (a) using other Indian languages' SentiWordNets, (b) inclusive of all Marathi words, classified as positive, negative, and neutral, and (c) accumulating negations for more adequate coverage.

References

1. Indian languages defining India's internet. https://assets.kpmg/content/dam/kpmg/in/pdf/2017/04/Indian-languages-Defining-Indias-Internet.pdf. Accessed 29 July 2022
2. Wikipedia contributors, 22 February 2022. IndoWordNet. In Wikipedia, The Free Encyclopedia. https://en.wikipedia.org/w/index.php?title=IndoWordNet&oldid=1073451318. Accessed 29 July 2022
3. Patil, R.S., Kolhe, S.R.: Supervised classifiers with TF-IDF features for sentiment analysis of Marathi tweets. Soc. Netw. Anal. Min. **12** (2022). https://doi.org/10.1007/s13278-022-00877-w
4. Asghar, M.Z., Khan, A., Bibi, A., Kundi, F.M., Ahmad, H.: Sentence-level emotion detection framework using rule-based classification. Cogn. Comput. **9**(6), 868–894 (2017)
5. Thet, T.T., Na, J.C., Khoo, C.S.G.: Aspect-based sentiment of movie reviews on discussion boards. J. Inf. Sci. **36**(6), 823–848. (2010)

6. Rani, S., Kumar, P.: A journey of Indian languages over sentiment analysis: a systematic review. Artif. Intell. Rev. **52**(2), 1415–1462 (2018). https://doi.org/10. 1007/s10462-018-9670-y
7. Das, A., Bandyopadhyay, S.: Sentiwordnet for bangla. Knowledge Sharing Event-4: Task, 2, pp. 1–8 (2010)
8. Panjwani, R., Kanojia, D., Bhattacharyya, P.: Pyiwn: a Python based API to ACCESS Indian language wordnets. ACL Anthology (n.d.). https://aclanthology. org/2018.gwc-1.47/. Accessed 28 Sept 2021
9. Bhattacharyya, P.: Indowordnet. The WordNet in Indian Languages, pp. 1–18 (2016). https://doi.org/10.1007/978-981-10-1909-8_1
10. De Vries, E., Schoonvelde, M., Schumacher, G.: No longer lost in translation: evidence that Google Translate works for comparative bag-of-words text applications. Polit. Anal. **26**(4), 417–430 (2018)
11. Xu, G., Yu, Z., Yao, H., Li, F., Meng, Y., Xu, W.: Chinese text sentiment analysis based on extended sentiment dictionary. IEEE Access **7**, 43749–43762 (2019)
12. Asghar, M.Z., Sattar, A., Khan, A., Ali, A., Masud Kundi, F., Ahmad, S.: Creating sentiment lexicon for sentiment analysis in Urdu: the case of a resource-poor language. Expert Syst. **36**(3), e12397 (2019)
13. Lahoti, P., Mittal, N., Singh G.: A survey on NLP resources, tools and techniques for Marathi. Lang. Process. Trans. Asian Low-Resource Lang. Inf. Process. (2022)
14. Baccianella, S., Esuli, A., Sebastiani, F.: SentiWordNet 3.0. An enhanced lexical resource for sentiment analysis and opinion mining. In: Proceedings of the Seventh Conference on International Language Resources and Evaluation (LREC 2010), pp. 2200–2204. European Languages Resources Association (ELRA), Valletta, Malta (2010)
15. Joshi, A., Balamurali, A., Bhattacharyya, P.: A fall-back strategy for sentiment analysis in Hindi: a case study. In: Proceedings of the 8th International Conference on Natural Language Processing, pp. 1–6 (2010)
16. Stone, P.J., Hunt, E.B.: A computer approach to content analysis. In: Proceedings of the May 21–23, 1963, Spring Joint Computer Conference on - AFIPS 1963 (Spring) (1963). https://doi.org/10.1145/1461551.1461583
17. Hatzivassiloglou, V., Kathleen R.M.: Predicting the semantic orientation of adjectives. In: Proceedings of the 35th Annual Meeting of the ACL and Eighth Conference of the European Chapter of the ACL, pp. 174–181 (1997)
18. Turney, P.D.: Thumbs up or thumbs down? Semantic orientation applied to unsupervised classification of reviews. In: proceedings of the 40th Annual Meeting of the Association for Computational Linguistics, pp 417–434 (2002)
19. Wiebe, J.M.: Learning subjective adjectives from corpora. In: Proceedings of the 17th National Conference on Artificial Intelligence, pp. 735–740 (2000)
20. Riloff, E., Wiebe, J., Wilson, T.: Learning subjective nouns using extraction pattern bootstrapping. In: Proceeding of the 7th Conference on Natural Language Learning, pp. 25–32 (2003)
21. Riloff, E. Wiebe, J.: Learning extraction patterns for subjective expressions. In: Proceedings of the 2003 Conference on Empirical Methods in Natural Language Processing, pp. 105–112 (2003)
22. Bakliwal, A., Arora, P., Varma, V.: Hindi subjective lexicon: a lexical resource for Hindi adjective polarity classification. In: Proceedings of the Eighth International Conference on Language Resources and Evaluation (LREC 2012), pp. 1189–1196 (2012)
23. Das, A., Bandyopadhyay, S.: SentiWordNet for Indian languages. In: Proceedings of the Eighth Workshop on Asian Language Resources, pp. 56–63 (2010)

24. Bakliwal, A., Arora, P., Varma, V.: Hindi subjective lexicon: a lexical resource for Hindi adjective polarity classification. In: Proceedings of the Eighth International Conference on Language Resources and Evaluation (LREC 2012), pp. 1189–1196, Istanbul, Turkey. European Language Resources Association (ELRA) (2012)

25. Popale, L., Bhattacharyya, P.: Creating Marathi WordNet. In: Dash, N.S., Bhattacharyya, P., Pawar, J.D. (eds.) The WordNet in Indian Languages, pp. 147–166. Springer, Singapore (2017). https://doi.org/10.1007/978-981-10-1909-8_8

26. Mohanty, G., Kannan, A., Mamidi, R.: Building a SentiWordNet for Odia. In: Proceedings of the 8th Workshop on Computational Approaches to Subjectivity, Sentiment and Social Media Analysis, pp. 143–148, Copenhagen, Denmark. Association for Computational Linguistics (2017)

27. Bo, P., Lillian, L., Shivakumar, V.: Thumbs up? Sentiment classification using machine learning techniques. In: Proceedings of the Conference on Empirical Methods in Natural Language Processing (EMNLP), pp. 79–86 (2002)

28. Patil, R.S., Kolhe, S.R.: Inflectional and Derivational Hybrid Stemmer for Sentiment Analysis: A Case Study with Marathi Tweets. In: Santosh, K., Hegadi, R., Pal, U. (eds.) RTIP2R 2021. CCIS, vol. 1576, pp. 263–279. Springer, Cham (2022). https://doi.org/10.1007/978-3-031-07005-1_23

29. Patil, R.S., Kolhe, S.R.: Resource creation for sentiment analysis of under-resourced language: Marathi. In: Santosh, K.C., Gawali, B. (eds.) RTIP2R 2020. CCIS, vol. 1380, pp. 445–457. Springer, Singapore (2020). https://doi.org/10.1007/978-981-16-0507-9_37

30. Jurafsky, D., Martin, J.H.: Speech and Language Processing. Pearson Prentice Hall, Harlow (2014)

A Computational Study on Calibrated VGG19 for Multimodal Learning and Representation in Surveillance

Pranav Singh Chib[1]([✉]) [iD], Manju Khari[1] [iD], and KC Santosh[2] [iD]

[1] Jawaharlal Nehru University, New Delhi 110067, India
pranavchib59@gmail.com, manjukhari@jnu.ac.in
[2] Applied AI Research Lab, Computer Science Department,
University of South Dakota, Vermillion, USA
Santosh.KC@usd.edu

Abstract. This research discusses the pre-trained deep learning architecture for the multimodal learning and representation in surveillance system. This framework generates a single image from the integration of the multi sensor information, which includes the infrared and visible. We use visible and infrared as the information in different spectrum of light, in term of contrast ratio and visibility. We start with image registration to align coordinates so the decomposition of the source image into the sub bands is possible. The VGG-19 and the weighted averaging are utilized for the feature extraction and transfer learning task. This is conducted thorough empirical research by implementing a series of methodology studies to evaluate how pre-trained deep learning techniques enhance overall fusion performance and improve recognition and detection capability. This study also contains a comparison of the performance of spatial and frequency algorithms in contrast to the deep learning based method for the surveillance system. The research work is concluded by evaluating the performance measure of the proposed fusion algorithm with the traditional algorithm.

Keywords: VGG19 · Multimodal learning · Image fusion · Surveillance system

1 Introduction

Image fusion is the process of integrating the image information obtained from varied kinds of image acquisition devices into single for capturing the different aspects of a scene. In this way, the different image information can be represented into a single or fewer image with more accurate information having compact and precise information. In recent years, the increasing interest in the visual surveillance of the scene or the abnormality in the military, public, and commercial scenario are emphasizing the need to have an intelligent visual surveillance system. In this direction, developing the methods for robust surveillance systems

KC Santosh et al. (Eds.): RTIP2R 2022, CCIS 1704, pp. 261–271, 2023.
https://doi.org/10.1007/978-3-031-23599-3_19

for tasks such as object detection, recognition, and tracking are crucial. In order to get the better clarity and depth of scene, a single image sensor device is not sufficient for better active surveillance technique. One sensor is not able to give clarity, depth of the field of the view, and design disadvantage is why the multi sensor approach will give the complete and much more information about the scene; for example, the infrared image [1] contains the much more information about the contrast and can be used to capture the target recognition but the visible image can able to get much more understanding about the scene in term of human understanding. The infrared measures the heat radiating that forms the base for image mapping, while the visible can show the colorized topography, their image fusion can provide better spatial resolution. In this scenario, the fusion of both the sensor input into the single fused image can be the better information. Image fusion can provide better recognition and detection ability in surveillance and can be very much reliable. It gathers the important features and information from the multiple images and includes it into a single source image. The image contains much more relevant information and is more approachable for human understanding. In the Multi modal approach for surveillance, In this work, integrate the multiple images from the different models to enhance the quality of visual surveillance. The model image can be visible, infrared, thermal, and panchromatic [2]. The better image fusion is the one that can combine important features into the source image without any inconsistencies. The image is better suitable for visual representation and understanding.

Image Fusion can be of the frequency domain [3] or that of the spatial domain. The spatial technique involves the manipulation of the pixel level of the image to get desired result. DWT techniques are very much used in fusion techniques under the frequency domain. Deep learning methods [13] have recently been used in image fusion, which has the huge potential in improving the fusion process, whether in terms of image representation or studying the fusion image. So, in this work a novel image fusion technique in visual surveillance for better object detection, tracking, and recognition has been proposed.

1.1 Research Gap

Visual surveillance has suffered because of the quality issues and the human understanding issue that lead to a lack of clarity and depth of the scene, which hinder the decision making [11]. Thus the system must provide accurate data about the scene for better visual perception. There must be Minimal spectral distortion, Better representation, Reliability and robustness to noisy environment.

- There is a lack of effective fusion management and representation techniques which have better evaluation matrices and performances.
- The fused image has the tendency of image edge loss which perform poor for the real time application also the process of transformation is a slower process.

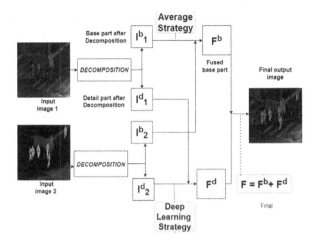

Fig. 1. Proposed schema

- Establishing an effective processing of the surveillance multimodal images to improve target detection and recognition capability is not the focus of much of research on fusion.

2   Proposed Methodology

The technique utilities a pre-trained deep learning - VGG-19 [22] for the feature extraction. The strategy comprises four significant model stages (see Fig. 1):

- Registration Process: Transforming our source images into a standard coordinate system as a step of pre-processing.
- Decomposition: The optimization method [3] for the process of effective decomposition of the input image as compared to that of the other decomposition methods like DWT.
- Fusion: Simple weighted average and the VGG-19 is employed to get the weights map for the for Final fusion
- Reconstruction: The Process of getting the Final image from the base and detail part which is obtained from previous step.

2.1   Registration Process

Image registration is the process of transforming images into a standard coordinate system, so corresponding pixels represent homogeneous points. The image is banded from 8 to 14 micron, so we apply the image registration that select the several pair points that needed to be aligned in between the two images. A number of points (landmarks) are defined on the identical locations in two volumes as part of the straightforward procedure known as image landmark registration

[6]. The volumes are then registered when an algorithm matches the landmarks. For the purposes of registration, the two volumes are referred to as fixed and movable.

2.2 Decomposition

For our method we choose K be 2 Which is our pre registered image as a input from the surveillance sensors, it can also be extended to multiple sensorial information were K greater than 2. The images is represented as Ik (k = 1,2) We use the optimization method [4] for the process of effective decomposition of the input image as compared to that of the other decomposition methods. From the decomposition of the source image we obtain the I_b and I_d which represents the base part of the image and the detail part of the image, We only obtain base part by using this optimization method. Next, I_d k the detail part is obtained using

$$I_d = \text{Intensity} - I_b, \tag{1}$$

where I_1 and I_2 denote the source image. To begin, for each source image, Eq. (1) are solved to produce the base component and the detail component. One is fused by the weighted averaging and the other through DL framework. The final image is generated through reconstruction by summing the base and the detailed part.

2.3 Image Fusion

The Base part and the Detailed part are fused through different pipelines one by the weighted average strategy and other by the VGG-19 strategy to get the fused image.

Base Parts Fusion. In our methodology we use the averaging of the weights to get the fusion of the base part. The base part is one which we extract from the input image which has redundant and common features Eq. 2 shows the calculation:

$$F_b = \alpha_1 I_1^b + \alpha_2 I_2^b, \tag{2}$$

where I corresponding to the image intensity $\alpha 1$ and $\alpha 2$ are the value of the weights in i_1^b and i_2^b. We choose $\alpha 1 = 0.5$ and $\alpha 2 = 0.5$.

Detail Content Fusion. I_1^d and I_2^d are the detail content. We proposed the Dl framework (VGG-19 model) for the deep feature extraction and the fusion strategy Fig. 2 illustrate the procedure.

LAYER	WEIGHT LAYERS	FILTERS	OUTPUT
	Input 224 × 224 × 3		
1	• Conv1_1 • Conv1_2	[3 × 3 conv] × 64 [3 × 3 conv] × 64	224 × 224 × 64 224 × 224 × 64
Max-pooling 2 × 2, stride = 2			112 × 112 × 64
2	• Conv2_1 • Conv2_2	[3 × 3 conv] × 128 [3 × 3 conv] × 128	112 × 112 × 128 112 × 112 × 128
Max-pooling 2 × 2, stride = 2			56 × 56 × 128
3	• Conv3_1 • Conv3_2 • Conv3_3 • Conv3_4	[3 × 3 conv] × 256 [3 × 3 conv] × 256 [3 × 3 conv] × 256 [3 × 3 conv] × 256	56 × 56 × 256 56 × 56 × 256 56 × 56 × 256 56 × 56 × 256
Max-pooling 2 × 2, stride = 2			28 × 28 × 256
4	• Conv4_1 • Conv4_2 • Conv4_3 • Conv4_4	[3 × 3 conv] × 512 [3 × 3 conv] × 512 [3 × 3 conv] × 512 [3 × 3 conv] × 512	28 × 28 × 512 28 × 28 × 512 28 × 28 × 512 28 × 28 × 512
Max-pooling 2 × 2, stride = 2			14 × 14 × 512
5	• Conv5_1 • Conv5_2 • Conv5_3 • Conv5_4	[3 × 3 conv] × 512 [3 × 3 conv] × 512 [3 × 3 conv] × 512 [3 × 3 conv] × 512	14 × 14 × 512 14 × 14 × 512 14 × 14 × 512 14 × 14 × 512
Max-pooling 2 × 2, stride = 2			7 × 7 × 512

(a)   (b)

Fig. 2. Specific configuration of VGG-19 and feature map

The detailed content is fed into the VGG-19 to get the deep feature. After obtaining the feature map we use the multi layer FS to get the corresponding weight. Finally the reconstruction is employed to reconstruct the detail content and corresponding weight map.

Let the detail content be I_d and the $\phi_k^{i,m}$ be the feature map of the detail with the ith layer and that of k image and the channel is m, $m \in 1, 2, ..., M$, $M = 64 \times 2^{i-1}$ is the layer in the VGG-network and i i∈ 1, 2, 3, 4. These are relu1 up to the relu4 as there are the four layers. $\phi^i, 1 : m(x,y)$ denotes the content, positioned in the pixel map, it is a vector. Figure 3 shows the strategy. As the Fig. 3 after the features the activation map Ci, k is obtained with the help of the l1-norm and the averaging operators on the each blocks. K range from 1 and

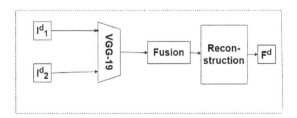

Fig. 3. Detail part fusion

2 and that of i in the range of 1,2,3,4. We know from [10] that the l1-norm is the measure of the activity of the detailed part. Thus, map Ci,k calculated by

$$\left\| \phi_k^{i,1:M}(x,y) \right\| 1. \tag{3}$$

To avoid our fusion technique resilient to misregistration, we employ the average block by block operation to compute the final map $C_{i,k}$.

Block size is determined by r. If the r is bigger, the fusion approach will be more resistant to misregistration, but some information may be lost. As a result, r = 1 in our method. We will apply the soft-max operator to produce weight maps for the features at each layer, thus a detailed fused content is obtained. Wi,k(x, y) in Eq. (4) is in range of [0,1]. We will apply the same operation at multiple layers and obtain different fused detailed content:

$$W_k^i = \frac{\hat{C}_i^{bk}}{\sum_{n=1}^{K} \hat{C}_n^i}. \tag{4}$$

Pooling in the VGG19 is a down sampling operation, this operator re sizes the map to $1/s$ times where it is dependent on the stride "s". VGG19 have the stride "s" that of the size 2 so it is $1/2$ time when ever the pooling is applied on the feature map. At different layers the FM $1/2$ $(i-1)$ times that of the

Detail part size, i range is 1,2,3,4 which represents the layers of the Relu1.1, Relu2.1, Relu3.1 and Relu4.1, respectively. Pooling in the VGG19 is a down sampling operation, this operator re sizes the map to $1/s$ times where it is dependent on the stride "s". VGG19 have the stride "s" that of the size 2 so it is $1/2$ time when ever the pooling is applied on the feature map. At different layers the FM $1/2$ $(i-1)$ times that of the Detail part size, i range is 1,2,3,4 which represents the layers of the Relu1.1, Relu2.1, Relu3.1 and Relu4.1, respectively. We employ an up sampling to adjust the weight map dimension to the source detail part size once we acquire Wi,k which is weight map. Equation 5 illustrates the calculation of the weight map.

$$\hat{W}_i^k(x+p, y+q) = W_i^k(x,y). \tag{5}$$

We now get the 4 pairs of Wi,k, $k \in 1,2$ and i is in range of 1, 2, 3, 4. Finally, Eq. 6 is used to calculate the F_d, which is calculated by selecting the highest value from the 4 initial Fd content for each location or the position:

$$F_d = MAX[F_d^i | i \epsilon 1, 2, 3, 4]. \tag{6}$$

The final out put image is given by the submission of the detailed f_d and the base f_b fused images in the reconstruction process.

3   Experimental Setup and Results

This section deal with the quantity and quality evaluation of the result obtained by the proposed methodology. The result are analyses with the set of generated

Table 1. Experimental observation

Method methods	RMSE reduction	Average MAE reduction	PSNR reduction	SF reduction	MI improvement	Increased similarity	MG
DWT	57%	61%	30%	18%	18%	8.5%	10%
DWPT	56%	62%	30%	14%	18.16%	8.25%	11%
SWT	50.1%	56%	24%	63%	5%	5.6%	45%
SWPT	50%	57%	23.5%	45%	5.33%	5.5%	46%
DTCWT	51%	59%	24.6%	21%	12.3%	6%	18%
PCA	44.3%	53%	20%	81%	5.8%	5.3%	75%
Ensemble	37%	-	13.2%	30%	-	5%	25%
MST	20.3%	-	10%	23%	-	5.3%	41%

images and the naturally obtain images using the testing parameters on the real images.

The result are analyses with the set of generated images and the naturally obtain images using the testing parameters on the real images. The fused result of various images as per the data set from the algorithm like the dwt, swt, pcs, mst [11] and our proposed algorithm are analyses and the result are shown in the Fig. 4.

The subjective analysis of the fused image that is produced from the proposed method is compared with the fused image that is generated from the traditional methods.

Our technique has shown reduction in RMSE value as compared to other methods, the 57%, 56%, 50%, 50%, 51%, 44.3%, 37%, 20.3%, as shown in Table 1. Our methodology have also achieve reduction in MAE Compared to others. The method also perform better in other measures. Like SF, MI, SSIM, and MG. The table below signifies the overall reduction in the relative value of the each measure in comparison to the other algorithms.

As in Fig. 5, it is clear that the our methodology have improved results in term of better visualization of the scenario. We use bar graph to represent the variation in the performance of the proposed methodology with the traditional one.

Wang et al. (2011) have proposed one of the earliest multiresolution transform, named Laplacian Pyramid to merge multi-focus images; this fusion scheme provides information on the sharp contrast changes but fails to preserve the low contrast features.

Neha et al. (2014) used an average fusion after that morphological pyramid is used combine multi-focus pictures. The drawback of pyramid-based fusion is that it produces a blocking effect in the fused image and has a poor Signal to Noise Ratio (SNR) as seen in the bar graph result shown in Fig. 5. Wavelet transforms have a superior shift-invariance and also the directional selectivity that enables wavelet transform in the correct transfer at more directional

Fig. 4. Qualitative comparison - surveillance input sample (left) and output (right).

and edge features into the fused picture. DWT has two significant drawbacks, restricted directionality and shift sensitivity, quite apart from the choice for its non-redundant character and perfect reconstruction characteristics in many domains. Furthermore, the conspicuous low contrast elements of the original picture are not preserved by this method because of the maximum selection fusion

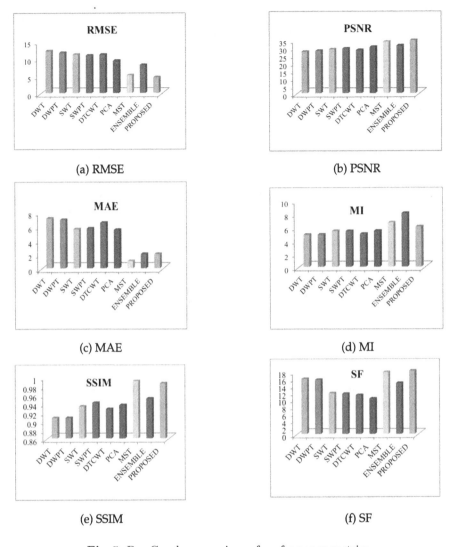

(a) RMSE

(b) PSNR

(c) MAE

(d) MI

(e) SSIM

(f) SF

Fig. 5. Bar Graph comparison of performance metrics

criterion. The Undecimated Discrete Wavelet Transform (UDWT) has been pro-posed for overcoming the shift-invariance problem associated with DWT.

Multi-scale geometric transform such as Dual Tree Discrete Wavelet Trans-form (DTDWT), Contourlet Transform (CT), and Shearlet Transform (ST) for overcoming the drawbacks of traditional DWT. They do suffer from the No shift invariance and produce Gibbs phenomena, Low computational efficiency; Low contrast features are not preserved.

The proposed method overcomes these disadvantages and producing high spatial and spectral information from the source image with Reliability and robustness in a noisy environment, as observed in the following experimental observatios. Less value of RMSE [15] which is best in class than other traditional methods like DWT, DWPT, SWT etc. In terms of PSNR, the proposed method has one of the highest values, also greater than mst and ensemble. Also, our proposed has the least value of Mean absolute error. Mutual information is relatively higher than the DWT, DWPT, SWT, PCA, etc. The similarity index proposed and MST has the highest similarity value. Spatial frequency also has the highest value in the proposed algorithm.

4   Conclusion and Future Scope

The traditional image fusion algorithms have not been addressed to different challenges posed by the surveillance system. Our methodology mainly focused on the VGG19 implementation with the weighted average strategy to maximize the feature extraction and the fusion of detailed content for our multi-sensor input. Prior to using a multilayer fusion technique based on a pre-trained VGG-19 network, the input picture is first decomposed. At last, the softmax function is used to get the final weight map. Experimental results showed that the performance in terms of measures like PSNR, SSIM, FI, MI, and ENTROPY, have better and robust result.

The Research can be further investigated in the future for various domain applications, and many further improvements and solutions can be implemented in the method. The further optimization can be provided for efficient working of the fusion technique. Further research is needed in the further improvement of the model selection, of the parameter required for optimizing the algorithm.

References

1. Paramanandham, N., Rajendiran, K.: Multi sensor image fusion for surveillance applications using hybrid image fusion algorithm. Multimedia Tools and Applications **77**(10), 12405–12436 (2017). https://doi.org/10.1007/s11042-017-4895-3
2. Azam, M.A., et al.: A review on multimodal medical image fusion: compendious analysis of medical modalities, multimodal databases, fusion techniques and quality metrics. Comput. Biol. Med. **144**, 105253 (2018)
3. Tang, L., Yuan, J., Ma, J.: Image fusion in the loop of high-level vision tasks: a semantic-aware real-time infrared and visible image fusion network. Inf. Fusion **82**, 28–42 (2022)
4. Alseelawi, N., Hazim, H.T., Salim ALRikabi, H.T.: A Novel method of multimodal medical image fusion based on hybrid approach of NSCT and DTCWT. Int. J. Online Biomed. Eng. **18**(3) (2022)
5. Zhang, H., Xu, H., Tian, X., Jiang, J., Ma, J.: Image fusion meets deep learning: a survey and perspective. Inf. Fusion **76**, 323–336 (2021)
6. Kaur, H., Koundal, D., Kadyan, V.: Image fusion techniques: a survey. Arch. Comput. Methods Eng. **28**(7), 4425–4447 (2021). https://doi.org/10.1007/s11831-021-09540-7
7. Huang, B., Yang, F., Yin, M., Mo, X., Zhong, C.: A review of multimodal medical image fusion techniques. Comput. Math. Methods Med. **144** (2020)

8. Ma, J, .Ma, Y., Li, C.: Infrared and visible image fusion methods and applications: a survey. Inf. Fusion. **45**, 153–178 (2019). https://doi.org/10.1016/j.inffus.2018.02.004

9. Ma, J., Tang, L., Fan, F., Huang, J., Mei, X., Ma, Y.: SwinFusion: cross-domain long-range learning for general image fusion via swin transformer. IEEE/CAA J. Automat. Sin. **9**(7), 1200–1217 (2022)

10. Hermessi, H., Mourali, O., Zagrouba, E.: Multimodal medical image fusion review: theoretical background and recent advances. Signal Process. **183**, 108036 (2021)

11. Li, Y., Zhao, J., Lv, Z., Li, J.: Medical image fusion method by deep learning. Int. J. Cogni. Comput. Eng. **2**, 21–29 (2021)

12. Li, G., Lin, Y., Qu, X.: An infrared and visible image fusion method based on multi-scale transformation and norm optimization. Inf. Fusion **71**, 109–129 (2021)

13. Xu, H., Ma, J., Jiang, J., Guo, X., Ling, H.: U2Fusion: a unified unsupervised image fusion network. IEEE Trans. Pattern Anal. Mach. Intell. **44**(1), 502–518 (2020)

14. Anandhi, D., Valli, S.: An algorithm for multi-sensor image fusion using maximum a posteriori and nonsubsampled contourlet transform. Comput. Electr. Eng. **65**, 139–152 (2018)

15. Cai, J., Cheng, Q., Peng, M., Song, Y.: Fusion of infrared and visible images based on nonsubsampled contourlet transform and sparse K-SVD dictionary learning. Infrared Phys. Technol. **82**, 85–95 (2017)

16. Tong, Y.: Visual sensor image enhancement based on non-sub-sampled shearlet transform and phase stretch transform. EURASIP J. Wirel. Commun. Netw. **2019**(1), 1–8 (2019). https://doi.org/10.1186/s13638-019-1344-1

17. Wang, Z., Ziou, D., Armenakis, C., Li, D., Li, Q.: A comparative analysis of image fusion methods. IEEE Trans. Geosci. Remote Sens. **43**(6), 1391–1402 (2005)

18. Pajares, G., De La Cruz, J.M.: A wavelet-based image fusion tutorial. Pattern Recogn. **37**(9), 1855–1872 (2004)

19. Li, S., Kang, X., Hu, J.: Image fusion with guided filtering. IEEE Trans. Image Process. **22**(7), 2864–2875 (2013)

20. Li, S., Kang, X., Fang, L., Hu, J., Yin, H.: Pixel-level image fusion: a survey of the state of the art. Inf. Fusion **33**, 100–112 (2017)

21. Zhang, Y., Liu, Y., Sun, P., Yan, H., Zhao, X., Zhang, L.: IFCNN: a general image fusion framework based on convolutional neural network. Inf. Fusion **54**, 99–118 (2020)

22. Simonyan, K., Zisserman, A.: Very deep convolutional networks for large-scale image recognition. arXiv preprint arXiv:1409.1556 (2014)

Automated Deep Learning Based Approach for Albinism Detection

Rahul Nijhawan[1], Manya Juneja[1], Namneet Kaur[1], Ashima Yadav[2(✉)], and Ishan Budhiraja[2]

[1] School of Computer Science, University of Petroleum and Energy Studies, Dehradun, Uttarakhand, India
rahul.nijhawan@ddn.upes.ac.in
[2] School of Computer Science Engineering and Technology, Bennett University, Greater Noida, India
ashimayadavdtu@gmail.com, Ishan.budhiraja@bennett.edu.in

Abstract. As we all know, Albinism is a condition in which a person is born with a deficiency in melanin pigment. The colour (shade) of skin, hair, and eyes is a symptom of having a molecule called melanin. Pale skin, hair, and eyes are signs of Albinism. People with Albinism are more likely to get skin cancer, and their skin is highly prone to sunburn. In our dataset, which contains data on people with or without Albinism, deep learning frameworks like inception V3, VGG 19, VGG 16, and many more were used. In this paper, we have employed different hybrid combinations of pre-trained deep learning architecture for deep feature extraction in combination with different hand-crafted based classifiers for classification. After a detailed analysis of the various hybrid architectures, the best one was proposed that outperformed the other state-of-the-art architectures. We further performed accuracy assessment on several statistical measures such as AUC, accuracy, precision, recall and others. Our proposed hybrid architecture was compared with other architectures using ROC (receiver operating characteristic curve). Our approach produced an accuracy of 99.8% compared to other models.

Keywords: Random forest · Logistic regression · Inception V3 · VGG16 · VGG19 · Albinism

1 Introduction

Albinism is a category of genetic illness in which the pigment called melanin which affects the color of the skin, hair, and eyes, is produced in minimal quantity or not produced at all. This condition affects the function and development of the eyes in every form. It happens because melanin has a unique role in developing particular optical nerves. The symptoms of Albinism are pale complexion varying with age and exposure to the sun, which can lead to an elevated risk of getting skin cancer. The leading cause of Albinism is mutations in one or more genes, and most cases are auto-summary recessive. The Latin word Albus, which means white, is where the word Albinism originates. As a result, the name "Albinos" is used to refer to those who have Albinism. Clinical phenotypic heterogeneity suggests that expressiveness varies [1].

Due to albinos' heightened sensitivity to the sun's rays and susceptibility to developing skin cancer, minor variations in a person's skin, hair, and eye colour might occur. Albinism rarely and barely has some treatment, although those who have it can make efforts to protect their skin and eyes from improving their vision. Albinism may have different inheritance patterns depending on the genetic cause. Oculocutaneous Albinism affects the skin, hair, and eyes. Less often occurring, ocular Albinism only affects the eyes; however, the skin and hair are either of the same color or somewhat lighter than other family members. Numerous distinct gene mutations on various chromosomes result in Albinism. A healthcare provider may conduct a physical examination and a skin, hair, and eye assessment [2].

On the other hand, a genetic test will provide the most accurate findings and identify the changed gene. This DNA test aids in identifying the type of Albinism that one possesses. Because of the societal stigma associated with Albinism, people with the condition are likelier to be alone. Albino persons, for the most part, have an expected lifespan. Due to linked diseases, people with Hermansky-Pudlak syndrome and Chediak-Higashi syndrome have a higher risk of dying very young.

In this paper, we proposed a hybrid framework based on the pre-trained deep learning architectures for computing the deep features, in combination with the hand-craft algorithms employed for classification. We created a vast library of such combinations to identify the most suitable combination. Intense analysis of the results confirmed the performance of the proposed model. Accuracy assessment was done, employing a wide range of statistical parameters such as AUC, precision, recall, specificity, ROC curves and so on. Our developed framework outperformed the state-of-the-art algorithms, as shown in detail in the results and discussion section of the paper.

The structure of the paper is as follows: Sect. 1 talks about the introduction to Albinism, Sect. 2 provides the details of created dataset and methods employed, Sect. 3 gives details of results achieved and its discussion, and the Sect. 4 provides the conclusion and future scope.

2 Materials and Methods

2.1 Dataset Acquired

We gathered the images from Google. Two partitions were created for the dataset; the first contained images with Albinism disease and the second without Albinism. The dataset collected was split into training and testing, where 75% of the total images were included in the training set, whereas the remaining 25% were included in the testing set. Our proposed approach produced an accuracy of 99.8%. The number of images with Albinism was 145 and without Albinism was 134. The total images collected were 279. All the images were resized into a uniform size matrix for final processing. The details of the created dataset are given in Table 1.

Table 1. Details of the sample images collected

Types of images	Number of images
Images with Albinism	145
Images without Albinism	134
Total number of images	279

2.2 Classifiers

2.2.1 Convolution Neural Network (CNN/ConvNet)

ConvNet is a class of deep neural networks used for image analysis and visualization. ConvNet is a network made up of wholly connected, pooling, and convolutional layers. In our research, we used two different types of CNN network frameworks (VGG-16 and VGG-19). These structures aid in object detection, the classification of images, and the localization of objects. Convolutional, max pooling, and Dropout are among the 19 trained layers in the VGG-19. VGG19 is a 19-layer variation of the VGG model (three completely connected layers, five max pool layers, sixteen convolution layers, and one SoftMax layer). VGG11, VGG16, and various variations of VGG are among them. VGG19 has 19.6 billion FLOPs in total. A predefined size (224 * 224) image was used as the network's input, indicating that the matrix was rectangular (224, 224, 3). The sole pre-processing was to take each pixel from the complete training set and subtract its mean RGB value. They used kernels with the size of stride of 1 pixel and a dimension of (3 * 3), covering the whole visual idea.

2.2.2 SVM

SVM is a supervised learning model with both uses like request and backslide issues. Regardless, it is essentially used in ML for Classification problems. The SVM's computation will presumably find the best line or decision limit for arranging n-layered space with the objective that we can, without a doubt, place new components in the correct arrangement later on. A hyperplane is the ideal decision limit. SVM selects the outstanding centres and vectors that help build the hyperplane. These models are algorithmic applications of statistical learning concepts [3], which deal with the challenge of creating a reliable estimation method from given data: how can the efficacy of a model be predicted using merely its attributes and its results on a training set? Support vector machines address a constrained quadratic optimization problem to create the optimum separation bounds between data sets [4, 5]. Different levels of non-linearity and adaptability can be incorporated into the model by employing other kernel functions.

2.2.3 K-Nearest Neighbor

K-Nearest Neighbor is among the most straightforward machine learning model compared to supervised learning systems. The new case is characterized in a way that is most similar to the arrangements that are already available via K-NN computation, which predicts the equivalence between new case/data and open cases. K-NN computation stores all open data and portrays another data point considering the comparability. This infers that when new data appears, it will generally be helpfully gathered into a good suite order using the K-NN calculation. K-NN estimation can be used for regression, too, concerning classification. However, for the most part, it is used for Classification issues. The k-nearest neighbour technique for classification differs from the previous approaches we have looked at since it classifies data directly without first developing a model [6, 7].

2.2.4 Binary Variable

A binary variable, such as True/False or 0/1, serves as the dependent variable in the Logistic Regression (LR) model, which is a relapsing model. Regarding the value of the reaction variables for the numeric condition that links it to the indicator components, it genuinely establishes the possibility of a paired response. Instead of fitting a relapsing line, we provide a calculated "S" shape that foretells the two essential characteristics of strategy relapse (0 or 1). The calculated capacity bend shows the probability of anything, including if the cells are harmful or whether a mouse is overweight, among other things. Maximizing $i = 1nP(yi|xi)$ is necessary for the ideal parameter values with maximum likelihood. The logistic (sigmoidal) activation function can transform a network without a hidden layer into a logistic regression model, even though the functional forms of the two models differ significantly [8, 9].

2.2.5 Decision Tree

This algorithm divides the data set frequently to enhance data isolation, producing a tree-like architecture [9, 10]. The most used parameter is information gain, which implies that each split maximizes the amount of lost entropy. The ratio of the elements belonging to the y class to all other parts in the leaf node that holds the data item x is the estimate of $P(y|x)$. The greedy construction strategy of decision trees, which chooses the optimum variable and split point combination at each stage, is a primary disadvantage. However, a multi-step integrated lookahead that considers combinations of the input variables can produce different (and more significant) outcomes. Another issue is that the splitting procedure inadvertently discretizes continuous variables, which results in the loss of information.

2.3 Proposed Framework

This study proposes a method for Albinism detection. This paper proposes a hybrid architecture that employs pre-trained Inception-V3 module for deep features extraction and Logistic Regression for classification. The first layer of the Inception v3 network is based on substantial learning-based component extraction. We used pre-trained deep learning architecture for performing feature extraction. The most optimal results have come from LR. An LR model analyses the link between at least one existing independent variable to predict a dependent information variable. Using the Inception-V3 deep learning architecture, an image embedding technique was used. The total number of layers in the inception V3 model is 42, slightly increasing over the inception V1 and V2 models. However, this model's effectiveness is genuinely astounding. We will get to it momentarily, Examining the parts of the Inception V3 model in more detail (See Fig. 1).

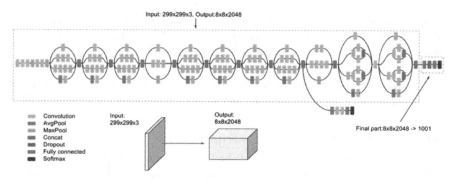

Fig. 1. Proposed pre-trained Inception V3 framework

3 Experimental Results

Two folders served as our inputs, one containing 134 photographs of individuals without Albinism and the other arresting images of individuals with Albinism (145 images). The second phase involved image embedding (also known as "image pre-processing"), which was applied to improve the raw data (here, images of people with Albinism and those without it), suppress image distortions, and improve various aspects of the images for processing. After completing the pre-processing image step, we focused on the testing and scoring technique to assess our datasets. We used a variety of deep learning architectures while picture embedding in this step (SqueezeNet, InceptionV3, VG16, VG19), providing the inputs as different classification algorithms or classifiers (SVM, KNN, Logistic Regression, Ada-Boost). We demonstrated the performance of different hybrid combination architectures using ROC curves.

3.1 Inception V3

A convolutional neural network with 48 layers is called Inception V3. Using the ImageNet database, one can load a network that has already been trained using more than a million images. Using pre-trained weights from ImageNet, the Keras image classification algorithm Inception V3 can be used. It is a CNN Framework trained on more than one million images. Thousand object categories have been used to pre-train images to read and classify. The GoogLeNet network is known as the Inception network since it primarily comprises the Inception network architecture [11–15] (See Table 2).

We looked at the ROC curves as well as the outcomes. The AUC showed that the LR algorithm has the best output accuracy at 99.8%. The F1 score in Table 1 shows how well our classifier performs utilizing the recall and precision ratings. The table above demonstrates that while AdaBoost performs best in the F1 score, F2 score and AUC, LR performs best in the F1 score, precision score, AUC, and Recall (Area Under the Curve) (See Fig. 2).

Table 2. ML classifier comparison results using the Inception V3 model

Model	Inception V3				
	AUC	CA	F1	Precision	Recall
KNN	0.939	0.885	0.885	0.887	0.885
SVM	0.980	0.930	0.930	0.933	0.930
Proposed Approach (LR)	**0.998**	**0.998**	**0.955**	**0.955**	**0.955**
AdaBoost	0.720	0.720	0.720	0.721	0.720

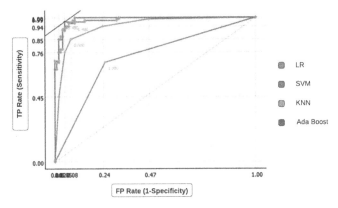

Fig. 2. ROC curve using different classifiers for the Inception v3 model.

3.2 VGG16

Convolutional neural network (CNN) framework VGG-16 is used to improve the precision of large-scale image categorization and identification. The artificial neural architecture features 16 layers, each of which has some weights and pooling layers. For every layer, the pool is 2×2, and the kernel is 3×3. VGG16 is widely used in deep learning image categorization methods because of how simple it is to use. Due to its benefits, VGG16 is frequently used in educational applications. ImageNet, a dataset with more than 14 million images, is divided into thousand classes. After this, it was observed that this model performed with 92.7% accuracy in the top-5 test [16–18] (See Table 3).

We looked at the ROC curves and the outcomes. The area under the roc curve of 99.4% indicates that the LR algorithm provided us with the best output. The best accuracy obtained by LR is 96.5%. For F1, Precisions, and Recall scores, LR performed best (See Fig. 3).

3.3 VGG19

VGG19 is an image classification deep learning convolutional network (CNN) architecture. The subsequent significant development came with the VGG architecture, which has 16 convolution layers and three fully linked layers, after Alexnet's victory in the

Table 3. Comparing the output of vgg16 model-based machine learning classifiers

Model	VGG16				
	AUC	Accuracy	F1	Precision	Recall
KNN	0.959	0.910	0.910	0.916	0.910
SVM	0.949	0.885	0.885	0.892	0.885
LR	**0.987**	**0.995**	**0.995**	**0.995**	**0.995**
AdaBoost	0.810	0.810	0.810	0.810	0.810

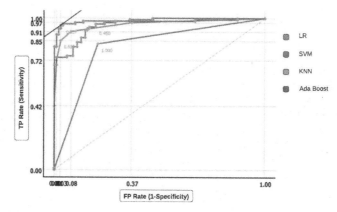

Fig. 3. ROC curve plotted using VGG16 model and different classifier.

2012 ImageNet Challenge competition. It is referred to as a VGG-19 since there are 19 layers (See Table 4).

Table 4. Evaluating and contrasting the results of VGG 19 model-based machine learning (ML) classifiers

Model	VGG19				
	AUC	Accuracy	F1	Precision	Recall
KNN	0.950	0.880	0.880	0.886	0.880
SVM	0.941	0.860	0.880	0.882	0.880
LR	0.974	0.915	0.915	0.915	0.915
AdaBoost	0.810	0.810	0.810	0.812	0.810

After observing the ROC curve chart and the outcomes, we learned that the LR algorithm performed the best in all five parameters. The highest AUC value is 87.4% (See Fig. 4). Table 5 gives a comparison of performance of our proposed approach with

Table 5. Comparison of our proposed approach with state-of-the-art algorithms

Model	AUC	Accuracy	F1	Precision	Recall
CNN [17]	0.902	0.897	0.865	0.911	0.896
Deep CNN [16]	0.901	0.879	0.910	0.867	0.891
Inception [14]	0.911	0.921	0.897	0.887	0.896
ResNet [15]	0.845	0.821	0.802	0.811	0.839
Proposed approach	**0.998**	**0.998**	**0.955**	**0.955**	**0.955**

state-of-the-art algorithms. It was observed that our proposed approach has outperformed the previous architectures as could be seen in Table 5.

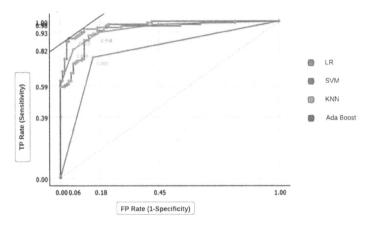

Fig. 4. ROC curve chart derived using VGG19 model and various classifier

4   Conclusion

This paper proposes a hybrid framework that computes the deep features using pre-trained deep learning architecture and employs a hand-crafted classifier for Albinism detection. We have created a vast library of such combination architectures, from which our proposed combination produced the highest performance compared to state-of-the-art algorithms. Our algorithm can correctly categorize any given image after already being trained on a dataset containing both categories. The method we suggest employees Inception-V3 architecture for computing deep features and Logistic Regression for classification. The dataset collected was split into training and testing, where 75% of the total images were included in the training set, whereas the remaining 25% were included in the testing set. Our proposed approach produced an accuracy of 99.8%. We performed a detailed comparison of our hybrid architecture with other state-of-the-art deep learning-based architectures. It was observed that our approach outperformed the previously employed techniques.

The genes that produce melanin alter in individuals with Albinism. People with Albinism lack pigmentation because melanin is the cause of skin, hair, and eye colour. Albinism is a genetic condition that occurs in the family. Depending on the genes involved, different kinds of Albinism have symptoms of varying severity. Melanin affects the development of healthy eyes, so people with Albinism have vision problems. They are also prone to sunburn and skin cancer. Although there is no treatment for this condition, management focuses on sun protection for the skin and eyes and monitoring skin changes. Our proposed approach could be further extended in detecting other diseases such as diabetic retinopathy and hair and nail infections.

References

1. Summers, C.G.: Albinism: classification, clinical characteristics, and recent findings. Optom. Vis. Sci. **86**(6), 659–662 (2009)
2. George, A., et al.: In vitro disease modelling of oculocutaneous albinism type 1 and 2 using human induced pluripotent stem cell-derived retinal pigment epithelium. Stem Cell Rep. **17**(1), 173–186 (2022)
3. Vapnik, V.N.: The Nature of Statistical Learning Theory. Springer, New York (2000). https://doi.org/10.1007/978-1-4757-3264-1
4. Andrew, A.M.: An introduction to support vector machines and other kernel-based learning methods by Nello Christianini and John Shawe-Taylor, Cambridge University Press, Cambridge, 2000, xiii+ 189 pp., ISBN 0-521-78019-5 (Hbk, £ 27.50). Robotica **18**(6), 687–689 (2000)
5. Schölkopf, B., Smola, A.J., Bach, F.: Learning with Kernels: Support Vector Machines, Regularization, Optimization, and Beyond. MIT Press, Cambridge (2002)
6. Dasarathy, B.: Nearest neighbour pattern classification techniques. IEEE Computer Society Press, Silver Spring, MD (1991)
7. Ripley, B.: Pattern Recognition and neural networks. Cambridge University Press, Cambridge. UK Google Scholar (1996)
8. Bishop, C.M.: Neural Networks for Pattern Recognition. Oxford University Press, Oxford (1995)
9. Hastie, T., Tibshirani, R., Friedman, J.: The Elements of Statistical Learning: Data Mining, Inference, and Prediction. Springer, New York (2001). https://doi.org/10.1007/978-0-387-21606-5
10. Breiman, L., et al.: Classification and regression trees. Wadsworth, 1984. Google Scholar (1993)
11. Abadi, M., et al.: Tensorflow: large-scale machine learning on heterogeneous distributed systems. arXiv preprint arXiv:1603.04467 (2016)
12. Szegedy, C., et al.: Going deeper with convolutions. In: 2015 IEEE Conference on Computer Vision and Pattern Recognition (2015)
13. Ioffe, S., Szegedy, C.: Batch normalization: accelerating deep network training by reducing internal covariate shift. In: International Conference on Machine Learning. PMLR (2015)
14. Szegedy, C., et al.: Rethinking the inception architecture for computer vision. In: Proceedings of the IEEE Conference on Computer Vision and Pattern Recognition (2016)
15. Szegedy, C., et al.: Inception-v4, inception-resnet and the impact of residual connections on learning. In: Thirty-First AAAI Conference on Artificial Intelligence (2017)

16. Simonyan, K., Zisserman, A.: Very deep convolutional networks for large-scale image recognition. arXiv preprint arXiv:1409.1556 (2014)
17. Yadav, N., et al.: A modern replica for COVID-19 pestilential disease identification. In: 2022 3rd International Conference on Intelligent Engineering and Management (ICIEM). IEEE (2022)
18. Kaur, D., et al.: Analysis of brain tumor using pre-trained CNN models and machine learning techniques. In: 2022 IEEE International Students' Conference on Electrical, Electronics and Computer Science (SCEECS). IEEE (2022)

A Deep Learning-Based Regression Scheme for Angle Estimation in Image Dataset

Tejal Rane[✉] [ID] and Abhishek Bhatt [ID]

College of Engineering Pune, Pune, India
{ranetd20.extc,bhatta.extc}@coep.ac.in

Abstract. A machine needs to recognize orientation in an image to address various rotation related problems. To calculate this rotation, one must require the information about different objects that present into the image. Hence this becomes a pattern recognition task. By using Deep Learning this issue of calculation of image rotation can be addressed as deep learning possess excellent ability of feature extraction. This paper proposes a novel deep learning-based approach to estimate the angle of rotation very efficiently. Kaggle dataset (Rotated Coins) and Caltech-256 has been used for this research, but the data available was limited hence this research utilize data augmentation by rotating the given dataset at random angles. Initially the unlabeled image has been rotated at different angles and store the values to be used as training dataset. Finally at the output a regression layer has been used to identify the angle of rotation for input image. The proposed deep learning approach provides a better result in terms of validation parameters like R-square, MSE, MAE. With proposed approach the value of R-square, MSE, and MAE for Kaggle dataset (Rotated Coins) obtained is 0.9846, 0.0013 and 0.0127 respectively. While for Caltech-256 Dataset proposed approach reported R-square, MSE, and MAE of 0.9503, 0.0039 and 0.0240 respectively. The proposed approach also helps in finding the position of an object by calculating the angle of rotation in an image.

Keywords: Convolutional neural networks · Deep learning · Image orientation estimation · Linear regression · Mean squared error (MSE) · Mean absolute error (MAE)

1 Introduction

There are numerous developments in the field of computer vision and deep learning within a span of few decades. Computer vision includes wide range of tasks like Image classification, Object detection, Object Identification, Facial recognition, Optical character recognition (OCR), Content based image retrieval etc. Although a lot of algorithms perform well for translation and scaling while rotation poses as challenge. Therefore, to improve the performance it is required to investigate rotation characteristics of an object in the given image. Even, extracting rotation-based information is helpful in various scenarios. Such as, while capturing a scene the camera might be tilted resulting in tilted photograph. Moreover, considering scanning of documents, if document is not placed correctly the resultant may have a skew. To get any image in the right orientation it is necessary that the angle of rotation to be known. However, some cameras with inertial sensors like accelerometers and gyroscopes can correct image orientation, but they correct the image orientation in 90° steps only. There are some edge detection-based algorithms exist that can correct the image orientation by using the concept of rotation. Here, the given image will be rotated till the edges are completely aligned with the horizontal edges. Further, such approaches do not work on the images that are inverted. To address this issue the content of the image has to be taken into consideration. In context of rotation estimation of an image of some scenery the content that can be looked for is the sky and ground while for an image of a person face or head have to be considered. Furthermore, looking into an optical character recognition problem there are the instances in which rotations can lead to wrong recognition. To illustrate, in numbers the digit '9' when flipped by 180° it becomes digit 6. Similarly, some symbols change with application of rotation. Therefore, here it is necessary to get the right orientation of the target.

Few examples like biomedical microscopy images, astronomical data, satellite data where content from the data may be randomly oriented and needs to be located. While detecting an object if it is rotated by few degrees, then the system should also be able to calculate the angle by which the object has been rotated. This research work addresses this issue by calculating the angle of rotation. The proposed work, is able to detect equivariant of angle if the output undergoes same transformation as and when any rotation has been applied to the input image. To acquire the exact information of transformation the proposed work analyze input before and after transformation using deep learning-based Convolutional neural network (CNN) algorithm. Based on the elements present in the image, through CNN architecture the proposed work further enables to predict the angle easily using Linear regression-based Model. The problem is treated as a pattern recognition task where change in orientation is recognized using a machine learning algorithm. Hence, in this paper, a deep learning-based approach that estimates the angle of rotation and corrects the orientation of image is proposed.

The remainder of this paper is organized in following manner. Section 2 discusses the relevant Literature background. Section 3 describes the methodology and working of proposed method. Section 4 presents results of proposed methods and comparative results of other deep learning methods. Section 5 concludes the paper.

2 Literature Review

For estimating the angle of rotation most of the older methods used feature extractors as color moments, local binary patterns and further feeding these extracted features to learning algorithms to Bayesian learning, logistic regression [1, 2]. Fewer use horizon detection method but not all images have horizons [3, 4]. Fewer research papers focused on detection of skew in documents [5–7]. Newer methods include the use of CNN for the purpose.

For images with human faces the techniques with human face recognition can be used. The use of VGGface classifier was proposed by Ogiue et al. for automatically correcting inclination of images [8]. The VGGface classifier consists of 16 layers that classifies the people like actors and actresses. Four images of each person were used that consisted of images with four orientations (0°, 90°, 180°, 270°). The method is able to correct the image regardless of meta data. Experimentation began with the four images of two persons it worked on the principle that the response of classifier will be less if image is tilted. Thus, the image with most response is correctly oriented image. But for the people's images that were not in the label of classifier the response was small due to dispersion of response. These images have lesser accuracy than the images learned. But the method was able to detect orientation between 0°, + 90°, −90°,180° for both learned and not learned images.

The use of self-supervised approach to recognize rotation transform on input image was proposed in the paper titled Unsupervised representation learning by predicting image rotation [9]. Rotation transformation includes rotation of input by the multiples of 90° (0°, 90°, 180°, 270°). The basic idea behind the task is that the CNN to perform rotation recognition it should learn to recognize classes of objects as well as their semantic features in the image. To recognize the object the use of supervised method is used while predicting rotation is a self-supervised method. The model RotNet was implemented on AlexNet architecture. The datasets that were used for the research are PASCAL VOC, CIFAR-10, Places-205. The approach attained 72.97%mAP.

To perform objects recognition and angle estimation simultaneously while eliminating the need of additional network training Zhou et al. proposed incorporated matching criterion and kernel mapping in CNN) [10]. The method is tested on MNIST, GTSRB and Caltech-256 dataset. The network uses octagonal kernel as it provided better results than the square kernel. CNN is first trained and all weight parameters from each convolutional kernel is extracted. The parameters thus obtained are replaced by their rotated version based on the matching criterion these parameters. The new network constructed using these new parameters could recognize the rotated images and estimate the angle of rotation. But work gives accurate results for only the angles that are multiples of 45°. The accuracy for angle estimation for MNIST dataset is above 91.75%. For GTSRB dataset the accuracy is above 95.87% while for Caltech dataset it is around 92.25%.

A deep neural network that can automatically correct the orientation of image which makes use of rectangular-shaped convolutions was proposed in the paper titled A Fast Deep Learning Network for Automatic Image Auto-Straightening [11]. The rectangular-shaped convolutions are used have shape of M × N, where M is less than N instead of square convolutions as these are better for detecting long horizontal lines. The proposed network is similar to MobileNetV2 with added a set of Straighten Bottleneck Residual blocks that help to recognize the rotation angle of the image. The paper adds new term called as regression loss that penalizes the network when predicted orientation is incorrect. Two datasets were used. First of 508,859 images downloaded from the Pixabay web platform. Second of 1,500,000 images like Google Street images, images with buildings. Accuracy and MAE for first dataset is 98.36% and 0.21 respectively while, second has 92.46% accuracy and 0.62 MAE.

3   Methodology

The proposed work as stated earlier is going to calculate the angle of rotation from its initial position by using a deep learning framework. The process begins with generation of labelled dataset in the required form. After pre-processing the dataset, the dataset is split into three parts they are train, test and validation. Train and validation part is used for training the model while for evaluation the test part is used. After training the model training and validation MAE, MSE and R^2 is graphed. The figure below shows the block diagram of proposed methodology (Refer Fig. 1).

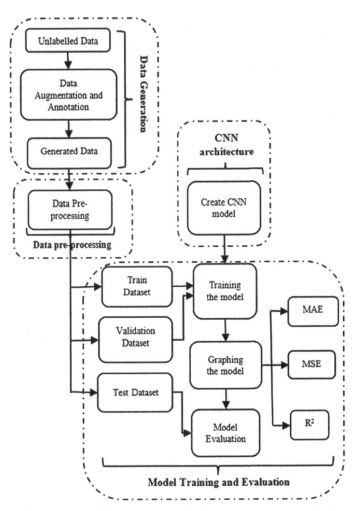

Fig. 1. Block diagram of the proposed methodology for estimating angle of rotation

3.1 Data Generation

Dataset required for training should be images rotated at random angle between 0° to 359° with the same as label. Such type of data can be gathered using cameras with inertial sensors so that we can get labelled data. CNN requires large amount of labelled data for training. Therefore, gathering large amount of data with such cameras can be time consuming as well as expensive. So here we use an unlabeled data and generate required labelled dataset. Initially we used the dataset from Kaggle (Rotated Coins) for the process [12]. The dataset contains images of one cent coins of varying shininess or color, mintmarks, and levels of wear. It consists of two classes the US Lincoln head one cent and the US Lincoln memorial tail one cent. From this dataset we selected all the image that were correctly oriented. The images then were rotated at any random angle and the angle is stored as the label for the image. The images were resized to 128×128 for faster processing. After rotating the image, the image is cropped to avoid the portion of black corners. So that the network can focus on the content information rather than the corners and the lines that form them as not every image may have it. Here the labelled dataset generated is of 25,000 images with the labels loaded into a JSON file. Further, to test the approach on complicated scenes Caltech-256 dataset was used [13]. Caltech dataset has 256 different categories. The images for the datasets were collected from Google images and then the images that does not fits categories are manually removed. From this dataset we selected images from 9 categories which were rightly oriented to create the dataset required. Similar to generation of coin dataset rotated Caltech dataset is prepared.

3.2 Data Pre-processing

Before feeding the dataset to the CNN one needs to pre-process it. Here we normalize the dataset before loading it. In normalization we rescale the values so that they can lie in the confined range. For the images the image pixels were normalized in the range of $[-0.5, 0.5]$ and for labels in the range $[-1, 1]$. Normalization helps neural network to perfom better on low range input output.

3.3 CNN Architecture

There are number of variants for CNN architecture. The model consists of following layers: Convolutional layer, Pooling layer, Dropout layer, Flatten layer, Dense layer. Each convolutional layer consists of the input feature map, the convolutional kernel, and the output feature map. The proposed model has 6 convolutional layers. Arguments to the convolutional layer consists of number of filters and kernel size. For the First layer kernel size is 5×5 while other use 3×3. The convolutional kernel convolves with the input feature map and outputs the two-dimensional feature map. During convolution operation the convolutional kernel slides over the input feature maps with a certain number of strides. Stride is the number of pixels that kernel will move in each step while moving across image. The convolutional layer is used to learn features of the inputs. The proposed network is as shown in the figure below (Refer Fig. 2).

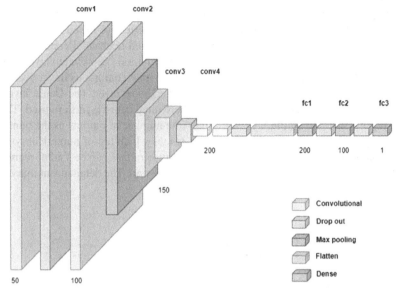

Fig. 2. Proposed CNN architecture. The numbers below the layer represents the number of filters used.

After convolving the input feature map with a convolutional kernel and applying activation function the new feature map is gained. If a neuron should be activated or not is decided by activation function depending on if a neuron's input to the network is important or not for the process of prediction. Activation Function helps to use important information while suppressing irrelevant data points. The proposed model uses Rectified Linear Unit (ReLU) activation function. ReLU eliminates all the values that are less than and equal to zero. The convolutional layer performs three operations, convolves the input feature map with convolutional kernel, compensates the resultant with offset term and activation function. Mathematically, the feature value at location (i, j) in the kth feature map of lth layer, $z^l_{(i,j,k)}$, after applying activation function f(.) is calculated as mentioned in Eq. (1)

$$z^l_{(i,j,k)} = f\left(w_k^{l^T} x^l_{(i,j)} + b^l_k\right) \tag{1}$$

where w^l_k and b^l_k are the weight vector and bias term of the kth filter of the lth layer respectively, and $x^l_{(i,j)}$ is the input patch centered at location (i, j) of the lth layer.

To decrease computational complexity, decrease in number of weights are required. This can be achieved using pooling layer. They are non-trainable as they do not have any weights. Common pooling types are Max Pooling, Average pooling. Here we are using Max Pooling. Max pooling layer contains small sliding kernels that takes the maximum value. As max pooling considers only one maximum value within the sliding window, any small change in the feature map is suppressed. Therefore, there would not be any significant changes in the output if there is small change in input with respect to spatial position. Thus, the network is enabled with certain amount of spatial invariance [14, 15].

If the network becomes too dependent on any one (or any small combination) of neurons then the network tends to overfit. Dropout is effective in reducing overfitting. During training dropout layer ignores randomly selected neurons. Dropout makes the network accurate even in the absence of certain information [16]. Flatten layer converts all the input feature maps provided to it into a single long continuous linear vector. The output of flatten layer is further fed as input to the Dense layer. The Dense layers are generally used at the end of the networks, and here three dense layers are used. The last Dense layer is also the output layer with the same number of outputs as the number of classes. Here for the output, we expect angle values which are of numerical type. We expect a value between 0° to 359° as output. This type of task can be said of regression. Therefore, we are connecting a regression layer at the end. The detailed summary of the model is shown in below figure (Refer Fig. 3).

```
Model: "sequential"
```

Layer (type)	Output Shape	Param #
conv2d (Conv2D)	(None, 64, 64, 50)	3800
dropout (Dropout)	(None, 64, 64, 50)	0
conv2d_1 (Conv2D)	(None, 64, 64, 100)	45100
max_pooling2d (MaxPooling2D)	(None, 32, 32, 100)	0
conv2d_2 (Conv2D)	(None, 15, 15, 150)	135150
conv2d_3 (Conv2D)	(None, 7, 7, 150)	202650
dropout_1 (Dropout)	(None, 7, 7, 150)	0
conv2d_4 (Conv2D)	(None, 4, 4, 200)	270200
conv2d_5 (Conv2D)	(None, 2, 2, 200)	360200
dropout_2 (Dropout)	(None, 2, 2, 200)	0
flatten (Flatten)	(None, 800)	0
dense (Dense)	(None, 200)	160200
dropout_3 (Dropout)	(None, 200)	0
dense_1 (Dense)	(None, 100)	20100
dropout_4 (Dropout)	(None, 100)	0
dense_2 (Dense)	(None, 1)	101

```
Total params: 1,197,501
Trainable params: 1,197,501
Non-trainable params: 0
```

Fig. 3. Summary for the proposed model

3.4 Model Training and Evaluation

Training is required for any CNN to work. A large amount of labelled data is fed to CNN for training. The different CNN architectures were trained on described the dataset. Before training the dataset is divided into two: training data and test data in 80–20 manner. The network performs well on the data they are trained on but to generalize the network on the data that is not seen the periodical testing on unseen data and monitoring of the performance on the same is required. Therefore, dataset is randomly split training and validation set. Therefore, the training set is again split into training and validation set. The dataset is randomly shuffled after every epoch. CNNs are generally trained on batches as training on a single image at a time optimizes network based on individual image while, using of batches makes weight updation more accurate. Here the network uses the batch size of 64. Early stopping enables to terminate training when model's performance on the validation dataset. The network was optimized with Adam optimizer using the MAE (mean absolute error) loss function. Mean absolute error is good option for a regression task such as predicting the angles. Adam optimizer is used as parameters with a small gradient change can be trained effectively [17]. MAE is calculated by taking the absolute difference between the predicted value of the model and the actual value, and then averaging it over the whole dataset. It is measured as mentioned in Eq. (2).

$$\text{MAE} = \frac{1}{n} \sum_{i=1}^{n} |y_i - \hat{y}_i| \tag{2}$$

where y_i indicates the angle predicted, $\hat{y}_i$ indicates the actual angle of the image and n indicates the total number of images.

We use mean squared error (MSE) and R2 score for evaluation. MSE is calculated by getting the square of the difference between the predicted value of the model and the actual value, and averaging it over the whole dataset. It is measured as mentioned in Eq. (3).

$$\text{MSE} = \frac{1}{n} \sum_{i=1}^{n} \left(y_i - \hat{y}_i\right)^2 \tag{3}$$

where y_i indicates the angle predicted, $\hat{y}_i$ indicates the actual angle of the image and n indicates the total number of images.

R2 score is the representation of how well the regression model fits with the data. It describes the amount of the variation in the output which is predicted from the input. It is used to check how well results are reproduced by the model. It is measured as mentioned in Eq. (4)

$$R^2 = 1 - \frac{\sum_{i=1}^{n} \left(y_i - \hat{y}_i\right)^2}{\sum_{i=1}^{n} \left(y_i - y_{\text{avg}}\right)^2} \tag{4}$$

where y_i indicates the angle predicted, $\hat{y}_i$ indicates the actual angle of the image, $y_{\text{avg}} = \frac{y_i}{n}$ where n is number of images.

4   Results and Analysis

From the original dataset images with no rotation were selected. Some rotation has been provided using python scripts. For the sake of introducing ambiguity into the rotation angle measurement each image belonging to a particular category has been rotated different amount. The dataset before rotation for each class has been shown in the first column and generated dataset after rotation has been shown in second column in the table below (Refer Table 1). Further, normalization has been carried out on the rotated image dataset which is shown in third column. Images are normalized as mentioned in equation.

$$Pixels = (Pixels/255) - 0.5 \qquad (5)$$

Hence, inter image anomalies has been reduced up to an extent that it becomes easier to process by the model. After predicting the angle of rotation, the image is rotated to get the correct orientation. Results obtained after rotating with the predicted angles are shown in fourth column.

Table 1. Results obtained.

Original Dataset (Before rotation)	Generated Dataset	Normalized Images	Corrected Image
Coin dataset			
(a1)	(a2)	(a3)	(a4)
(b1)	(b2)	(b3)	(b4)
Caltech Dataset			
(c1)	(c2)	(c3)	(c4)
(d1)	(d2)	(d3)	(d4)

(continued)

Table 1. (*continued*)

Original Dataset (Before rotation)	Generated Dataset	Normalized Images	Corrected Image
(e1)	(e2)	(e3)	(e4)
(f1)	(f2)	(f3)	(f4)
(g1)	(g2)	(g3)	(g4)
(h1)	(h2)	(h3)	(h4)
(i1)	(i2)	(i3)	(i4)
(j1)	(j2)	(j3)	(j4)
(k1)	(k2)	(k3)	(k4)

(a1) US Lincoln head one cent, (b1) US Lincoln memorial tail one cent, (c1) Buddha, (d1) Eiffel Tower, (e1) Ketch, (f1) Menorah, (g1) Tent, (h1) Refrigerator, (i1) Aero plane, (j1) Telephone booth, (k1) Car

The different six models with variations in Convolution layer, Max Pooling layer, Dropout, Fully Connected layers were trained on both the datasets. With every model, the number of convolution layers are increased. Max pooling layers with 2×2 kernel size were used in every model. For Model 1 only 1 max pooling layer is used whereas 2 layers are used for Model 2–4. Then again Model 5,6 uses single Max pooling layer. Initial two models used one dropout layer while a dropout layer goes on increasing with every new model from model 3. Initial 3 models have 2 fully connected layers while later 3 consists of 3 layers. The variations in the models and total number of parameters are in the below table (Refer Table 2).

Table 2. Model configuration with their parameters

Parameter (number of layers)	Model 1	Model 2	Model 3	Model 4	Model 5	Model 6
Convolution	1	2	3	4	5	6
Max Pooling	1	2	2	2	1	1
Dropout	1	1	2	3	4	5
Fully Connected	2	2	2	3	3	3
Number of parameters	525,217	480,257	785,537	1,669,701	852,151	1,197,501

Table 3 shows the results obtained for different models for both the datasets. For every model value of MAE, MSE and R^2 are calculated. Ideally values for MAE and MSE should be as low as possible whereas value for R^2 should be as high has possible. It can be seen that values of MSE and MAE for Model 6 are lower than other models whereas R^2 value of Model 6 are higher than other models.

Table 3. Calculation of MAE, MSE and R2

Dataset	Acc. Measure	Model 1	Model 2	Model 3	Model 4	Model 5	Model 6
Coin	MAE	0.053	0.040	0.041	0.073	0.035	0.013
	MSE	0.006	0.004	0.004	0.008	0.005	0.001
	R^2	0.91	0.94	0.94	0.88	0.94	**0.98**
Caltech	MAE	0.081	0.072	0.071	0.047	0.038	0.024
	MSE	0.016	0.013	0.012	0.007	0.006	0.004
	R^2	0.79	0.83	0.84	0.91	0.93	**0.95**

The Comparative results for MAE, MSE and R^2 are presented in graphical manner in 3 figures below (Refer Figs. 4, 5, and 6).

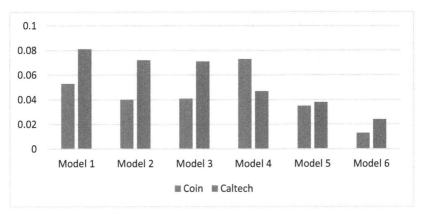

Fig. 4. Comparison between all models w.r.t. MAE

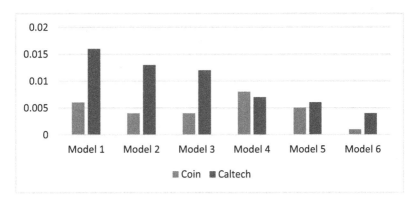

Fig. 5. Comparison between all models w.r.t. MSE

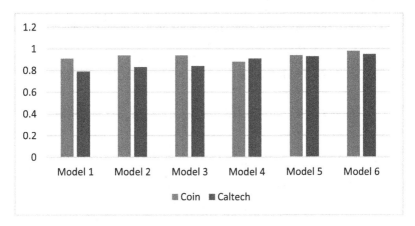

Fig. 6. Comparison between all models w.r.t. R2

Table 4. Training Graphs for MAE, MSE and R^2

	Coin	Caltech
MAE		
	(a)	(b)
MSE		
	(c)	(d)
R^2		
	(e)	(f)

In the above table (Refer Table 4) (a) shows the training and validation curve for MAE loss for coin dataset, (b) shows the training and validation curve for MAE loss for Caltech dataset, (c) shows the training and validation curve for MSE loss for coin dataset, (d) shows the training and validation curve for MSE loss for Caltech dataset, (e) shows the training and validation curve for R^2 for coin dataset, (a) shows the training and validation curve for R^2 for Caltech dataset.

In the approach [10] the author has used Caltech-256 dataset for the research and has only worked for angles that are equal to n x 45° (n = 1, 2, ...,7) (Table 5).

Table 5. Comparison between proposed method and KM-CNN.

Dataset		% R^2
Coin	Proposed approach	98.46
Caltech-256	Proposed approach	95.03
	KM-CNN [10]	-

We tested the proposed approach for the different ratios of train and test. The values of R^2 obtained for them are shown in the below table (Refer Table 6).

Table 6. Performance of proposed network for different train test split ratios.

Dataset	Train test split ratio (R^2)			
	50/50	60/40	70/30	80/20
Coin	0.9796	0.9771	0.9817	0.9846
Caltech	0.9148	0.9346	0.9395	0.9503

The results for the above tables are represented graphically in the figure given below (Refer Fig. 7). It is seen that for 80/20 train test ratio for both dataset the model performed better.

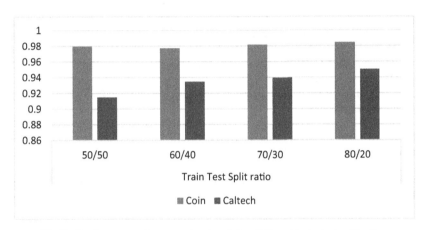

Fig. 7. Performance of proposed network for different train test split ratios.

5 Conclusion

This study proposed an approach that can predict the angle of rotation for an image effectively even if the image does not contain horizontal lines or vertical lines. Hence, such prediction also helps in getting the image back to its original position. The proposed approach, for prediction of angle by which the image has been rotated, is based on convolutional neural network architecture, later on linear regression has been applied for estimation of angle of rotation. Further, such an approach helps in generating large amount of training samples synthetically, that can be utilized by the network to enhance its capacity to learn features. As already discussed, in previous study carried out by authors [10] has not worked for angle estimation other than n × 45° (where n = 1, 2, …, 7). However, the proposed approach is able to quantify the angle for any value from 0° to 360°. Hence, the proposed approach is much robust while calculation for angle of rotation. Moreover, the value of R^2 obtained on two different datasets i.e., coin dataset which is adaptively new dataset, is 0.9846 and for Caltech dataset which is a widely used dataset the value of R2 is 0.9503. It signifies that, for both type of datasets the regression model performed well. Furthermore, in future some hybrid models could be developed that can be test with some other kind of datasets also. Hence, in future more focus will be on generalization of algorithm as well as real time prediction.

References

1. Vailaya, A., Zhang, H., Yang, C., Liu, F.I., Jain, A.K.: Automatic image orientation detection. IEEE Trans. Image Process. **11**, 746–755 (2002). https://doi.org/10.1109/TIP.2002.801590
2. Ciocca, G., Cusano, C., Schettini, R.: Image orientation detection using LBP-based features and logistic regression. Multimed. Tools App. **74**(9), 3013–3034 (2013). https://doi.org/10.1007/s11042-013-1766-4
3. Fefilatyev, S., Smarodzinava, V., Hall, L.O., Goldgof, D.B.: Horizon detection using machine learning techniques. In: Proceedings - 5th International Conference on Machine Learning and Applications, ICMLA 2006, pp 17–21 (2006)
4. Workman, S., Zhai, M., Jacobs, N.: Horizon lines in the wild. In: British Machine Vision Conference 2016, BMVC 2016. British Machine Vision Conference, BMVC, pp. 20.1–20.12 (2016)
5. Ávila, B.T., Lins, R.D.: A fast orientation and skew detection algorithm for monochromatic document images (2005)
6. Amin, A., Fischer, S.: A document skew detection method using the Hough transform (2000)
7. Huang, K., Chen, Z., Yu, M., Yan, X., Yin, A.: An efficient document skew detection method using probability model and Q test. Electronics (Switzerland) **9**, 55 (2020). https://doi.org/10.3390/electronics9010055
8. Ogiue, S., Ito, H.: Method of correction of rotated images using deep learning networks. In: Proceedings - 2018 7th International Congress on Advanced Applied Informatics, IIAI-AAI 2018. Institute of Electrical and Electronics Engineers Inc., pp. 980–981 (2018)
9. Gidaris, S., Singh, P., Komodakis, N.: Unsupervised representation learning by predicting image rotations (2018)
10. Zhou, Y., Shi, J., Yang, X., Wang, C., Wei, S., Zhang, X.: Rotational objects recognition and angle estimation via kernel-mapping cnn. IEEE Access **7**, 116505–116518 (2019). https://doi.org/10.1109/ACCESS.2019.2933673
11. Mironica, I., Zugravu, A.: A fast deep learning network for automatic image auto-straightening (2021)
12. Rotated Coins I Kaggle. https://www.kaggle.com/competitions/coins. Accessed 1 Aug 2022
13. Caltech 256 Image Dataset I Kaggle. https://www.kaggle.com/datasets/jessicali9530/caltech256. Accessed 1 Aug 2022
14. Lee, C.-Y., Gallagher, P.W., Tu, Z.: Generalizing pooling functions in convolutional neural networks: mixed, gated, and tree (2015)
15. Worrall, D.E., Garbin, S.J., Turmukhambetov, D., Brostow, G.J.: harmonic networks: deep translation and rotation equivariance (2017)
16. Srivastava, N., Hinton, G., Krizhevsky, A., Salakhutdinov, R.: Dropout: a simple way to prevent neural networks from overfitting (2014)
17. Kingma, D.P., Ba, J.: Adam: a method for stochastic optimization (2014)

The Classification of Native and Invasive Species in North America: A Transfer Learning and Random Forest Pipeline

Sayani Sarkar[1]($\boxtimes$)(iD) and Somenath Chakroborty[2](iD)

[1] Bellarmine University, Louisville, KY 40205, USA
ssarkar@bellarmine.edu
[2] West Virginia University Institute of Technology, Beckley, WV 25801, USA
somenath.chakraborty@mail.wvu.edu

Abstract. Data Analytic interpretation of plant species is not widely explored. The image variety of plant species can be investigated with the help of machine learning and deep learning techniques. Machine learning and deep learning make the plant species investigation automated and almost accurate. In this paper, we have proposed a novel native and invasive plant species classification technique. We use the pre-trained deep convolution neural networks (transfer learning) to extract features from plant species and classify them into Native and Invasive. Here, state-of-the-art deep convolution neural network models like *InceptionV3*, *MobileNetV2*, *ResNetV2*, *VGG*16, and *Xception* have been explored to extract the feature vectors from images. Furthermore, the features of the images have been used for image classification using the Random Forest algorithm. The performance of the proposed system is verified on the proposed dataset (Native-Invasive) with aerial view images of native and invasive species. Results were obtained using cross-validation techniques. Our experiments demonstrate the potential of our proposed method for achieving excellent performance with a 95% accuracy using Xception with data augmentation, hyper-parameter optimization, and the Random Forest classification technique. The aerial images were captured and labeled by us which is very novel to our experimental setup. After using deep learning models we got promising results. The dataset used to train the plant species classifier will be made available on request.

Keywords: Feature extraction · Transfer learning · Random Forest · Deep learning · Image classification · Native plant species · Invasive plant species

1 Introduction

In our environment, there are various kinds of plant species around. Some of them are good for the environment and ecology but many species are harmful as well [1]. Native species are born and evolved in a particular area without

KC Santosh et al. (Eds.): RTIP2R 2022, CCIS 1704, pp. 297–307, 2023.
https://doi.org/10.1007/978-3-031-23599-3_22

much human intervention. Native plants like Butterfly weed, Black-eyed Susan, Purple Coneflower, and many more blooms very well and the color and smell attracts various kind of insects that help pollination [2]. Native plant fruits are a good source of food and medicine for humans and animals [3]. These species also survive extreme climate conditions. On the other hand, there are invasive species that avert the growth of native species [4]. These species don't provide any nutrients for native habitats and bring ecological disharmony. The very common invasive species we can find are Daylily, Petunia, Lantana, and many more. Some of the invasive species are also harmful to animals like St. John's wort which causes skin irritations for animals [5].

These automated applications very efficiently classify native and invasive species in North America by only looking at the plant or taking a picture. In this experimental design, we have proposed Transfer Learning (TL) with Machine Learning-based Native and Invasive species classifications from aerial view RGB images. Tr We have created a dataset named *Native-Invasive* of 5000 images with 30 native and 25 invasive species. We implemented TL in which pre-trained deep convolutional neural networks (DCNN) weights were used for feature extraction of the images to overcome the size of the input dataset. The Machine learning-based Random Forest classification algorithm is used for binary classification of native and invasive species.

The structure of the paper is as follows. In Sect. 2 we have discussed various related studies of the implementation of AI on plant species classification. Next, in Sects. 3 and 4 we have elaborated the experimental design techniques and experimental findings respectively. Finally, in conclusion, we have discussed all of the advantages, limitations, and future research directions.

2 Background

The application of machine learning approaches to environment and ecology sustainability has been discussed in various kinds of research. In a recent review, plant disease detection using various classification techniques like Support vector machine, artificial neural network, K-Nearest Neighbourhood, CNN, and Fuzzy logic was discussed. The experimental result shows that the CNN classifier is able to detect more diseases than the rest [6]. In another research, plant leaf classification was performed by TL-based deep neural network on public datasets [7]. The experimental results demonstrated that TL in addition to traditional CNN improved the performance of plant classification. In another study, the support vector machine (SVM) algorithm was used for leaf classifications on the Swedish leaf dataset [8]. Convolution Neural Network (CNN) was used in another research for plant classification and the model was tested on the images collected from smart agro stations in Turkey [9]. In another approach, a combination of image processing and machine learning-based random forest classifier was used for invasive plant classification [10]. In a recent study, machine learning techniques like Boosted Logistic Regression, Naive Bayes (NB), Neural Network, Random Forest, and Support Vector Machine were used for invasive plant detection on Sentinel-2 and AVIRIS Dataset [11]. In another research, deep learning with pre-trained model weights was used for aquatic invasive plant species classification. In the study, RGB and hydroacoustic sensors were used for data collection and the result had 84% classification accuracy [12]. Mukti et al. proposed a deep learning-based plant disease detected approach. The researchers used an open-source dataset to test the model performance. The result shows that the Resnet50 model performed best on the training and validation datasets [13]. A recent review on horticultural research discussed how different deep learning algorithms are currently days using due to the advancement of big data [14].

All of the studies indicated the huge potential of artificial intelligence in horticultural research. The researchers mostly used open source datasets for their research. In our experimental design, we have proposed a hybrid deep transfer learning and machine learning-based model to classify native and invasive plants. Our model uses pre-trained DCNN model weights for image feature extractions due to the limited size of the dataset and TL also helped to improve the efficiency of the trained model. Next, the image feature vectors are fed into a machine learning-based Random Forest classifier. The model was tested on a proposed dataset named *Native-Invasive* that contains aerial view images of popular native and invasive plants that can be found in North America.

3   Experimental Design

The proposed method comprises the *training* and *testing* phases. The weights of the model are determined in the training phase and then the trained model is employed to classify input signals into native or invasive categories. Figure 1 illustrates the proposed model-aided classification system. The plant image dataset is split randomly into 80/20 ratios where the training set has 80% images to learn the image properties and a model is created during *training phase*. The model performance is tested on the remaining 20% images during *test phase*. In the training phase, the training images are preprocessed and augmented. Next, the feature extraction was performed using pre-trained DCNN models. Finally, the Random Forest classification algorithm is used for species classification. In

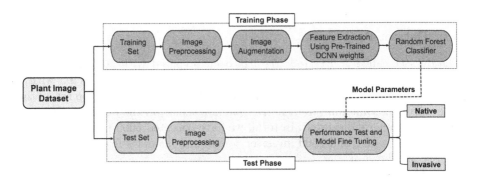

Fig. 1. Flow of diagram of the proposed model.

the testing phase, the images are preprocessed and training model parameters are used for performance tests. Training models were fine-tuned to improve classification accuracy. Each step of the training and test phase is described in the following sections.

Fig. 2. Sample images of native (top row) and invasive species (bottom row), (a) Purple Coneflower, (b) Aromatic Aster, (c) Butterfly Weed, (d) Bandana Lantana, (e) Summersweet, (f) Daylily.

3.1 Dataset Preparation

The dataset called *Native-Invasive* has been prepared with 30 native and 25 invasive popular plant images. The top view of the images is collected with a high-resolution RGB camera. Sample images from the dataset The top row of the figure displays some full-grown native plants whereas, in the bottom row, some invasive plants are displayed. In total, we have collected 5000 plant images out of that 2500 native and 2500 invasive. Some image samples from our proposed dataset are shown in Fig. 2.

3.2   Image Preprocessing

The captured images are at a very high resolution of $2{,}532 \times 1{,}170$ pixels. In image pre-processing, we have preliminary resized all of the training and test set images into 224*224 pixels. The images are labeled correctly into two groups called *Native* and *Invasive*. Images that are not captured properly or captured during low light conditions are removed from the dataset. The image sizes were finetuned using *parameter-tuning* based on the model performance.

3.3   Image Augmentation

In the image augmentation process, the training set images rotated 90°, shifted, sheared, zoomed in, and flipped horizontally. This augmentation process generated 5000 native and 5000 invasive plant images. The augmentation process helps to reduce the overfitting of the model in the training set. It also reduced system memory overhead and added additional time costs at the time of model training.

3.4   Image Feature Extraction

Standard and Pre-trained deep convolutional neural networks (DCNN) have been used to feature extraction of Native and Invasive plant species images. In the case of standard DCNN, the augmented images are fed into a sequential model consisting of four CNN layers with ReLU activation function with max pooling layers. The final layer of the standard DCNN model is the flattened layer. The architecture of the Standard DCNN is shown in Fig. 3. In transfer learning (TL), the input images are fed into a pre-trained DCNN network such as *InceptionV*3, *MobileNetV*2, *ResNetV*2, *VGG*16, and *Xception*. The two final layers of such pre-trained networks (the classifier and its previous layers) are removed because they are highly related to the target classes of their original dataset. The architecture of pre-trained networks is detailed in Fig. 4. The

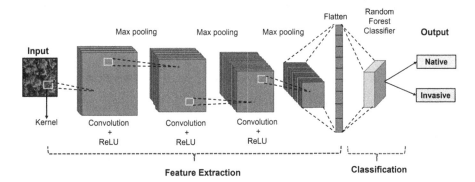

Fig. 3. The architecture of standard DCNN feature extractor with Random Forest classifier for Native and Invasive species classification.

pre-trained DCNN block performs the feature extraction task using pre-defined weights which are determined through training procedures on large-scale image datasets like ImageNet [15]. Pre-trained $InceptionV3$ has 48 deep layers [16]. Whereas, MobileNetV2 has 55 pre-trained layers trained layers on the Imagenet dataset [17]. A pre-trained $VGG16$ model consists of 16 convolution and max pooling layers [18]. $Xception$ model is designed by taking inspiration from the Inception model in which the number of deep layers is the same as $InceptionV3$ [19]. Xception is designed with depthwise separable convolution whereas Inception has pointwise convolution. Pre-trained $Resnet - 152v2$ network designed with 152 residual network designs rather than the sequential design Inception, MobileNet, VGG16, and Xception to overcome the vanishing gradient problem [20]. The *training set* images from the *Native-Invasive* dataset are fed into the pre-trained DCNN models for image feature extraction. The output of the DCNN model from a layer prior to the Dense layer of the model is used as input to a new classifier.

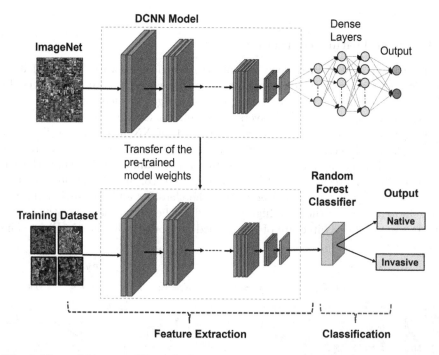

Fig. 4. The architecture of Transfer Learning with Random Forest classifier for Native and Invasive species classification.

3.5   Random Forest Classification

Random Forest (RF) is a supervised machine learning model designed with multiple Decision Tree classifiers. Ensemble of multiple Decision Tree classifiers using bagging techniques, reducing the over-fitting in the classification process. It is a very effective machine learning model both for regression analysis and classification model. Especially for our classification work, it is more effective in the experiment as we use our generated data set to use different machine learning models than for classification state, we use an RF classifier. RF not only helps in reducing over-fitting but is very flexible as it is very effective for handling missing values in the parameters. It helps to identify feature importance through many decision trees and that helps to identify more valuable feature aspects, hence helping to generate a more robust classification. Image parameters from DCNN models are fed into the RF classifier shown in Fig. 4. The RF classifier generated the results of the classification of Native and Invasive species from the proposed dataset. The RF classifier was also finetuned using *Parameter-Tuning*.

3.6   Parameter-Tuning

We have performed parameter tuning on the experimental design to generate better performance of the DCNN and RF models. The list of best parameters for each of the models after hyperparameter tuning for DCNN and RF models is shown in Table 1 and Table 2 respectively. The hyperparameter list for the images are $[128 \times 128, 156 \times 156, 196 \times 196, 224 \times 224, 256 \times 256, 296 \times 296]$. The VGG16 model performed best even in a 128×128 size image whereas MobilNet, Resnet, and Xception performed well on a larger image size of 296×296 shown in Table 1. In the case of the RF classifier, a n_estimator 20, max_depth of 30, min_sample_split of 2 and Gini Criterion performed best for model validations.

4   Experimental Setup and Results

4.1   Experimental Setup

Various experiments have been performed on the proposed *Native-Invasive* dataset to evaluate the proposed TL-RF pipelined approach. RGB images were

Table 1. Selected image size for the models input after parameter tuning.

DCNN model	Image size
InceptionV3	256×256
MobilNetV2	296×296
ResNetV2	296×296
VGG16	128×128
Xception	296×296

Table 2. List of parameters for tuning for the RF machine learning model.

RF parameters	Parameter values
n_estimator	10, 20, 30, 40, 50
max_depth	10, 20, 30, 40, 50
min_samples_split	2, 3, 4, 5
Criterion	Entropy, Gini

captured using iPhone 12 pro max with a 12MP camera and f/2.2 aperture. Images were collected during the months of June and July in full bloom conditions under daylight. The aerial view of plant images was captured at 3 ft distance. Images were processed using a Dell Alienware X17 R1 laptop with GeForce RTX 3070 Ti GPU, and 16 GB RAM. The images were processed using Python programming language and TensorFlow framework for pre-trained DCNN models and Sciket Learn library for Random Forest algorithm in the Anaconda environment using Spyder IDE.

4.2   Evaluation Criteria

We evaluated standard performance metrics for our *Native-Invasive* dataset including accuracy, precision, recall, and F1 score. Precision helps us to understand the number of correct Invasive species out of all of the correct predictions of both Native and Invasive species. Whereas Recall helps to understand the number of Invasive class predictions made out of all positive examples in the dataset. F-Measure provides a single score that balances the concerns of precision and recall in one number. The formulae for performance metrics are shown below:

$$Accuracy = \frac{TP + TN}{TP + FP + TN + FN} \tag{1}$$

$$Precision = \frac{TP}{TP + FP} \tag{2}$$

$$Recall = \frac{TP}{TP + FN} \tag{3}$$

$$F_1 score = 2 \times \frac{Precision \times Recall}{Precision + Recall} \tag{4}$$

where TP is the number of true positives, FP is the number of false positives, TN is the number of true negative cases and FN is the number of false negative instances.

4.3   Experimental Result

The results of different state-of-the-art machine learning models are shown in Table 3. Standard DCNN feature extractor with RF classifier performed poorly among all of the feature extractors with 83% accuracy. Whereas the TL-based feature extractors showed better performance. We got the highest accuracy of 95% for the Xception neural network model with 50 estimators, a depth of 30, a min split of 4, and an Entropy Criterion for the RF model. The Xception model had 98% precision on the Native species and 98% recall on Invasive species. The next good fit DCNN model is MobileNet. It showed 93% overall accuracy.

Table 3. Performance measures of RGB images from *Native-Invasive* dataset obtained via proposed CNN-TL-RF pipelines.

Feature extractor	Class	Precision	Recall	F1-score	Accuracy
Standard DCNN	Invasive	81	85	83	83
	Native	83	87	85	
InceptionV3	Invasive	88	94	90	90
	Native	93	87	90	
MobileNetV2	Invasive	95	91	93	93
	Native	92	96	94	
ResnetV2	Invasive	85	91	88	88
	Native	91	85	87	
VGG16	Invasive	89	91	90	90
	Native	91	89	90	
Xception	Invasive	92	98	95	**95**
	Native	98	91	94	

5 Conclusion

This research study is fascinating and distinctive from the other literary work that happens on the native and invasive species of trees found in North America. This is a transfer-machine learning approach that was built using different state-of-the-art techniques. The results are shown in the comparative analysis with the different frameworks of application with different techniques. The results indicated that the Xception-DCNN feature extractor with the RF classifier generates 95% classification accuracy of Native and Invasive species which is 12% than a standard DCNN feature extractor with an RF classifier. The most important part of this research work is that we have created a novel data set that will be publicly available on request. The data set is mainly captured through aerial view so that drone applications could be designed using this research work. In the future, we will update the data set with a more variety of samples and more advanced techniques and develop the system with web apps and mobile app applications.

References

1. Zettlemoyer, M.A., Schultheis, E.H., Lau, J.A.: Phenology in a warming world: differences between native and non-native plant species. Ecol. Lett. **22**(8), 1253–1263 (2019)
2. Nackley, L.L., West, A.G., Skowno, A.L., Bond, W.J.: The nebulous ecology of native invasions. Trends Ecol. Evol. **32**(11), 814–824 (2017)
3. Shelef, O., Weisberg, P.J., Provenza, F.D.: The value of native plants and local production in an era of global agriculture. Front. Plant Sci. **8**, 2069 (2017)
4. Welch, K.: Plant toxins. Toxicon **168**, 140 (2019)
5. Drummond, F.A.: Common St. John's Wort (Malpighiales: Hypericaceae): an invasive plant in Maine wild blueberry production and its potential for indirectly supporting ecosystem services. Environ. Entomol. **48**(6), 1369–1376 (2019)
6. Shruthi, U., Nagaveni, V., Raghavendra, B.K.: A review on machine learning classification techniques for plant disease detection. In: IEEE 5th International Conference on Advanced Computing & Communication Systems (ICACCS), pp. 281–284 (2019)
7. Kaya, A., et al.: Analysis of transfer learning for deep neural network based plant classification models. Comput. Electr. Agric **158**, 20–29 (2019)
8. Ali, R, Hardie, R., Essa, A.: A leaf recognition approach to plant classification using machine learning. In: IEEE National Aerospace and Electronics Conference, pp. 431–434 (2018)
9. Yalcin, H., Razavi, S.: Plant classification using convolutional neural networks. In: IEEE Fifth International Conference on Agro-Geoinformatics (Agro-Geoinformatics), pp. 1–5 (2016)
10. Baron, J., Hill, D.J., Elmiligi. H.: Combining image processing and machine learning to identify invasive plants in high-resolution images. Int. J. Remote Sens. **39**(15–16), 5099–5118 (2018)
11. Jensen, T., Hass, F.S., Akbar, M.S., Petersen, P.H., Arsanjani, J.J.: Employing machine learning for detection of invasive species using sentinel-2 and aviris data: The case of Kudzu in the United States. Sustainability **12**(9), 3544 (2020)
12. Perrin, J.E., et al.: Sensor Fusion with deep learning for autonomous classification and management of aquatic invasive plant species. Robotics **11**(4), 68 (2022)
13. Mukti, I.Z., Biswas, D.: Transfer learning based plant diseases detection using ResNet50. In: IEEE International Conference on Electrical Information and Communication Technology (EICT), pp. 1–6 (2019)
14. Yang, B., Xu, Y.: Applications of deep-learning approaches in horticultural research: a review.. Horticult. Res. **8** (2021)
15. Krizhevsky, A., Sutskever, I., Hinton, G.E.: Imagenet classification with deep convolutional neural networks. Commun. ACM **60**(6), 84–90 (2017)
16. Xia, X., Xu, C., Nan, B.: Inception-v3 for flower classification. In: IEEE 2nd International Conference on Image, Vision and Computing (ICIVC), pp. 783–787 (2017)
17. Gujjar, J.P., Prasanna Kumar, H.R., Chiplunkar, N.N.: Image classification and prediction using transfer learning in colab notebook. Glob. Transit Proc. **2**(2), 382–385 (2019)
18. Giraddi, S., Seeri, S., Hiremath, P.S., Jayalaxmi, P.S.: Flower classification using deep learning models. In: IEEE International Conference on Smart Technologies in Computing, Electrical and Electronics (ICSTCEE), pp. 130–133 (2020)

19. Wu, X., Liu, R., Yang, H., Chen, Z.: An exception based convolutional neural network for scene image classification with transfer learning. In: IEEE 2nd International Conference on Information Technology and Computer Application (ITCA), pp. 262–267 (2020)
20. Han, D., Liu, Q., Fan, W.: A new image classification method using CNN transfer learning and web data augmentation. Expert Syst. Appl. **95**, 43–56 (2018)

Internet of Things and Security

Towards a Digital Twin Integrated DLT and IoT-Based Automated Healthcare Ecosystem

Prodipta Promit Mukherjee[1]([✉]) [iD], Maharin Afroj[2] [iD], Sohaima Hossain[2] [iD], and Milon Biswas[3] [iD]

[1] zBack Systems Limited, 441/6A, Mirpur DOHS, Dhaka 1216, Bangladesh
prodipta.promit@ieee.org
[2] Bangladesh University of Business and Technology, Rupnagar R/A, Mirpur-2, Dhaka 1216, Bangladesh
{19203103021,19203103012}@cse.bubt.edu.bd
[3] University of Alabama, Birmingham, 1720 University Blvd, Birmingham, AL 35294, USA
milon@ieee.org
http://www.zbacksys.com/, https://www.bubt.edu.bd/, https://www.uab.edu/

Abstract. The concept of Digital Twin technology unlocks a higher potential for a sustainable healthcare ecosystem, and disruptive technologies like Machine Intelligence, Blockchain, Internet of Things are taking over the industries beyond any logical assumptions. In the field of the medical industry, Blockchain and Digital Twin stands the most popular buzzwords, and there also be a valid explanation for this. Integration of Blockchain and Digital Twin with an intelligent eHealth Solution allows data consistency, immutability, transparency, security, and sophisticated medical services to patients with improved research, development, and innovation platform for medical professionals and researchers. It has the scope to be used in various ways in the medical industry, resulting in significant cost savings and new methods for patients to obtain healthcare. We often wonder how time is becoming more and more expensive day after day. In this race, all audience groups are required to optimize time in comparison to medical services, research advances, medical professionals' training to achieve sustainable development goals in healthcare. Now we have the necessary technologies to do so. And here we are, proposing a futuristic Digital Twin integrated IoT, and Blockchain-based sophisticated eHealth system solution by which the automation of medical operational processes ensures satisfactory service to all parties. This solution will allow the research advances and continuous development of medical industry resources and build-up a win-win ground among all participants.

Keywords: Digital Twin · Cyber-physical asset · IoT · ML · Blockchain · dApp · Smart contracts · Truffle · Infura · IPFS · eHealth · Ecosystem

1   Introduction

Optimization of the services requires optimized operational processes and management. In terms of the healthcare industry, research advances and continuous development are also required. The fact is, patients never had enough time, and they still don't. Not even in their day-to-day life. Time has become more precious than ever before, and it's continuously increasing. To face this reality, this is where we found a vision of complete automation in the healthcare industry. Figure 1 is the visualization of the vision we've made. A patient will get the highest possible medical services [1] remotely in zero downtime. From health monitoring to getting prescribed utility support, everything will be easy to get to the doorstep. This will increase the rate of the healthy population as well as a higher rate of cash flow in the healthcare and related industries which will lead to a win-win situation among all parties.

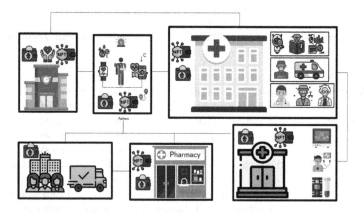

Fig. 1. The vision of a completely automated healthcare ecosystem where patients can get adequate services within zero downtime.

Stepping towards this vision, we got branches of computer science that already have started to contribute in medical research advancement. The application of Artificial Intelligence (AI) [2–8] is consistently providing significant contributions over the last five years in the healthcare industry and it's expected to go beyond our logical assumptions [9]. Parallelly, Blockchain or Distributed Ledger Technology (DLT) is showing great potential [10–13], and experts started to believe that it has enough capacity and ability to transform the healthcare industry. Day after day, DLT is proving itself by presenting highly feasible and sophisticated secure telehealth solutions to us. According to reports, Estonia has successfully established a sophisticated culture with EHR system [14] where citizens can get on-demand medical services more adequately than other cultures by relying on technologies.

In 1991, the concept of the Digital Twin (DT) technology was originally introduced by David Gelernter in his book *Mirror Worlds* [15]. For more than two decades, this was just a concept until manufacturers entered into the game [16]. Since then, a strong academic and industrial research continuum has been established. Tao, F. et al. [17] explained the state-of-the-art of this technology and outlined key technologies, promising areas, and existing industrial applications of the concept of DT. Wu, Y. et al. [18] performed a survey of DT Networks and shows that not only encapsulated in manufacturing industries, but it also has an enormous potential to transform every industry by bringing them together with enabling technologies such as DLT [19–21], AI [20,22–24], Augmented and Virtual Reality [25], etc., and so on [26–28] with its promising technological aspects.

To achieve the vision we made, now we have enough technologies to step forward, and here we are, proposing a DT, DLT, AI/ML, and IoT-enabled [29] futuristic eHealth solution that will provide a strong contribution towards a completely automated healthcare ecosystem. Contributions to this research are listed below.

1. The proposed solution is designed by segregating independent systems and services without interrupting each other by using segregated cross-functional disruptive technologies such as DT, DLT-based dApp System, and machine learning (ML) service that will remain integrated with the existing Hospital's Information Management System. The concept of the single responsibility principle has been applied while designing the proposed solution. It assures zero inter-dependencies that make the solution fail-safe and resilient. Business perspectives are considered during the solution design to make the investment worthy, feasible, and adaptable to healthcare institutes.
2. Real-time implementation of this proposed solution will directly impact by accelerating the transformational process of the healthcare industry. From health informatics to core medical research, more aspects will be identified, and the advancement of medical research and more effective professional training will bring satisfactory medical facilities. This will establish a common ground of mutual gain among all participants and results an increased amount of cash flow in the industry. In aggregate, we'll get a healthy, wealthy, and happy society by advancing this research of Healthcare Ecosystem.
3. For experimental purposes, a segregated DT model of a patient has been implemented by applying advanced level AI based on GNNs and GANs to inspect patient health conditions. For operational purposes, another segregated ML service has been developed to collect internal and external data. Both of these modules are developed by using the python programming language. For transaction and record exchange purposes, a dApp has been developed within the TruffleSuit framework on Ethereum by using Solidity, NodeJs, Web3.0, and ReactJs based on ERC20 and ERC721 token-base where medical and institutional records are stored into IPFS and integrated with existing system via Infura API [30].

2   Proposed Solution

We depict our working model for digital healthcare including IoT, DLT, and DT which is like a package of the total healthcare arena. In Fig. 1, we can observe the vision of a healthcare solution that provides satisfactory automation to us all the necessary medical services with the help of DT, DLT, AI/ML, and IoT. The Fig. 2 explains the proposed eHealth solution. In ideal conditions, a patient can request telemedicine services to a hospital first. The hospital will redirect that patient to a doctor or consultant or physician. After consultation, the medical professional updates that patient's medical profile and the prescription document into an institute-authenticated distributed file system (DFS). From this DFS, the medical professional send that prescription document by signing it digitally to the patient directly via a specified private blockchain network in the NFT approach. In the same way, the smart contract will also send it to the pharmacy. The pharmacy will prepare the order including delivery charges and send the bill to the hospital. At the same time, the delivery service provider will deliver the prescribed pharmaceutical products to that patient. The hospital accounts

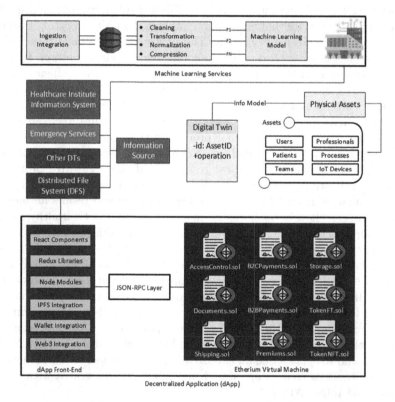

Fig. 2. A top-level architectural design of the proposed eHealth Solution by applying segregated DT, IoT, AI/ML, and Blockchain modules, that will be executed together to achieve common goals and objectives and governed by existing system.

will segregate financial matters for that patient, then sign the document digitally, and then store it in the DFS and send it to the insurance company via the private blockchain network. The insurance company will perform all necessary wallet-to-wallet transactions for all bills at the end of the business day. Along with these, this system will monitor the patients' health parameters (heartbeat, pulse rate, blood pressure, oxygen saturation, sensor ECG, body temperature) through the sensor and transfer them to the hospital for observation. Here the data transmission can be accessible for multiple devices and DT. At the same time, a patient can communicate or transmit data to an ambulance and hospital. The medical profiles of all patients and other pieces of information like patients' device data, internal service performance, and other technical information will access by the DT system to create exact virtual copies of potential participants. These DT models will allow the healthcare institute to train medical professionals by predictive simulations and pre-defined problem solutions for continuous improvement in medical facilities and institutional services. The DT module processes these pieces of information including all of the dynamics and sends them to researchers and AI/ML modules. Putting full effort into all visible potential scopes will achieve desired and deserving medical services for patients. According to this Fig. 2, we can observe different segregated systems, modules and services are integrated by considering Institutional Information System as a middleware in the proposed solution architecture. Later in this section, we'll see each of these segregated systems, modules and services in brief details.

2.1   Blockchain-Based dApp System

This decentralized application (dApp) system is designed for end-to-end fungible and non-fungible transactions among parties in zero downtime. In ideal conditions, a patient's smart device picks up his or her health information by using several sensors and communicates with the system via Infura API. The Infura API will store this information into the patient profile on IPFS and start communication with smart contracts. These smart contracts encrypt these data, and then store it into a block, perform a non-fungible transaction with medical professionals or institutes or ambulance services, and add these blocks to the private Ethereum Blockchain. We believe that transparent transactions will make every party's services more effective and efficient. Potential audiences inside and outside from healthcare industry are identified by considering domain-specific dependencies and accountabilities in recent practices. This number of participants could be extended in case of an increase in solution scope depending on the specific organizations or ecosystems or cultures. While performing experimental validation, the dApp has been developed in a limited scope [30].

dApp Front-End. The dApp front-end consists of a mobile app or a web app or both, which contains React Components, Redux Libraries, Node Modules including IPFS, Wallet, and Web3.js integration. In this case, we've chosen

IPFS-InterPlanetary File System, the most popular DFS system to store records. The React app has been chosen for the front-end due to its popularity, and maintainability during real-time usage.

JSON-RPC Communication. The dApp front-end communicates with smart contracts (back-end) via the JSON-RPC layer, by using Web3.js, which is a widely used JSON-RPC application. JSON-RPC is a JSON-encoded remote procedure call protocol. It's similar to the XML-RPC protocol in that it merely specifies a handful of data types and actions. JSON-RPC supports alerts (data delivered to the server that does not require a response) as well as multiple calls to the server that can be answered asynchronously. Web3 API, often known as web3.js, is an Ethereum JavaScript API that we're employing here. It's a set of libraries that let you use HTTP, IPC, or WebSocket to communicate with a local or distant Ethereum node. The Web3 API makes it simple to link a dApp or wallet to the most widely used smart contract blockchain.

dApp Back-End. The smart contracts are written in the solidity programming language, stored on Ethereum Virtual Machine (EVM), executed on a blockchain network, and allow users to interact with the application interface through a web browser or a mobile app. All these layers are deployed to the Ethereum private consortium network. In another word, the encrypted data of a patient profile or prescription or emergency calls are stored in a block and the block is added to the blockchain. Finally, the information is stored in the IPFS platform for read-typed operations. Alongside this, the Infura API is also connected with the patient's smart devices where these devices get health data from patients and send it to the dApp to store and process by medical professionals for taking necessary actions.

Record Storage. Distributed File System is the most common platform for storing and transferring records and documents securely. We have chosen IPFS which is the most popular and widely used distributed file system. The InterPlanetary File System (IPFS) is a distributed file system protocol and peer-to-peer network for storing and distributing data. This platform is being used to hold the most important readable patient profiles, which have already been encrypted and saved on the Ethereum blockchain.

2.2 Digital Twin Service

DT refers an exact copy of a physical object including its dynamics in virtual world. In another words, it is a logical representation of any physical object. In recent days, it is showing great potential for research advances in almost every industry, specially in healthcare. Faster advances of medical science and technologies will provide more reliable medical services. From training up professionals to research and innovations, DT technology will help the medical science to achieve next level faster than expectation. The concept of DT is based on Internet of Things (IoT). IoT devices are continuously collecting data. In this proposed solution, the DT service is collecting data from all potential participants and creating their exact copy with dynamics using various sources. Predictive simulation will unlock more dimensions, perceptions, and aspects for medical researchers.

IoT Devices and Integration. It is often refers that the concept of IoT is the backbone of DT. In this proposed model, continuous data collection from IoT devices has been considered from every audience. From patient to medical professionals and other participants, various sensors, embedded modules, and smart devices can provide potential dynamics and behavioural pattern of every recognizable entities. These pieces of information are crucial for DT to provide them to AI/ML services and creates exact reflections of each entities.

Role of AI. It has been observed that AI is the most vital part of the puzzle. Machine learning and deep learning methods such as Graph Neural Networks (GNNs) are used within ML frameworks like Generative Adversarial Networks (GANs) to create DT models from data that are collected from IoT devices. During experimental validation, GNNs and GANs are applied to implement patient DT model [30]. Similar to this, AI is required to utilize all related object data and utilize them by learning their physical and logical behaviour with real-time dynamics, and implement their exact virtual copy. Not only limited to DT model creation, but AI is also important for conducting medical research and development advancements by implementing supporting tools such as predictive simulation, AR/VR based training modules, etc., and so on.

DT Models and Its Application. It is intended to create DT models of all potential objects such as patient, medical professional, researchers, physical and logical infrastructure, utility vehicles, etc. and so on. Predictive simulation on the behavioural and executional pattern of all models will assure satisfactory medical services from the root. For experimental purposes, it's been only tested with patient DT model [30] to validate the proposed solution.

2.3   Machine Learning Service

A segregated ML service has been developed to analyze the interaction from all end-user groups and identifies their behavioural pattern of system usage. This service will continuously learn from end-users and plays a partial role of system analyst by identifying problems of existing system from end-users perspectives. This will consistently push Institution's IT section to accelerate their continuous development process efficiently. On the other hand, it will assist specific end-users for their healthcare routine that will save patients time to get healthcare facilities to the doorstep. Alongside with this, this service will provide these behavioural result analysis to the DT service. This approach will make the entire solution more sophisticated where accuracy of predictive simulation from DT will be more reliable. In simple terms, it'll provide digital eHealth assistance services and simplify peoples day-to-day lifestyle for healthcare. During experimental validation, end-user interaction has been observed in a limited scope [30].

3   System Analysis

Applying the concepts of DT, AI/ML, IoT, and DLT, the proposed solution has been designed to become an adaptable, secured, improved quality sustainable, and sophisticated eHealth application system. It provides a simplified and optimistic way for healthcare professionals and consumers to automate and fasten processes which will save procedural time significantly and reduce the probability of blunders in medical profile management. The solution design is completely feasible, operationally, technically, and economically. In this section, the analysis and observation are described based on scope, performance, cost, and impact.

3.1   Scope Analysis

The scope of the proposed solution is covered several technical and technological areas to support the development, implementation, and real-time management of highly sustainable information system solutions. The solution architectural design assure an extensive flexibility that assures the scope of the proposed solution to become expandable to multiple dimensions of software engineering. Based on vision, objectives, and technical dependencies, on-demand basis changes can be performed. As a result, it allows more cross-functional technological integration such as Solid-Pod for system betterment without interrupting existing system. It helps the solution to remain sustainable for a long-run.

3.2   Design Analysis

The proposed solution architectural has been designed by following several concepts and principles. The observation of the solution architecture is given below:

- The Domain-Driven Design paradigm has been followed strictly.
- Segregated independent systems and services are designed with single specific responsibility.
- It eradicates the degree of inter-dependencies to zero.
- Psychology behind the business has been considered by keeping the existing system constant.
- Integration of cross-functional modules has performed externally, without violating the existing system.
- Its architectural facilities reduces the project risk and make the solution adaptable in all aspects.
- It is highly maintainable, fail-safe and resilient.
- On-demand real-time support and solution can provide without any failure and delay.

3.3   Performance Analysis

It's been observed the performance of the blockchain-based decentralized application system at the machine level. In this paper, we've considered the number of transactions and the number of participants or nodes to justify the real-time performance with other modules, components, and systems. Figure 3 clearly indicates the higher number of consortium members using a higher number of machines or blockchain nodes impacts faster transactions. This is applicable for both fungible and non-fungible transactions. Everything performed in a blockchain is recorded into the distributed ledger, considering each change or modification as a transaction. Applying this concept allows the proposed solution to use a highly consistent resource of information which is mandatory for information systems like eHealth. Figure 3 also shows the quantity of upload data and the respective time consumption, of the IPFS-InterPlanetary File System, a distributed file system we've chosen for the proposed solution. It has been used to store medical records. While uploading data into IPFS returns the uploaded file's hash value and delegated Document.sol smart contract stores it into the blockchain.

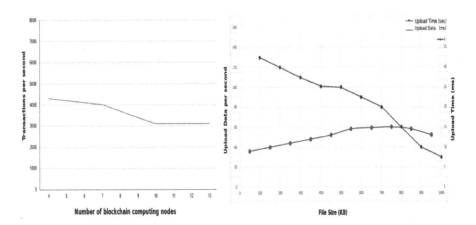

Fig. 3. Performance analysis of the experimental prototype in aspects of a) blockchain transaction performance as per no. of transaction per second and number of computing nodes and b) IPFS data storage performance as per data size and upload time.

3.4   Cost Analysis

As per the theory of the project management triangle, the time, cost, and scope has a relation of direct proportion. An increase in any of them results in an increase in the rest of them. Moreover, the increase in quality causes an increase in time, scope, and cost. According to this theory, the proposed solution is expensive. It consists of a complex architectural design to become a top-most quality eHealth system. As a result, the project budget will increase. But, end-of-the-day, it's worth it.

3.5   Impact Analysis

Integration of DT technology allows continuous improvement of any health-care institute to optimize their medical service and internal processes, and faster research advancements. It'll impact directly people's everyday lifestyles by redefining the telehealth service into a new dimension. It will allow a patient to get medical services, reports, and prescriptions in zero downtime. That patient can purchase prescribed medicines online, and receive them at home. All the financial matters will remain automated, and transactions will perform as per the conditions defined. By using it, getting healthcare services will become much faster, easier, and better. This will impact the continuous improvement and research advancement by accelerating them. Putting things together, this idea of proposed solution will be a significant contribution to the healthcare industry by empowering the automation the healthcare ecosystem completely from root.

4   Observation

Stepping towards the vision we've made, in this proposed solution, cross-functional technologies have been used to develop independent systems and services by applying the single responsibility principle and segregating them from the existing system. This architectural design strategy allows the project to expand its scope by integrating on-demand basis most feasible new solution with it. In simple words, the proposed eHealth system has the architectural endurance of accepting rapid business changes toward 4IR and remains sustainable for a long run. A sustainable and sophisticated application system always signifies a higher RoI by lowering risk factors in all aspects while adapting new solutions like the proposed one. Industrial adaptability will impact an increasing interaction of the end-consumers' with application systems by reducing digital literacy tends to zero, and to accelerate the process of transformation of the healthcare industry. The idea of the proposed solution is an initiative to step forward with our vision of a completely automated healthcare ecosystem that will simplify our lifestyle and lead us towards a healthy, wealthy, and happy society.

5   Recommendation

IT Solutions now-a-days requires maturity and quality to become sustainable. It is strongly recommended for vendors to practice CMMI V2.0 process areas and achieve ISO/IEC 27001 standards of security and ISO/IEC 25010:2011 SQuaRE standard of deliverable quality during production level development and implementation. Practicing Agile methodology in Scrum framework will be highly effective. The total number of development teams must be equal to the total number of segregated modules. Agile clean coding practice is mandatory. Violation of standard practices can cause severe damage to deliverable quality, as an impact during real-time live operation, more bugs and issues will arise, which will increase the project expenses beyond estimation.

6 Conclusion

Every moment in medical service operations is much more valuable beyond our logical assumptions. Delays in service often take lives or cause potential damages. In our everyday busy life, it is really hard for any individual to maintain their own medical profile accurately. With the blessings of technological progression, now we have the opportunity to take care of ourselves and make medical services more optimistic than ever before. We've found our vision of a completely automated healthcare ecosystem. With this vision and motivations, we are here stepping towards this vision by proposing this DT integrated futuristic eHealth system solution, where the prime objective of this system becomes to utilize the medical system for remote patients with satisfactory automated medical services with zero downtime in every aspect. It'll allow continuous improvement, and medical research advancements parallelly from an information system. By inclusion of ISO/IEC 27001 standards of security, compatibility, integrity, flexibility, and ISO/IEC 25010:2011 SQuaRE model, the proposed solution will stands as a sophisticated DT and DLT-based smart healthcare system where automation of the process makes the service to patients faster and in an effective and efficient way, by managing patients' medical profiles appropriately. Overall, we are confident to state that this system will simplify an individual's healthcare routine, optimize the medical service processes, and brings satisfaction to all parties.

Future Directions

- It is required to define a collection of software engineering standards and practices to perform appropriate integration of cross-functional technologies.
- An increased amount of investment is required, although it's worth it. But it is also important to perform deep research on cost reduction within this level of project scope without compromising the product quality.
- Further research on the scope expansion of DT in the Healthcare Industry is necessary to perform to keep all participants of the industry together with the help of AI and DLT to achieve a common ground of mutual gain.

Proposed solution is an initiative. Its contribution to the healthcare industry will impact the continuum of progression of medical information systems. Our philosophy is to present the blessings of technology in a satisfactory way to make things easier, smarter, and better. This is the demand of time to grab these blessings, and now we have what we need to step forward, toward an automated healthcare ecosystem. Let's begin the change.

References

1. Biswas, M., et al.: An enhanced deep convolution neural network model to diagnose Alzheimer's disease using brain magnetic resonance imaging. In: Santosh, K., Hegadi, R., Pal, U. (eds.) Recent Trends in Image Processing and Pattern Recognition. RTIP2R 2021. CCIS, vol. 1576, pp.42–52. Springer, Cham (2022). https://doi.org/10.1007/978-3-031-07005-1_5

2. Santosh, K.C., Ghosh, S.: Covid-19 imaging tools: how big data is big? J. Med. Syst. **45**(7), 1–8 (2021)
3. Kamal, Md.S., Dey, N., Chowdhury, L., Hasan, S.I., Santosh, K.C.: Explainable AI for glaucoma prediction analysis to understand risk factors in treatment planning. IEEE Trans. Instrum. Measur. **71**, 1–9 (2022)
4. Mahbub, Md.K., Biswas, M., Gaur, L., Alenezi, F., Santosh, R.C.: Deep features to detect pulmonary abnormalities in chest x-rays due to infectious disease: Covid-19, pneumonia, and tuberculosis. Inf. Sci. **592**, 389–401 (2022)
5. Mahbub, Md.K., et al.: Mobapp4infectiousdisease: classify covid-19, pneumonia, and tuberculosis. In 2022 IEEE 35th International Symposium on Computer-Based Medical Systems (CBMS), pp. 119–124 (2022)
6. Biswas, M., Kaiser, M.S., Mahmud, M., Al Mamun, S., Hossain, M.S., Rahman, M.A.: An XAI based autism detection: the context behind the detection. In: Mahmud, M., Kaiser, M.S., Vassanelli, S., Dai, Q., Zhong, N. (eds.) BI 2021. LNCS (LNAI), vol. 12960, pp. 448–459. Springer, Cham (2021). https://doi.org/10.1007/978-3-030-86993-9_40
7. Biswas, M., et al.: Accu3rate: a mobile health application rating scale based on user reviews. PLoS ONE **16**(12), e0258050 (2021)
8. Biswas, M., et al.: Indoor navigation support system for patients with neurodegenerative diseases. In: Mahmud, M., Kaiser, M.S., Vassanelli, S., Dai, Q., Zhong, N. (eds.) BI 2021. LNCS (LNAI), vol. 12960, pp. 411–422. Springer, Cham (2021). https://doi.org/10.1007/978-3-030-86993-9_37
9. Shehab, M., et al.: Machine learning in medical applications: a review of state-of-the-art methods. Comput. Biol. Med. **145**, 105458 (2022)
10. Yang, L.: The blockchain: state-of-the-art and research challenges. J. Ind. Inf. Integr. **15**, 80–90 (2019)
11. Ahmad, R.W., Salah, K., Jayaraman, R., Yaqoob, I., Ellahham, S., Omar, M.: The role of blockchain technology in telehealth and telemedicine. Int. J. Med. Inform. **148**, 104399 (2021)
12. Gambril, J., et al.: Application of nonfungible tokens to health care. Comment on "blockchain technology projects to provide telemedical services: Systematic review". J. Med. Internet Res. **24**(5), e34276 (2022)
13. Nguyen, D.C., Pathirana, P.N., Ding, M., Seneviratne, A.: Blockchain for 5g and beyond networks: a state of the art survey. J. Netw. Comput. Appl. **166**, 102693 (2020)
14. Koppel, A., Kahur, K., Habicht, T., Saar, P., Habicht, J., van Ginneken, E.: Estonia: Health System Review. World Health Organization (2008)
15. Gelernter. D.: Mirror Worlds: Or the Day Software Puts the Universe in a Shoebox... How It Will Happen and What It Will Mean. Oxford University Press, Oxford (1993)
16. Siemens and General Electric gear up for the internet of things—The Economist, 3 December 2016. Accessed 31 Aug 2022
17. Tao, F., Zhang, H., Liu, A., Nee, A.Y.C.: Digital twin in industry: State-of-the-art. IEEE Trans. Ind. Inform. **15**(4), 2405–2415 (2019)
18. Yiwen, W., Zhang, K., Zhang, Y.: Digital twin networks: A survey. IEEE Internet Things J. **8**(18), 13789–13804 (2021)
19. Yaqoob, I., Salah, K., Uddin, M., Jayaraman, R., Omar, M., Imran, M.: Blockchain for digital twins: recent advances and future research challenges. IEEE Netw. **34**(5), 290–298 (2020)

20. Yunlong, L., Huang, X., Zhang, K., Maharjan, S., Zhang, Y.: Low-latency federated learning and blockchain for edge association in digital twin empowered 6g networks. IEEE Trans. Industr. Inf. **17**(7), 5098–5107 (2020)
21. Altun, C., Tavli, B., Yanikomeroglu, H.: Liberalization of digital twins of IoT-enabled home appliances via blockchains and absolute ownership rights. IEEE Commun. Mag. **57**(12), 65–71 (2019)
22. Tao, F., Cheng, J., Qi, Q., Zhang, M., Zhang, H., Sui, F.: Digital twin-driven product design, manufacturing and service with big data. Int. J. Adv. Manuf. Technol. **94**(9), 3563–3576 (2018)
23. Dai, Y., Zhang, K., Maharjan, S., Zhang, Y.: Deep reinforcement learning for stochastic computation offloading in digital twin networks. IEEE Trans. Industr. Inf. **17**(7), 4968–4977 (2020)
24. Barbiero, P., Torné, R., Lió, P.: Graph representation forecasting of patient's medical conditions: toward a digital twin. Front. Genet. **12**, 289 (2021)
25. Schroeder, G., et al.: Visualising the digital twin using web services and augmented reality. In: 2016 IEEE 14th International Conference on Industrial Informatics (INDIN), pp. 522–527. IEEE (2016)
26. Zheng, Yu., Yang, S., Cheng, H.: An application framework of digital twin and its case study. J. Ambient. Intell. Humaniz. Comput. **10**(3), 1141–1153 (2019)
27. Tuegel, E.J., Ingraffea, A.R., Eason, T.G., Spottswood, S.M.: Reengineering aircraft structural life prediction using a digital twin. Int. J. Aerosp. Eng. **2011**, 154798 (2011)
28. Söderberg, R., Wärmefjord, K., Carlson, J.S., Lindkvist, L.: Toward a digital twin for real-time geometry assurance in individualized production. CIRP Ann. **66**(1):137–140 (2017)
29. Biswas, M., Whaiduzzaman, M.D.: Efficient mobile cloud computing through computation offloading. Int. J. Adv. Technol **10**(2), 32 (2018)
30. Afroj, M.: Github - maharinafroj/eHealth. 1 September 2022. [Online; Accessed 1 Sep 2022]

Enabling Edge Devices Using Federated Learning and Big Data for Proactive Decisions

Abishi Chowdhury$^{(\boxtimes)}$, A. Swaminathan, Rajan R. Ashoka, and Amrit Pal

School of Computer Science and Engineering, Vellore Institute of Technology,
Chennai 600127, Tamil Nadu, India
abishi.chowdhury@gmail.com

Abstract. Big data and cloud computing lay a new paradigm of data analytics and pave an insight for new types of intelligent devices. These smart devices continuously capture, store, and transfer data to the centrally controlled devices. In recent years, there has been an exponential increase in smart devices, which has increased the amount of data generated by these devices. The communication of the generated data to the central nodes results in a high communication rate. This type of data communication is vulnerable to network intrusions and multiple security threats. Realtime processing of the data is also a huge challenge, and it is an arduous task to provide support to the applications working on realtime decision making. This paper proposes a message passing approach among intelligent edge devices, which leverages the advantages of the big data analytics and federated learning to tackle the challenges as mentioned above. The experimental analysis of several benchmark datasets supports the proposed approach's theoretical base. The proposed approach with suitable number of edge devices reduces the overall training time maximum by one third while maintaining a significant amount of accuracy.

Keywords: Federated learning · Big data · Edge computing · Prediction model · Fault prediction

1 Introduction

The computation power of the edge devices like mobile phones, wearable smart devices, intelligent vehicles, and smart monitoring devices is increasing day by day. There are cloud based solutions to store and process data generated by these devices. However, this paradigm is changing due to the increase in the amount of data and demand for time-sensitive processing. The existing cloud based solutions are getting inferior in routing data from end devices to the cloud and then processing the data at the cloud and sending the decision or trained model to the end device. It is evident that sharing the data captured or generated by these devices is costly and not secure. It is very efficient to store and process the data locally at the edge devices.

KC Santosh et al. (Eds.): RTIP2R 2022, CCIS 1704, pp. 324–336, 2023.
https://doi.org/10.1007/978-3-031-23599-3_24

The distributed processing of the data using commodity hardware [1] is not a very new concept. However, there is still a sufficient gap in developing efficient algorithms which leverage the advantage of distributed computing. The concept of edge computing is a milestone in that direction and encourages the use of federated learning. Federated learning (FL) [2] can help utilize the edge devices' storage and processing power. It can perform the training of a machine learning model in a collaborative manner orchestrated by a control unit while using the distributed and decentralized data available at the edge devices. It can handle the challenges of communication overheads, and security of the data.

FL starts with the selection of the model which needs to be trained. The model parameters are initialized and shared among the edge devices. The edge devices work on the server's received model and its parameters. The edge devices use the local data to improve the model further and share the updated model parameters with the server. No exchange of original data takes place. The server receives the updated model parameters from the edge devices, aggregates them to generate the global parameters, and shares those updated parameters with the edge devices for further model training.

Detection of critical events like component failure [3,4], equipment failure [5], security threat [6], and commercial frauds is essential for ensuring the overall reliability and robustness of a system. Detecting an event and taking proactive measures in the context of that event is very important and can ensure the overall system's effectiveness.

The Internet of Things, along with wireless sensor networks, plays a crucial role in collecting and processing data for the detection of critical events. There are a variety of applications like surveillance, monitoring of the traffic, and monitoring for network faults.

This paper proposes an approach for predicting critical events while considering distributed data collection and edge computing. A distributed incremental learning model has been proposed based on the federated learning approach. Following are the main objectives achieved through this work.

- A data collection model over independent learners
- Generation of the local learners
- Combining local learners to generate a global model and passing that global model to the edge devices
- Updation and communication of the global model

2   Related Work

The concept of federated learning [7] is often used for learning the models over distributed edge devices. With its continuous expansions, federated learning solves data communication challenges over the computing nodes along with data security and privacy [8,9]. The increase in the amount of raw data is very high compared to the good quality data. This results in a lack of good quality data that can be used to train the centralized machine learning models. Organizations that are benefited from applied data analytics find it very difficult to share their data with other organizations or competitors. There is an urgent need to develop machine learning and data analytics models to overcome these challenges. Faults can occur at any time in a system and subsequently result in the degradation of the overall process [10,11].

In a production line, faults can occur at any time, prediction of these faults will eventually enhance the overall production and reduce the production cost. Ge et [12] have presented fault prediction models for such industrial operations using federated random forest and support vector machine models. A deep learning based method has also been proposed for the prediction of machine faults [13]. A critical event like a total device failure can occur for an edge device; also, detecting such events is essential to ensure reliable data capturing and processing. A CNN and LSTM based model has been proposed by [14] to detect anomalies in the edge devices. Detection of a critical event like an intrusion in a network or on a local computer is also crucial. Machine and deep learning based approaches [15] are proposed for the detection of such events using techniques like support vector machine [16–18], random forest, and deep belief network [19,20]. Although multiple approaches are proposed for fault predictions there is sufficient research gap in context of processing data at the edge nodes and communicating the compressed information to all decision makers. The proposed approach targets the challenge of maintaining independence among the edge devices while minimizing the amount of data communication required to train a global model.

3   Proposed Approach

The overall approach is four fold. In the first phase, the edge nodes estimate their model; in the second phase, the edge nodes share their trained model. The models collected from the edge devices are combined to generate a global model in the third phase. The global model is then shared with the edge nodes and performs the global model training in the final phase. Figure 1 presents an overview of the proposed approach. Table 1 shoes the important notations used in this paper.

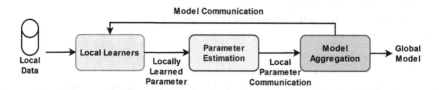

Fig. 1. An overview of the proposed model

Table 1. Notation description

Notation	Description
X	A d dimension vector for representing a point
X_i	A specific point from the data
D	The complete dataset
D^t	Data available to the tth edge node
E	Set of edge devices
e^t	t^{th} edge device
C^t	Information generation at t^{th} edge device
c_{ji}	Association of X_i point with j^{th} class
η	Linear sum for variance estimation
η_j	Linear sum for variance estimation over j^{th} class
l	Number of class labels
μ	An $l \times d$ mean matrix
σ	An $l \times d$ variance matrix
τ	Used for representing time instance
τ_t	Time instance at t^{th} edge node
$prosum$	Estimated parameter generated by each edge device
sum	Estimated parameter generated by each edge device

3.1 Local Training

Each edge device works as a sensing node and collects the data generated by its sensors. The edge device also has processing capabilities for making decisions based on a given model, and the edge device can also find the updates for the local model. The local edge device stores the localized data and stores the local model. The predictions are being performed for the new data using the model available with the edge device. The model update process starts with the estimation of the new model parameters.

Model Updation Consider that a total of m number of d dimension points are available at an edge device. The collection of points $D^t = \{X_1, X_2, X_3, ..., X_m\}$, t^{th} edge device. The global parameters$< (c, \tau), \mu, \sigma >$ are communicated to the edge device. The duplet (c, τ) works as an identifier for synchronizing the cycle of the updates. Each class has a unique identifier denoted by c, c_j for the jth class, and τ is the number used for referencing the cycle of the updation. As the edge device receives this information, it compares the received (c, τ) with its existing (c, τ_t) for each class. If the τ_t is less than the received τ then a possible update can be performed to estimate the posterior probability for the points available to an edge device. Iterating over all the local data (D^t) for each class(j) the posterior probability$(c_j i)$ is estimated as shown in the Eq. 1.

$$P(X_i | c_j) = \frac{1}{\sqrt{(2\pi)^d \sigma_{c_j}^2}} exp \left(-\frac{(X_i - \mu_{c_j})^2}{2\sigma_{c_j}^2} \right) \tag{1}$$

It results in an $l \times m$ matrix.

$$C^t = \begin{bmatrix} c_{11} & \cdots & c_{1m} \\ \vdots & \ddots & \vdots \\ c_{l1} & \cdots & c_{lm} \end{bmatrix} \tag{2}$$

Each edge device generates the results as mentioned in Eq. 2. This informa-

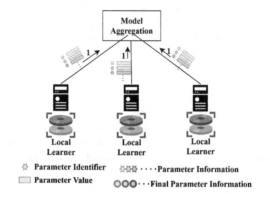

Fig. 2. Communication of the model parameter from the edge devices to the central node for aggregation process

tion is further used for the calculation of the shared parameters. Edge devices prepare a compressed form of information to reduce data communication and preserve the data's privacy. After estimating the posterior information for each point and class, the edge device increments τ_t by one. The edge device performs compression of this generated information before sharing it with the server using a parameter sharing approach as shown in Fig. 2.

3.2   Communicating Estimates

Each edge device uses the generated C^t to calculate the parameters to be shared. The edge devices compress the complete posterior estimation in the form of $< (c, \tau), prosum, sum >$. For each point in the local data, its weight associated for a particular class is multiplied with the point. A linear sum is performed as shown in Eq. 3. This sum helps in two ways, first, it restricts the communication to one parameter. Secondly, it helps in privacy preservation of the data. The estimation of *prosum* communicating parameter is done using Eq. 3.

$$prosum = c_{j1}^t * X_1 + c_{j2}^t * X_2 + ... + c_{jm}^t * X_m \tag{3}$$

c_{ji} ranges from 0 to 1, 0 signifies that the ith point does not belong to j^{th} class. A fraction value signifies bias of the point towards a particular class. Iterating over

Algorithm 1. Model updation

Require: $\{\mu_1, \mu_2, ...\mu_d\}, \{\sigma_1, \sigma_2, ...\sigma_d\}$
Ensure: $y = x^n$
    for $X_i \in D^t$ **do**
        Estimate $P(X_i|c_j) \rightarrow c_{ji}$
    end for
    for $X_i \in D^t$ **do**
        Estimate $\sum_{i=1}^m c_{ji} * X_i \rightarrow prosum_j$
        Estimate $\sum_{i=1}^m c_{ji}^t (X_i - \mu_j^t)^2 \rightarrow \eta_j$
    end for
    for $i = 1$ *to* m **do**
        $sum_j = +c_{ji}^t$
    end for
        return $prosum_j, \eta_j, sum_j$

all points product of the scalar c_{ji} and the vector X_i is maintained in memory, and a linear sum is performed. The quadruple consists of parameter sum, which is estimated as shown in Eq. 4.

$$sum = c_{j1}^t + c_{j2}^t + ... + c_{jm}^t \tag{4}$$

Each edge node generates a quadruple as a result as shown in the equation below

$$< (\mu_j^t, \tau), prosum, sum > \tag{5}$$

The first parameter of the quadruple is the identifier for the parameter, τ is an incremental parameter to synchronize the parameters. Parameter $prosum$ is a d dimension vector and sum is a scalar.

Another parameter η is also estimated; this parameter is used as input for calculating the global variance for a particular class. The calculation of the η is done using Eq. 6.

$$\eta_j = c_{j1}^t(X_1 - \mu_j^t)^2 + c_{j2}^t(X_2 - \mu_j^t)^2 + ... + c_{jm}^t(X_m - \mu_j^t)^2 \tag{6}$$

The sharing of this parameter is done as $< (\eta_j, \tau), \eta_j, sum >$. This phase ends with the generation of two quadruples from each edge device. Both the quadruples have unique identifiers as a pair at the front. These identifiers help in aggregating the parameters from different edge devices.

Model Aggregation. The edge devices communicate the generated information to a central coordinating node as shown in Fig. 3. The collected information is processed to generate the global variables, which are further shared back with the edge devices as shown in Fig. 4. Algorithm 2 presents the procedure for aggregating of the information and the final generation of the estimated value for μ and σ. The estimation of the parameter μ is done as shown in Eq. 7 and

Algorithm 2. Model aggregation

Require: $\{< (\mu_j^t, \tau), prosum, sum >, < (\eta_j^t, \tau), \eta_j, sum >\}$
Ensure: μ, σ
  $S_j = 0$
  $Total_j$
  for each $t \in T$ **do**
    $S_j = S_j + prosum_j^t$
    $total_j = +sum$
  end for
  for each $j \in l$ **do**
    $\mu_j = \frac{S_j}{total_j}$
  end for
  for each $t \in T$ **do**
    $Vsum = +\eta_j^t$
  end for
  for each $j \in l$ **do**
    $\sigma_j = \sqrt{\frac{Vsum}{total_j}}$
  end for
  return μ, σ

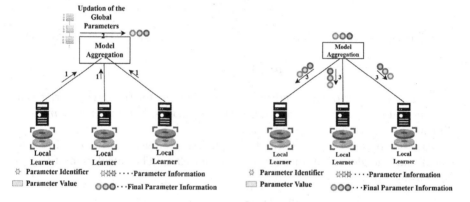

Fig. 3. Aggregation of the model parameter at the central node

Fig. 4. Communication of the aggregated parameters to the edge devices

the same is reflected in Algorithm 2.

$$\mu_j = \sum_{t=1}^{T} \frac{prosum^t}{sum^t} \qquad (7)$$

The estimation of another parameter σ using Eq. 8 is done using the shared information from all edge devices.

$$\sigma_j^t = \sqrt{\frac{c_{j1}^t (X_1 - \mu_j^t)^2 + c_{j2}^t (X_2 - \mu_j^t)^2 + ... + c_{jm}^t (X_m - \mu_j^t)^2}{c_{j1}^t + c_{j2}^t + ... + c_{jm}^t}} \qquad (8)$$

The complete process of generation of the global parameters is presented in Algorithm 2. These results are further communicated to all edge nodes for the next update iteration. The edge devices use the newly received parameters to estimate the new parameters using the Algorithm 1. The edge devices pass the generated information to the central node, and the model parameters are updated using Algorithm 2.

4 Result Analysis

To test the proposed approach analysis has been performed over several benchmark datasets like network fault [21], credit card fraud detection [22], machine fault detection [23], and Amazon IoT data [24]. The description of the datasets is given in Table 2.

Table 2. Dataset used for the analysis of the proposed approach

S. No.	Dataset	Classes	Features	Instances
1	IoT monitoring	7	4	105846
2	Credit cards	2	28	284807
3	Machine faults	4	20	30352
4	Amazon IoT	2	7	6319485

Table 3. Analysis of the obtained accuracy with increasing number of iterations and edge devices using Amazon IoT dataset

Iterations	Edge 2	Edge 4	Edge 6	Edge 8	Edge 10	Edge 12	Edge 14	Edge 16	Edge 18	Edge 20
2	72	65	63.05	60	62	65	65	62	62	60
4	76	67	65	60.45	64	69	70	68	65	63
6	80	64	66	65	65	73	74	70	69	68
8	82	70	67.9	69	72	76	75	73	72	70
10	84	75	73	72	75	78	77	75	76	73
12	85	78	76	78	79	82	83	82	80	76
14	86	80	82	80	82	84	83	82	83	84
16	88	83	84	83	85	85	86	84	85	88
18	89	86	85	84	83	87	87	86	87	88
20	92	88	85	86	89	89	89	88	88	88

4.1 Accuracy Analysis

As the accuracy of the proposed model is an important parameter for classification, an analysis of the accuracy of the model with respect to the increasing number of iterations along with an increasing number of edge devices is presented. It has been observed that as the number of edge devices increases, which

results in an increase in the number of partitions of the data, the accuracy of
the prediction model decreases. However, it has been observed that as the number of iterations increases, there is a potential gain in prediction accuracy. For
instance as shown in Table 3, consider the number of edge devices as 12. There
is an average gain of 3% over an increasing number of iterations. It has also been
observed that it is essential to decide the number of iterations for the learning
process as it directly affects the accuracy and the communication cost, which is
discussed in the next section. It is observed that there is an average gain of 4%
in the accuracy during the first 50% of the training cycle however, it decreases
to 2% after that.

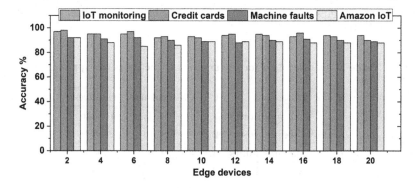

Fig. 5. Accuracy analysis with respect to increasing number of edge devices for different
datasets

Another analysis has been performed to analyze the accuracy of the proposed
approach over different datasets, as shown in Fig. 5. It has been observed as the
number of edge devices increases. As the number of edge devices increases, there
is a slight deflection in the overall accuracy of the model. For example, in the
credit card dataset, there is a 1% deflection among 10 and 14 edge devices.
However, the gain in the context of the training time is very high, as discussed
in the following subsection.

Figure 6 shows the accuracy analysis with respect to the increasing number of
communication iterations among the edge devices over the Amazon IoT dataset.
Two scenarios are considered to perform this analysis, one with two edge devices
and another with twenty edge devices. It has been observed that in both cases,
the accuracy of the model increase as the number of communication iterations
increases. The model is able to achieve high accuracy in both cases. However,
there is a deflection of accuracy in the case of twenty edges. Because there is no
significant improvement in the model parameter after the 14 iterations, due to
which there is a slight change in the accuracy in the case of 20 edge devices.

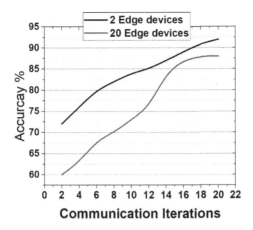

Fig. 6. Accuracy Analysis for fault analysis over Amazon IoT dataset with two edges vs 20 edges

Table 4. Analysis of the training time (sec.) with increasing number of edge devices while keeping number of iterations as twenty

Edge devices	IoT monitoring	Credit cards	Machine faults	Amazon IoT
1	3215	4187	426	1206
2	2647	3624	384	845
4	1678	2864	366	649
6	1065	2179	358	635
8	948	1816	278	612
10	916	1535	256	579
12	885	1289	224	564
14	826	1235	198	522
16	806	1198	169	513
18	798	1127	162	489
20	754	1098	156	468

4.2 Training Time Analysis

An analysis has been presented over different datasets to analyze the training time of the proposed approach. Table 4 presents the training time analysis of the proposed model over different datasets. The number of iterations considered for this analysis is 20. It has been observed that the overall training time reduces as the number of edge devices increases. In the case of the IoT monitoring dataset, there is a reduction of almost 75% in training time. There is a reduction of 73%, 63%, and 61% for credit cards, machine faults, and the Amazon IoT dataset. It should be observed that the amount of reduction in the training time is not proportional to the increase in the number of edge devices.

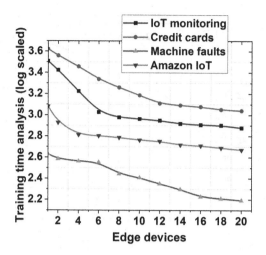

Fig. 7. A log scaled time analysis of the proposed approach with varying number of edge devices

As the number of edge devices increases, it has been observed that the reduction in the training time is not linear, as shown in Fig. 7. For instance, in the case of the IoT monitoring dataset, the average rate of reduction is approximately 30% till 6 edge devices and reduced to an average of 26% for 8 edge devices. Similarly, The rate of reduction for credit cards, machine faults, and Amazon IoT datasets is 18%, 5%, and 18% respectively.

5   Conclusion

In this paper, federated learning based critical event detection model has been proposed with the aid of distributed edge devices. The proposed approach consists of multiple local learners over the edge devices that learn from locally available data. These local learners generate model parameters, which are aggregated to calculate global model parameters. A parameter exchange message format has been proposed to exchange the learned parameters from the local data. The aggregation process for the model's parameters is also presented. Experimental results over four datasets demonstrated the ability of the proposed approach while maintaining a reasonable accuracy with significant gain in terms of training time.

References

1. Lee, K.H., Lee, Y.J., Choi, H., Chung, Y.D., Moon, B.: Parallel data processing with MapReduce: a survey. ACM SIGMOD Rec. **40**(4), 11–20 (2012)
2. McMahan, B., Moore, E., Ramage, D., Hampson, S., y Arcas, B.A.: Communication-efficient learning of deep networks from decentralized data. In: Artificial Intelligence and Statistics, pp. 1273–1282. PMLR, April 2017

3. Spachos, P., Hatzinakos, D.: Real-time indoor carbon dioxide monitoring through cognitive wireless sensor networks. IEEE Sens. J. **16**(2), 506–514 (2015)
4. Van der Geest, M., Polinder, H., Ferreira, J.A., Veltman, A., Wolmarans, J.J., Tsiara, N.: Analysis and neutral voltage-based detection of interturn faults in high-speed permanent-magnet machines with parallel strands. IEEE Trans. Industr. Electron. **62**(6), 3862–3873 (2015)
5. Mahmood, M.A., Seah, W.K., Welch, I.: Reliability in wireless sensor networks: A survey and challenges ahead. Comput. Netw. **79**, 166–187 (2015)
6. Mehmood, A., Mukherjee, M., Ahmed, S.H., Song, H., Malik, K.M.: NBC-MAIDS: Naïve Bayesian classification technique in multi-agent system-enriched IDS for securing IoT against DDoS attacks. J. Supercomput. **74**(10), 5156–5170 (2018). https://doi.org/10.1007/s11227-018-2413-7
7. Konečný, J., McMahan, H.B., Yu, F.X., Richtárik, P., Suresh, A.T., Bacon, D.: Federated learning: Strategies for improving communication efficiency. arXiv preprint arXiv:1610.05492 (2016)
8. Li, T., Sahu, A.K., Talwalkar, A., Smith, V.: Federated learning: Challenges, methods, and future directions. IEEE Signal Process. Mag. **37**(3), 50–60 (2020)
9. Yang, Q., Liu, Y., Cheng, Y., Kang, Y., Chen, T., Yu, H.: Federated learning. Synthesis Lectu. Artifi. Intell. Mach. Learn. **13**(3), 1–207 (2019)
10. Tsang, Y.P., Lee, C.K.M.: Artificial intelligence in industrial design: A semi-automated literature survey. Eng. Appl. Artif. Intell. **112**, 104884 (2022)
11. Pandey, S.K., Mishra, R.B., Tripathi, A.K.: Machine learning based methods for software fault prediction: A survey. Expert Syst. Appl. **172**, 114595 (2021)
12. Ge, N., Li, G., Zhang, L., Liu, Y.: Failure prediction in production line based on federated learning: an empirical study. J. Intell. Manufact. 1–18 (2021)
13. Zhang, W., Li, X., Ma, H., Luo, Z., Li, X.: Federated learning for machinery fault diagnosis with dynamic validation and self-supervision. Knowl.-Based Syst. **213**, 106679 (2021)
14. Liu, Y., et al.: Deep anomaly detection for time-series data in industrial IoT: A communication-efficient on-device federated learning approach. IEEE Internet Things J. **8**(8), 6348–6358 (2020)
15. Thakkar, A., Lohiya, R.: A review on machine learning and deep learning perspectives of IDS for IoT: recent updates, security issues, and challenges. Arch. Comput. Methods Eng. **28**(4), 3211–3243 (2021)
16. Manzoor, M.A., Morgan, Y.: Real-time support vector machine based network intrusion detection system using Apache Storm. In 2016 IEEE 7th Annual Information Technology, Electronics and Mobile Communication Conference (IEMCON), pp. 1–5. IEEE (Oct 2016)
17. Omrani, T., Dallali, A., Rhaimi, B. C., Fattahi, J.: Fusion of ANN and SVM classifiers for network attack detection. In 2017 18th International Conference on Sciences and Techniques of Automatic Control and Computer Engineering (STA), pp. 374–377. IEEE (Dec 2017)
18. Chang, Y., Li, W., Yang, Z.: Network intrusion detection based on random forest and support vector machine. In 2017 IEEE International Conference On Computational Science and Engineering (CSE) and IEEE International Conference on Embedded and Ubiquitous Computing (EUC), vol. 1, pp. 635–638. IEEE (Jul 2017)
19. Ferrag, M.A., Maglaras, L., Moschoyiannis, S., Janicke, H.: Deep learning for cyber security intrusion detection: Approaches, datasets, and comparative study. J. Inf. Sec. Appli. **50**, 102419 (2020)
20. Dixit, P., Silakari, S.: Deep learning algorithms for cybersecurity applications: A technological and status review. Comput. Sci. Rev. **39**, 100317 (2021)

21. Telstra, Telstra network disruptions. www.kaggle.com/c/telstra-recruiting-network/data
22. M.L. Group, Credit card fraud detection (Mar 2018). www.kaggle.com/mlg-ulb/creditcardfraud
23. Loparo, K.A.K.A.: Loparo, Bearing data center, case western reserve university. www.csegroups.case.edu/bearingdatacenter/pages/download-data-file
24. Aws-Samples, aws-samples/aws-iot-examples (Apr 2016). www.github.com/aws-samples/aws-iot-examples/tree/master/predictionDataSimulator

IoT and Blockchain Oriented Gender Determination of Bangladeshi Populations

Md.Akkas Ali[1,2(✉)] and Rajesh Kumar Dhanaraj[2]

[1] Bangabandhu Sheikh Mujibur Rahman Science and Technology University, Dhaka, Bangladesh
akkas.gu@gmail.com

[2] School of Computing Science and Engineering, Galgotias University, Greater Noida, India

Abstract. Forensic and medical-legal investigations depend heavily on sex identification. The most precise and trustworthy evidence of a person's identity are regarded to be their fingerprints and sexual identity determination. This test's goal was to find any gender-specific variations in the Gopalganj district of Bangladesh's population between the number of fingerprint ridges between male and female hands. To determine the topological, age demographic, and gender variability inside the number of fingerprints inside the aforementioned population is the purpose of this research. Whether the individual is male or female can be determined with accuracy by our technology. 800 unrelated volunteers, 400 men and 400 women, were fingerprinted. We have discovered through experimentation that the Ridge Density (RD) of humans varies with age. As a result, we divided the population of people into four groups, each consisting of individuals between the ages of 12 and 17; 18 to 36; 37 to 55; and 56 to 73, all of whom were collected from the Gopalganj district of Bangladesh. After conducting an experiment with 200 people from each of two groups (men = 100 and women = 100) totaling 8000 individuals, we determined and set the threshold values to detect humans. For men, we discovered a range of RD from 10 to 15 with a mean equal to 12.75, while for women, we found a range of RD from 15 to 21 with a mean equal to 18.25. As a result, we've established a threshold of 10 to 15 for males and 15 or more for women. Age and sex groups both showed significant disparities. Females have narrower crests and higher RD than males. Age-related decreases in RD levels were also noted. All groups met the RD criterion for sex discrimination, which was determined using Bayes' theorem, allowing for its use in forensic inquiry.

Keywords: IoT · Blockchain technology · Decentralized database · Ridge density · Gender determination

1 Introduction

The ridges and valleys that make up a person's fingerprints are dermatoglyphic traits that can be used to identify them [1]. Numerous genes, as well as the embryo's surroundings during development, influence ridge creation. Amniotic fluid composition during the first month of pregnancy. Except in circumstances of injury, ridges do not change further after they are produced. Dermatoglyphics research is typically qualitative or quantitative. In contrast to the quantitative examination of fingerprints, which focuses on factors such crest finger ridge (RD) count and density, qualitative dermatoglyphics examines fingerprint patterns and minutiae kinds. Even identical twins' fingerprints are not identical because each person has a unique fingerprint. As a result, different fingerprint patterns and distinctive traits have been utilized for personal identification all across the world. The first piece of evidence that detectives need to gather at the crime scene is latent fingerprints. Numerous groups have been the subject of constant reporting regarding the research of RD for forensic purposes. One research showed on RD evaluation in northeast Thailand where teenagers was just not included in their subject populations. Teenagers urgently require RD assessments, [2] according to the reports from the Department of Observation and Protection of Minors, who were involved in 36,763 instances in Thailand. According to the World Health Organization, an adolescent is someone who is between the ages of 15 and 24. However, the Royal Law of Thailand and the Royal Institute of Thailand define adolescents differently. According to the dictionary, these terms refer to people who are between the ages of 14 and 24 and 15 and 25 respectively. We determined the age range for the study's teenage population to be 14 to 25 years old by combining all three categories. In this study, our primary goals are to assess whether there are any differences in RD between adolescents of the same sex and between adolescents of the two sexes [3]. We also contrasted our results from the RD with the data already available from other populations. Although the number of ridges has been proven to be predominantly inherited genetically, genes and amniotic fluid content-controlled ridge formation, with up to 90–95 percent of genes contributing. Consequently, it is possible that RD will differ amongst the groups if they are genetically dissimilar.

2   Background

The determination of gender is crucial to forensic science, judicial inquiries. Identification is the definition of an individual's uniqueness may be finished or unfinished. The complete fixation of a person's personality is referred to as full identification [4]. When an individual is only partially identified, only a few details about them are known, such as their gender, age, height, etc. The best strategy for individualization combines a number of techniques [5]. Among the many factors that may be used to identify a person, The most accurate and dependable indicators of personal and gender orientation are thought to be fingerprints [6]. Never two fingers have the same fingerprints, which increases the tremendous statistical possibility which no other two fingerprints would ever match [7]. Among all living things on earth, identical twins descended from the same human embryo are possibly the most alike. They have the same DNA profile since they started out as a unit, yet their fingerprints are as unique as those of any unrelated person [8]. Examiners of fingerprints often look at the number of ridges and the features of the ridges when comparing suspects' fingerprints with latent fingerprints discovered at the crime scene [9]. As a result, academics, analysts, and researchers have investigated these two unique traits in great detail. Fingerprinting has become a vital instrument in the hands of investigators due to the rising crime rate. The investigator's workload will be lighter if the gender of the subject can be precisely identified [10]. In Spanish Caucasians, Spanish populations, Sardinian population, Egyptians, Chinese and Malaysians, several Indian populations, including the South American population, it has recently been demonstrated that fingerprinting ridge density is hermaphroditic, the Indian community in Mauritius, etc. [11–15]. It has also been investigated in the past whether imprint crest density differs among the genders. Throughout the present study, a middle Indian public's ridge density from fingerprint being utilized to try to determine a person's sex [16]. In a variety of scientific disciplines, including forensic science, medicine, and technology, dermatoglyphs are investigated [17]. However, there is still a lack of agreement on how to interpret some dermatoglyphic traits. The width of the epidermal ridges was the starting point for studies on it. Since then, there have been various changes made to the methodology for this kind of study [18]. The most used approach for determining the breadth of the epidermal ridge. In adulthood, friction ridges are created in the skin [19]. Age determination might be possible with more knowledge of this mechanism of an unidentified subject based solely on fingerprints. The first researcher to demonstrate a link between adult anthropometric measurements and epidermal ridges [20]. He discovered a connection between the quantity of epidermal ridges and the length of the distal phalanges.

3 Motivation

After studying literature review, we have found that few works done on this research along with Spanish Caucasians, Spanish populations, Sardinian population, Egyptians, Chinese and Malaysians, several Indian populations but not yet for Bangladeshi populations. As a result, we have done this work so that Bangladesh Police, NSI, Investigation Bureau, Anti-Corruption Commission etc. department can be used in their investigation.

4 Objectives and Specific Aims

The primary goals and precise objectives of this study are:

- To study as well as analyze of fingerprint ridge density (RD) of Bangladeshi peoples.
- To study and count the fingerprint ridge density (RD) of Bangladeshi peoples both men and women.
- To assess the differences between Bangladeshi males and females' fingerprint ridge densities (RD).
- To maintain data as a byte stream in a decentralized Blockchain database
- To create a system for determining gender based on IoT and Blockchain
- To ascertain Bangladeshi peoples' genders
- To identify the gender of the human.

5 Methodology

We have collected the fingerprint from human of different area of Gopalganj district of Bangladesh by using the electronic device called scanner (See Fig. 1).

Fig. 1. Fingerprint Sensor (IoT device)

We have hashed the fingerprint data using the Secure Hash Algorithm and encrypted by using AES and saved it into the decentralized Blockchain system as a byte string for data security, availability, and integrity (See Fig. 2).

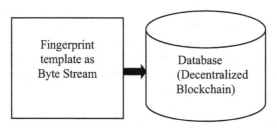

Fig. 2. Data storing process in our system

We have created two 5 × 5 mm^2 squares and from one corner to the diagonally opposite corner on the edge of each square, they were tallied and positioned above the core on the second peak. Points were not included in the calculation, but forks and lakes were, just like two crests. Each fingerprint on a card of gathered fingerprints was scanned into an image format file in order to count the ridges. On the two 5 × 5 mm^2 squares, one of which featured a diagonal line, the image was then superimposed. (See Fig. 3).

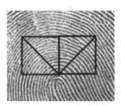

Fig. 3. A fingerprint image was cut into two 5 × 5 mm^2 squares by putting just above the core.

We have used the Ridge Density based algorithm to determine the ridge density of both male and female. This algorithm is as following:

Step 1: We have set each 5 × 5 mm^2 of two squares above the core of fingerprint image.

Step 2: A diagonal line has drawn for each square.

Step 2: We have counted the ridge passing through diagonal line for calculating the Ridge Density (RD).

In order to count the ridges more precisely, the overlay fingerprint have been enlarged five times. The RD values of all fingers were determined for the statistical analysis. The average of both sexes was calculated using the means in each subject. Additionally calculated was the mean RD across all fingers. The probability density in males (C) and females (C_0) in each specified RD density was calculated using observed RD. Following the calculation of the likelihood ratio (LR) using these two values in each individual RD density. Let C be the male donor and C0 be the female donor, and let RD be the ridge density.

$$LR = P(RD/C) / P(RD/C_0)$$

LR value represented the degree of support for either hypothesis, C or C_0. Let P(C) and P(C_0) stand in for the prior probability for men and women, respectively in order to calculate the posterior probability.

$$\text{Posterior Probability} = \{P(C) \times P(RD/C)\}/[\{P(C) \times P(RD/C)\} + \{P(C_0) \times P(RD/C_0)\}]$$

For the purpose of computing the posterior probability the two sets of P(C) and P(C_0) in this investigation. The total RD data as well as each categorization group were used for all the analyses that were indicated above. Four groups were statistically examined for RD.

6 Results Analysis and Discussion

Fingerprints were taken from 800 unrelated volunteers, 400 men and 400 women. We have discovered through experimentation that the ridge density (RD) of humans varies with age. As a result, we divided the population of people into four groups, each consisting of people between the ages of 12 and 17 is the first group; 18 to 36 is the second group; 37 to 55 is the third group; and 56 to 73 is the fourth group, all of which were collected in the Gopalganj district of Bangladesh. From all groups, RD mean as shown in Table 1.

Table 1. RD means from all groups

Age (Years)	RD Mean		No. of human	
	Male	Female	Male	Female
5–17	14.21	20.41	100	100
18–36	13.37	18.11	100	100
37–55	11.68	17.09	100	100
56–73	9.56	14.55	100	100
		Total = 800		

After conducting an experiment with 200 people from each of the two groups (men = 100 and women = 100) with a total of 8000 individuals, we determined and established the threshold values to determinate human's sex. For men we found a range of RD from 10 to 15 with a mean equal to 12.75, while for women we found a range of RD from 15 to 21 with a mean equal to 18.25. As a result, we have set a threshold of 10 to 15 for men and 15 or more for women as shown in Table 2.

Table 2. Calculation of threshold values.

Age (Years)	RD		No. of human	
	Male	Female	Male	Female
5–17	15	21	100	100
18–36	14	19	100	100
37–55	12	18	100	100
56–73	10	15	100	100
Average	12.75	18.25	Total = 800	
Thresholding	10–15	> = 15		

7   Future Recommendation

When a human provides RD equal to exactly 15, our algorithm is unable to determine whether the person is a male representing group 1 or a female representing group 4. This is how our suggested system is constrained. We will solve this single problem in our next research. We are recommending to other researchers to solve this single problem.

8   Conclusion

According to this study, women from Bangladesh's Gopalganj district have much more ridges than men do. It is statistically significant that the male and female fingerprint ridge densities differ. The ability to suppositionally predict the gender of an unidentified print left at a crime scene makes it a useful tool for forensic professionals and law enforcement. This could be accomplished through immediately quantifying the ridge density using techniques similar to those outlined in this article after qualitatively determining whether the traces appear coarse or fine. The results of a medicolegal investigation on a bloody finger can also be helpful in locating remains that have been damaged.

References

1. Ali, M.A., Balamurugan, B., Sharma, V.: IoT and blockchain based intelligence security system for human detection using an improved ACO and heap algorithm. In: 2022 2nd International Conference on Advance Computing and Innovative Technologies in Engineering (ICACITE), IEEE Xplore, pp. 1792–1795 (2022)

2. Premakumar, P., Azeez, M., Sivakumar, R., Deepa, M.S., Siraj, S.E.: Gender determination using morphological analysis of palatal rugae patterns–a retrospective study. Online J. Health Allied Scs. **21**(1), 9 (2022)

3. Ebrahimi, B., Ghaffari, N., Alizamir, T., Jaberi, K.R., Nazmara, Z.: Gender determination using Nasofacial anthropometry in the Iranian population. Iraq Med. J. **6**(2), 1–10 (2022)

4. Santosh, K.C., et al.: Machine learning techniques for human age and gender identification based on teeth X-ray images. J. Healthcare Eng. **2022**, 5302674 (2022)

5. Anarte, L.F.: The right to gender self-determination in Spain. Lessons from autonomous communities. Age Human Rights J. **18**, 83–104 (2022)

6. Cheema, S.N., Jamal, W.N.: An empirical study on gender based discrimination at Pakistani workplaces: determination of the causes of gender based discrimination in Pakistan's private service sector workplaces. Sustain. Bus. Soc. Emerg. Econ. **4**(2), 227–238 (2022)

7. Akman, M., Uçar, M.K., Uçar, Z., Uçar, K., Baraklı, B., Bozkurt, M.R.: Determination of body fat percentage by gender based with photoplethysmography signal using machine learning algorithm. IRBM **43**(3), 169–186 (2022)

8. Astuti, E.R., Iskandar, H.B., Nasutianto, H., Pramatika, B., Saputra, D., Putra, R.H.: Radiomorphometric of the jaw for gender prediction: a digital panoramic study. Acta Medica Philippina. **56**(3), 1–9 (2022)

9. Rad, B., Ahmad, S., Anbiaee, N., Moeini, S., Bagherpour, A.: Sex determination using human sphenoid sinus in a Northeast Iranian population: a discriminant function analysis. J. Dentistry (2022)

10. Sebo, P.: Are accuracy parameters useful for improving the performance of gender detection tools? A comparative study with western and Chinese names. J. Gener. Intern. Med. **27**, 1–4 (2022)

11. Gutiérrez-Redomero, E., Alonso, C., Romero, E., Galera, V.: Variability of fingerprint ridge density in a sample of Spanish Caucasians and its application to sex determination. Forensic Sci. Int. **180**, 17–22 (2008)

12. Nayak, V.C., et al.: Sex differences from fingerprint ridge density in the Indian population. J. Forensic. Leg. Med. **17**, 84–86 (2010)

13. Nayak, V.C., et al.: Sex differences from fingerprint ridge density in Chinese and Malaysian population. Forensic Sci. Int. **197**, 67–69 (2010)

14. Eshak, G.A., et al.: Sex identification from fingertip features in Egyptian population. J. Forensic Leg. Med. **20**, 46–50 (2013)

15. Nithin, M.D., et al.: Gender differentiation by finger ridge count among South Indian population. J. Forensic Leg. Med. **18**, 79–81 (2011)

16. Mota, L.F., Fernandes, B.S.: Debating the law of self-determination of gender identity in Portugal: composition and dynamics of advocacy coalitions of political and civil society actors in the discussion of morality issues. Soc. Polit. Int. Stud. Gend. State Soc. **29**(1), 50–70 (2022)

17. Malik, S., Nayak, M.T., Goyal, M., Sanath, A.K., Malik, U.: Determination of sexual dimorphism using tongue prints–a prospective cross-sectional study. Univ. J. Dental Sci. **8**(1), 1–5 (2022)

18. Aboim, S.: Fragmented recognition: gender identity between moral and legal spheres. Soc. Polit. Int. Stud. Gend. State Soc. **29**(1), 71–93 (2022)

19. Stites, S.D., Cao, H., Harkins, K., Flatt, J.D.: Measuring sex and gender in aging and Alzheimer's research: results of a national survey. J. Gerontol. Ser. B **77**(6), 1005–1016 (2022)

20. Souza, M.A., Santos, A.S., da Silva, S.W., Braga, J.W.B., Sousa, M.H.: Raman spectroscopy of fingerprints and chemometric analysis for forensic sex determination in humans. Forensic Chem. **27**, 100395 (2022)

Federated Learning Based Secured Computational Offloading in Cyber-Physical IoST Systems

Shivani Gaba[1(✉)], Ishan Buddhiraja[1], Vimal Kumar[1], and Aaisha Makkar[2]

[1] School of Computer Science Engineering and Technology, Bennett University, Greater Noida, U.P., India
{e20soe822,ishan.budhiraja,vimal.kumar}@bennett.edu.in
[2] College of Science and Engineering, Department of Computing and Mathematics, University of Derby, Derby, UK
a.makkar@derby.ac.uk

Abstract. In the past years, there has been fast growth in various applications which generates penetrating and personal information dependent on the Internet of things (IoT). The Softwarization of a network may improvise its inclusive flexibility. The software-enabled proficiency has made it functional for mobile devices, wireless, and telecommunication networks through the progression of technologies like software-defined network (SDN), and mobile edge networks. The applications of cyber-physical systems have also increased with the rise of cyber-physical Internet of softwarized things (IoST) systems. To maintain the quality among users, managing the applications for latency of cyber-physical system (CPS) is mandatory. Though edge computing and cloud computing have performed well in achieving latency-aware resource allocation, sometimes it fails to do secure computation offloading in cyber-physical IoST systems. This paper presents a novel federated scheme based on deep learning for fast computation offloading. Secondly, we develop a federated learning framework that allows cyber physical IoST systems to build a model in a privacy-preserving way.

Keywords: Internet of softwarized things (IoST) · Cyber physical systems (CPS) · Federated learning · Offloading

1 Introduction

As we are aware with this thing that one of the futuristic designs of the Internet for the Internet of things architecture (IoT) and platform of cyber-physical systems (CPS) is enhanced in several areas such as intelligent homes, and smart cities, and many more. Cyber-physical systems have gained massive consideration for connecting the physical domain with the cyber domain [1]. However,

KC Santosh et al. (Eds.): RTIP2R 2022, CCIS 1704, pp. 344–355, 2023.
https://doi.org/10.1007/978-3-031-23599-3_26

cyber-physical systems gather massive consenting data in the design, which rely on both cyber and physical spaces. The method of Internet of Things intends to envision or examine the numerous sensing data for helping control equipment to generate appropriate responsive instructions. At the same time, the huge quantity of data may exaggerate bottleneck among networks [2,12] and stimulates secure decision-making whenever it is transmitted via networks. Presently a fusion approach comprising software-defined networking (SDN) and the Internet of things (IoT) called as Internet of Softwarized Things (IoST) concerning cyber-physical systems (Cyber-Physical IoST systems) has been planned for providing global visualization management and coordinating the decision-making capacity for the networks [3] via effectively parted control and data flow.

In Cyber-Physical IoST systems, the physical devices produce the appreciated data, which is accordingly progressed to the controllers of software-defined networks for making the decisions. The controllers of SDN want to share the gathered information for making the decisions globally [4]. As the various controllers of SDN could not believe in one another, this resulted in the rise in the prospect of uncertain exchange of data and delays in secured information sharing. So IoT is embraced for performing secure offloading and protecting data security. The techniques enable software defined network controllers to manage massive and extensively distributed plans proficiently and provide secure communication [6].

As per the authors [5], the total quantity of associated devices in the internet of things will reach nearly 16 million by 2021, and a market of around 900 billion will be created by industry in America by 2022 [13]. Such access to pervasive devices has controlled a rise in the volume of data, diversity, and rapidity [4,5]. To our knowledge, cyber-physical systems present an emergent model where a tight connection is accomplished among the physical and cyber domains [1].

With the growing occurrence of physical devices in the IoTs, the paradigm of CPSs could result to numerous issues in existing operations of manufacturing, such as compacted flexibilities, restricted scalabilities, low efficient data, and deficiency of acceptable intelligence. Whereas various works have deliberated the undesirable effects and provocation that have been come across regarding the exchange of data among IoT/CPS applications and cloud suffers from weaknesses in latency, bandwidth, and security. For overcoming these kinds of issues, the various solutions have processed data at the edge [1,2,9]. Softwarization of the network is one of the standard ways to manage networks. It is becoming advanced in the quick expansion of the internet of Things (IoT), Artificial Intelligence (AI), and fifth-generation technology (5G). The computer program is executed in the network environment for a definite persistence, known as a software process [4].Though all discussed methods attained computations and caches on the edge server, they don't rely on the federated learning in cyber-physical IoST systems.

In Cyber-Physical IoST systems, the transmission and computational offloading are starving for resources with explosive data growth. Previous works process vast amounts of data in edge networks [7] which can suggest terminating the load of bandwidth and security. The cyber-physical IoST systems deliver powerful computational capacity, decrease latency, and improve scalability [8]. So the cohabitation of edge and cloud computing produces an impressive network standard for simplifying offloaded computations [9] via dispensing the computations load between various computations anchors. Besides this, the multiple strategies of offloading assist in streamlining the edge system for making the optimum decisions about allocating resources for wireless communication. However, the computational offloading may improvise the processing speed of tasks and encounter the needs of a task having limited latency in cyber-physical IoST systems.

1.1 Contribution

The main contributions of the paper are brief below:

- We suggest a framework for cyber-physical IoST systems for achieving protected computational offloading by integration of edge and cloud computing. The planned approach provisions the adaptable offloaded applications approaches for edge nodes for determining, is there a need to offloaded communication-intensive responsibilities towards edge servers and cloud servers.
- Secondly, a federated learning framework is developed, which tradeoff to computational offloading strategies for cyber-physical internet of softwarized things. This framework supports federated learning and slows secure computation offloading of data sources.

The rest of the paper is ordered as follows. The system model is described in Sect. 2. Then the proposed federated approach is defined in Sect. 3. The results and discussions have been deliberated in Sect. 4. Finally, Sect. 5 concludes the paper.

2 System Model

In this segment, authors have presented scenario of fedrated learning cyber physical IoST systems. Firstly we discuss the Softwarization Network Architecture Layers and then discuss on an instinctive mathematical definition of our system model.

2.1 Softwarization Architecture Layers

The softwarization architecture comprises four different layers; application layer, control layer, orchestration layer, and physical resources layer. In contrast, various authors have other names for the layers [5]. The physical resource layer is also named SDN data plane and NFV infrastructure; the control layer is called the SDN control plane, the orchestration layer is called NFV Orchestration and Management MANO, whereas, in the application layer, some of the applications of healthcare have advised deprived of identification of the layer [9]. The architecture of IoT softwarization is shown in Fig. 1, summarized in Table 1. The various layers of the architecture are as follows: However, IoT softwarization architecture is adopted in the figure, summarized in Table 1, and explained as follows:

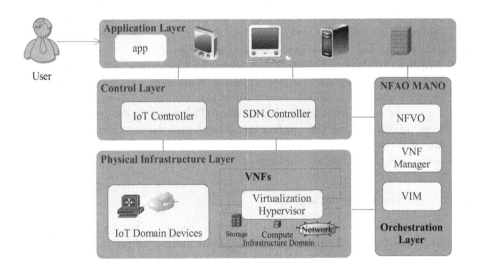

Fig. 1. IoT softwarization architecture

- **Physical infrastructure layer:** This layer comprises physical resources of the system such as IoT devices and sensors, devices of network connectivity, and environmental infrastructure of virtualization, called as VNF domain. This layer communicates with the controller layer and gathers data on the user's demand and from the real-world atmosphere.
- **Control layer:** This layer comprises SDN and IoT controllers, which are responsible for registering things and strategies within the scope of their ser-

vices in the system, monitoring and controlling the entities, and allocating possessions and design as per the requested [10] services of demand of the real world. It contains SDN controllers and IoT controllers, which are responsible for registering entities and devices with their service scopes in the system and controller, monitoring and controlling entities, and allocating resources and devices according to the requested services of real-world demand [5]. It summarizes the physical layer with the orchestration layer and suggests the part of the interface among these two layers [7].

- **Orchestration layer:** This layer has the management layer components of virtualization systems like VIM, VNFM, and NFV MANO. It is accountable for the management of the virtualization function. It allocated the possessions for the on-demand services and organized the capabilities of tasks of devices in concern to on-demand services. Whenever the user requests the services via the application layer, this layer accepts the request, matches the task among the devices and services requested, and finally sends the request to the controller. Finally, the controller gives the requested services by generating data for the IoT devices in the infrastructure layer [13].

- **Application layer:** This layer comprises the applications used for processing and managing the data that is useful for the end-user. This may be considered the user interface in which users request the service and browse the services. This layer is the front of the IoT system. The users may categorize the services interpreted via the application, which must be comprehensible for the orchestration layer. Finally, the resultant of requested services to the user has been shown via a suitable interface.

2.2 System Formulation

On the basis of the its architecture layers, authors deliberate cyber physical internet of softwarized things system having M number of physical devices and N number of edge servers symbolized as $M = 1, 2, 3 \ldots P$ and $N = \{1, 2, 3..Q\}$, correspondingly. Every edge servers are arranged in base stations. There are N number of modules for software defined network controller and which are integrated with edge servers and all of this manages confined domains X_i of the network. We presume that physical devices q produces computational tasks $T_{q,j} = B_{q,j}, E_{q,j}, T_{q,j}^{max}$, where $B_{q,j}$ is considered as the data size of task (in bits), $E_{q,j}$ is the essential amount of computational resources for accomplishing the task (in CPU cycles), $T_{q,j}^{max}$ is the maximum rate [10] for tolerant latency (in ms). The computational task of physical devices must be managed locally or could be offload towards other servers. Even every edge server acts as entity for cyber physical IoST system for the secure transmissions and computations between physical devices, edge nodes and cloud server for the security of systems. We present the decision for offloading for the task j of physical devices q in the time slot t as binary variable $0_{q,t} \in [0,1]$ where $0_{q,t}$ shows task of physical devices j will be processed locally and $0_{q,t} = 1$ shows task would offload to edge server (Fig. 2).

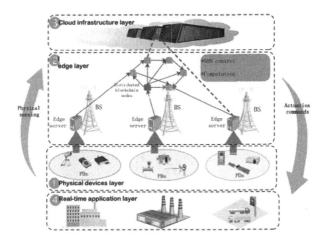

Fig. 2. Illustration of the cyber physical IoST framework [6]

2.3   Transmission Model

We suppose that the latency required for transmission is having two components: latency for uplink transmission and downlink transmission. The downlink transmission is trivial when it compared with uplink latency [10]. The channels are firstly divided into N number of subchannels in our planned model. In this model, we deliberate the orthogonal subchannels are allotted to physical devices. Whenever physical devices q disseminates computational task to edge serve and the base station assigns orthogonal spectrums to various physical devices and so there is no as such interference among physical devices. As per "Shannon Hartley formula, the uplink transmission rate of physical devices q at the time slot t is specified by":

$$S_{PB,q}(t) = w_{PB,q}log_2(1 + \frac{p_q g_q^{(t)}}{\alpha^2})$$

(1)

where $w_{PB,q}$ defines bandwidth of base station allocated to physical devices q. ($Y_q = \frac{p_q g_q^{(t)}}{\alpha^2}$) presents signal to interreference plus noise ratio (SINR) from physical devices q to base station, where p_q is the transmission power of physical devices q and α^2 is the additive white gaussian noise. At this time, $g_q^{(t)}$ is the gain of channel from physical devices q to the base station which may reflect the quality of channel. Practically, the channel is a continuous variable. Moreover, channel gain's range $g_q^{(t)}$ is discrete and quantified into level L in the model. We suppose that data may be transmitted effectively when the value of signal to interreference plus noise ratio is above some threshold.

2.4 Computational Model

Every computational task could be either implemented locally or offloaded to edge server or cloud server. The computational latency can be of three types: local, edge and cloud computational latency. Even the processing latency comprises of latency of transmission and computations [11].

- Local Processing Latency: When physical devices q processes the task j, this latency is equivalent to computational latency and it is distinct as

$$Z_{q,j}^l = \frac{F_{q,j}}{\omega_{q,j}^l} \tag{2}$$

- Edge Processing Latency: Suppose ω_m is the computational capacity of edge server m and $m \in M$. Whenever the task is divested to edge server m, the dispensation latency for the task j of physical devices q is denoted as

$$Z_{q,j}^m = \frac{D_{q,j}}{S_{PB,q}} + Z_{q,j}^{co} + \frac{F_{q,j}}{\omega_{q,j}^l} \tag{3}$$

Where $\omega_{q,j}^l$ is the number of allocated computational resources to physical devices q by edge server m. $\frac{D_{q,j}}{S_{PB,q}}$ is the latency of transmission, $\frac{F_{q,j}}{\omega_{q,j}^l}$ is the computational latency

- Cloud Processing Latency: Formerly computational task could be performed by cloud server, the edge nodes should firstly process the data, leveraging the hash function. The actual $D_{q,j}$ and h_q could be transmitted to cloud. The processing latency for task j of physical devices q is

$$Z_{q,j}^c = \frac{D_{q,j}}{S_{PB,q}} + Z_{q,j}^{co} + \frac{D_{q,j} + h_k}{S_{BC,q}} + D_{0.k} \tag{4}$$

Where $S_{BC,q}$ is the rate of transmission from base station to cloud server,k is the rate of backhaul from cloud server to base station, and D_o is the data size of the result calculated by cloud server.

3 Proposed Approach

In this segment, we intricate on the proposed approach by demarcation of the workflow's scheme first, and then presenting the deep fedrated-based [11] model, surveyed by the secure communication protocol.The workflow of secure federated learning approach is the general idea of the scheme is to build deep learning model which is based on federated learning for secure offloading. The complete workflow is explained in Algorithm 1.

Algorithm 1. Secured federated learning approach

Input: The parameter of security s, set of industrial agents I, resources of data for all its industrial agents $\{D_s | s \in S\}$, total amount of communications rounds C .

Output: An inclusive fedrated learning model.

Initialize

The authenticated authority delivers the key pair by $\{PS, QS\} = KeyGenerate(s)$;

The trusted authority creates a protected channel for the cloud server and every industrial agent

The cloud server sets $\eta, \tau_1, \tau_2, \nu, L, B$ and primary model constraints w_0 Every P_s generates a size X_s to cloud server, where $s \in S$; then, the cloud server computes every contribution ratio by $\beta_s = \frac{X_k}{X_1 + X_2 + \ldots + X_S}$;

Prepare the round index of communication by $c = 1$.

Procedure:

for $c \leqslant C$ do

For industrial agents:

for $\forall s \in S$ do

P_s evaluates the c-th round local model parameters w_s^c with inputs: $\eta, \tau_1, \tau_2, \nu, L, B$,w^{c-1}, D_s;

for $\forall_i \in T$ do

$E_{Pai}(w_{s,i}^c) = ParaEncrypt(w_{s,i}^c, PS)$;

end

P_s uploads the encrypted model parameters $\{E_{Pai}(w_{s,i}^c) | i \in T\}$ to the cloud server;

end

For cloud server :

for $\forall_i \in T$ do

$r_i = ParaAggregate(w_{1,i}^c, \ldots\ldots, w_{S,i}^c, \ldots, \beta_1, \ldots\ldots, \beta_S)$;

end

The cloud server distributes the aggregated ciphertexts $r = \{r_i | i \in T\}$ to all $P_s (s \in S)$;

For all industrial agents:

for $\forall_s \in S$ do

for $\forall_i \in T$ do

$w_{s,i}^c = ParaDecrypt(r_i, QS)$;

end

P_s alters its local model using its updated parameters $w^c = \{w_{s,i}^c | \in T\}$;

end

$c = c + 1$.

end

returns The appropriate deep fedrated model with parameters w^C.

4   Results and Discussions

In this segment, we have performed extensive experiments for evaluating the performance of our planned fedrated approach. Firstly, the experimental settings have been done including experimental settings, performance settings such as accuracy, precisiom, f-score, recall etc. Then, we have compared the number of experiments for comparing the analysis of our planned fedrated approach with respect to authors Schneble's [11], Nguyen's [12] and under our developed

Table 1. Comparitive Analysis of our work with other authors. Note*: A: Accuracy, P: Precision, R: Recall, F: F-Score

[11]				[12]				The proposed federated approach			
A	P	R	F	A	P	R	F	A	P	R	F
0.981	0.987	0.963	0.974	0.981	0.988	0.962	0.974	0.991	0.992	0.969	0.980
0.981	0.987	0.964	0.975	0.990	0.988	0.967	0.977	0.991	0.993	0.969	0.981
0.981	0.988	0.964	0.975	0.990	0.988	0.967	0.977	0.99	0.993	0.969	0.980
0.981	0.988	0.964	0.975	0.991	0.988	0.967	0.978	0.992	0.994	0.968	0.981
0.98	0.988	0.965	0.976	0.991	0.988	0.967	0.977	0.992	0.988	0.974	0.981
0.9801	0.986	0.961	0.973	0.981	0.987	0.964	0.975	0.991	0.992	0.968	0.979
0.981	0.987	0.964	0.975	0.99	0.992	0.963	0.977	0.991	0.987	0.974	0.981
0.982	0.987	0.964	0.975	0.991	0.992	0.963	0.977	0.992	0.994	0.969	0.981
0.982	0.987	0.964	0.975	0.991	0.992	0.963	0.977	0.992	0.988	0.974	0.981
0.982	0.988	0.964	0.976	0.991	0.992	0.964	0.978	0.992	0.988	0.974	0.981
0.981	0.987	0.963	0.974	0.981	0.987	0.964	0.975	0.985	0.986	0.968	0.977
0.981	0.987	0.964	0.975	0.990	0.993	0.963	0.978	0.992	0.994	0.968	0.981
0.981	0.987	0.964	0.975	0.990	0.992	0.963	0.977	0.992	0.994	0.969	0.981
0.982	0.987	0.964	0.975	0.991	0.993	0.963	0.977	0.992	0.989	0.973	0.981
0.982	0.988	0.964	0.976	0.991	0.993	0.963	0.978	0.992	0.9885	0.975	0.981

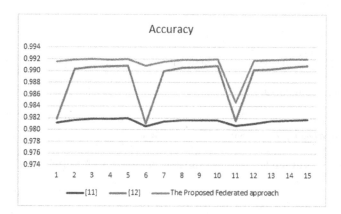

Fig. 3. Comparitive analysis of accuracy of [11, 12], proposed fedrated approach

federated learning framework. So we have analyzed that the planned approach is performs secure computational offloading in cyber physical internet of softwarized things systems.

Figure 3 shows the Comparitive Analysis of Accuracy of [11,12], Proposed Fedrated Approach. This shows how accuracy is coming better in Proposed Fedrated Approach when it is compared with Schneble's [11] and Nguyen's [12].

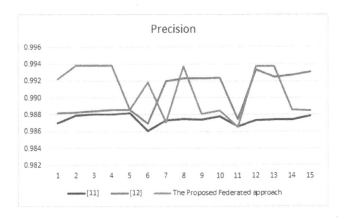

Fig. 4. Comparitive analysis of precision of [11,12], proposed fedrated approach

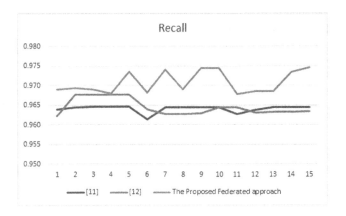

Fig. 5. Comparitive analysis of recall of [11,12], proposed fedrated approach

Figure 4 shows the Comparitive Analysis of Precision of [11,12], Proposed Fedrated Approach. This shows how Precision is coming better in Proposed Fedrated Approach when it is compared with Schneble's [11] and Nguyen's [12].

Figure 5 shows the Comparitive Analysis of Recall of [11,12], Proposed Fedrated Approach. This shows how Recall is coming better in Proposed Fedrated Approach when it is compared with Schneble's [11] and Nguyen's [12].

Figure 6 shows the Comparitive Analysis of F-Score of [11,12], Proposed Fedrated Approach. This shows how F-Score is coming better in Proposed Fedrated Approach when it is compared with Schneble's [11] and Nguyen's [12].

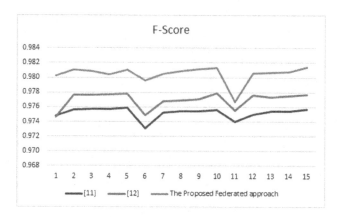

Fig. 6. Comparitive analysis of F-score of [11,12], proposed fedrated approach

5   Conclusion and Future Scope

Here in this paper we have novel federated scheme based on deep learning for fast computation offloading and a federated learning framework is designed that allows cyber physical internet of softwarized things systems to build a model in a privacy-preserving way. The results are also compared with other works and we have justified that our approach is better then the current approaches. As the Cyber Physical systems are mandatory for mainatining quality among users and for managing the applications. So we can elaborate the work in the terms of securing the cyber physical systems using deep learning by detecting and mitigating the attacks.

References

1. Ye, C., Li, G., Cai, H., Gu, Y., Fukuda, A.: Analysis of security in blockchain: case study in 51%-attack detecting. In: 5th International Conference on Dependable Systems and Their Applications (DSA), pp. 15–24. IEEE (2018)
2. Chen, H., Pendleton, M., Njilla, L., Xu, S.: A survey on ethereum systems security: vulnerabilities, attacks, and defenses. ACM Comput. Surv. (CSUR) **53**, 1–43 (2000)
3. Atzei, N., Bartoletti, M., Cimoli, T.: A survey of attacks on ethereum smart contracts (SoK). In: Maffei, M., Ryan, M. (eds.) POST 2017. LNCS, vol. 10204, pp. 164–186. Springer, Heidelberg (2017). https://doi.org/10.1007/978-3-662-54455-6_8
4. Usman, M., Jan, M.A., He, X., Chen, J.: A survey on representation learning efforts in cybersecurity domain. ACM Comput. Surv. (CSUR) **52**, 1–28 (2019)
5. Sharma, A., Gaba, S., Singla, S., Kumar, S., Saxena, C., Srivastava, R.: Recent Trends in Communication and Intelligent Systems, pp. 47–54. Springer, Heidelberg (2020). https://doi.org/10.1007/978-981-19-1324-2
6. Garg, D., Verma, G.K.: Emotion recognition in valence-arousal space from multi-channel EEG data and wavelet based deep learning framework. Procedia Comput. Sci. **171**, 857–867 (2020)

7. Liu, B., Zhang, Y., He, D.J., Li, Y.: Identification of apple leaf diseases based on deep convolutional neural networks, Symmetry, Multidisciplinary Digital Publishing Institute, vol. 11 (2018)

8. Alom, M.Z., et al.: The history began from alexnet: a comprehensive survey on deep learning approaches. arXiv preprint arXiv:1803.01164 (2018)

9. Gaba, S., Budhiraja, I., Makkar, A., Garg, D.: Machine learning for detecting security attackson blockchain using software defined networking. In: 2022 IEEE International Conference on Communications Workshops (ICC Workshops), pp. 260–264 (2022)

10. Aggarwal, A., Gaba, S., Nagpal, S., Arya, A.: A deep analysis on the role of deep learning models using generative adversarial networks. In: Ahmed, K.R., Hexmoor, H. (eds.) Blockchain and Deep Learning. SBD, vol. 105, pp. 179–197. Springer, Cham (2022). https://doi.org/10.1007/978-3-030-95419-2_9

11. Schneble, W., Thamilarasu, G.: Attack detection using federated learning in medical cyber physical systems. In: 28th International Conference on Computer Communications and Networks (ICCCN), pp. 1–8 (2019)

12. Nguyen, T.D., Marchal, S., Miettinen, M., Fereidooni, H., Asokan, N., Sadeghi, A.-R.: Dïot: a federated self-learning anomaly detection system for IoT. In: IEEE 39th International Conference on Distributed Computing Systems (ICDCS), pp. 756–767. IEEE (2019)

13. LeCun, Y., Bengio, Y., Hinton, G.: Deep learning. Nature 521(7553), 436–444 (2015)

A Hybrid Campus Security System Combined of Face, Number-Plate, and Voice Recognition

Abu Sayeed[1(✉)], Azmain Yakin Srizon[1], Md. Mehedi Hasan[1], Jungpil Shin[2], Md. Al Mehedi Hasan[2], and M. Rasel Mahmud[3]

[1] Rajshahi University of Engineering and Technology, Rajshahi 6204, Bangladesh
abusayeed.cse@gmail.com
[2] The University of Aizu, Aizuwakamatsu, Fukushima 965-8580, Japan
jpshin@u-aizu.ac.jp
[3] The University of Texas at San Antonio, San Antonio, TX 78249, USA
mrasel.mahmud@my.utsa.edu

Abstract. Campus or institution security has been a prominent area of study in recent decades. Facial identification, voice verification, and vehicle license plate recognition have all been used individually in the literature to prevent attackers from entering the facility. Although several academics have agreed that a hybrid recognition system may significantly increase security, hybrid systems are not often discussed in the literature. To overcome this issue, we presented a hybrid driver and vehicle identification module in this study, which can detect both the driver and the vehicle. We applied face recognition and speech verification for driver recognition. Multi-task Cascaded Convolutional Networks were used to crop the faces for facial recognition, while FaceNet was employed for face identification. A three-layer Long Short-Term Memory model was used for voice verification. Finally, Tesseract has been used for car number plate identification. According to the results of the experiments, the suggested approach is capable of detecting both drivers and cars with 0 percent mistake every time, which is a critical improvement for assuring the security of the institutions.

Keywords: MTCNN · FaceNet · LSTM · Tesseract · Hybrid campus security system

1 Introduction

With the increase in crimes and thefts, campus security has become one of the biggest concerns throughout the last decade [25]. To ensure the entry of only valid drivers and vehicles, many systems have been proposed previously [3,35]. For driver identification, the most used technique in literature is the facial recognition technique. A few years ago, facial recognition was applied by using machine learning techniques. However, with the increase in the usage of deep learning models and convolutional neural networks, different deep models for

© The Author(s), under exclusive license to Springer Nature Switzerland AG 2023
KC Santosh et al. (Eds.): RTIP2R 2022, CCIS 1704, pp. 356–368, 2023.
https://doi.org/10.1007/978-3-031-23599-3_27

facial recognition have been introduced. Although facial recognition is simple, it has some downsides too. If the face has any coverings or if the faces are identical, the faces can't be recognized with the same precision. Another problem with facial recognition is that the face images need enough light exposure. However, at night, there is often not enough light [18, 32].

These problems don't occur in the voice verification task. Unlike facial recognition, the voice verification task doesn't need any light exposure [5, 27]. However, if there are noises, voice verification can be hampered. Moreover, text-independent voice verification is more difficult than voice-dependent voice verification. As text-independent voice verification is more secure, it is often advised to use this type of voice verification, and therefore, the verification process gets complex. Furthermore, the voice signals can be changed due to sickness, weather conditions, or environmental variables as well. Keeping all these advantages and disadvantages in mind, the best solution is to utilize both facial recognition and voice verification for the driver recognition process.

Previously, many works have focused solely on facial recognition or voice verification. However, not many works have contributed with hybrid models where two different recognition processes have been utilized for driver verification. In our study, we have considered both facial recognition and voice verification for recognizing the driver. For the facial recognition task, first, we have cropped the faces from the captured images by using the Multi-task Cascaded Convolutional Networks (MTCNN). After that, the cropped faces were recognized by using FaceNet architecture. For voice verification, a 3-layer Long Short-Term Memory (LSTM) has been employed.

In campus security management, vehicle recognition is as important as driver recognition [23, 24]. The driver of the vehicle may be verified, but the vehicle he or she who is driving may not be registered. To solve this dilemma, we started with the captured photos of vehicle number plates. With the help of Tesseract, the texts of the number plates can be recognized and matched with the numbers stored in the database. Thus, driver and vehicle recognition can be arranged. In the next section, more literature on the face, voice, and number-plate recognition has been presented. After that, dataset description and proposed methodologies such as MTCNN, FaceNet, LSTM, and Tesseract have been described along with performance matrices. Finally, experimental results have been illustrated.

2   Literature Review

Previously, facial recognition, voice recognition, and number-plate recognition had been used separately, but in our study, we are focusing on a hybrid approach where we have integrated all of them. In the next subsections, each of the recognition processes has been addressed via existing works.

2.1   Face Recognition

Facial recognition has been and is still a very popular way of human verification. Recently, many studies considered facial recognition for different tasks. A study focused on cropping and an attention-based approach for masked face recognition that could not only recognize normal faces but also recognize masked faces [19]. Filters such as the Gabor filter bank with a deep autoencoder-based facial recognition system had been proposed previously as well [9]. Moreover, age-invariant face recognition using a multi-task learning framework had also been proposed recently [12]. Joint segmentation and identification feature learning for occlusion face recognition was also proposed recently [11]. Furthermore, new loss functions such as self-restrained triplet loss for accurate masked face recognition were being proposed as well [6]. However, none of the approaches were able to achieve a decent performance due to the lack of relevant extracted face features.

2.2   Speaker Recognition

Speaker verification can be achieved in many ways. Recently, ASV-Subtools, an open-source toolkit for automatic speaker verification had been proposed [31]. ResNeXt and Res2Net structures for speaker verification had been presented recently as well [39]. Another study focused on adversarial defense for automatic speaker verification by cascaded self-supervised learning models [33]. Speaker verification was also be done by improving the adversarial robustness through self-supervised learning [34]. A neural acoustic-phonetic approach for speaker verification with a phonetic attention mask had been proposed recently too [21]. The main issue with speaker recognition is that the performance is lower than facial recognition. However, combining face and speaker recognition can boost performance which has not been discovered in previous works.

2.3   Vehicle Number Plate Recognition

Vehicle number-plate recognition has been present in the literature for a long time now. Machine learning and deep learning are now being used for automatic number plate recognition [8,17]. Recently, YOLO-Darknet had been proposed for number-plate recognition as well [29]. Furthermore, area-specific number plate recognition is becoming more popular now such as Saudi license car plate recognition [2] and Oman number plate recognition [1]. Previously, number plate recognition has only been used as the sole recognition process. In this study, we have combined it with face and speaker recognition.

3   Materials and Methods

In this section, first, the dataset description has been presented for face recognition, speaker verification, and vehicle number plate recognition. Next, the proposed methodology has been described in detail. After that, the methods needed for each recognition process have been explained. Finally, performance matrices utilized for outcomes measurements have been illustrated.

3.1   Dataset Description

Previously, many researchers have focused on face verification, voice recognition, and vehicle number plate recognition separately. However, in this study, we focused on a hybrid recognition system where both vehicle and the driver of the vehicle need to be recognized. For driver recognition, both face recognition and voice recognition have been utilized. Therefore, to successfully recognize both driver and vehicle, we considered 3 separate datasets: 20-celebrity faces dataset for face recognition, CSTR VCTK Corpus (English Multi-speaker Corpus for CSTR Voice Cloning Toolkit) for voice recognition, and a custom dataset built of the Google images for the vehicle plate recognition.

For the face recognition task, we have used 5 images per celebrity for training and 1 image for testing per celebrity. For the speaker recognition, a variable number of train images per class have been used, however, 1 sample per class has been used for testing. While recognizing the number plate recognition, no training was needed. Testing was applied directly to the collected images.

3.1.1   20-Celebrity Dataset

The CelebFaces Attributes Collection (CelebA) [22], a large-scale face attributes dataset with over 200K celebrity photos, is used to create the CelebFaces Attributes Dataset (CelebA). The photos in this collection span a wide range of position variants as well as background clutter. CelebA contains a broad variety, huge quantity, and rich annotations, including - 10,177 identities, - 202,599 face pictures, and - 5 landmark locations, 40 binary characteristics annotations per image. However, due to machine limitations, we have used 20 classes for experimenting in this case.

3.1.2   CSTR VCTK Corpus

The CSTR VCTK Corpus [37] contains speech data from 109 native English speakers with varied accents. Each speaker reads around 400 phrases, the majority of which were chosen from a newspaper, as well as the Rainbow Passage and an elicitation paragraph designed to detect the speaker's accent. The Herald (Glasgow) newspaper texts were used with permission from the Herald & Times Group. Each speaker reads a separate collection of newspaper sentences, which were chosen using a greedy algorithm to optimize contextual and phonetic coverage. All speakers have the identical Rainbow Passage and elicitation paragraph. In our investigation, we used 20 classes from the celebrity faces dataset, as well as 20 classes from the VCTK dataset.

3.1.3   Vehicle Number Plate Dataset

We gathered 40 different photos from the Internet for vehicle number plate identification. Following that, the real values of the number plate were manually retrieved, and the machine-encoded texts were compared with the true values to determine the outcome.

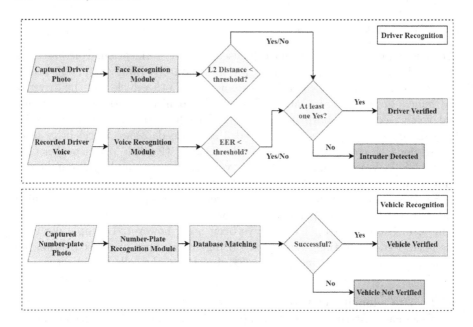

Fig. 1. Proposed workflow diagram for the hybrid architecture.

3.2 Proposed Methodology

Two types of security measures or recognition systems are required to provide maximum security at an institution's main entrance. The first is vehicle recognition, and the second is driver recognition. For driver recognition, we explored facial recognition and speech verification in our research. The camera will collect the driver's picture, and just the driver's face can be retrieved using Multi-task Cascaded Convolutional Networks (MTCNN). Following that, the FaceNet architecture may be used for facial recognition. The driver will be confirmed if the L2 distance determined by FaceNet architecture is smaller than the threshold.

A microphone will also record the driver's voice. Voice verification was performed using a 3-layer Long short-term memory (LSTM). The driver will be verified if the Equal Error Rate (EER) is less than the threshold. The driver is validated if one of the verifications (face recognition or voice verification) delivers a true result.

However, for the vehicle number plate identification, a database containing the vehicle plate numbers of the permitted vehicles was first created. Tesseract was then used to recognize the text on the number plates. The detected text is then compared to the database numbers. The car is validated whether the plate numbers match one of the vehicle number plates in the database. In this investigation, both vehicle number plate recognition and driver verification were used. Figure 1 illustrates the proposed workflow diagram for the hybrid architecture.

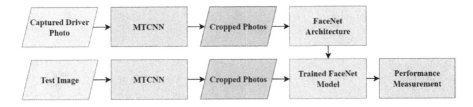

Fig. 2. Detailed view of face recognition module.

3.3   Driver Face Recognition

We employed two primary phases for driver facial recognition. For starters, we used Multi-task Cascaded Convolutional Neural Networks to detect faces in images (MTCNN). Second, we used FaceNet to recognize the faces. Figure 2 illustrates detailed view of the face recognition module.

3.3.1   Multi-task Cascaded Convolutional Networks

Multi-task Cascaded Convolutional Networks (MTCNN) [36] is a framework designed to solve both face identification and face alignment problems. The method comprises of three levels of convolutional networks capable of recognizing faces and landmark locations such as the eyes, nose, and mouth.

MTCNN is proposed in the study as a method for integrating both tasks (recognition and alignment) utilizing multi-task learning. In the first stage, it employs a shallow CNN to generate candidate windows fast. The recommended candidate windows are refined in the second step using a more advanced CNN. Finally, in the third step, it employs a third, more complicated CNN to further refine the result and output face landmark positions.

3.3.2   FaceNet

FaceNet [28] is the term given to the facial recognition system presented by Google researchers in the paper FaceNet: A Unified Embedding for Face Recognition and Clustering published in 2015. It obtained cutting-edge performance in a variety of benchmark face recognition datasets, including Labeled Faces in the Wild (LFW) and YouTube Face Database.

They suggested a method for generating high-quality face mapping from photos using deep learning architectures like ZF-Net and Inception. Then, as a loss function, it employed a method known as triplet loss to train this design. Let's take a closer look at the architecture.

FaceNet's design incorporates end-to-end learning. Its fundamental architecture is ZF-Net or Inception. It also includes a number of 1*1 convolutions to reduce the number of parameters. These deep learning models provide an embedding of the picture f(x) with L2 normalization. These embeddings are then sent into the loss function, which computes the loss. The purpose of this loss function is to minimize the squares distance between two picture embeddings that are independent of image condition and pose of the same identity, while increasing the squared distance between two images of different identities. As a result,

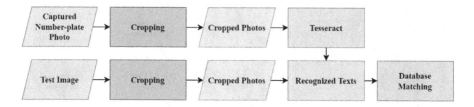

Fig. 3. Detailed view of vehicle number-plate recognition module.

a novel loss function known as Triplet loss is employed. The use of triplet loss in our design allows the model to impose a boundary between faces of distinct identities.

3.4   Driver Voice Recognition

We deployed a three-layer Long short-term memory (LSTM) architecture for driver speech recognition and computed the Equal Error Rate (EER). The speakers are differentiated based on the value of EER.

3.4.1   3-Layer LSTM

Long short-term memory (LSTM) [16] is a type of artificial neural network used in artificial intelligence and deep learning. Unlike traditional feedforward neural networks, LSTM has feedback connections. A recurrent neural network of this type may analyze not just single input points (such as photos), but also complete data sequences (such as speech or video). LSTM, for example, is useful for unsegmented, linked handwriting recognition, speech recognition, machine translation, robot control, video games, and healthcare. The LSTM neural network has become the most mentioned neural network of the twentieth century.

The basic LSTM model consists of a single hidden LSTM layer followed by a conventional feedforward output layer. The Stacked LSTM is a model extension that features many hidden LSTM layers, each of which contains multiple memory cells. Stacking LSTM hidden layers deepen the model, more correctly defining it as a deep learning approach. The depth of neural networks is often ascribed to the approach's performance on a wide range of difficult prediction tasks. We employed 3-layer LSTM in this work.

3.5   Vehicle Number Plate Recognition

Tesseract was used here for vehicle number plate recognition. After we finished the recognition, we transformed it into machine-encoded text and compared it to the true values kept in a database for matching photographs. Figure 3 illustrates detailed view of the vehicle number-plate recognition module.

3.5.1   Tesseract

Tesseract [30] is an optical character recognition engine that works with a variety of operating systems. It is open-source software distributed under the Apache License. Originally created as commercial software by Hewlett-Packard in the 1980s,s, it was published as open source in 2005 and has been sponsored by Google since 2006. Tesseract was regarded as one of the most accurate open-source OCR engines available in 2006. For the text recognition on the license plate, we utilized Tesseract.

3.6   Performance Matrices

For face recognition, accuracy was considered as the main performance matrix. For speaker verification, Equal Error Rate (EER) [7,10,26] was utilized. EER is a biometric security system algorithm that predicts the threshold values for its false acceptance and false rejection rates. The common value is referred to as the equal error rate when the rates are equal. The figure shows that the percentage of erroneous acceptances equals the percentage of false rejections. The smaller the equal error rate number, the greater the biometric system's accuracy. For vehicle number plate recognition, text-matching from database was used for performance measurement.

4   Experimental Analysis

4.1   Experimental Setup

For cropping the faces from the photos, MTCNN version 0.0.9 was used. The FaceNet architecture's input size was $160 \times 160 \times 3$. The confidence was calculated using the L2 distance. For voice verification, the hop size was set to 0.01, the window length to 0.025, and the sampling rate to 8000. According to the model, there were three layers, with the hidden state dimension of lstm set to 128 and the projection dimension of lstm set to 64. The number of speakers in each batch and utterances per speaker were adjusted to four and five, respectively. The stochastic gradient descent optimizer was combined with the softmax loss type. The model was run for a total of 10000 iterations with a decay-enabled starting learning rate of 0.01. The input size for vehicle number plate identification was varied.

It should be noted that the camera resolution to capture the picture of the driver is the same as the resolution of the camera which is usually 1920×1080. However, after applying MTCNN, the cropped face is resized to 160×160. The resolution of the car number plate image is variable as Tesseract allows variable image size. The distance to capture the above pictures is not more than 100 m or 328 ft.

Fig. 4. Some test examples of vehicle number-plate recognition.

4.2   Implementation and Results

As previously stated, we used both face recognition and speech verification in this study for driver verification. A camera initially captures a picture of the motorist. The shot was then submitted to the MTCNN architecture, which retrieved the driver's cropped face from the image. The retrieved image was then scaled to $160 \times 160 \times 3$ and sent to the FaceNet architecture. The FaceNet architecture learns from example faces and trains using L2 distances. When a test image is supplied as input during the testing phase, the trained FaceNet architecture calculates the L2 distance and compares it to the set threshold. If the threshold exceeds the L2 distance, the driver is validated. In our analysis, we discovered that facial recognition attained an overall accuracy of 100 percent.

We used the three-layer LSTM model for speech verification. The trained model was used for testing once it had been trained. It was discovered that the voice verification testing accuracy was likewise 100 percent. Finally, we used Tesseract to recognize car license plates. We began by removing the number plate from the supplied picture. The outlines were then identified and recognized. The identified texts were then compared to the database. The car is validated if it matches. In our example, the identified texts always matched with the database, giving in a total accuracy of 100 percent. Figure 4 illustrates some test examples of vehicle number-plate recognition. It should be noted that if either the face or voice verification is successful, the driver is validated.

Table 1. Comparison between proposed work and previous works.

Methods/Approaches	Face?	Speaker?	Number-plate?	Overall accuracy
Ensembled CNN [13]	No	Yes	No	55.00%
Custom CNN [14]	Yes	Yes	No	85.03%
CNN [38]	No	No	Yes	98.71%
Proposed methodology	Yes	Yes	Yes	**100.00%**

Table 1 illustrates the comparison between the proposed work and previous works mentioning if the studies have considered face, speaker, and vehicle number-plate recognition. It can be noticed that the previous works have achieved 55% [13] and 85.03% [13] accuracy whereas we have achieved 100% accuracy. As we have applied both MTCNN and FaceNet, our proposed approach discards the unnecessary portions of face images and extracts only the important points of faces. The previous approaches focused on ensembled CNNs or custom CNNs and tried to find important edges rather than facial points. The speaker verification also produced 100% accuracy due to working with text-independent verification as in text-independent verification, there is a higher probability of finding distinguishable features. Finally, the vehicle number-plate recognition achieved 100% accuracy due to applying Tesseract rather than CNNs.

5 Limitations

Although we achieved 100% accuracy, it might perform less in other scenarios. For example, it has been previously observed that face recognition suffers from race discrimination [4,15]. Therefore, assessing the performance of faces of different races may produce lower accuracy. In this work, it has been assumed that the users will provide face, voice records, and vehicle numbers to the concerned party for further recognition. However, in reality, a vast sample of our population does not want to share images of their face and vehicle number plates as well as records of their voices [20].

6 Conclusion

We concentrated on creating a hybrid campus security structure in this study. In this case, we examined both driver verification and vehicle recognition. Facial recognition and voice recognition were used for driver verification. MTCNN and FaceNet architecture were used to perform facial recognition, while 3-layer LSTM was employed for speech verification. Tesseract, on the other hand, was used for car number plate identification. The experimental findings for all three recognition methods were encouraging. We expect that by integrating all of these recognition processes, campus security can be improved significantly. In the future, we will concentrate on scaling up the suggested approach and calculating the risk variables for actual application. Moreover, the focus will be provided on developing a low-cost CNN that will fuse the extracted features of face and speech for final verification.

Acknowledgement. This research is funded and supported by the 'Research and Extension' section of Rajshahi University of Engineering & Technology, Rajshahi-6204, Bangladesh.

References

1. Al Awaimri, M., Fageeri, S., Moyaid, A., Thron, C., ALhasanat, A.: Automatic number plate recognition system for Oman. In: Alloghani, M., Thron, C., Subair, S. (eds.) Artificial Intelligence for Data Science in Theory and Practice. SCI, vol. 1006, pp. 155–178. Springer, Cham (2022). https://doi.org/10.1007/978-3-030-92245-0_8
2. Antar, R., Alghamdi, S., Alotaibi, J., Alghamdi, M.: Automatic number plate recognition of Saudi license car plates. Eng. Technol. Appl. Sci. Res. **12**(2), 8266–8272 (2022)
3. Azadani, M.N., Boukerche, A.: Driverrep: driver identification through driving behavior embeddings. J. Parallel Distrib. Comput. **162**, 105–117 (2022)
4. Bacchini, F., Lorusso, L.: Race, again: how face recognition technology reinforces racial discrimination. J. Inf. Commun. Ethics Soc. (2019)
5. Bimbot, F., et al.: A tutorial on text-independent speaker verification. EURASIP J. Adv. Signal Process. **2004**(4), 1–22 (2004)
6. Boutros, F., Damer, N., Kirchbuchner, F., Kuijper, A.: Self-restrained triplet loss for accurate masked face recognition. Pattern Recogn. **124**, 108473 (2022)
7. Cheng, J.M., Wang, H.C.: A method of estimating the equal error rate for automatic speaker verification. In: 2004 International Symposium on Chinese Spoken Language Processing, pp. 285–288. IEEE (2004)
8. Gnanaprakash, V., Kanthimathi, N., Saranya, N.: Automatic number plate recognition using deep learning. In: IOP Conference Series: Materials Science and Engineering, vol. 1084, p. 012027. IOP Publishing (2021)
9. Hammouche, R., Attia, A., Akhrouf, S., Akhtar, Z.: Gabor filter bank with deep autoencoder based face recognition system. Expert Syst. Appl., 116743 (2022)
10. Hofbauer, H., Uhl, A.: Calculating a boundary for the significance from the equal-error rate. In: 2016 International Conference on Biometrics (ICB), pp. 1–4. IEEE (2016)
11. Huang, B., et al.: Joint segmentation and identification feature learning for occlusion face recognition. IEEE Trans. Neural Netw. Learn. Syst. (2022)
12. Huang, Z., Zhang, J., Shan, H.: When age-invariant face recognition meets face age synthesis: a multi-task learning framework. In: Proceedings of the IEEE/CVF Conference on Computer Vision and Pattern Recognition, pp. 7282–7291 (2021)
13. Ivanko, D., Ryumin, D., Axyonov, A., Kashevnik, A.: Speaker-dependent visual command recognition in vehicle cabin: methodology and evaluation. In: Karpov, A., Potapova, R. (eds.) SPECOM 2021. LNCS (LNAI), vol. 12997, pp. 291–302. Springer, Cham (2021). https://doi.org/10.1007/978-3-030-87802-3_27
14. Ivanko, D., Ryumin, D., Markitantov, M.: End-to-end visual speech recognition for human-robot interaction (2022)
15. Jung, S.G., An, J., Kwak, H., Salminen, J., Jansen, B.J.: Assessing the accuracy of four popular face recognition tools for inferring gender, age, and race. In: Twelfth International AAAI Conference on Web and Social Media (2018)

16. Kim, J., El-Khamy, M., Lee, J.: Residual lstm: design of a deep recurrent architecture for distant speech recognition. arXiv preprint arXiv:1701.03360 (2017)
17. Kumar, J.R., Sujatha, B., Leelavathi, N.: Automatic vehicle number plate recognition system using machine learning. In: IOP Conference Series: Materials Science and Engineering, vol. 1074, p. 012012. IOP Publishing (2021)
18. Li, M., Huang, B., Tian, G.: A comprehensive survey on 3D face recognition methods. Eng. Appl. Artif. Intell. **110**, 104669 (2022)
19. Li, Y., Guo, K., Lu, Y., Liu, L.: Cropping and attention based approach for masked face recognition. Appl. Intell. **51**(5), 3012–3025 (2021). https://doi.org/10.1007/s10489-020-02100-9
20. Lin, S.W., Liu, Y.C.: The effects of motivations, trust, and privacy concern in social networking. Serv. Bus. **6**(4), 411–424 (2012)
21. Liu, T., Das, R.K., Lee, K.A., Li, H.: Neural acoustic-phonetic approach for speaker verification with phonetic attention mask. IEEE Signal Process. Lett. **29**, 782–786 (2022)
22. Liu, Z., Luo, P., Wang, X., Tang, X.: Large-scale celebfaces attributes (celeba) dataset. Retr. August **15**(2018), 11 (2018)
23. Patel, C., Shah, D., Patel, A.: Automatic number plate recognition system (anpr): a survey. Int. J. Comput. Appl. **69**(9), 21–33 (2013)
24. Puranic, A., Deepak, K., Umadevi, V.: Vehicle number plate recognition system: a literature review and implementation using template matching. Int. J. Comput. Appl. **134**(1), 12–16 (2016)
25. Raharja, N.M., Fathansyah, M.A., Chamim, A.N.N.: Vehicle parking security system with face recognition detection based on eigenface algorithm. J. Rob. Control (JRC) **3**(1), 78–85 (2022)
26. Rajasekar, V., et al.: Enhanced multimodal biometric recognition approach for smart cities based on an optimized fuzzy genetic algorithm. Sci. Rep. **12**(1), 1–11 (2022)
27. Rosenberg, A.E.: Automatic speaker verification: a review. Proc. IEEE **64**(4), 475–487 (1976)
28. Schroff, F., Kalenichenko, D., Philbin, J.: Facenet: a unified embedding for face recognition and clustering. In: Proceedings of the IEEE Conference on Computer Vision and Pattern Recognition, pp. 815–823 (2015)
29. Setiyono, B., Amini, D.A., Sulistyaningrum, D.R.: Number plate recognition on vehicle using yolo-darknet. In: Journal of Physics: Conference Series, vol. 1821, p. 012049. IOP Publishing (2021)
30. Smith, R.: An overview of the tesseract ocr engine. In: Ninth International Conference on Document Analysis and Recognition (ICDAR 2007), vol. 2, pp. 629–633. IEEE (2007)
31. Tong, F., et al.: Asv-subtools: open source toolkit for automatic speaker verification. In: ICASSP 2021–2021 IEEE International Conference on Acoustics, Speech and Signal Processing (ICASSP), pp. 6184–6188. IEEE (2021)
32. Verma, A., Goyal, A., Kumar, N., Tekchandani, H.: Face recognition: a review and analysis. In: Computational Intelligence in Data Mining, pp. 195–210 (2022)
33. Wu, H., Li, X., Liu, A.T., Wu, Z., Meng, H., Lee, H.y.: Adversarial defense for automatic speaker verification by cascaded self-supervised learning models. In: ICASSP 2021–2021 IEEE International Conference on Acoustics, Speech and Signal Processing (ICASSP), pp. 6718–6722. IEEE (2021)
34. Wu, H., Li, X., Liu, A.T., Wu, Z., Meng, H., Lee, H.Y.: Improving the adversarial robustness for speaker verification by self-supervised learning. IEEE/ACM Trans. Audio Speech Lang. Process. **30**, 202–217 (2021)

35. Xia, H., Xu, S., Liu, Y., Wei, X., Jia, H.: Research on the construction of intelligent vehicle verification system for road transportation. In: Jain, L.C., Kountchev, R., Hu, B., Kountcheva, R. (eds.) Smart Communications, Intelligent Algorithms and Interactive Methods. SIST, vol. 257, pp. 97–103. Springer, Singapore (2022). https://doi.org/10.1007/978-981-16-5164-9_12

36. Xiang, J., Zhu, G.: Joint face detection and facial expression recognition with mtcnn. In: 2017 4th International Conference on Information Science and Control Engineering (ICISCE), pp. 424–427. IEEE (2017)

37. Zen, H., et al.: Libritts: a corpus derived from librispeech for text-to-speech. arXiv preprint arXiv:1904.02882 (2019)

38. Zhang, Q., Zhuo, L., Zhang, S., Li, J., Zhang, H., Li, X.: Fine-grained vehicle recognition using lightweight convolutional neural network with combined learning strategy. In: 2018 IEEE Fourth International Conference on Multimedia Big Data (BigMM), pp. 1–5. IEEE (2018)

39. Zhou, T., Zhao, Y., Wu, J.: Resnext and res2net structures for speaker verification. In: 2021 IEEE Spoken Language Technology Workshop (SLT), pp. 301–307. IEEE (2021)

Signal Processing and Machine Learning

Single-Trial Detection of Event-Related Potentials with Artificial Examples Based on Coloring Transformation

Hubert Cecotti[✉]⊕ and Steve Jaimes⊕

Department of Computer Science, California State University, Fresno, CA, USA
hcecotti@csufresno.edu

Abstract. Non-invasive Brain-Computer Interfaces (BCIs) using electroencephalography (EEG) recordings are the most common type of BCI. The detection of Event-Related Potentials (ERP) corresponding to the presentation of visual stimuli is one of the main paradigms in BCI, such as for the detection of the P300 ERP component that is used in the P300 speller. The typing speed and the information transfer rate in a BCI speller are directly related to the single-trial detection performance. It corresponds to the binary classification of brain evoked responses corresponding to the presentation of stimuli representing targets vs. nontargets. Many techniques have been proposed in the literature, ranging from shallow approaches using linear discriminant analysis to hierarchical and deep learning methods. For BCIs that require a calibration session, reducing its duration is critical for the implementation of BCIs in clinical settings. For this reason, data augmentation approaches allowing to increase the size of the training database can improve performance while keeping the same number of trials for the calibration session. In this paper, we propose to generate artificial trials based on the properties of the distribution of the signals after spatial filtering using the coloring transformation. The approach is compared with other approaches on the single-trial detection of ERPs from a public database of 8 subjects with amyotrophic lateral sclerosis. The results support the conclusion that artificial trials based on the coloring transformation can be used for training a classifier. However, they do not provide a substantial improvement then added as a data augmentation technique, compared to data augmentation using examples shifted temporally.

Keywords: Brain-Computer Interface · Event-Related Potentials · Artificial examples

1 Introduction

Non-invasive Brain-Computer Interface (BCI) using electroencephalography (EEG) signals have been studied and enhanced in the last decades thanks to the

This study was supported by the NIH-R15 NS118581 project.

KC Santosh et al. (Eds.): RTIP2R 2022, CCIS 1704, pp. 371–382, 2023.
https://doi.org/10.1007/978-3-031-23599-3_28

advance of signal processing and machine learning algorithms. Yet, their reliability over time and across users, and their relatively low performance prevent them from being fully deployed in clinical settings or in private homes for the main target users: people with severe disabilities. It is still necessary to research approaches that can mitigate the effects of non-stationarity of the EEG signal, where regular calibrations are required. Machine learning approaches such as deep learning methods can require a large number of training examples.

Single-trial detection performance is one of the most important aspects in BCI based on ERP detection. Single-trial detection is essential in different paradigms using the oddball paradigm, from the P300 speller to Rapid Serial Visual Presentation tasks [9]. In these paradigms, the user has to pay attention to different visual stimuli occurring on the screen. Visual stimuli are categorized into two categories: targets and non-targets. When the user pays attention to a stimulus corresponding to a target, we expect different ERP components to have different characteristics than for the presentation of a stimulus corresponding to a non-target. Because of the oddball paradigm where the presentations of sequences of repetitive stimuli are infrequently interrupted by a deviant stimulus, there is a significant unbalance between the target and non-target examples. The number of examples corresponding to a target are therefore limited based on the total number of examples that are recorded. It is therefore important to find ways to find ways to limit the number of needed target examples.

In this paper, we propose to assess different data augmentation techniques for ERPs. In addition, we propose to generate fully artificial data by considering original data after spatial filtering and then describing its distribution after coloring transformation. We show that the projection of the EEG data after spatial filtering using coloring allows to create artificial trials that lead to similar results as the original EEG data. This hypothesis stems from the success of shallow approaches using linear discriminant analysis taking into account the covariance matrices of the data from each class, and the success of density based approaches using Riemannian geometry with covariance matrices as input features.

The remainder of the paper is organized as follows: The background and rationale of the approach are given in Sect. 2. The methods and the descriptions of the dataset are detailed in Sect. 3. The results are presented in Sect. 4. Finally, the main contributions, results and future scope of the project are summarized in Sect. 5.

2   Background

Data augmentation approaches are critical in machine learning and pattern recognition. They substantially improve the performance of some classifiers. The goal is to increase the size of the training dataset by adding transformed artificial training examples [1]. The machine learning algorithm will then extract the information from both the training data and the artificially generated training data. The creation of artificial training examples increases the size of the database and has the advantage of being readily implemented for multiple classifiers.

Data augmentation may require some knowledge about the problem and the possible variations that are acceptable between examples belonging to the same class. For instance, it is possible to rotate or mirror images in problems where such deformations have no impact on the label of the objects presented in the image. Geometric deformations and image warping approaches to acknowledge local deformations in images, such approaches led to state-of-the-art results in handwritten digit recognition with deep learning [18], and density-based approaches [7]. In the case of EEG signals, and in particular for ERPs, it can be necessary to separate classes (targets and non-targets) before generating artificial signals. The properties of ERP components within an evoked brain response have some well-defined meanings in cognitive neuroscience and they cannot be ignored [10,13]. Each ERP component can be defined by its latency and its peak, these measurements vary across participants and across trials. The variability of the latency in some late ERP components can be directly correlated with the response time for processing the stimuli [8].

A recent trend for the generation of artificial data is to use Generative adversarial networks (GANs). These models have been highly successful in generative applications involving images such as medical imaging [19], and they have been applied to time series [11]. They have been applied on EEG and motor imagery signals [5,20]. A key question is to know if it is really necessary to use GANs, i.e., to have generative models that require deep architecture and non-linearity for the generation of artificial data in BCI and if the underlying distribution of the brain evoked responses cannot be described in more simple terms.

3 Methods

3.1 Data Generation

We consider a set of examples $X \in \mathbb{R}^{N_e \times N_f}$ corresponding to a unique class of objects and containing N_e examples. $X = [\mathbf{x}_1, \ldots, \mathbf{x}_{N_e}]$. each example being defined by N_f features. We define the mean (μ) across the examples, and the covariance matrix by:

$$\mu = \frac{1}{N_e} \sum_{i=1}^{N_e} \mathbf{x}_i \tag{1}$$

$$K_{XX} = \frac{1}{N_e - 1} X^T \cdot X \tag{2}$$

The approach is directly related to the whitening transformation and Principal Component Analysis (PCA). A coloring transform is a reversed procedure of the corresponding whitening transform. It is a linear transformation that transforms a vector of random variables with a known covariance matrix (K_{XX}) into a set of new variables whose covariance is the identity matrix. It means that they are uncorrelated, and each have variance 1. Here, we use seeds from the standard normal distribution that we scale in relation to the standard deviation of each uncorrelated variable, and then we go back to the original space (rotation from the eigenvectors and shift from the mean μ). From the covariance matrix K_{XX}, we extract the diagonal matrix D of eigenvalues λ and matrix V whose columns are the corresponding right eigenvectors, so that $K_{XX} \cdot V = V \cdot D$. The eigenvectors in V are normalized so that the 2-norm of each is 1.

Each artificial example is created based on random values extracted from a standard normal distribution ($\mu = 0$ and $\sigma = 1$, i.e., zero mean and unit standard deviation). We define the function f_r that generates a number that follows the standard normal distribution:

$$f(z) = \frac{1}{\sqrt{(2\pi)}} e^{-\frac{z^2}{2}} \qquad (3)$$

for a random real variable z with mean 0 and variance 1. We define a vector of random values of size N_f, $\mathbf{r} = [f_r(), \ldots, f_r()]$.

A new example $\mathbf{x}'$ can be created with:

$$\mathbf{x}' = \mu + (r \circ \sqrt{\lambda}) \cdot V^T \qquad (4)$$

The approach can be resumed in the following steps: shift, rotate, and scale to have white noise; create white noise for new examples then scale, rotate, and shift back to the original dataset. A toy example with 2 dimensions is depicted in Fig. 1. In addition to this approach, we create artificial trials by shifting the signals in the time with ± 1 time points (the approach depends on the sampling rate and the temporal shift that we wish to allow in the examples) [2].

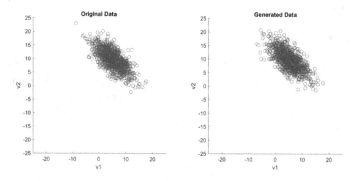

Fig. 1. Toy example with a dataset in 2 dimensions. Left: original data; Right: generated data.

3.2   Database

We consider a dataset that represents a complete record of P300 evoked potentials recorded with BCI2000 [17] using the P300 speller [4]. In these sessions, 8 users with amyotrophic lateral sclerosis (ALS) focused on one out of 36 different characters. Scalp EEG signals were recorded from eight channels ($N_s = 8$)

according to 10–10 standard (Fz, Cz, Pz, Oz, P3, P4, PO7, and PO8) using active electrodes. All the channels were referenced to the right earlobe and grounded to the left mastoid. The original EEG signal from the dataset was digitized 256 Hz and band-pass filtered between 0.1 30 Hz. Participants were required to copy spell seven predefined words of five characters each, by using a P300 speller displayed as a matrix of size 6 × 6. Each character was repeated 10 times, with 12 (2 targets + 10 non-targets) different stimuli (6 rows and 6 columns). Hence, each subject has entered 35 characters ($N_{char} = 35$), and with 10 repetitions ($N_{rep} = 10$), leading to 3500 examples ($10 \times N_{rep} \times N_{char}$) corresponding to non-targets and 700 examples corresponding to targets ($2 \times N_{rep} \times N_{char}$).

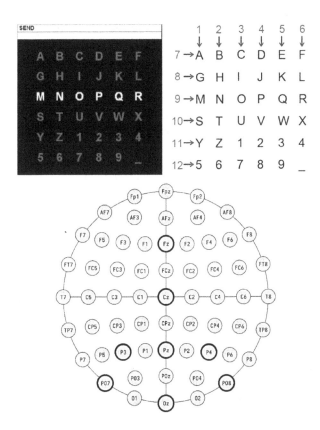

Fig. 2. P300 speller experimental paradigm **top** and electrode placement **bottom**.

3.3 Features Extraction and Classification

The signal was low-pass filtered with a zero-phase Butterworth filter of order 5 using a cutoff frequency 21 Hz. The signal was then downsampled by a factor of 4 to have a frequency 64 Hz.

After temporal filtering, we apply the xDAWN spatial filtering approach to enhance the signal-to-signal plus noise ratio (SSNR) [3,15,16]. Spatial filters are estimated through the Rayleigh quotient by maximizing the SSNR, where the signal corresponds to the information contained in the ERPs corresponding to the presentation of a target. The result provides N_f spatial filters that are ranked in terms of their SSNR [14]. The enhanced signal XU is composed of three parts: the ERP responses on a target class (D_1A_1), a response common to all stimuli, i.e., all targets and non-targets confound (D_2A_2), and the residual noise (H), that are all filtered spatially with U.

$$XU = (D_1A_1 + D_2A_2 + H)U. \tag{5}$$

where $\{D_1, D_2\} \in \mathbb{R}^{N_t \times N_1}$ are two Toeplitz matrices, N_1 is the number of sampling points representing the target and superimposed evoked potentials (640 ms), and $H \in \mathbb{R}^{N_t \times N_s}$. The spatial filters U maximize the SSNR:

$$\text{SSNR}(U) = \arg\max_{U} \frac{\text{Tr}(U^T \hat{A}_1^T D_1^T D_1 \hat{A}_1 U)}{Tr(U^T X^T X U)} \tag{6}$$

where $\hat{A}_1$ represents the least mean square estimation of A_1:

$$\hat{A} = \begin{bmatrix} \hat{A}_1 \\ \hat{A}_2 \end{bmatrix} = ([D_1; D_2]^T [D_1; D_2])^{-1} [D_1; D_2]^T X \tag{7}$$

where $[D_1; D_2] \in \mathbb{R}^{N_t \times (N_1+N_2)}$ is obtained by concatenation of D_1 and D_2, and Tr(.) denotes the trace operator.

Each time segment related to the presentation of a visual stimulus is set to 1 s after the stimulus onset, corresponding to 64 time points ($N_t = 64$). We consider as many spatial filters as sensors. Therefore, the number of features is $N_s \times N_t = 512$.

Performance evaluation for the binary classification task (target vs. non-target) was assessed for each subject using cross-validation with 5 folds. We report the Area Under the ROC curve (AUC) for determining the single-trial performance. Bayesian linear discriminant analysis (BLDA) [6,12] was used for the binary classification of the ERPs corresponding to the presentation of a target versus non-target visual stimuli. This classifier has been used successfully in different studies for the same type of problem [3,15].

3.4   Conditions

We consider two main conditions, with and without data augmentation. Without data augmentation, we evaluate the data or the artificial data. The default condition represents the original dataset. The coloring condition represents data that have been created using normal distributions for the different time points and are then scaled and rotated in relation to the eigenvalues and eigenvectors obtained from coloring. The STD condition represents data that have been generated using the average mean for each class on which we are adding $\pm$ random values coming from a uniform distribution (from -1 to $+1$) and weighted by the standard deviation of the feature, obtained from the examples of the original dataset. In the data augmentation condition, we combine the original data with the artificial examples, i.e., default+coloring, default+temporal shifts, default+coloring+temporal shifts, and with default+artificial trials on which we add noise based on the standard deviation of each feature. In each condition with data augmentation, we add for each class as many examples as examples that were originally present in the database.

4   Results

The AUC for the different experimental conditions with spatial filtering are presented in Tables 1 and 2; without spatial filtering in Tables 3 and 4. For the evaluation with spatial filters, the mean AUC across subjects is 0.857, 0.838, 0.524 for the default data, coloring (shift/rotate/scale), and the noise only approaches (shift/scale), respectively. With data augmentation, the AUC is 0.855, 0.874, 0.872, and 0.861 for coloring, temporal shifts, coloring+temporal shifts, and the addition of noise based on the standard deviation of each feature. Pairwise Wilcoxon signed-rank tests revealed a difference between the default and coloring conditions ($p = 0.0078$), and between the default and noise condition ($p = 0.0078$). While the artificial examples based only on the mean and the standard deviation provide a bad performance, i.e., random decision, the artificial examples based on coloring provide a performance of 0.838 which is very close to the performance with the original data. With the data augmentation, Wilcoxon signed-rank tests indicated an improvement of performance with data augmentation for all the conditions except the one with coloring. The best performance was reached with the shifts condition, suggesting that the variability in latency of the ERPs is a key element for capturing the variability of the trials between the training and test sessions. The same pattern of performance is observed without using spatial filters, where the default performance is with an AUC of 0.857, the best performance with data augmentation is with the temporal shifts (AUC $= 0.74$), and the coloring transformation provides artificial trials that can be used to train the classifier with an AUC $= 0.838$.

Table 1. AUC for the different conditions (with spatial filters) - No Data Augmentation.

Subj.	Default	Coloring	STD
1	0.838 ± 0.019	0.818 ± 0.024	0.513 ± 0.034
2	0.812 ± 0.012	0.793 ± 0.012	0.500 ± 0.020
3	0.881 ± 0.020	0.857 ± 0.019	0.492 ± 0.029
4	0.801 ± 0.119	0.766 ± 0.109	0.491 ± 0.041
5	0.858 ± 0.020	0.831 ± 0.022	0.509 ± 0.009
6	0.887 ± 0.019	0.865 ± 0.019	0.497 ± 0.025
7	0.876 ± 0.042	0.856 ± 0.043	0.515 ± 0.027
8	0.954 ± 0.011	0.945 ± 0.012	0.502 ± 0.017
Mean	0.863 ± 0.033	0.841 ± 0.033	0.502 ± 0.025
SD	0.048 ± 0.036	0.054 ± 0.032	0.009 ± 0.010

Table 2. AUC for the different conditions (with spatial filters) - Data Augmentation.

Subj.	Coloring	Shifts	Coloring+Shift	STD
1	0.829 ± 0.022	0.854 ± 0.020	0.849 ± 0.021	0.829 ± 0.016
2	0.808 ± 0.012	0.830 ± 0.010	0.829 ± 0.004	0.811 ± 0.005
3	0.870 ± 0.022	0.889 ± 0.019	0.885 ± 0.024	0.876 ± 0.020
4	0.796 ± 0.112	0.814 ± 0.126	0.814 ± 0.123	0.800 ± 0.120
5	0.851 ± 0.021	0.868 ± 0.018	0.864 ± 0.021	0.857 ± 0.018
6	0.883 ± 0.022	0.897 ± 0.018	0.895 ± 0.016	0.884 ± 0.021
7	0.875 ± 0.041	0.887 ± 0.044	0.886 ± 0.045	0.873 ± 0.043
8	0.950 ± 0.011	0.960 ± 0.009	0.957 ± 0.009	0.952 ± 0.009
Mean	0.858 ± 0.033	0.875 ± 0.033	0.872 ± 0.033	0.860 ± 0.032
SD	0.049 ± 0.033	0.045 ± 0.039	0.045 ± 0.038	0.048 ± 0.037

Table 3. AUC for the different conditions (without spatial filters) - No Data Augmentation.

Subj.	Default	Coloring	STD
1	0.829 ± 0.019	0.810 ± 0.025	0.520 ± 0.031
2	0.803 ± 0.010	0.781 ± 0.022	0.519 ± 0.043
3	0.874 ± 0.021	0.853 ± 0.026	0.518 ± 0.044
4	0.788 ± 0.111	0.769 ± 0.111	0.528 ± 0.026
5	0.849 ± 0.020	0.824 ± 0.027	0.535 ± 0.024
6	0.883 ± 0.023	0.867 ± 0.015	0.523 ± 0.037
7	0.873 ± 0.048	0.856 ± 0.049	0.523 ± 0.033
8	0.953 ± 0.008	0.946 ± 0.010	0.527 ± 0.029
Mean	0.857 ± 0.033	0.838 ± 0.036	0.524 ± 0.033
SD	0.052 ± 0.034	0.056 ± 0.033	0.006 ± 0.007

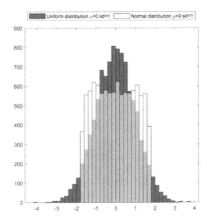

Fig. 3. Histograms of the standard normal distribution and the uniform distribution ($\mu = 0$ and $\sigma = 1$).

Table 4. AUC for the different conditions (without spatial filters) - Data Augmentation.

Subj.	Coloring	Shifts	Coloring+Shift	STD
1	0.827 ± 0.021	0.851 ± 0.022	0.852 ± 0.024	0.835 ± 0.022
2	0.809 ± 0.005	0.831 ± 0.009	0.831 ± 0.008	0.814 ± 0.007
3	0.868 ± 0.022	0.887 ± 0.021	0.886 ± 0.026	0.876 ± 0.020
4	0.787 ± 0.118	0.812 ± 0.124	0.810 ± 0.125	0.798 ± 0.117
5	0.847 ± 0.016	0.866 ± 0.019	0.862 ± 0.019	0.854 ± 0.019
6	0.884 ± 0.021	0.896 ± 0.020	0.894 ± 0.018	0.886 ± 0.021
7	0.872 ± 0.047	0.887 ± 0.046	0.884 ± 0.049	0.875 ± 0.045
8	0.949 ± 0.012	0.960 ± 0.007	0.959 ± 0.008	0.953 ± 0.010
Mean	0.855 ± 0.033	0.874 ± 0.034	0.872 ± 0.035	0.861 ± 0.033
SD	0.050 ± 0.037	0.046 ± 0.038	0.045 ± 0.039	0.048 ± 0.036

In Fig. 3, we display an example of the differences between the standard normal distribution and the uniform distribution where both distributions have a zero mean and unit standard deviation. We propose to compare these distributions with the AUC when considering only artificial trials for training the classifiers. In addition, we assess the effect of scaling the random values to different standard deviations (from 1 to 2). The performance is depicted in Fig. 4. The mean AUC drops from 0.843 to 0.817 with the normal distribution while it drops from 0.847 to 0.815 with the uniform distribution. There are no differences of performance between random trials generated from the normal and uniform distributions.

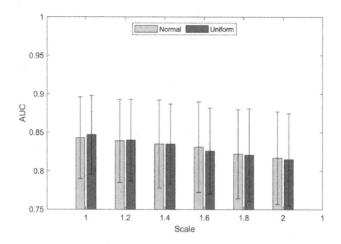

Fig. 4. Classification performance with artificial trials for training the classifiers.

5   Discussion and Conclusion

EEG data acquisition is a time-consuming and expensive task that is required for training BCI systems. While it is possible to create systems that are calibrated using data from a large number of participants, the most common approach is to calibrate a system for a specific individual. Reducing the calibration session or improving the performance with a limited number of trials is critical for enhancing the user experience and usability of BCI, so users spend only a limited amount of time in the calibration session. Data augmentation can be used in BCI paradigms, EEG super-sampling, or for the restoration of corrupted data segments. The ability to generate signals of a certain class, or having specific properties, provides a new research direction for better understanding brain signals and how they are generated. We have shown the artificial data using the coloring transform can provide a high AUC (0.841) for the classification of ERPs. It indicates that all the information contained in the ERPs corresponding to targets and non-targets can be synthesized within their mean and covariance matrices. While there is statistical difference of performance between the coloring and the default trials, the gap in performance is low and suggests that the artificial trials can be simply generated using a coloring transform and it would not be necessary to have more complex approaches for creating examples. However, the results show as well that such an approach is not sufficient for improving the performance of the classifier then used as a data augmentation technique: it leads to the same performance. It creates additional examples but coming from the same distribution. The approach doesn't learn the type of variations that are embedded with the trials and how it could improve the performance. The classification performance is better with the examples that are shifted in time.

In this paper, we have shown that fully artificial signals based on the coloring transformation can be used to train and discriminate targets from non-target visual stimuli with an AUC $\approx$ 0.84. Further work will investigate the relationships between the type of classifiers and the type of data augmentation.

References

1. Baird, H.: Document image defect models. In: Proceedings of the IAPR Workshop on Syntactic and Structural Pattern Recognition, pp. 38–46 (1990)
2. Cecotti, H., Marathe, A., Ries, A.: Optimization of single-trial detection of event-related potentials through artificial trials. IEEE Trans. Biomed. Eng. **62**(9), 2170–2176 (2015)
3. Cecotti, H., et al.: A robust sensor selection method for P300 brain-computer interfaces. J. Neural Eng. **8**, 016001 (2011)
4. Farwell, L.A., Donchin, E.: Talking off the top of your head: toward a mental prosthesis utilizing event-related brain potentials. Electroencephalogr. Clin. Neurophysiol. **70**(6), 510–523 (1988)
5. Hartmann, K.G., Schirrmeister, R.T., Ball, T.: EEG-GAN: Generative adversarial networks for electroencephalograhic (EEG) brain signals (2018)
6. Hoffmann, U., Vesin, J., Diserens, K., Ebrahimi, T.: An efficient P300-based brain-computer interface for disabled subjects. J. Neurosci. Meth. **167**(1), 115–125 (2008)
7. Keysers, D., Deselaers, T., Gollan, C., Ney, H.: Deformation models for image recognition. IEEE Trans. Patt. Anal. Mach. Intell. **29**(8), 1422–1435 (2007)
8. Kutas, M., McCarthy, G., Donchin, E.: Augmenting mental chronometry: the p300 as a measure of stimulus evaluation time. Science **197**(4305), 792–795 (1977)
9. Lees, S., et al.: A review of rapid serial visual presentation-based brain–computer interfaces. J. Neural Eng. **15**(2), 021001 (2018)
10. Luck, S.J., Kappenman, E.S.: The Oxford Handbook of Event-Related Potential Components. Oxford University Press, USA (2011)
11. Luo, Y., Cai, X., Zhang, Y., Xu, J., et al.: Multivariate time series imputation with generative adversarial networks. Adv. Neural Inf. Process. Syst. **31** (2018)
12. MacKay, D.J.C.: Bayesian interpolation. Neural Comput. **4**(3), 415–447 (1992)
13. Polich, J., Kokb, A.: Cognitive and biological determinants of P300: an integrative review. Biol. Psychol. **41**, 103–146 (1995)
14. Rivet, B., Cecotti, H., Maby, E., Mattout, J.: Impact of spatial filters during sensor selection in a visual p300 brain-computer interface. Brain Topogr. **25**(1), 55–63 (2012)
15. Rivet, B., Souloumiac, A.: Optimal linear spatial filters for event-related potentials based on a spatio-temporal model: asymptotical performance analysis. Signal Process. **93**(2), 387–398 (2013)
16. Rivet, B., Souloumiac, A., Attina, V., Gibert, G.: xDAWN algorithm to enhance evoked potentials: application to brain-computer interface. IEEE Trans. Biomed. Eng. **56**(8), 2035–2043 (2009)
17. Schalk, G., McFarland, D.J., Hinterberger, T., Birbaumer, N., Wolpaw, J.R.: BCI 2000: a general-purpose brain-computer interface (bCI) system. IEEE Trans. Biomed. Eng. **51**(6), 1034–1043 (2004)
18. Simard, P.Y., Steinkraus, D., Platt, J.C.: Best practices for convolutional neural networks applied to visual document analysis. In: Proceedings of the 7th International Conference on Document Analysis and Recognition, pp. 958–962 (2003)

19. Yi, X., Walia, E., Babyn, P.: Generative adversarial network in medical imaging: a review. Med. Image Anal. **58**, 101552 (2019)
20. Özdenizci, O., Erdoğmuş, D.: On the use of generative deep neural networks to synthesize artificial multichannel EEG signals. In: 2021 10th International IEEE/EMBS Conference on Neural Engineering (NER), pp. 427–430 (2021). https://doi.org/10.1109/NER49283.2021.9441381

Identifying the Relationship Between Hypothesis and Premise

Srishti Jhunthra[1(✉)], Harshit Garg[1], and Vedika Gupta[2]

[1] Department of Computer Science and Engineering, Bharati Vidyapeeth's College of Engineering, New Delhi, India
jhunthrasrishti@gmail.com, gargharshit2000@gmail.com
[2] Jindal Global Business School, O. P. Jindal Global University, Sonipat, Haryana, India
vgupta2@jgu.edu.in

Abstract. Natural language processing is one the most interesting study leading to huge research solutions in the modern era. Multilingual toxic comment classification can be served as a huge benefit to the existing social media life where comments, tweets, etc. can be analyzed when a topic is known to the system. This would help in the prevention of false commenting and better interpretation and analysis of the miscommunication that occurred on different social media platforms over a certain issue. Multilingual toxic comment classification refers to the analysis of a hypothetical sentence proposed given a premise. This classification is divided into three categories are the hypothetical sentence proposed can be either an entailment to the premise, neutral, or contradictory to the known premise statement. Natural language inference is considered as one of the most trending problems under the field of natural language processing which helps to determine how two statements given the premise and hypothesis are related to each other. Thus, the paper proposes different models such as CBOW, ESIM, BiLSTM and fine-tuned XML-RoBERTa model to predict the relationship between two statements. The prediction helps in the determination of whether the given hypothesis is in an entailment, neutral, contradictory relation with the given premise. The paper shows a study over various algorithms that can be used to solve the natural language inference problem. After analysis, the paper also proposes a model that obtained an accuracy of 95.35% with a ROC score of 0.9629 for the entailment relationship, 0.97076 for the neutral relationships, and 0.9797 for the contradictory relationships between the sentence pairs.

Keywords: Natural language processing · Natural language inference · Multilingual toxic comment · XLM-RoBERTa · Comments · Prediction

1 Introduction

Social media [1] is one of the most rising sources of entertainment incorporated in recent times. Due to the coronavirus pandemic situation social media, online suffering, internet usage has reached their maximum heights. Along with this rise there comes certain opinions and objections also referred to as a discussion served by the people all across the world. The social media platforms like Twitter, Facebook, Instagram have gained a lot of publicity from people all across the world where every issue occurring anywhere across the globe is being discussed. Knowing the hot topic swirling around people tend to re-tweet, comment, like, and share to extend the topic and gain insights from every person out there. This sometimes leads to various conflicts and misunderstandings of the situation. Natural language processing (NLP) [2] which is considered as one of the most emerging topics over the past few years can be used to resolve such problems. Natural language inference (NLI) [3] is a popular problem that falls under the category of natural language processing where a model can be trained to predict the relation between two sentences. Given a premise that is, information regarding a topic the proposed NLI based model can predict whether the given hypothesis is in an entailment, neutral or contradictory relation with the known premise. Therefore, the paper proposes an NLI [9] based model using the combination of the multi-genre natural language inference (MultiNLI) dataset and TensorFlow dataset to predict whether the given hypothesis is in an entailment, neutral, or a contradictory relation with the premise. The MultiNLI dataset[1] is a collection of 433k sentence pairs. The dataset is analyzed and trained on the proposed model in the paper below. After training the multi-genre natural language inference dataset on various algorithms and models, the prediction was made to predict the multilingual toxic comment classification across different languages using the test dataset to obtain the results. Thus, the fine-tuned XML-RoBERTa based proposed model obtained an accuracy of 95.35% with a receiver operating characteristic (ROC) score of 0.9629 for the entailment relationship, 0.97076 for the neutral relationships, and 0.9797 for the contradictory relationships between the sentence pairs.

The organization of the paper is as follows: Sect. 2 presents the background work. Section 3 comprises the methodology used to train and predict the multilingual toxic comment classification from the proposed model. Section 4 consists of the results and discussion enclosed after predicting the multilingual toxic comments from the proposed model using the multi-genre natural language inference dataset. Further, Sect. 5 comprises the conclusion and future work proposed after analyzing the results and conclusion obtained by implementing the proposed NLI-based model.

2   Background

In literature, some researchers have been made on NLI-based problems using different methodologies and proposed models. In early 2020, Lees et al. [6] proposed their study on the problem of hate speech detection (HaSpeeDe2). The study shows the fine-tuning pre-trained comment-domain bidirectional encoder representations from transformers (BERT) model. The proposed model was successfully able to predict the multilingual toxicity in comments. Nie et al. [7] also proposed a study on natural language inference using the hierarchical bidirectional long short-term memory (BiLSTM) max-pooling architecture methodology to solve the natural language processing problem and predict the multilingual toxicity in comments. The study proposes a multilayer perceptron (MLP) based model with a SoftMax activation layer to make predictions using the MultiNLI

---

[1] https://cims.nyu.edu/~sbowman/multinli

dataset for training and testing of the proposed model. After making a prediction using various models the study acquired a maximum accuracy of 86.0% using the hierarchical BiLSTM max polling (HBMP) model.

The study also concludes that the results could be further improved considering the error percentage and evaluating the performance of the hierarchical BiLSTM max-pooling (HBMP) architecture on other natural language inference problems. In late 2020, Du et al. [8] also came up with their study for testing natural language inference on word-pair comparison and local content. The study uses deep neural networks and long short-term memory (LSTM) concepts to predict the natural language inference with a famous novel enhanced relation-head-dependent (RHD) triplet. The study proposes that the RHD triplet was the first novel to be proposed for NLI comparison. The study made it possible to develop an enhanced RHD triplet by the integration of all the structured information and the local context information more accurately and with great precision. The study also proposes to use the cross-comparison technique to predict corresponding words while making comparisons in premise and hypothesis sentences. As shown in Fig. 1, the study uses a 3-way Softmax classifier, proposing the general architecture of NLI. The study also concludes that the proposed study obtains the highest accuracy of 87.5% on testing the proposed model on multiple languages but the performance can be further improved and analyzed.

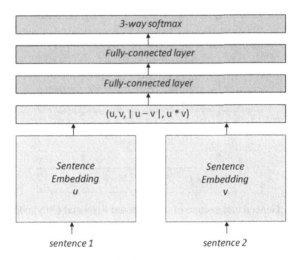

Fig. 1. Architecture of NLI [8]

In 2019, Guo et al. [9] used the concept of natural language inference for fake news detection. The study used individual convolutional neural network (CNN), recurrent neural network (RNN) layers to train the strongest NLI models along with the BERT model to make predictions for fake news detection. The study used a dataset consisting of over 1,000 foreign dissect children premise sentences and around 1,000 humor statements of humans stealing the children's organs as the hypothesis statements. Based on the observation recorded from the obtained dataset the researchers considered BERT and neural network models for training the NLI model as the best methodology for detecting fake news. The proposed NLI models included dense CNN, RNN layers, enhanced sequential inference model (ESIM), gated CNN layer, SoftMax activation layer as well as decomposable attention layer for making various levels of NLI models. Figure 2 depicts the overall flow of the RNN and CNN models used. On training and testing the proposed model, the prediction accuracy came out to be 88.06%. [10] The study thereby concluded that ensemble along with gradient boosting and fine-tuning can be used as an advantage for revolving the NLI problems. The paper also concluded that the work can be extended by looking towards a transitive method for data augmentation from which results can be further improved and analyzed. [11].

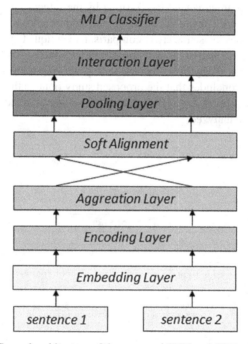

Fig. 2. General architecture of the proposed RNN and CNN models [9]

3   Methodology Adopted

The MultiNLI dataset [4] is a collection of 433k sentence pairs. The dataset is analyzed and trained on the proposed model in the paper below. The MultiNLI dataset also known as the multi-genre natural language inference dataset is a crowdsourced collection of around 433k sentence pairs with different types of relationships information also with the sentence pairs. The MultiNLI dataset is an advanced version of SNLI also known as the Stanford natural language inference corpus (SNLI). After training the multi-genre natural language inference dataset on various algorithms and models, the prediction was made to predict the multilingual toxic comment classification [5] across different languages using the test dataset to obtain the results. The proposed model obtained an accuracy of 95.35% with a receiver operating characteristic (ROC) score of 0.9629 for the entailment relationship, 0.97076 for the neutral relationships, and 0.9797 for the contradictory relationships between the sentence pairs.

Table 1 shows the complete description of the final dataset obtained by combining the MultiNLI dataset and TensorFlow dataset. Figure 3 shows the overall descriptions of the proposed methodology used for training and testing the proposed model for predicting the labels of multilingual toxic comments classification.

Table 1. Dataset available for each level

S.no	Label	Count
1	Neutral	141032
2	Entailment	142017
3	Contradiction	141420

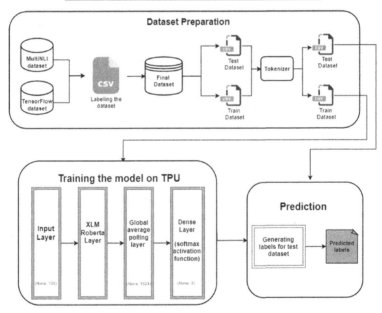

Fig. 3. Overall description

Thus, in order to predict the multilingual toxic comment classification, the exiting pre-trained XLM – RoBERTa model has been fine-tuned with different layers. The XLM-RoBERTa model [22] is an encoder that has been pre-trained over different languages, but the model cannot detect the relationship between the hypothesis and premise.

4   Results and Discussion

In this study, the final dataset was divided into training and test dataset to train various models and the tuned XLM-RoBERTa model. [12, 13] The model was trained over a tensor processing unit (TPU) taking a time of 4 s to 5 s. TPU [25] is an accelerator that usually helps to fasten up the training process. After training the model the results were obtained by testing various models and tuned XLM-RoBERTa model [19] in the form of the confusion matrix and ROC curve [21, 22, 23] to analyze the results and predict the accuracy of the model [24]. [17] After the computation of accuracy, error approximation is calculated for different models in three forms: mean average error (MAE), mean square error (MSE), and root mean square error (RMSE). Mean average error, also known as MAE refers to the average error calculated from the predicted and the originally known values as shown in Eq. 1.

$$MAE = \frac{1}{n}\sum |y - \hat{y}| \tag{1}$$

Mean square error, also known as MSE [15] is the error calculated by finding the mean square of difference obtained from the predicted and the actual value calculated using Eq. 2.

$$MSE = \frac{1}{n}\sum (y - \hat{y})^2 \tag{2}$$

Root means square error, also known as RMSE [14] is considered best over calculating MAE and MSE when there are chances of some large errors. It is calculated by finding the square root of MSE as shown in Eq. 3. RMSE provides a higher weight or value to large errors as it considers the square of predicted and actual values.

$$RMSE = \sqrt{MSE}$$

$$RMSE = \sqrt{\frac{1}{n}\sum (y - \hat{y})^2} \tag{3}$$

Table 2 shows the tabular representations of the results obtained i.e., accuracy, roc score, RMSE, MSE, and MAE scores obtained by implementing different models and algorithms. It also shows the comparison of all the models/algorithms implemented to predict the relationship between the hypothesis and premise.

Table 2. Results obtained

S. No	Model	Accuracy (%)	MAE	MSE	RMSE	AUC		
						Label: 0	Label: 1	Label: 2
1	BiLSTM	86.31	0.1676	0.2290	0.4785	0.8934	0.8976	0.9109
2	CBOW	80.23	0.2472	0.3463	0.5885	0.8617	0.8407	0.8578
3	ESIM	88.63	0.1365	0.1821	0.4267	0.9096	0.9161	0.9285
4	XLM-RoBERTa	95.53	0.0508	0.0594	0.2437	0.9629	0.9706	0.9797

5 Conclusion

The paper proposes a detailed description of the overall proposed model using the XLM-RoBERTa model [18] to predict labels of multilingual toxic comments. The paper also discusses the datasets used for training and testing the proposed model. After training the model, the paper shows the results acquired by the model on testing the dataset on various models and algorithms. Upon testing, the proposed model acquired an accuracy of 95.35% with a ROC score of 0.9629 for the entailment relationship, 0.97076 for the neutral relationships, and 0.9797 for the contradictory relationships outperforming all the exiting models/algorithms. Further, for future more such models and algorithms can be used to identify the relationship between hypothesis and premise given two statements using NLI.

References

1. Fuchs, C.: Social media: A critical introduction. SAGE publications Limited (2021)
2. Arbieu, U., Helsper, K., Dadvar, M., Mueller, T., Niamir, A.: Natural language processing as a tool to evaluate emotions in conservation conflicts. Biol. Cons. **256**, 109030 (2021)
3. Zhang, K., et al.: Multilevel image-enhanced sentence representation net for natural language inference. IEEE Trans. Syst. Man Cybern. Syst. **51**(6), 3781–3795 (2019)
4. Li, Z., Ding, X., Liu, T.: TransBERT: a three-stage pre-training technology for story-ending prediction. ACM Trans. Asian Low-Resour. Lang. Inf. Process. (TALLIP) **20**(1), 1–20 (2021)
5. Saeed, H.H., Ashraf, M.H., Kamiran, F., Karim, A., Calders, T.: Roman Urdu toxic comment classification. Lang. Resour. Eval. **55**(4), 971–996 (2021). https://doi.org/10.1007/s10579-021-09530-y
6. Lees, A., Sorensen, J., Kivlichan, I.: Jigsaw@ AMI and HaSpeeDe2: Fine-Tuning a Pre-Trained Comment-Domain BERT Model. In: Proceedings of Seventh Evaluation Campaign of Natural Language Processing and Speech Tools for Italian. Final Workshop (EVALITA 2020), Bologna, Italy (2020). http://ceur.org
7. Nie, Y., Wang, Y., Bansal, M.: Analyzing compositionality-sensitivity of NLI models. In: Proceedings of the AAAI Conference on Artificial Intelligence, vol. 33, No. 01, pp. 6867–6874, July 2019
8. Du, Q., Zong, C., Su, K.Y.: Conducting natural language inference with word-pair-dependency and local context. ACM Trans. Asian Low-Resour. Lang. Inf. Process. (TALLIP) **19**(3), 1–23 (2020)
9. Guo, M., Zhang, Y., Liu, T.: Gaussian transformer: a lightweight approach for natural language inference. In: Proceedings of the AAAI Conference on Artificial Intelligence, vol. 33, no. 01, pp. 6489–6496, July 2019
10. Naik, A., Ravichander, A., Sadeh, N., Rose, C., Neubig, G.: Stress test evaluation for natural language inference (2018). arXiv preprint arXiv:1806.00692
11. Poliak, A., et al.: Collecting diverse natural language inference problems for sentence representation evaluation (2018). arXiv preprint arXiv:1804.08207
12. Schmidt, A., Wiegand, M.: A survey on hate speech detection using natural language processing. In: Proceedings of the Fifth International Workshop on Natural Language Processing for Social Media, pp. 1–10, April 2017
13. Chen, Q., Zhu, X., Ling, Z., Wei, S., Jiang, H., Inkpen, D.: Enhanced lstm for natural language inference (2016). arXiv preprint arXiv:1609.06038
14. Parikh, A.P., Täckström, O., Das, D., Uszkoreit, J. A decomposable attention model for natural language inference (2016). arXiv preprint arXiv:1606.01933

15. Tanana, M.J., et al.: How do you feel? Using natural language processing to automatically rate emotion in psychotherapy. Behav. Res. Methods **53**(5), 2069–2082 (2021). https://doi.org/10.3758/s13428-020-01531-z
16. Stewart, R., Velupillai, S.: Applied natural language processing in mental health big data. Neuropsychopharmacology **46**(1), 252–253 (2021)
17. Sabarmathi, K.R., Gowthami, K., Kumar, S.S.: Fake news detection using machine learning and Natural Language Inference (NLI). In: IOP Conference Series: Materials Science and Engineering, vol. 1084, No. 1, p. 012018. IOP Publishing (2021)
18. Abzianidze, L.: Solving textual entailment with the theorem prover for natural language. AMIM **25**(2), 114–136 (2020)
19. Pathak, A., Manna, R., Pakray, P., Das, D., Gelbukh, A., Bandyopadhyay, S.: Scientific text entailment and a textual-entailment-based framework for cooking domain question answering. Sādhanā **46**(1), 1–19 (2021). https://doi.org/10.1007/s12046-021-01557-9
20. Zhao, R., Yongquan, Y., Zeng, T.: The identification of main contradictory information. In: Wei, L., Cai, G., Liu, W., Xing, W. (eds.) Proceedings of the 2012 International Conference on Information Technology and Software Engineering, pp. 945–953. Springer Berlin Heidelberg, Berlin, Heidelberg (2013). https://doi.org/10.1007/978-3-642-34522-7_99
21. Sai, S., Jacob, A.W., Kalra, S., Sharma, Y.: Stacked embeddings and multiple fine-tuned XLM-roBERTa models for enhanced hostility identification. In: Chakraborty, T., Shu, K., Bernard, H.R., Liu, H., Akhtar, M.S. (eds.) Combating Online Hostile Posts in Regional Languages during Emergency Situation. CCIS, vol. 1402, pp. 224–235. Springer, Cham (2021). https://doi.org/10.1007/978-3-030-73696-5_21
22. Macková, K., Straka, M.: Reading comprehension in Czech via machine translation and cross-lingual transfer. In: Sojka, P., Kopeček, I., Pala, K., Horák, A. (eds.) Text, Speech, and Dialogue. LNCS (LNAI), vol. 12284, pp. 171–179. Springer, Cham (2020). https://doi.org/10.1007/978-3-030-58323-1_18
23. Jain, N., et al.: Prediction modelling of COVID using machine learning methods from B-cell dataset. Results in Physics **21**, 103813 (2021)
24. Sameer, M., Gupta, B.: ROC analysis of EEG subbands for epileptic seizure detection using Naïve Bayes classifier. J. Mob. Multimed. 299–310 (2021)
25. Bunn, C., et al.: Application of machine learning to the prediction of postoperative sepsis after appendectomy. Surgery **169**(3), 671–677 (2021)

Data Poisoning Attack by Label Flipping on SplitFed Learning

Saurabh Gajbhiye[1]([✉]) [iD], Priyanka Singh[2] [iD], and Shaifu Gupta[1] [iD]

[1] Indian Institute of Technology Jammu, Nagrota, India
{2020pcs2028,shaifu.gupta}@iitjammu.ac.in
[2] Dhirubhai Ambani Institute of Information and Communication Technology,
Gandhinagar, India
priyanka_singh@daiict.ac.in

Abstract. In the distributed machine learning scenario, we have Split Learning (SL) and Federated Learning (FL) as the popular techniques. In SL, the model is split between the clients and the server for sequential training of clients, whereas in FL, clients train parallelly. The model splitting in SL provides better overall privacy than FL. SplitFed learning (SFL) combines these two popular techniques to incorporate the model splitting approach from SL to improve privacy and utilize the generic FL approach for faster training. Despite the advantages, the distributed nature of SFL makes it vulnerable to data poisoning attacks by malicious participants. This vulnerability prompted us to study the robustness of SFL under such attacks. The outcomes of this study would provide valuable insights to organizations and researchers who wish to deploy or study SFL. In this paper, we conduct three experiments. Our first experiment demonstrates that data poisoning attacks seriously threaten SFL systems. Even the presence of 10% malicious participants can cause a drastic drop in the accuracy of the global model. We further perform a second experiment to study the robustness of two variants of SFL under the category of targeted data poisoning attacks. The results of experiment two demonstrate that SFLV1 is more robust than SFLV2 the majority of times. In our third experiment, we studied untargeted data poisoning attacks on SFL. We found that untargeted attacks cause a more significant loss in the global model's accuracy than targeted attacks.

Keywords: SplitFed Learning · Federated Learning · Adversarial machine learning · Label flipping · Data poisoning

1 Introduction

Machine learning (ML) has become an inseparable part of most of the companies, be it big tech giants like Amazon, Google, Facebook, and Microsoft, or small-scale startups. ML models are employed almost everywhere, in trivial problems like product recommendation systems, movie rating platforms or complex problems like forecasting prices of stocks, natural gas price prediction, etc.

© The Author(s), under exclusive license to Springer Nature Switzerland AG 2023
KC Santosh et al. (Eds.): RTIP2R 2022, CCIS 1704, pp. 391–405, 2023.
https://doi.org/10.1007/978-3-031-23599-3_30

These models demand vast amounts of data that is fetched either by combining multiple data repositories or exploiting public crowd-sourcing platforms. This raises alarms to the reliability of data that is used to train these models and hence poses questions to the achieved performance accuracy. Injection of corrupted or poisoned data can badly affect these models and pave the way to misleading results. Another aspect to training these ML models is the privacy concerns for the shared data [1,2]. This may work as an inhibiting factor for applications dealing with crucial data that may involve sharing medical histories, military documents, or finance centric problems. Recently, various distributed learning frameworks are proposed to enable participation of thousands of people and collaboratively train a deep learning model.

Federated Learning (FL) [3] is one such approach, where the training is distributed among a set of clients and a central server. The entire training process is done in multiple rounds where each round consists of the following: sampling of clients, sharing of global model with the sampled clients, training of the received model at the client's end using their local training data and sending back the model updates to the central server. Thereafter, the aggregation of the updates happens at the central server to obtain the updated model. This process continues until the global model achieves the desired accuracy. From machine learning predominantly neural networks are used in federated learning procedure. But there are some pitfalls of FL, for instance, computational requirement at the client-side to run the full ML model during training. Also, if an adversary compromises any client or the server, then it can access the entire model [5]. This raises privacy concerns. To address these shortcomings, Split Learning (SL) [4] was introduced.

SL splits the entire model into smaller networks, contrary to FL. The smaller networks can be trained separately on distributed clients with local training data. This significantly reduces the computational needs at client-side in comparison to a client-side computational requirement during the training as per FL procedure. This is a big advantage for the resource constrained devices like mobile phones and edge devices. Moreover, it improves upon the security of the model, even if an attacker compromises a client, it cannot get hold of the entire model. However there is a downside to these independent small networks in terms of training time of the model. At one instance, only one participant is engaged in training with the server while other participants remain idle waiting for their turn. This causes significant training time overhead as the number of training participants increase. To address the issues of SL and FL, another distributed model called SplitFed Learning (SFL) [6] was proposed.

In SplitFed learning, the parallel federated training procedure of FL is merged with the model splitting nature of the SL. It aims to provide better privacy than FL while being faster than SL. There are two variants of SFL: SFLV1 [6] and SFLV2 [6]. Consider a scenario where some malicious participants are involved in training the model. These malicious participants can train the model on the poisoned data and send the updates to the server-side model. SFL has no control over the training data of participants and there is no way for the aggregator to detect the malicious participants. This makes SFL vulnerable to data poisoning attack.

Data poisoning attacks are broadly classified into two types clean label attacks [7] and dirty-label attacks [8]. In clean label attack the attacker does not tamper with the labels of the training data. The poisoning is done by injecting tampered data in the training dataset. Whereas in dirty label attack the attacker manipulates the labels of training data. The data poising attack can be targeted [9–11] or untargeted [12,13] in nature. In the targeted attacks the focuse of attacker is on manipulating the behaviour of model for a specific target class on the other hand while performing untargeted attack the attacker can target multiple classes. Label flipping attack [14] in an example of dirty-label attack where an attacker flips the labels of training data.

In this paper, we focus on studying the robustness of SFL against the targeted and untargeted data poisoning attacks. We assume that the adversary has control only over the training data of the compromised clients. With such constraint in mind, it becomes easier for a novice attacker to formulate a targeted label flipping attack or a untargeted label flipping attack. Specifically, we focused on the following:

- There are studies conducted on the effects of data poisoning attacks on FL [14], but there is a lack of such studies relating to SFL. We wish to bridge this gap in our paper.
- We demonstrate empirically through experiments that SFL is prone to the targeted data poisoning attacks during the training procedure. We observe that the effectiveness of the threat is dataset dependent.
- We analyze the robustness of SFLV1 and SFLV2. Our empirical data from the experiments 1 and 2 show that SFLV1 is more robust than SFLV2 for majority of the scenarios.
- We also study the performance of untargeted data poisoning attacks on SFL. Through our empirical data, we observe that untargeted attacks cause a higher drop in model accuracy compared to targeted data poisoning attacks. Hence, untargeted attacks are a serious threat to SFL training procedure.

2   Background Work

In this section, we briefly give an overview of SplitFed learning. SFL is based on integrating the SL and FL models to give a better model. In SL, the biggest advantage is of model splitting between the server-side and the client-side. On the other hand, FL's strength lies in the parallel processing of the clients in the distributed setting. Both the aforementioned characteristics are combined in SFL. Several variants of SFL are proposed thereafter, but for our experimentation we consider the SFLV1 and SFLV2 which are based on server-side aggregation. In SFL, the client can be resource-constrained while the main server must have high computational capabilities. The client-side local updates will be passed to the fed server, where FedAvg [3] will be computed for the collected client updates during each global epoch. The computation of FedAvg is not computationally intensive.

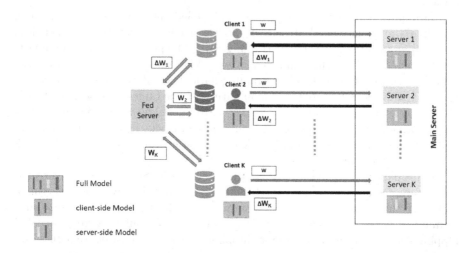

Fig. 1. Overview of SFLV1 learning system model.

2.1 SFLV1 Workflow

An overview of SFLV1 is shown in Fig. 1. All the clients from client 1 to client k undergo forward propagation on their client-side local networks. Thereafter, the smashed data of each client is passed to the main server. Smashed data are the weights generated when the training data is passed through client-side network. Forward and back-propagation are performed on the server-side network of each client in parallel, by processing the smashed data of each client. The gradients generated on the server-side network are then sent back to the clients so that each client can complete its back-propagation.After sending the gradients to clients, the main server does the FedAvg on the gradients generated during the back-propagation on the server-side. In the next epoch, the computed FedAvg acts as the updated weights for the server-side network. Each client completes its back-propagation on the client-side local network after receiving gradients from the main server. The local updates generated by each client are sent to the fed server, where FedAvg is computed. This newly computed FedAvg acts as the updated weights for each client in the next epoch.

2.2 SFLV2 Workflow

An overview of SFLV2 is shown in Fig. 2. In this version, the model aggregation on the server-side is dropped. A set of clients are selected in random order and forward propagation and back-propagation are performed on each client's smashed data sequentially. The server-side network gets updated while

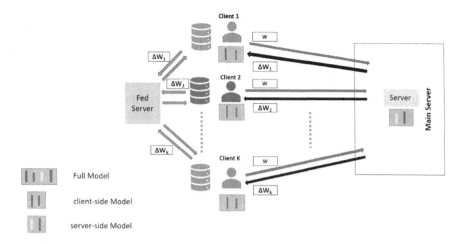

Fig. 2. Overview of SFLV2 learning system.

processing each client's smashed data. The smashed data of all the clients is received by the server-side synchronously. The procedure on the client-side remains unchanged. The fed server is the entity which does the FedAvg on the local updates received from the clients. The order of clients does not affect the operation of fed server as the aggregation is done by FedAvg.

3 System Model

In this section, we discuss the basic assumptions and the main entities of the considered system.

3.1 Threat Model

In the SFL setting, we have four main entities: the client, the FedServer, the Main-server, and the adversary. The role of each of these actors is briefed as follows:

- Client: The role of the client is to participate in the training process, where it will start training with its respective server-side network. Once the client has finished its training procedure, it will send updated weights to the FedServer.
- FedServer: During each global epoch, the FedServer receives the updated weights from the participants. The received weights are aggregated as per FedAvg algorithm. These aggregated weights will be used as the starting weights for participants in the following round.
- MainServer: In SFLV1, the MainSever needs to create a parallel server-side copy for every client-side network during the training. In the case of SFLV2 will only create a single copy of the server-side network. The participants will

work with the server-side network to train the model. The MainServer will require higher computational capacity if the number of participants in SFLV1 is more.

- Adversary/Attacker: The attacker will compromise the participants or inject the already compromised participants or incentivize benign participants to act maliciously. It will poison the training data of the compromised participants. The adversary will act maliciously and conducts a data poisoning attack on the SFL training process.

3.2 Assumptions in the Model Setting

Attacker's Capability. The attack done by the adversary is independent of any loss function, optimization function, and the deep neural network (DNN) architecture used in SFL. The malicious client cannot manipulate the other clients learning processes, e.g., optimization algorithm, aggregation process of FedServer and main server, and loss function. Neither can it manipulate the training data of other clients. It can only manipulate its own training data.

Attacker's Goal. The attacker's goal is to make a targeted data poisoning attack that only causes the global model to have high error rates for a specific target class. In order to achieve this goal the attacker will consider targeted label flipping attack. In this attack the attacker manipulates the training data of the compromised client by flipping the labels of the training data. This is contrary to untargeted attacks that brings down the accuracy of the overall global model across all classes. The targeted attacks are more stealthy and more challenging to detect than the untargeted data poisoning attack.

4   Experimental Setup

In this section we will discuss the assumptions and the constraints considered by us while conducting our experiments.

4.1   Datasets and DNN Architecture Setup

To conduct the experiments, we have used two popular benchmarking datasets, CIFAR10 [15] and MNIST [16]. The CIFAR10 consists of 10 object classes such as ship, deer, bird, and airplane. There are 60000 images in total, with 6000 images per class. These images are divided into 50,000 training images and 10,000 testing images. The size of these images is 32×32 pixels.

The MNIST dataset contains images of handwritten digits. These images are of size 28×28 pixels and are grayscale in nature. A total of 6000 training images are present in the dataset, and for testing, there are 10000 images. While using CIFAR10 for experiments, we utilize ResNet18 [18] which has 18 layers with kernel size (7×7), (3×3), and for experiments based on MNIST, we utilize

LeNet [19] having five layers with kernel size (5×5), (2×2). For both SFLV1 and SFLV2 experiments, the network layers are split. In the case of ResNet, split is done at the third layer (after 2D BatchNormalization layer), and for the LeNet split is done at second layer (after the 2D MaxPool layer).

4.2 SplitFed Setup

In the experiments, the global epoch limit for the model convergence was set to 200. The total number of participants in the entire SFL process was set to 50. For each global epoch, we randomly sample 5 participants out of 50 available participants and each of these participants complete 1 local epoch. The training data is independent and identically distributed (IID). Every participant receives a unique subset of training data. SFL is implemented using Pytorch [17] library in Python. The testing data is only used for model evaluation, it is not a part of participants' training data.

4.3 Label Flipping

Label flipping attack is the most common attack in FL [14,20] and centralized machine learning procedure [21–24]. The adversary utilizes label flipping to implement the targeted data poisoning attack, allowing the attacker to manipulate the training data by flipping it's label. The attack was effective in the FL scenario even when less than 10% of the clients where compromised by the attacker [14]. Hence this attack becomes suitable for SFL since it fulfills all the adversarial objectives and capabilities. Moreover, it is easier for the non-expert attacker to carry out the attack since it does not require the adversary to know SFL's internal working, loss function, underlying DNN architecture, etc. The attacker does not need to modify or alter the internal SFL process, only the training data of the malicious participants will be tampered.

Out of all the available classes in the dataset, the attacker selects a source class and target class. The goal is to compel the global model to misclassify the source class as the target class. Each malicious client will modify it's training data by changing all instances of source class labels to target class labels. For example in MNIST image classification, if the source class is 0 and target class is 1, each malicious participant will poison it's training data by mislabelling all the images of class 0 as 1. This process of mislabelling is called label-flipping. For the label flipping attack we consider that out of the 50 participants, m% are malicious, and the rest are honest. To evaluate the experiments, we use the accuracy of the global model and class recall as the metrics.

Global Model Accuracy ($M_{accuracy}$): Let D_t be the testing dataset. M_{200} is the global model after 200 rounds of training. $M_{accuracy}$ is the percentage of instances $y \in D_t$ for which M_{200} predicts its class as C and C is actual true label of y.

Class Recall (c_{recall}): For any class C, the recall is calculated as follows:

$$\frac{TruePositive_c}{TruePositive_c + FalseNegative_c} \times 100 \tag{1}$$

where $TruePostive_c$ and $FalseNegative_c$ indicates the number of instances of class C for which the global model correctly predicted them as C and incorrectly predicted them as not equal to C.

The baseline accuracy of SFLV1 and SFLV2 on CIFAR-10 without any poisoning is 77.29% and 76.16%, and for MNIST, it is 98.8% and 98.67% respectively. Likewise, the baseline class recall for CIFAR-10 without any poisoning on SFLV1 and SFLV2 is 76.1% and 75.96%, and for MNIST, it is 98.4% and 98.26%.

5   Analysis of Label Flipping Attack on SFL

For analysis of label flipping attack on SFL we conducted three experiments. We will discuss these experiments in this section.

5.1   Experiment 1: Targeted Data Poisoning Attack on SFL

Aim of this experiment is to study the fall of global model's accuracy when the targeted data poisoning attack is performed. To better understand how this experiment was done, we explain a experimental scenario where $m\% = 10$ and SFLV1 is paired with MNIST. A similar flow will be followed for SFLV2 as well.

Experiment 1 Scenario. Fixed parameters or constraints considered for this scenario were MNIST dataset, LeNet5 model, 200 global epochs of training, malicious participants $m\% = 10\%$ and a total of 50 participants. The distribution of training data was done in IID fashion amongst the participants. Malicious participants will undergo label flipping attack. For each global round 5 clients are randomly sampled out of 50 participants. Since the clients are randomly selected the appearance of malicious clients can vary in each round.

Flow of experiment 1:

1. We set the $m\%$, if the $m\% = 10$ then a total of 5 participants will be malicious out of 50, while the remaining 45 will be honest participants.
2. Repeat the below steps 10 times:
   (a) We repeat the below steps for 200 epochs:

       i. Randomly sample 5 participants to take part in SFLV1 training process.

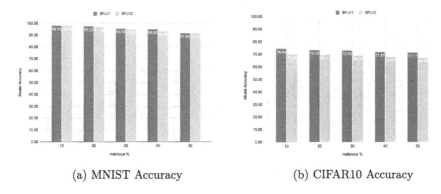

(a) MNIST Accuracy   (b) CIFAR10 Accuracy

Fig. 3. Effectiveness of attack on global model accuracy with varying number of malicious clients. For MNIST experiments source class is 4 and target class is 9, in case of CIFAR-10 source class is deer and target class is truck.

    ii. The first set of participants will start their training procedure with the random initial weights, while the rest of the participants will receive the starting weights from FedServer. The participants train for one local epoch with their respective server-side copies as per SFLV1 procedure.

    iii. Participants send the newly generated updates to the FedServer.

    iv. FedServer aggregates the update received from the participants, and it will send the aggregated weights as the starting weights to the next set of participants.

  (b) We note down the reading of the Model accuracy and the class recall after 200 global epochs are completed for SFLV1.

3. Report the average of 10 readings.

Attack Strategy. We record our results by doing the above procedure for different values of $m\%$ varying from 10% to 50%. The SFL version, dataset and ML model are changed. We report the average of 10 readings to accommodate the random appearance of malicious participants.

Attack Findings. The feasibility of the attack on the final global model with a varying percentage of malicious participants from 10% to 50% is shown in Fig. 3. It is observed that in both the datasets as the number of malicious participants in the training process increases the global model accuracy (test accuracy) decreases.

The impact of malicious participants on the class recall of the source class can be observed in Fig. 4. Here we see that as the number of malicious participants increases the source recall also decreases in the case of both the datasets. Attack shows stealth, for $m = 10\%$ we see a smaller decrease in model accuracy in Fig. 3 and an even larger reduction in class recall as seen in Fig. 4. So it justifies that

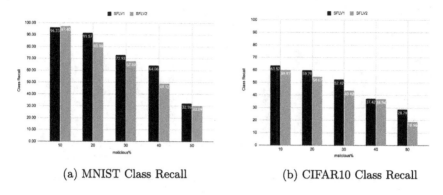

(a) MNIST Class Recall   (b) CIFAR10 Class Recall

Fig. 4. Impact of varying number of malicious clients on the class recall under Experiment 1 setting

Table 1. Class Recall fall % compared to baseline in CIFAR10

SFL version	Malicious participants percentage ($m\%$)				
	10	20	30	40	50
CIFAR-10					
SFLV1	12.58%	16.31%	23.68%	38.68%	47.31%
SFLV2	15.99%	21.29%	32.14%	39.02%	57%

even if the adversary has control of a smaller percentage of malicious clients involved in the training process, it can still cause a substantial effect on the source class. Table 1 and Table 2 shows us how by many percentages the class recall dropped with respect to baseline. Each drop percentage is averaged over 10 readings. The vulnerability of the dataset with respect to attack can be studied from Table 1 and Table 2. We see that CIFAR-10 is much more vulnerable to attack than MNIST. The class recall drop percentage for CIFAR-10 is much higher than the MNIST majority of the time. Therefore we can say that the effect of attack would vary across different datasets.

The robustness between the two versions of SFL also becomes clear in Table 1 and Table 2. We see that the SFLV2 suffered a higher class recall drop compared to SFLV1 in both the datasets majority of the time. This suggests that SFLV1 is more robust against the label flipping attack. From an attacker's point of view, the label flipping attack will be more successful and would cause severe effects on model accuracy if the underlying structure follows SFLV2. The insights into the robustness of two versions of SFL would aid the organization determine the right version for their use case.

The trend of the robustness of SFLV1 is also seen in Fig. 3a. where we see that SFLV2 suffered more and has lower model accuracy. This becomes much more clear in Fig. 3b in the case of CIFAR-10, where the difference between the robustness is much clearer. Since CIFAR-10 is more vulnerable to attack than MNIST.

Table 2. Class Recall fall % compared to baseline in MNIST

SFL version	Malicious participants percentage ($m\%$)				
	10	20	30	40	50
MNIST					
SFLV1	2.17%	6.83%	25.47%	34.34%	66.24%
SFLV2	0.86%	14.68%	30.67%	49.14%	68.87%

5.2 Experiment 2: Robustness of SFL Against Targeted Data Poisoning Attacks

To better compare the robustness of the different versions of SFL against the targeted data poisoning attacks, we decided to conduct an experiment where all the parameters will be identical. The only difference will be in the training procedure one will follow the SFLV1, and the other will follow SFLV2. To better understand how this experiment is conducted, we demonstrate below the process for one scenario in the case of SFLV1 and SFLV2 paired with the MNIST dataset where $m\% = 10$.

Experiment 2 Scenario. We want the appearance of malicious participants to be identical in every round of experimental reading of SFLV1 and SFLV2 to make a fair robustness comparison. We will consider the fixed parameters from Experiment 1 scenario and extend it with additional constraints. Participants Starting weights will be kept the same in each experimental reading of SFLV1 and SFLV2. The data distribution between clients will also be identical for SFLV1 and SFLV2. The final accuracy of the SFLV1 and SFLV2 experiments will be tested on identical testing data.

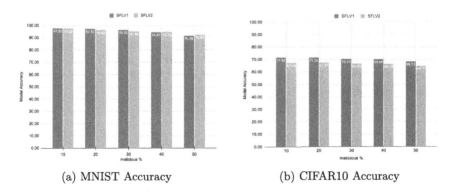

(a) MNIST Accuracy   (b) CIFAR10 Accuracy

Fig. 5. Effectiveness of attack on global model accuracy under Experiment 2 setting.

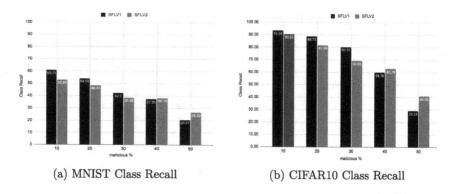

(a) MNIST Class Recall   (b) CIFAR10 Class Recall

Fig. 6. Impact of varying number of malicious clients on the class recall under Experiment 2 setting

Flow of Experiment 2:

1. We set the $m\%$, if the $m\% = 10$ then a total of 5 participants will be malicious out of 50, while rest of the 45 will be honest participants.
2. Repeat the below steps 10 times:
   (a) We repeat the below steps for 200 epochs:
      i Randomly sample 5 participants to take part in the training process. The same set of participants is sampled for SFLV1 and SFLV2. The SFLV1 and SFLV2 will have the same clients in identical order.
      ii The participant's starting weights will be the same for SFLV1 and SFLV2. The only difference is that participants of SFLV1 will follow the SFLV1 training procedure. The participants of SFLV2 will follow the SFLV2 training procedure.
      iii Participants send the newly generated updates to the FedServer.
      iv FedServer aggregates the updated weights received from the participants, and it will send the aggregated weights as the starting weights to the next set of participants.
   (b) We note down the reading of the Model accuracy and the class recall after 200 global epochs are completed for both SFLV1 and SFLV2.
3. Report the average of 10 readings taken for SFLV1. Similarly, we will report the average of 10 readings taken for SFLV2.

Attack Strategy. Repeat the above procedure for the varying value of $m\%$ from 10% to 50%. Conduct the experiment with different dataset, SFL version and ML model. Record the observation by taking the average of 10 readings.

Attack Findings. Under this attack setting, in Fig. 5 we see that as the number of malicious participants increases the model accuracy decreases. Analogous to the trend in experiment 1 we see that majority of the time the accuracy of the

SFLV1 was higher than the SFLV2 suggesting that the SFLV2 suffered more under the attack across both datasets. In Fig. 6a and Fig. 6b we see that the class recall of the source class gives a little higher accuracy for SFLV2 when the number of malicious participants is more than 40%. In a more realistic scenario, the attacker will only be able to compromise 10–20% of the total participants in the SFL training process. This suggests us to say that SFLV1 will act more robustly in the majority of realistic scenarios.

5.3   Experiment 3: Untargeted Attack on the SFL

Here we assumed that the primary objective of the attacker is to bring down the global model. In such a scenario, we assume that the adversary will poison the entire training dataset of compromised clients. This experiment was done similar to the experiment 1, with only difference being that the malicious clients have all of their training data poisoned. In order to poison the entire training data, we assume that the adversary will randomly mislabel all classes present in the training data.

Attack Strategy. The central focus of our study in experiment 1 and experiment 2 concentrated on the targeted data poisoning attack due to its stealthy nature, but for an attacker whose primary objective is to bring down the accuracy of the global model, the targeted data poisoning does not serve the purpose. In that scenario, the adversary will favor untargeted data poisoning. In untargeted data poisoning, the attacker has the flexibility of poisoning multiple classes by mislabeling them. We performed our experiments with a varying number of malicious participants. The number of malicious participants out of the total participants is varied from $m = 10\%$ to 50%. We recorded our reading by changing datasets, SFL version and ML models. We report average of 10 readings.

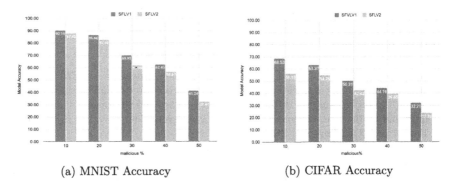

(a) MNIST Accuracy   (b) CIFAR Accuracy

Fig. 7. Effectiveness of untargeted data poisoning attack on global model accuracy

Attack Findings. We observed that the damage done by this attack is significantly more than that of the targeted attack. This can be seen in Fig. 7 where for both the datasets the global model accuracy of SFLV1 and SFLV2 is lower in all the $m\%$ cases compared to the targeted attack in Fig. 3.

We see that in the case of MNIST, for targeted data poisoning attack in Fig. 3a global model accuracy for $m = 10\%$ is 98.10% and 98.12%, whereas in the case of untargeted attack in Fig. 7a it is 90.16% and 87.85%. This shows that the attacker can do substantial damage to the model accuracy even with a small number of malicious clients. The untargeted attack is a serious threat due to its effectiveness. It is also followed that model accuracy was lower for the SFLV2 than SFLV1 in Fig. 7 which suggest SFLV2 suffered more damage as compared to the SFLV1.

6   Conclusion

In this paper, our major focus was to study the impact of the data poisoning attack against SFL systems. In our experiments, we found that both SFLV1 and SFLV2 are vulnerable to the label flipping attack. These label flipping attacks can significantly reduce the accuracy of the global model. Based on the experiments, we found that SFLV1 is more robust compared to SFLV2 for majority of the times. In SFLV1 due to the presence of multiple server-side networks which are trained parallelly the poisoning is less as opposed to SFLV2 where the a single server-side newtork is trained sequentially. This understanding will allow decision-makers to choose the right version of SFL. We also found that for the attacker, it is possible to do more damage in the untargeted data poisoning scenario compared to targeted one. In the future, we plan to continue the work by checking the impact of other kinds of attacks such as inference attacks, model poisoning attacks, backdoor attacks etc. on the SFLV1 and SFLV2. Also, we want to work on finding new strategies to strengthen the SFL process against the variety of possible attacks.

References

1. Mathews, K., Bowman, C.: The California consumer privacy act of (2018)
2. Regulation, G.D.P.: Regulation of the European parliament and of the council of 27: on the protection of natural persons with regard to the processing of personal data and on the free movement of such data, and repealing directive 95/46. Off. J. Eur. Union (OJ) **59**(1–88), 294 (2016)
3. McMahan, B., Moore, E., Ramage, D., Hampson, S., Arcas, B.: Communication-efficient learning of deep networks from decentralized data. In: Proceedings Of the 20th International Conference on Artificial Intelligence and Statistics, vol. 54, pp. 1273–1282 (2017)
4. Vepakomma, P., Gupta, O., Swedish, T., Raskar, R.: Split learning for health: distributed deep learning without sharing raw patient data. CoRR. abs/1812.00564 (2018)

5. Bouacida, N., Mohapatra, P.: Vulnerabilities in federated learning. IEEE Access **9**, 63229–63249 (2021)
6. Thapa, C., Chamikara, M., Camtepe, S, Sun, L.: Splitfed: when federated learning meets split learning. ArXiv Preprint ArXiv:2004.12088 (2020)
7. Shafahi, A., et al.: Poison frogs! targeted clean-label poisoning attacks on neural networks. Adv. Neural Inf. Process. Syst. **31** (2018)
8. Chen, X., Liu, C., Li, B., Lu, K., Song, D.: Targeted backdoor attacks on deep learning systems using data poisoning. ArXiv Preprint ArXiv:1712.05526 (2017)
9. Biggio, B., Nelson, B., Laskov, P.: Poisoning attacks against support vector machines. ArXiv Preprint ArXiv:1206.6389 (2012)
10. Chen, X., Liu, C., Li, B., Lu, K., Song, D.: Targeted backdoor attacks on deep learning systems using data poisoning. ArXiv Preprint ArXiv:1712.05526 (2017)
11. Koh, P., Liang, P.: Understanding black-box predictions via influence functions. In: International Conference on Machine Learning, pp. 1885–1894 (2017)
12. Liu, Y., et al.: Trojaning attack on neural networks (2017)
13. Bagdasaryan, E., Veit, A., Hua, Y., Estrin, D., Shmatikov, V.: How to backdoor federated learning. In: International Conference on Artificial Intelligence and Statistics, pp. 2938–2948 (2020)
14. Tolpegin, V., Truex, S., Gursoy, M., Liu, L.: Data poisoning attacks against federated learning systems. In: European Symposium on Research in Computer Security, pp. 480–501 (2020)
15. Krizhevsky, A., Nair, V., Hinton, G.: CIFAR-10 (Canadian Institute for Advanced Research). http://www.cs.toronto.edu/kriz/cifar.html
16. LeCun, Y., Cortes, C.: MNIST handwritten digit database (2010). http://yann.lecun.com/exdb/mnist/
17. Paszke, A., et al.: PyTorch: an imperative style, high-performance deep learning library. Adv. Neural Inf. Process. Syst. **32**, 8024–8035 (2019)
18. He, K., Zhang, X., Ren, S., Sun, J.: Deep residual learning for image recognition. In: Proceedings of the IEEE Conference on Computer Vision and Pattern Recognition, pp. 770–778 (2016)
19. LeCun, Y., et al.: LeNet-5, convolutional neural networks. http://yann.Lecun.Com/exdb/lenet 20, 14 (2015)
20. Li, D., Wong, W., Wang, W., Yao, Y., Chau, M.: Detection and mitigation of label-flipping attacks in federated learning systems with KPCA and K-Means. In: 2021 8th International Conference on Dependable Systems and their Applications (DSA), pp. 551–559 (2021)
21. Shen, S., Tople, S., Saxena, P.: AUROR: defending against poisoning attacks in collaborative deep learning systems. In: Proceedings of the 32nd Annual Conference on Computer Security Applications, pp. 508–519 (2016)
22. Steinhardt, J., Koh, P., Liang, P.: Certified defenses for data poisoning attacks. Adv. Neural Inf. Process. Syst. **30** (2017)
23. Xiao, H., Xiao, H., Eckert, C.: Adversarial label flips attack on support vector machines. ECAI **2012**, 870–875 (2012)
24. Xiao, H., Biggio, B., Nelson, B., Xiao, H., Eckert, C., Roli, F.: Support vector machines under adversarial label contamination. Neurocomputing **160**, 53–62 (2015)

A Deep Learning-Powered Voice-Enabled Math Tutor for Kids

Arnab Banerjee[1,2](✉), Srijoy Paul[1], Tisu Priya[1], Anamika Rohit[1],
and Nibaran Das[2]

[1] Dr. B. C. Roy Polytechnic, Durgapur 713206, West Bengal, India
`researchwork.arnab@gmail.com`
[2] Jadavpur University, Kolkata 700032, West Bengal, India
`nibaran.das@jadavpuruniversity.in`

Abstract. In this study, a voice enabled math tutor system is proposed
that enables children to practice math problems on their own. For this,
we have developed numerical sound dataset targeting the application.
In the application, when the system is turned on, a math problem is
generated, and the child will respond verbally to it. The system will
categorize the audio data (user-provided answer) and produce a text
number, which will then be further analysed and generate output as
either a correct or erroneous answer. Any toy can be equipped with the
proposed system, allowing a kid to practice problems while engaging
with the system. A dataset named JUDVLP-BCRP: numeralSound.v1
is prepared, with 2315 audio data of numerals in the range of 0 to 9. In
a typical setting, the audio data were collected from people in the age
range of 10 to 60 from West Bengal, Jharkhand, Delhi, Assam, Bihar,
and Orissa. After pre-processing the audios, Mel spectrograms were produced which acts as input by the deep neural network algorithms. The
audio data has been classified using a number of well-known deep learning algorithms, including DenseNet-121, VGG-16, modified DenseNet121
(DenseNet-41), and modified VGG-16 (VGG-12). Using DenseNet-121,
VGG-16, DenseNet-41, VGG-12, 94.60%, 98.70%, 98.27%, and 98.48%
accuracy was obtained. The networks were run for 100 epochs using a
learning rate of 0.0001, and categorical cross-entropy loss function. The
VGG-16 produced the highest precision of 98.9%, and the VGG-12 produced the second-best precision of 98.6%. The outcomes are positive and
influence a workable system design.

Keywords: Sound classification · Deep learning · Math tutor ·
Numeral sound classification · Voice enabled

1 Introduction

The classification of audio signals is a burgeoning field of study with many practical applications such as speech recognition, music genre classification, automated

Supported by Dr. B. C. Roy Polytechnic and Jadavpur University.

KC Santosh et al. (Eds.): RTIP2R 2022, CCIS 1704, pp. 406–417, 2023.
https://doi.org/10.1007/978-3-031-23599-3_31

music tutor, and voice-based phone lock systems, etc. Classifying sound means to separate it into various groups specific to a problem domain. Automatic speech recognition (ASR) is a technology that breaks down human speech into text so that a computer can understand it and handle it appropriately. Based on ASR technology, various voice bots are available in the market such as Amazon Alexa, Apple Siri, Google Assistant etc. Users are able to do a wide range of tasks, including entertainment, automatic preparation of shopping list, online shopping without navigating the website, smart home management, asking various queries, etc. The use of these ASR-based gadgets has made human life easier and smarter. The purpose of this study is to help kids in practicing simple math problems by designing an automated math tutor, based on deep learning. Here, the user will be asked to provide a response to a straightforward mathematical problem by the system. The system recognize the user speech and produces an audio output designating whether it is right or wrong. This method can be applied to any electronic item that encourages kids to practice math problems in an enjoyable manner. They'll enjoy the experience while also picking up some new knowledge. Some of the voice bots that are now on the market can answer mathematical questions by either using a backend system or an internet search. Installing certain third-party software makes it feasible to practice arithmetic problems, however they are error-prone and only support extremely elementary mathematical expressions. The proposed system does not need internet, whereas the existing speech bots require an internet connection to function. Only the English language is taken into account in this study, but it might be expanded to include additional languages in the future to make it a globally acceptable solution. The sound numerals 0 through 9 are the major subject of this study. There is no public dataset available for the proposed experiment that we are aware of. From different Indian states, a total of 2315 audio files of 10 English numbers from 0 to 9 were collected. The inclusion of data in multiple languages can transform this system into a multilingual audio classification system that can be used globally.

Convolutional neural network (CNN) is a popular tool nowadays for solving image classification problems because of their high performance in terms of accuracy and precision. CNN requires image data to function, whereas audio classification works with audio data rather than image data. It is not possible to feed audio data directly to CNN. Frequency and time are the two fundamental parameters that describe sound. The main issue is determining how to convert audio input into image data and build a CNN-based model to categorise sounds. The project's goal is to use advancements made in deep learning to classify numerical sounds. There are some studies in the literature on sound classification for various applications. Aditya et al. [1] used a customized CNN to address the sound categorization on the ESC-10 [4] and ESC-50 [4] datasets, and achieved 77% and 49% accuracy, respectively. Another study by Wenjie et al. [2] developed a sound categorization system based on a CNN network with temporal frequency attention on the two public datasets UrbanSound8K [3] and ESC-50 [4]. The study used a simple network structure and feature processing, and it performed well on the UrbanSound8K and ESC-50 datasets, with accuracy of 93.1% and 94.4%. Detecting individual sound occurrences, such as identifying dog barking, gunshots, and air conditioner noises, have been the subject of recent research on categorising environmental sounds. The study by Shivam et al. [5] addressed the classification of three security threat sounds such as, glass break, gun shots and smoke alarms using CNN based approach. Accuracy of 90% was achieved on the test dataset. This system identifies the various security sound event using microphone enabled camera surveillance system to track the unusual events in emergency situation. In the music industry, there are some applications of sound classification. The music genre classification using machine learning was proposed by Anirudh et al. [6]. A four layer CNN structure was used to identify the ten genres from the 1000 sound files in the GTZAN dataset [7], with an overall accuracy of 91%. Recently Vishnu et al. [8] proposed an automated Indian classical music tutor using deep learning. The long term short memory (LSTM) technique was employed in the study to find the similarity between the actual classical music, and the music file submitted by the music learner. The highest accuracy of 78% was achieved by their proposed Deep BiLSTM RNN network. The primary contribution of this study is the preparation of the JUDVLP-BCRP: numeralSound.v1 dataset, which contains 2315 audio samples of 10 numerals in the range of 0 to 9, pre-processing the audio data in the appropriate format for feeding into several prominent CNNs, and using some popular deep neural networks for the experiment. A light-weight network that is suitable for a real-world sound categorization challenge is created by modifying the conventional VGG-16 and DenseNet-121.

The remaining sections of the study are structured as follows: Sect. 2 describes the procedure for gathering data and pre-processing steps; Sect. 3 describes the proposed methodology; Sect. 4 presents the experiment protocol and results; and Sect. 5 describes the conclusion and future scope.

2   Dataset Description

In this study, ten numerical sounds (0, 1, 2, 3, 4, 5, 6, 7, 8, 9) were considered. Sound recordings were collected from persons ranging in age from 10 to 60 in states like West Bengal, Jharkhand, Delhi, Assam, Bihar, and Odisha. The data were gathered from residents in the areas close to our hometown. Our goal was to gather data from several locations across India, however the pandemic scenario prevented us from travelling to different places to do so. A total of 2315 sounds were gathered in a general setting with normal noise in the background. The proposed dataset includes more than 200 samples across all classes. The audio data were captured using common smartphone voice recorders including the Samsung M30/J6, Mi A3, Redmi y2/note 7 pro, and Vivo y35i/z1 pro. The average age of the participants in the data collecting process was 38, and 53.17% of the total data were obtained from male participants and 46.83% from female participants. Many participants in the 45–60 age range who were asked to participate in the data collection procedure declined for security-related reasons. Each participant was asked to provide ten sounds (ranging from 0 to 9), with the exception of a few who declined to provide all ten sounds. Table 1 lists the class-wise number of data collected as well as the number of female and male data. After the sounds were collected, they were in various different formats like m4a, 3gpp, and mp3. During the pre-processing stage, these files were changed to the mp3 format. All of those mp3 files were subsequently converted to .wav format. The .wav files were then converted into Mel spectrograms with a size of 224×224 using the Mel spectrogram package of the Librosa library. The sounds clippings were 2–3 s long. Following pre-processing, the dataset is split into training, validation, and testing components in a 60:20:20 ratio. At first, after shuffling the entire dataset, randomly 60% data were taken as training data, and the remaining data were then randomly divided into validation and test dataset, one by one, in the same proportion. No duplicates elements were present into training, validation, and test dataset. The proposed dataset is named as JUDVLP-BCRP: numeralSounddb.v1[1] because it was created in collaboration between the Dr. B. C. Roy Polytechnic in West Bengal, Durgapur, India and the DVLP Lab at Jadavpur University in West Bengal, Kolkata, India. In the dataset name, JU stands for Jadavpur University, DVLP stands for Deep Learning in Vision and Language Processing, and BCRP stands for Dr. B. C. Roy Polytechnic. Figure 1 displays a few of the images from the proposed dataset.

Table 1. Number of female and male data per class-wise in the JUDVLP-BCRP: numeralSounddb.v1 dataset

Class	0	1	2	3	4	5	6	7	8	9
Female	115	103	107	113	104	110	105	103	111	113
Male	125	119	130	119	125	116	121	126	117	133
Total	240	222	237	232	229	226	226	229	228	246

3 Methodology

The goal of the proposed study is to develop a method that will let kids of a certain age practice and learn the fundamental arithmetic operations such as addition, subtraction, multiplication, and division of numbers and more while engaging with the system. The proposed automated math tutor can be deployed into an electronic toy, that generates different mathematical problems and recognize the kid's audio answer and verify the result. A dataset JUDVLP-BCRP: numeralSounddb.v1 is developed, which consists of 2315 Mel spectrogram images, was split into training, validation, and testing datasets at a ratio of 60:20:20. The process adopted to divide the dataset into training, testing, and validation without any data leakage is discussed in the Sect. 2. Several well-known deep learning

---

[1] Click here to place a request to access the JUDVLP-BCRP: numeralSounddb.v1 dataset.

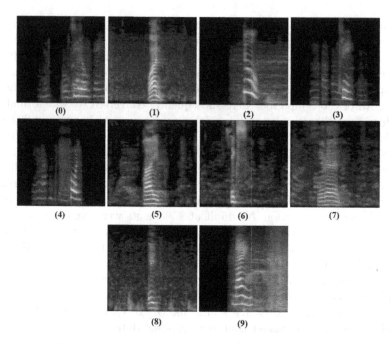

Fig. 1. Some spectrogram images of JUDVLP-BCRP: numeralSounddb.v1 dataset

networks, including VGG-16, DenseNet-121, VGG-12, and DenseNet-41, were used to train the system using the training and validation dataset. Next, this technique is employed to categorise the unseen numerical sound data. After the user's response was recognized, it was evaluated to see if it was the right one or not, and the user was then provided with feedback. Figure 2 depicts the flow diagram of the proposed approach. The different deep learning networks used in the proposed study are briefly introduced with the relevant diagrams in this section.

3.1 Deep Learning

Machine learning, a branch of artificial intelligence, is the foundation for deep learning. Deep learning mimics the human brain in a similar way to neural networks. Deep learning uses a large number of nonlinear processing units to extract features from the input data. Here each of the subsequent layers takes the output from the previous layer as an input. Transfer learning is a popular choice in deep learning-based approach, when a small dataset is used. ANN known as a deep neural network (DNN), that has numerous hidden layers between the input and output layers. Numerous applications use various DNN models for supervised learning, unsupervised learning, and reinforcement learning.

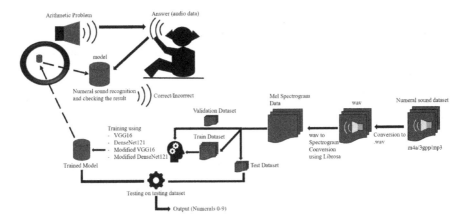

Fig. 2. Flow diagram of the proposed technique for the classification of numerical sound

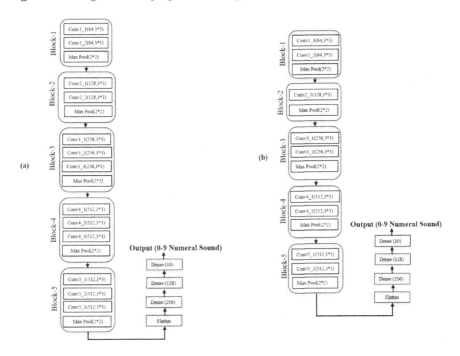

Fig. 3. Structure of (a) VGG-16 and (b) Modified VGG-16 (VGG-12) network

3.2 VGG-16 [9]

VGG-16 consists of 16 convoluted layers with 3×3 layers (Fig. 3). Conv-1 layer has 64 filters, Conv-2 layer has 128 filters, Conv-3 layer has 256 layers, Conv-4 and Conv-5 layer has 512 filters, just like the conventional VGG-16. After the stack of convolutional and pooling layers, a total of three fully connected

(FC) layers are used in this work. To identify a total of 10 different numerical sounds, the first FC layer has 256 channels, the second FC layer has 128 layers, and the final FC layer has 10 channels. Here the input data dimension is set to (224×224). The quantity of feature mappings or convolution also rises as the network's depth does.

3.3   DenseNet-121 [10]

Convolutional layer, pooling layer, dense blocks, and transition layer are all components of the convolutional neural network design known as DenseNet-121 (Fig. 4). Each layer in this instance receives input from the layer before it and passes the feature map to the layers after it. In contrast to conventional CNNs, this network requires less parameters and can be applied to interactive real-world applications where human and system interaction is frequent.

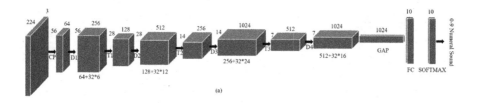

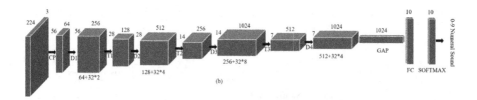

Fig. 4. Structure of (a) DenseNet-121 and (b) DenseNet-41

3.4   Modified VGG-16 (VGG-12)

To create a lightweight VGG network, the standard VGG-16 network is modified. Block 1, Block 2, and Block 3 of the traditional VGG-16 network are changed with 2, 3, and 6 repetitions (Fig. 3). The altered network is known as the VGG-12 network since it contains a total of 12 convolutional blocks. Blocks 1, 2, and 3 of the original VGG-16 have 3, 4, and 8 repeats, respectively. The rest of the structure is same as conventional VGG-16.

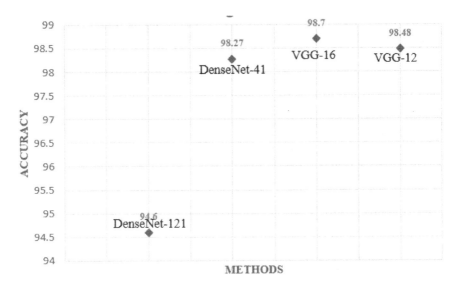

Fig. 5. Performance comparison of different deep learning algorithms used in this study

3.5 Modified DenseNet-121 (DenseNet-41)

In this work, a lighter variant of the standard DenseNet-121 is proposed. Dense Block 1, Dense Block 2, Dense Block 3, and Dense Block 4 of the standard DenseNet-121 are modified by 2, 4, 8, and 4 repetitions, respectively (Fig. 4). Dense Block 1, Dense Block 2, Dense Block 3, and Dense Block 4 of the standard DenseNet-121 each have 6, 12, 24, and 16 repetitions. Because there are 41 layers in the modified DenseNet-121, it is called DenseNet-41. Since it contains fewer parameters than the standard DenseNet-121, training takes less time. To categorise the sound data, DenseNet-41 is applied to the JUDVLP-BCRP: numeralSounddb.v1 dataset.

4 Experiment Protocol and Results

In this study, experiments were carried out using the proposed dataset JUDVLP-BCRP: numeralSounddb.v1, which contains 2315 spectrogram images of audio recordings of 10 digits from 0 to 9. The training, validation, and testing datasets were split up into a 60:20:20 ratio. The dataset used in this study comprises a total of 10 classes, hence all deep learning techniques used in this study uses 10 channels in the final SoftMax layer. In all of the experiments, categorical entropy loss function, batch size of 16 and learning rate 0.0001 was used. The model was trained over 100 epochs and retained for deployment. On Google Colab with GPU support, the Keras environment was used for all the experiments. On the test dataset, traditional VGG-16 and DenseNet-121 achieved accuracy of 98.70% and 94.60%, respectively. VGG-12 and DenseNet-41, a proposed, more compact

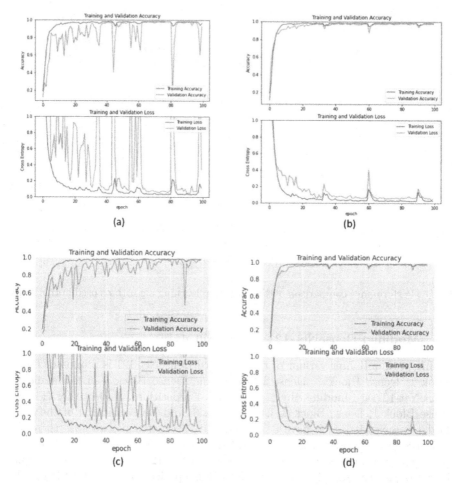

Fig. 6. Accuracy and loss graph of the used deep neural networks, (a) DenseNet-121 (b) VGG-16 (c) DenseNet-41 (d) VGG-12

version of VGG-16 and DenseNet-121, performed with 98.48% and 98.27% accuracy on the test dataset. Despite having fewer parameters than the conventional versions of these networks, DenseNet-41 achieved improved accuracy of 3.67% while the VGG-12 fell short by 0.22% accuracy (refer Fig. 5). Because the final system must be fast and interactive, the lighter version is crucial in this particular application. In Fig. 6, the loss and accuracy graph of the networks is shown. The loss and accuracy graph of DenseNet-121 on the validation dataset exhibits ups and downs with a minimal difference between training and validation loss. Due to the large size of the DenseNet-121 network and the modest size of the dataset used in this study, oscillations do occur in many sections in the graph. When DenseNet-41 was employed with fewer parameters than DenseNet-121, slight oscillations were observed. In the cases of VGG-16 and VGG-12, the same

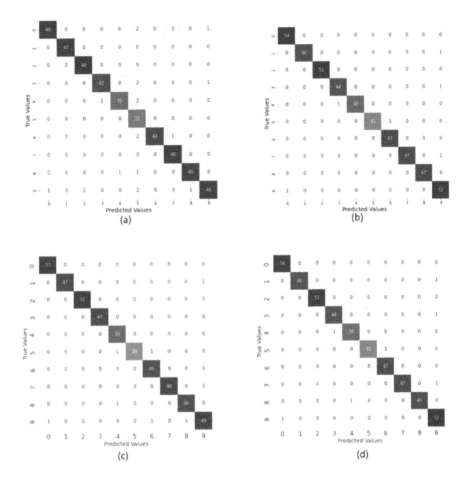

Fig. 7. Confusion matrix of the networks used in the proposed study: (a) DenseNet-121 (b) VGG-16 (c) DenseNet-41 (d) VGG-12

type of phenomenon occurs. In contrast to DenseNet, the VGG networks' loss and accuracy graphs are stable and the training and validation graphs have a small gap, which results in better generalisation. The confusion matrices for the four networks are shown in Fig. 7. The confusion matrix provides the information about the miss-classifications occurred on the test dataset. Table 2 presents certain statistical parameters, such as precision, recall, and F1-score, that were calculated.

Table 2. Class wise precision, recall, and F1-score of all the deep learning networks applied in this study

Method	Statistics	0	1	2	3	4	5	6	7	8	9	Accuracy(%)
DenseNet-121	Precision	0.98	0.96	0.98	0.98	0.97	0.73	1.00	0.92	0.98	0.96	94.60
	Recall	0.89	1.00	0.96	0.93	0.90	1.00	0.94	1.00	0.96	0.91	
	F1-score	0.93	0.98	0.97	0.95	0.93	0.84	0.97	0.96	0.97	0.93	
VGG-16	Precision	0.98	1.00	1.00	0.98	1.00	1.00	0.98	1.00	1.00	0.95	98.70
	Recall	1.00	0.98	1.00	0.98	0.97	0.97	1.00	0.98	1.00	0.98	
	F1-score	0.99	0.99	1.00	0.98	0.99	0.98	0.99	0.99	1.00	0.96	
DenseNet41	Precision	0.98	1.00	1.00	1.00	0.95	1.00	0.96	1.00	0.98	0.96	98.27
	Recall	1.00	0.98	1.00	1.00	1.00	0.94	1.00	0.98	0.98	0.94	
	F1-Score	0.99	0.99	1.00	1.00	1.00	0.94	1.00	0.98	0.98	0.94	
VGG-12	Precision	0.98	1.00	1.00	0.98	0.97	1.00	0.98	1.00	1.00	0.95	98.48
	Recall	1.00	0.98	1.00	0.98	0.97	0.97	1.00	0.98	0.98	0.98	
	F1-Score	0.99	0.99	1.00	0.98	0.97	0.98	0.99	0.99	0.99	0.96	

5   Conclusion

The main focus of this study is on practicing and learning math skills while having fun with the system. The proposed technique could be incorporated into a tool that kids can use to have fun and independently practise a variety of mathematical problems. Participants in this study ranged in age from 10 to 60 and lived in West Bengal, Jharkhand, Delhi, Assam, Bihar, and Odisha. A total of 2315 sound data of the numbers in the range of 0 to 9 were gathered, and a dataset known as JUDVLP-BCRP: numeralSounddb.v1 was developed. The system was trained to recognize the sound numerals using some well-known deep learning networks, including VGG-16, DenseNet-121, VGG-12, and DenseNet-41. A kid's response to a mathematical issue can be recognised by the trained model, which can then determine whether the response is accurate or incorrect and produce audio feedback accordingly. No internet connection is required for the proposed technique to function. The proposed method recognizes numerical sounds with 98.70% accuracy when using VGG-16. Additionally, 98.27% accuracy was achieved utilising the lightweight DenseNet-41, which is more feasible to implement in a system to obtain the result quickly. Future extensions of this research could incorporate two-digit numerical sounds. In the future, data will also be gathered in different languages, in order to create a comprehensive dataset.

References

1. Khamparia, A., Gupta, D., Nguyen, N.G., Khanna, A., Pandey, B., Tiwari, P.: Sound classification using convolutional neural network and tensor deep stacking network. IEEE Access **7**, 7717–7727 (2019). https://doi.org/10.1109/ACCESS. 2018.2888882

2. Mu, W., Yin, B., Huang, X., et al.: Environmental sound classification using temporal-frequency attention based convolutional neural network. Sci. Rep. **11**, 21552 (2021). https://doi.org/10.1038/s41598-021-01045-4
3. Salamon, J., Jacoby, C., Bello, J.P.: A dataset and taxonomy for urban sound research. In: MM 2014 Proceedings of the 22nd ACM International Conference on Multimedia, no. 3, p. 1041–1044 (2014)
4. Piczak, K.J.: ESC: Dataset for environmental sound classification. In: Proceedings of the 23rd ACM International Conference on Multimedia, pp. 1015–1018 (2015)
5. Agarwal, S., Khatter, K., Relan, D.: Security threat sounds classification using neural network. In: 2021 8th International Conference on Computing for Sustainable Global Development (INDIACom) 2021, pp. 690–694 (2021)
6. Ghildiyal, A., Singh, K., Sharma, S.: Music genre classification using machine learning. In: 2020 4th International Conference on Electronics, Communication and Aerospace Technology (ICECA) 2020, pp. 1368–1372 (2020). https://doi.org/10.1109/ICECA49313.2020.9297444
7. Tzanetakis, G., Cook, P.: Musical genre classification of audio signals. IEEE Trans. Speech Audio Process. **10**(5), 293–302 (2002). https://doi.org/10.1109/TSA.2002.800560
8. Pendyala, V.S., Yadav, N., Kulkarni, C., Vadlamudi, L.: Towards building a deep learning based automated Indian classical music tutor for the masses, systems and soft computing, vol. 4, p. 200042, ISSN 2772-9419 (2022). https://doi.org/10.1016/j.sasc.2022.200042
9. Simonyan, K., Zisserman, A.: Very deep convolutional networks for large-scale image recognition. In: 3rd International Conference on Learning Representations, ICLR 2015, 7–9 May 2015, San Diego, CA, USA, Conference Track Proceedings (2015)
10. Huang, G., Liu, Z., Van Der Maaten, L., Weinberger, K.Q.: Densely connected convolutional networks. IEEE Conference on Computer Vision and Pattern Recognition (CVPR) **2017**, 2261–2269 (2017). https://doi.org/10.1109/CVPR.2017.243

Author Index